HARVARD HISTORICAL STUDIES • 162

Published under the auspices
of the Department of History
from the income of the
Paul Revere Frothingham Bequest
Robert Louis Stroock Fund
Henry Warren Torrey Fund

NEXUS

STRATEGIC COMMUNICATIONS
AND AMERICAN SECURITY
IN WORLD WAR I

Jonathan Reed Winkler

HARVARD UNIVERSITY PRESS
Cambridge, Massachusetts
London, England
2008

Copyright © 2008 by the President and Fellows of Harvard College
All rights reserved
Printed in the United States of America

Library of Congress Cataloging-in-Publication Data

Winkler, Jonathan Reed, 1975–
 Nexus : strategic communications and American security in World War I / Jonathan Reed Winkler.
   p. cm.
 Includes bibliographical references and index.
 ISBN-13: 978-0-674-02839-5 (alk. paper)
  1. World War, 1914–1918—United States. 2. United States—Foreign relations—1913–1921. 3. World War, 1914–1918—Diplomatic history. 4. National security—United States—History—20th century. 5. Strategy—History—20th century. 6. World War, 1914–1918—Communications. 7. Communication, International—History—20th century. 8. Communication in politics—United States—History—20th century. I. Title.
 D619.W697 2008
 940.3'2273—dc22
                               2007043112

Contents

Maps and Figures *vii*

Introduction *1*

ONE The Information Network and the Outbreak of War *5*

TWO Neutrality and Vulnerability *34*

THREE Security and Radios *61*

FOUR At War in Europe *100*

FIVE In Pursuit of Cables to Asia and the Americas *136*

SIX Radio, the Navy, and Latin America *165*

SEVEN The Quest for Independence *206*

EIGHT The Illusion of Success *239*

Conclusion *266*

Abbreviations *283*

Primary Sources *285*

Notes *289*

Acknowledgments *337*

Index *339*

Maps and Figures

Maps

Principal Atlantic cables, 1914   *10*

Principal east Asian cables, 1914   *11*

German Atlantic communications, 1914   *18*

German east Asian communications, 1914   *19*

Principal South American cables, 1914   *54*

Principal North Atlantic cables, 1914   *106*

Figures

United States wavelength allocations, 1912–1916   *73*

U.S. Navy Proposal for hemispheric radio nework, 1916   *89*

Original cable lines   *223*

Severed cable lines   *223*

Nexus

Introduction

"THERE IS NO SOUND, no echo of sound, in the deserts of the deep," Rudyard Kipling once penned, "Or the great gray level plains of ooze where the shell-burred cables creep."[1] In paying tribute to underwater cables, the imperial odist honored one of the great marvels of his age. Submarine telegraph cables were an invention that, like the harnessing of steam and electrical power, transformed international communications and transportation. They bound the world together as never before, and intensified the nineteenth century worldwide economic, political, and cultural exchange that now bears the term globalization. Kipling understood that the words conveyed over these cables were a "Power," one that in disturbing "the Still" of the ocean depths had "neither voice nor feet":

> They have awakened the timeless Things; they have killed
>   their father Time;
> Joining hands in the gloom, a league from the last of the sun.
> Hush! Men talk to-day o'er the waste of the ultimate slime,
> And a new Word runs between: whispering, "Let us be one!"

Kipling's eloquent words are just as apt today as they were more than a century ago. In the subsequent years, the countries of the world have bound themselves more tightly together by ever more powerful submarine cables. The equally important development of radio, untouched by Kipling's poetic sentiments, also destroyed time and distance in ways imperceptible to the naked eye. The culmination of this technology has been a flock of communications satellites roosting in the icy darkness of outer space and exchanging radio signals from this lonely perch with the planet beneath. Though figuratively and often quite literally invisible to the average person, these two systems, cables and radios, through their power to make the world one, have become an essential part of global affairs in the modern era. It is not surprising, then, that countries intent on playing a leading role in the world have given especial attention to cables and radios throughout the twentieth century.

This is a study of United States foreign relations during the First World War and the transformation of U.S. diplomatic, military, and economic relations with the world at a critical moment from the viewpoint of these cables and radios. It was only during World War I that the United States first came to comprehend how a strategic communications network—the collection of submarine telegraph cables and long-distance radio stations used by a nation for diplomatic, commercial, and military purposes—was vital to the global political and economic interests of a great power in the modern world. Uncovering this story requires a deeper level of analysis, beneath more familiar subjects like U.S. behavior in the Western Hemisphere, Anglo-American relations during the war, the character of Wilsonian foreign policy, or the postwar fight over the ratification of the Treaty of Versailles. Complicated, geographically extensive, and relatively unknown to most historians of the period, this story rests at the intersection of diplomatic, military, technologic, intelligence, and business history. The story ranges chronologically, geographically, and topically from Latin America to Asia to Europe and moves between submarine cable telegraphy and radio. It has three principal sections. The first is a reconstruction of the global cable and radio network in existence in 1914, of the strategic importance of this to Great Britain and Germany, and of the measures taken by both against one another during the wars in what we today term information warfare. The second is an analysis of how U.S. officials, in light of these conditions, defined the strategic importance of cable and radio communications for the United States. The third part is the examination of the policies that these officials enacted to correct the problems they identified. Altogether, this study tells a tale of a country aware of its great potential yet not quite prepared to develop the infrastructure needed for lasting world power.

Despite a flirtation after the Spanish-American War in 1898, the first serious, sustained interest of the United States government in submarine telegraph cables and long-distance radio arose because of the outbreak of war in 1914. The British destruction of the German prewar global communications network and the corresponding imposition of censorship on British-controlled cables directly affected the ability of the United States to communicate freely with areas of commercial or political importance. At the same time, the ongoing development of radio and growing number of stations tied to Europeans across the Western Hemisphere led to security concerns for the U.S. Navy about the danger of signal interference or violations of neutrality. In an effort to redress these issues, State Department officials assisted companies seeking to expand their cable operations overseas and to bypass the British cables. Naval officers, meanwhile, worked to devise a centralized radio network to suit the service's strategic requirements. Political and ideological problems, however, frustrated efforts to build a larger public or private network throughout the Americas.

U.S. entry into the war in 1917 magnified the imbalances in world communications initially revealed in 1914 and raised a host of additional significant problems. The need for continual contact with the American Expeditionary Force in Europe in the face of a deteriorating transatlantic cable network and the danger of submarine attacks on the cables themselves led directly to a new high-power interallied radio network. The experience of censorship and the acquisition of intelligence passing by cable and radio also revealed to U.S. officials not only the tremendous value of such systems but also their potential vulnerability. When passing over other countries' networks abroad, this nation's diplomatic and military messages were open to interception and observation. The tremendous growth in overseas commerce during the war also raised the demand for rapidly improved communications links with South America and Asia as well. Altogether these issues led senior Wilson administration officials and military officers to accelerate efforts to link the country by submarine cable and long-distance radio with places of political and economic importance to the United States.

Following the experience of World War I, these efforts continued in earnest. At the Paris Peace Conference, President Woodrow Wilson and Secretary of State Robert Lansing fought to ensure that the Allied powers did not parcel out the former German cable network to America's further detriment. U.S. companies succeeded in expanding service to South America and developed plans for additional cables to Asia and Europe. Postwar supply problems complicated this, however, and a federal effort to jump-start a domestic cable manufacturing industry to support more cables failed as wartime momentum flagged. At the same time, U.S. Navy concerns over the future of radio technology and control of scarce wavelengths led to the creation of a new company, the Radio Corporation of America (RCA), by General Electric at the U.S. Navy's behest. RCA's initial purpose was to ensure that the nation's international radio connections remained under U.S. and not foreign control.

The motivation behind these efforts was a desire to realign world communications in ways that would minimize Great Britain's predominant position, move the United States from the periphery to the center of the global cable and radio network, and apply the benefits of this transformation to the nation's standing and influence in the world. Despite this ambition, the U.S. officials who planned these programs did not find the permanent changes they had envisioned. These would only come during another world war. Though of limited success in the short run, the efforts of officials at this time set important diplomatic, institutional, and technical precedents for later developments in telephony, shortwave radio, satellites, and eventually the Internet in the decades to come. The story of how the United States came to appreciate the strategic significance of communications amid the First World War is the first chapter in the larger history of how the United States created the global infrastructure, from cables to satellites to the Internet, that underlaid its predominance during the twentieth century.

ONE

❖ ❖ ❖

The Information Network and the Outbreak of War

JUST AFTER MIDNIGHT on August 4, 1914, the captain of the British General Post Office cable ship *Alert* received the special coded telegram he had been expecting. The *Alert*, restocked with provisions several days before, had already moved farther down the Dover docks to be ready to proceed to sea. This new order was to head at once into the English Channel. Britain's ultimatum to Germany to respect Belgian neutrality had expired at 11:00 PM. War with Germany had just begun. The fleet had already left Dover. The job assigned to the *Alert* would be a particularly hazardous one, for although a civilian ship, it too was about to engage in an act of war. There could be no escort—there was only one destroyer left at the Admiralty harbor. Shortly before two o'clock the ship steamed in the clear, fine weather under a nearly full moon toward the Varne lightship off the English coast.[1]

Passing several merchant ships but no warships, the *Alert* arrived at a patch of sea otherwise unremarkable save for the presence, on the ocean bottom, of Germany's five Atlantic submarine telegraph cables. These cables linked Germany to France, Spain, and the Azores. Through them Germany could reach the United States and the rest of the world. Shortly after three thirty in the morning, after steaming methodically back and forth for twenty minutes with a grappling hook over the side, the crew found first the cable to Spain. For the next two and a half hours the *Alert* continued its undulating way until it found three more cables and brought each aboard. Crewmen methodically hacked them apart with hatchets. The severed ends went back over the side, their position marked with a small buoy.

The work was difficult and fraught with danger. By half past six the weather had changed, and amid rising seas and wind a heavy rain squall passed over the ship. The crew had to replace the grapples one by one as they became damaged. After locating each cable, the ship went calm in the water as the crew raised the cable up from the muck of the channel bottom. Then, just after seven and amid the rising light, the lookouts spotted the distinctive profile of destroyers and submarines, steaming some five or six miles away. They were definitely not British. Were it to be a German flotilla, the *Alert* would be in a critical situation. The steady southerly wind and a change in the tide now began to work against the ship's maneuverability and slow speed. Still, the crew of the *Alert* kept at its work. Just as they cut the fifth cable, the destroyers arrived. To the crew's relief, the lookouts made out the French flags flying at the mast. Passing close by, the inquisitive destroyers signaled "What are you doing?" The captain of the *Alert* replied, "Cutting German cables." A round of cheers then came from the crew on the French destroyer, taken up as well by those of the *Alert*. Its work done, the cable ship turned back shortly after ten for the safety of Dover harbor.[2]

By its actions, the *Alert* had also rendered the United States virtually dependent upon Britain for communication with the rest of the world. Britain sat at the heart of a vast worldwide web of submarine telegraph cables, and the United States was on its periphery. By 1914 submarine telegraphy was still a relatively new technology. In 1844 Samuel Morse had demonstrated the first practical use of telegraphy on land between Washington, D.C., and Baltimore. Seven years later, British inventors laid the first commercial telegraph cable underneath the English Channel. The North Atlantic was a far more daunting obstacle. After several attempts, the first successful cable came into operation in 1866.[3] From this modest beginning sprang an ever-growing nexus of copper threads, insulated with a scarce tree sap called gutta-percha and wrapped in protective steel wire. British firms, the first in the field, quickly established themselves as the leading experts. They rapidly extended these cables from port to port, through the Mediterranean and across the Indian Ocean, to the Far East and Australia. By 1872 the Eastern Telegraph Company, the predominant firm, announced that it had linked Australia and Hong Kong with Britain by telegraph cable. This "all-red route" became the informational spinal cord of the British

Empire. When connected to land telegraph networks and other cables laid in Europe, the Americas, Africa, or Asia, it reinforced Britain's place at the hub of international shipping, trade, and finance.

Like their counterparts on land, submarine telegraph cables conquered time and space. In doing so, they revolutionized the modern world within the span of a single generation. Before the transatlantic cable, news could cross the Atlantic only at the speed of the fastest sailing vessel or steamship, a matter of weeks. Between Britain and Australia it was a matter of months. The cables reduced the speed of transmitting information across the oceans to a matter of minutes. In Jules Verne's 1873 classic *Around the World in Eighty Days,* the intrepid detective Fix used the cables to try to secure an arrest warrant for Phileas Fogg from London as Fix chased Fogg and his party east from Egypt. Despite Fix's best efforts, the replies arrived too late—Fogg always managed to move ahead. Most remarkable for readers of the time, however, was that Fix could remain in rapid contact with British authorities as he chased after Fogg, something which could not have occurred just a few years before.[4] Cables made the world smaller; linking the continents together, they launched the first phase of globalization.

Use of the cables was more widespread than many have realized. At first the high costs for sending messages limited their use to those people most interested in advance knowledge of important events, particularly newspapers, diplomats, bankers, and importers. Cable companies frequently subsidized their operation with contracts from governments and press agencies who guaranteed to send a daily minimum number of words. Governments appreciated the benefits of rapid communications with far-flung imperial administrators, diplomats, or distant military forces and so encouraged the use of cables in every corner of the globe. Defense of overseas territories became easier with the cable, as admirals and generals could coordinate the movement of warships and regiments from a central headquarters. When antiforeign sentiment in China welled up into the Boxer Rebellion of 1899–1900, for example, U.S. Minister Edwin Conger and other diplomats in Peking used the cable to summon international help swiftly.[5] At the same time, the telegraph on land and the cable at sea picked up the pace of international affairs. Because governments could quickly receive messages from seemingly insignificant parts of the world within minutes, however, diplomats soon suffered from a surfeit of information. At the same time, the high cost of messages forced officials to shorten messages when they could, even at the risk of ambiguity. The cables made participation in global affairs faster, even if it did not make it easier.[6]

As prices dropped and demand increased, nearly all parts of society began to make use of the cables. The cable transformed international trade and finance. Merchants based almost anywhere could simultaneously know the market prices for goods in Europe or North America as well as the availability of such goods in Latin America or Asia. With this knowledge they could direct the efforts of their agents in both places, so that ships sailed with the right cargo and went directly to the ports offering the best prices. Financiers could raise capital and arbitrageurs speculate on foreign currencies on a scale and speed previously unimaginable. Cables provided the information flow that, together with British capital and merchant shipping, made London the vital core of global trade.[7] At the same time, the press agencies such as Reuters, Havas, and Wolff distributed news and financial data throughout the world. Local newspapers could, through these press agencies, carry news only days old from the farthest reaches of the globe. By cable, explorers could alert their colleagues to exciting new discoveries. Academics researching abroad could secure additional funding from deep-pocket donors without having to wait for a letter to go by ship. The cables also allowed ordinary people to keep in touch when separated by great distances. Anxious mothers in London or Boston could receive regular, brief messages from their missionary sons in India or China. Immigrants in the Americas or Australia could remit money rapidly and safely back to their families in Europe. The cables even made it possible, by linking observers on different continents, to map the world and measure its size with an accuracy never before possible.[8] And when calamity struck— as it did in 1883 with the eruption of Krakatoa in Indonesia—the cables carried that news around the globe within hours. The messages borne by electrical impulse along the slender cables allowed the world to come together economically, culturally, and politically as never before.[9]

The importance of such a global network for administration and defense of the scattered empire did not go unnoticed in London. Unlike land telegraph lines, submarine cables could not be tapped or easily damaged and so provided a secure and rapid form of imperial communications. From the beginning, the British government had steadily encouraged the laying of cables. Official subsidies helped the operation of important cables that were otherwise of little commercial value. This in turn allowed the steady creation of a vast telegraphic network wholly independent of the whim of foreign countries. British cables soon ran to South America, through the Mediterranean, along the African coast, and throughout the Far East. By encouraging foreign firms to land their cables on British territory, Britain soon linked with Canada and the United States as well.

Another essential feature of the imperial cable network was redundancy. The more cables that interconnected different parts of the empire, the less likely it was that any individual place could be isolated easily in war. In 1898 a special governmental committee charged with considering submarine cables in wartime concluded that there should be additional cables linking Britain to South Africa and Australia. To reduce the danger of interruption, wherever possible these cables would land on remote islands. With subsidies to the Eastern Telegraph group of companies, the British government laid a new strategic line of cables at the turn of the century. These ran from Britain to South Africa via several islands in the Atlantic. Another spur then ran across the Indian Ocean to Singapore and down to Perth in Australia. When the Eastern Telegraph Company balked at a similar plan to construct a cable across the vast Pacific to link Canada with New Zealand and Australia, these colonies created the Pacific Cable Board to lay the cable anyway.[10] By 1902 Britain's thin copper strands permitted telegraphic messages to traverse the entire globe in less than an hour. This strategic backbone to the empire reinforced the disposition of British military and naval forces throughout the world. Together with the new technology of radio, cables allowed for a global coordination of force on a scale and speed never before imaginable.[11]

It was the wartime importance to Britain of this global network that would affect the United States. To isolate their opponents and impose an economic blockade, British officials had planned on the simultaneous destruction of certain enemy cables and the institution of censorship on their own network.[12] Unfortunately for the United States, the result of this strategy was to remove the only practical non-British-controlled connections to Europe and the rest of the world. Alone this might have been manageable, but the overwhelming wartime traffic and imposition of censorship on the remaining cables sowed mass confusion and antagonized the neutrals. The United States could not lay its own cables directly to Europe or other locations because the manufacturing expertise and essential raw materials were under British control and in limited supply. Restrictive concessions and discriminatory pricing on the cost of sending messages also helped to ensure British control of the cables in South America or Asia, where rival firms might challenge them. The only alternative, long-distance radio, was a technology still in its infancy. The latest advancements were in the hands of British and German firms. The existing stations were not powerful enough to supplant the cables. Altogether, this situation left the United

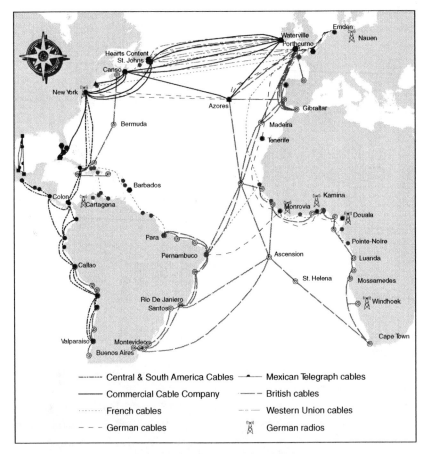

Principal Atlantic cables, 1914

States dependent upon foreign powers for its vital communications in a time of great need.

The voyage of the *Alert* and its implications caused officials in the United States eventually to realize the strategic necessity of having an independent cable and radio network linking the nation to its overseas interests. Whether as a neutral or a belligerent, the potential danger of the United States' being isolated from places of commercial, political, or military significance was now all too real. The gradual process by which the United States realized this vulnerability, fought for independence, and developed its first strategic communications network is the subject of this work.

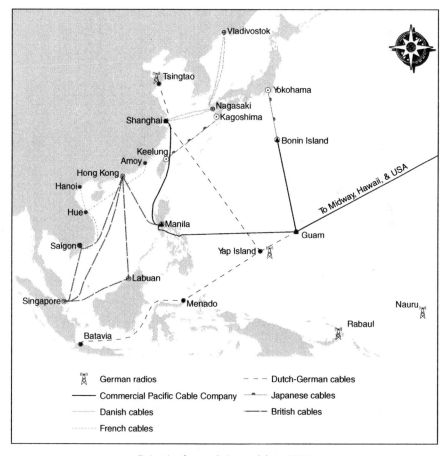

Principal east Asian cables, 1914

The United States' surprise at the effects of Britain's war on Germany's cables stemmed from the large gap between the United States and the warring powers in 1914 in appreciating the strategic importance of international communications. To understand this gap, we must first examine the background of Britain's prewar control over cables, Germany's efforts to circumvent this, the place of the United States in the cable web, and the efforts made by both Britain and Germany to destroy each other's networks in the opening months of the war. The effects and the policies the United States undertook to right the balance are largely unknown to historians. These efforts culminated in an ambitious but ultimately unsuccessful effort to place the United States at the center of the world's communications after the war. By the 1920s, the American turn to political isolation correspondingly led to a declining interest in the importance of cables and radio to the security of the nation. Still, the gains won by certain far-sighted public and private officials laid the foundation for continued commercial expansion in the interwar years, a foundation that would, ultimately, undergird the rise of the United States to global power in the mid-twentieth century.[13]

Challenging Britain's control over cables and its position in radio would not be easy. The world's cable industry was almost entirely in British hands. The major operating firms, all parts of the Eastern Telegraph group of interlocking companies controlled by Sir John Denison Pender, were British. The latest techniques for manufacturing cables and designing the necessary transmitting equipment were coming from British laboratories and workshops. The electrical insulation of the cables to ensure the quality of the signal over long distances required the use of a latex wrap, the best of which came from the sap of the gutta-percha tree. The principal market for gutta-percha was in Singapore. British firms controlled the brokerages and thus the supply. The best cable operators were all British trained, and most were British citizens.[14] All told, this meant that Britain had at its disposal the research and innovative capacity to improve cable design, manufacture and lay cables, and operate them primarily on British territory around the world. Furthermore, Britain had encouraged other countries to land their cables in Britain and its overseas colonies. This had the effect of ensuring that other countries remained on the cable periphery while their communications came under British control in wartime.[15] If any other country wished to have its own cable network, it had first to develop its own cable industry, train its own personnel, and secure its own supply of gutta-percha.

Like cables, radio was also an area of strong British commercial and strategic interest. Here the technological lead was not as great. Between 1900 and 1914, the Marconi Wireless Telegraphy Company of Britain had constructed dozens of short-range "ship-to-shore" radio stations along the principal shipping routes of the world.[16] Several Marconi subsidiaries also operated chains of coastal stations, the largest being those along the U.S. and Canadian coasts. Operators trained by Marconi served on board commercial ships, whose owners rented the radio equipment from the company as well. The Marconi firm also constructed high-power stations in Canada and the United States, to communicate directly with Britain. They built similar stations to link the United States to Japan and Asia. Encouraged by these developments, Britain and her colonies endorsed the idea in 1911 of having a chain of regional stations that would link the empire in a way independent of the cables.[17] The British General Post Office awarded Marconi a contract to build six of these high-power stations to form the imperial wireless chain from Britain to Australia, but political and technological problems plagued its development. By the outbreak of the war, only two of these stations, in Britain and Egypt, were under construction.

The Royal Navy gave particular attention to the strategic importance of wireless to the empire. The Admiralty, suspicious of Marconi's near monopoly in radio, had constructed its own network of medium- and long-range stations. These covered the North Sea and British Isles and linked Britain to Gibraltar and the Mediterranean by 1909. Similar stations were under construction at Malta and later Egypt. Each used the same type of transmitter and antennae installed on all battleships and first-rate cruisers.[18] Though the technology was still young, the military implications of wireless were readily apparent. Together with the cables, it could allow continual contact with the fleet and merchant shipping while they were at sea beyond sight of land. It would permit the Admiralty to control from the center the movements of its ships on the periphery of the empire. In the words of the Secretary of the Committee on Imperial Defense (CID), "The directing brain will consequently be a far more potent factor than formerly in determining success in naval war."[19] For the Admiralty and its "directing brain," it meant that they, not the General Post Office, would have to exercise the predominant influence over wireless policy in Britain.[20]

From this perspective, the Admiralty and officials from the Committee on Imperial Defense envisioned a global network of ship-shore stations, commercially self-sustaining and under British control, that would ensure continual contact with British merchant and naval ships along the major trade routes. These stations would collect sightings of enemy warships and direct merchant vessels away and vector British cruisers in to intercept. Financial and technical limitations hindered substantive work until 1914, when a special subcommittee of the CID finally considered the construction of several more medium-power stations (with a range of five hundred to one thousand miles).[21] Altogether, this expansive network of cables and wireless stations, combined with an extensive intelligence operation designed to track shipping throughout the world, was to form the basis for a comprehensive global information-communications system that would allow planners in the Admiralty to direct the defense of the empire from a single location—London.[22] In the end, war came before the chain of medium-power stations could be built. Nonetheless, the strategic significance of cables and wireless, and their importance to any power seeking a global role, had shaped how British imperial planners viewed the efforts of other powers to build their own networks.[23]

This gradual extension of Britain's global network had not gone unnoticed by the other great powers. In the decades before World War I, France, Germany, Japan, and the Netherlands had all considered projects to link their overseas territories and interests in ways that would minimize dependence upon Britain's cables. France, for example, subsidized private companies with hefty sums to lay cables to its colonies in North America, the Caribbean, Africa, and southeast Asia.[24] The Netherlands pursued a similar goal in the Far East. Before her alliance with Britain in 1902, so had Japan with the help of a Danish company. A shortage of suitable islands and an inadequate industry, however, left these countries still largely in need of Britain's cables to connect to the rest of the world.[25]

The country that did the most before World War I to free itself from British cable control was Germany. The need for an overseas communications system had deepened with Germany's economic and political expansion in the late 1890s. After British rejection of a proposed German cable touching at Cornwall and the infuriating experience of cable censorship during the Boer War, Germany realized that it would have to develop a network of its own. The German government encouraged the creation of a domestic cable industry to meet this challenge. Between 1896 and 1911, German companies ran cables to Spain, the Azores, and the Canary Islands. From these places they extended further cables to the United States, Liberia, Germany's west African colonies, and South America.[26] The steadily increasing demand for greater international cable capacity coincided with this boom in German cable-laying, to Germany's benefit. Not long after the opening of the first German transatlantic cable, over three hundred thousand messages had passed between the United States and Germany. To meet this demand, a second cable had to be laid within two years.[27]

Germany created a smaller cable network in the Pacific. Finding the Dutch government of a similar mind about the need for independent cables, the German firm Felten und Guilleaume formed a joint Dutch-German subsidiary in 1903 to lay and operate cables. Centered at Yap in the Caroline Islands, this network linked to the Dutch East Indies and China and through Guam to the United States, Japan, and Russia. While Germany could manufacture its own cables, British firms still controlled the vital gutta-percha latex, as well as the extensive supplies and repair ships essential for maintaining the global network in wartime.[28]

As radio developed in the first decade of the twentieth century, Germany saw in this technology a solution to its vulnerabilities in cables. Germany encouraged the development of its own radio industry to match that of Britain. In 1903 the German government enthusiastically supported the merger of the leading German radio firms into the conglomerate known as Telefunken.[29] Telefunken salesmen were soon selling ship-shore radio services from South America to Siberia. German engineers worked these stations and trained local operators. Diplomatically, Germany fought to limit Marconi's predominance in the industry and its refusal to exchange traffic with ships not using Marconi equipment. For this purpose, Kaiser Wilhelm II convened in Berlin two international conferences on radio. At the second, in 1906, the Marconi Company was unable to prevent the assembled countries from mandating the exchange of messages between radio stations in all instances, especially in emergencies. Signatories to the international accord also reserved certain wavelengths for government and military uses. With the number of available wavelengths seemingly limited, Germany ensured that Marconi—and thus Britain—could not control them all.[30]

Telefunken and the German government then undertook a mammoth project to connect Germany's colonies and overseas markets by long-distance radio. This would bypass the need to rely on the more vulnerable cables. Built between 1911 and 1914, the stations made use of a new arc transmitter technology that made longer-distance transmissions (greater than one thousand miles) more reliable and continual than the existing spark transmitters championed by Marconi. The German radio network centered on the high-power station at Nauen, near Berlin. A similar high-power station, in Kamina, Togoland, became the hub of the African colonial system. Kamina in turn linked stations in Liberia, German East Africa, Cameroon, and German Southwest Africa. The station at Monrovia in Liberia connected to the existing German cable to Brazil.[31] A subsidiary of Telefunken, the Atlantic Communications Company (ACC), had the responsibility of building a similar network of stations throughout the Americas. The ACC had built a high-power station near New York at Sayville, on Long Island, and smaller ones in Colombia and Peru. The full network was to have included stations in Mexico, Cuba, Venezuela, and Brazil. War broke out before they could be completed.[32] In the Pacific, another Telefunken subsidiary built stations at the German colony at Tsingtao (now Qingdao) in China, on Yap, and at other German island possessions. Telefunken also had plans to develop another high-power station in China. An ambitious project, the radio network ultimately proved as vulnerable to British attack as the cables. Many of the stations were located in places not otherwise worth defending. Few of the stations in neutral territory were complete.[33]

Alert to the steady expansion of Germany's network, Great Britain made plans to destroy it as quickly as possible. Doing so would choke off Germany's overseas military and economic contact during war. Members of a special subcommittee of the Committee of Imperial Defense considered the submarine cable situation in 1911. They recommended that certain measures be taken to protect British cables from attack and to cut the German cables from the very beginning of war. The Eastern Telegraph group was to guarantee additional cable supplies and cable-repair ships for the government at key locations around the world. The army worked out plans for defending the cable-landing sites against raiding parties. The Royal Navy and the General Post Office, meanwhile, agreed upon offensive action to locate and cut the five major German cables in the English Channel. Throughout the empire, military officers at cable stations would implement censorship. This would let them monitor traffic, suppress enemy messages, and glean any valuable intelligence. The Foreign Office would have the responsibility of putting diplomatic pressure on neutrals with German cable and radio stations in their territory to shut them down.

As Germany turned to high-power radio between 1911 and 1914, the British armed services very likely worked out similar plans for destroying the radio network in the German colonies but had not yet presented them before the CID. There was some thought given to the effects that the entire campaign might have on aggrieved neutrals, but the planners believed most of these neutrals could be disregarded. The Netherlands, Brazil, and the United States, they noted, might close British cables in retaliation, but the cable network had been designed to withstand such action. Thus, when the *Alert* steamed to sea in the morning of August 5, its actions were the culmination of many years of planning to gain predominant control over the world's communications networks and the information flowing through them in wartime.[34]

The United States was not without its own cable network before 1914 but was much more on the periphery of the global system than many Americans might have understood. To some extent, this was true because existing cables largely met the international financial and trading needs of the country. Seventeen cables connected the United States and Europe before August 1914. These included two German cables that touched at the Azores before passing through the English Channel toward Germany. Two more were French, but they were old and inefficient and were no substitute for the severed German cables.

Two U.S. companies, Western Union and the Commercial Cable Company, controlled the remaining thirteen. Commercial Cable owned its cables, while Western Union either owned theirs outright or had acquired extended leases of the others.[35] Because the strength of an electrical impulse weakens the farther it travels, the companies had laid their cables between Canada and Great Britain in order to minimize the distance. Though the U.S. companies largely controlled the North Atlantic cable business, the location of the cable stations in British territory meant that Great Britain exercised significant control over the content and operations on both sides of the Atlantic.[36] To the south, the entrepreneur James Scrymser had extended a chain of cables from Mexico through Central America and Panama down to the western coast of South America between 1879 and 1882. He had attempted to lay cables over to the eastern side of the continent, to the more important markets in Brazil, Argentina, and Uruguay, but found that his British rivals had already secured concessions that locked him out. De-

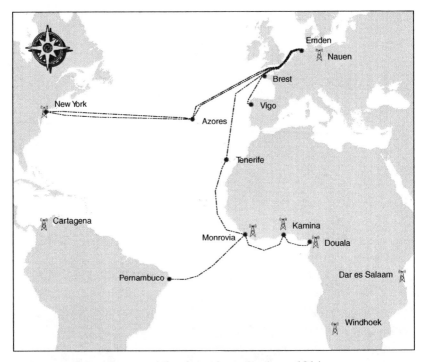

German Atlantic communications, 1914

spite Scrymser's difficulties and the high costs of sending messages, the American cabling public still had access, indirectly and expensively, through the British network to all the principal markets of the world.

In the United States official interest in cables and their extension arose after the war with Spain in 1898 but did not lead to significant changes. Presidents William McKinley and Theodore Roosevelt called publicly for a government-supported cable to connect with the new territories in the Pacific and the Caribbean. Indeed, there had been demand for such a cable across the Pacific to Asia since the 1860s, but financial difficulties and the depression of the 1890s prevented any private undertakings. The most spectacular effort had been Western Union's 1864 attempt with the Collins Overland Line to link California to Siberia via Russian Alaska and the Bering Strait.[37] After 1898 the matter became more urgent. The acquisition of Hawaii, Guam, and the Philippines determined the route the eventual cable would take. Congress appropriated federal funds to support such a project, but the clamor of competing firms and the lack of a clear encouragement from

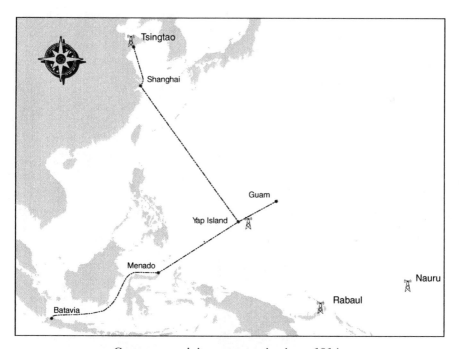

German east Asian communications, 1914

the executive branch prevented the selection of a recipient. The political importance of a cable to the Philippines was still not so great as to warrant the U.S. government laying the cable itself.

In the end, John Mackay, who also controlled the Commercial Cable Company in the Atlantic, offered to lay the entire cable without the subsidy.[38] This was a shocking offer, for only with the promise of a subsidy could a company have expected to survive the initial costs of laying the cable. What Mackay kept well hidden was that his new company, the Commercial Pacific Cable Company, had secret foreign backing. Half the ownership was in the hands of Eastern Extension, part of Pender's Eastern Telegraph group. One quarter was under the control of the Great Northern Telegraph Company. Together Eastern Extension and Great Northern contrived to keep the rates on the new Pacific cable artificially high. This allowed Great Northern and the Eastern Telegraph group to prevent their American and European customers from defecting to a cheaper alternative, and at the same time appear to satisfy the great demand for a reasonably direct Pacific cable. Over time, this arrangement preserved the predominance of the two companies in China and the rest of the Far East, at the expense of the United States, Japan, and others. Mackay's company laid the first section of cable between San Francisco and Manila between the summer of 1902 and April 1903. A subsequent extension linked the Philippines to Shanghai, and at the request of the Japanese, another cable linked Guam to Japan via the Bonin Islands in 1906. Mackay's project was an inadequate and indirect solution to the ever-growing demand for transpacific communications. Unsated, the public in Japan, China, and the United States clamored for more cables for years to come.[39]

The amount of sustained thinking that focused on cables, radio, and security came from a few individuals whose recommendations went largely unheeded in the absence of any immediate threat. Foremost among these was Captain George O. Squier of the U.S. Army Signal Corps. Squier had come to understand what the British could do with their cable network in wartime. Reflecting on the recent war with Spain, he noted in 1900 that this conflict and, by implication, those to come were, in his words, largely dependent upon "coal and cables." "Reliable submarine [cable] communications under exclusive control are not only absolutely necessary," he concluded, "but exercise a dominating influence upon the control of the seas, whether in commercial strategy or in military and naval strategy." Squier argued that the time saved by use of instantaneous communications over long sea-distances might give the decisive advantage if the United States had such a system to link its scattered possessions overseas. He strongly urged the immediate creation of a domestic cable industry and extension of a vast network of government cables to link the Philippines, Alaska, Cuba, and Puerto Rico with the United States.[40] Such cables, in Squier's view, were more important for linking together the naval bases and coaling stations to be located in these places than for expediting the limited commerce with those islands themselves. Squire's arguments, presented in a paper before the Naval War College in 1900, remained the principal American text on strategic communications for the next twenty years.[41]

Similar sentiments guided the young Lieutenant Stanford C. Hooper in his views on the role of radio in the U.S. Navy. During Hooper's early career, radio was still in its development stage in the navy. Foreign firms like Marconi and Telefunken held prominent places in equipment and operation, the navy's policy toward radio was to assemble the necessary equipment as components and then build its own sets so that no single supplier could hold influence. This was of limited success, however, and by 1912 over half of the navy's radio equipment was of German manufacture.

Following the *Titanic* disaster, which highlighted the importance of radio for safety at sea, an international conference issued guidelines for the development of radio for ship-shore work. Congress, considering the resolutions of the conference, passed the Radio Act of 1912, the first significant radio legislation in the country. Many in the public welcomed these initial efforts to regulate radio. Certain provisions limiting foreign ownership of stations in the United States and providing sanctions for improper operating procedures, however, had been set aside to speed the law's passage. Hooper, considered the father of naval radio in the United States, repeatedly raised concerns about these inadequacies and the strong position of foreign firms in the United States. Referring specifically to the ACC transatlantic station at Sayville, Long Island, he warned his superiors in 1913 that its German operators were in a position to intercept U.S. naval communications post for the German navy. Hooper was also concerned about the extensive influence of a Marconi subsidiary in the ship-shore radio industry, a field he believed should be the realm of the navy alone, as it was in many countries. Hooper's consistent attention to tactical and operational use of radio in the navy and his warning about U.S. vulnerabilities bolstered the belief among many in the fleet that it should control all radio operations in the United States. Both Squier and Hooper remained closely involved in cable and radio matters through the prewar period, but their limited influence did little to spur the formation of any consistent policy before the outbreak of war.[42] The actions of Britain and Germany in the opening months of the war showed Squier and Hooper to be prescient.

The daring effort by the crew of the *Alert* was only one part of the well-orchestrated offensive against Germany's global information network. In London, the General Post Office cleared each of the six cables between Britain and Germany of traffic around midnight on August 4. Another cable ship then cut each of these just beneath the low-water mark off the English coast. Beyond the North Sea and English Channel, British forces systematically captured or destroyed German radio stations throughout Africa and the Far East. Britain pressured neutrals with German- owned and -operated cable and radio stations in their territories to shut these facilities down and to ensure that they remained sealed. British consular officers and military attachés kept a close watch on interned German commercial ships throughout the world, to detect attempts to use sealed radio sets. Where these steps proved ineffective, British cable ships severed the remaining German cables landing on neutral territory and even destroyed radio station equipment through covert operations when all else failed. Although most of the fighting between Germany and Britain occurred on the Western Front, it was the struggle for control over worldwide communications that made the war global.

The overarching objective in this offensive was to isolate Germany militarily, politically, and economically. The Admiralty feared that Germany would use the radio and cable network to monitor the trade routes and direct German cruisers against British shipping. Capture or destruction of the cable and radio stations would prevent this. It would also contribute to the economic war against Germany. Without the cables, Germany would have to rely on the long-distance transmitter at

Nauen or attempt to pass information secretly through British or allied cables. Closure of the remaining receiving stations abroad would end Nauen's usefulness, while total censorship would stop German trade and financial transactions through sympathetic neutrals. The effect would be the evisceration of German influence outside Europe for long after the war itself was over. This was the plan the British put into motion on the night of August 4.[43]

Carrying out this operation was the responsibility of a special wartime subcommittee of the Committee of Imperial Defense. The Joint Naval and Military Committee convened on August 5 to consider further action—beyond the initial cable cuttings in the channel—against Germany's overseas colonies and its imperial communications. Headed by Admiral Sir Henry B. Jackson, the Chief of the Admiralty War Staff and himself a pioneer in wireless within the Royal Navy, the committee was a mixture of military, Colonial, and Foreign Office personnel. To them, it was "obvious from the first that the object . . . must be an organized attack upon the distant bases and intelligence centers of the enemy" in order to break up the cable and wireless-based information network, "which it was believed had been elaborated for the dislocation of [British] ocean trade." This required a concerted strategic operation to destroy these stations, to forestall their use against British trade or the concentration of imperial forces in Europe. Lest its intentions be misunderstood, the CID explicitly enunciated two principles that would guide the planning: the operations were designed not for territorial conquest but for defense of trade, and these campaigns would have to rely upon Colonial and Dominion forces, because all British units were already committed to the fighting on the Continent. The Cabinet approved the general outlines of the strategy the following day, with action coming shortly thereafter.[44]

In Africa, the principal target was the German high-power station at Kamina, the key to the African network. Messages exchanged with Germany could pass through Kamina to other African colonial stations or to South America by cable from Liberia. Without Kamina, the rest of the stations were isolated. Jackson's subcommittee directed African and Indian colonial forces to capture the radio stations in German East Africa, German South-West Africa, Togoland, and the Cameroons. On August 8, three days after the committee first met, the cruiser *Astraea* attacked the wireless station at Dar es Salaam in German East Africa, but the Germans themselves destroyed it first. On August 24, the besieged German defenders at Kamina blew up their station as well. By the beginning of September, British colonial troops were in control of the colony. In mid-September, South African forces captured one station, while a British warship destroyed another with shell fire. Douala, in the Cameroons, fell to a joint Anglo-French force on September 27. The last station, Windhoek in German South-West Africa, lasted until May 1915. Although Britain could not touch the German cable and radio station in Liberia, British action had silenced all of the others in Africa.[45]

In the Far East, the two main objectives were the German colony at Tsingtao and the island of Yap, in the Carolines. The forces available to the British were too weak to reduce Tsingtao, but the colony was of little significance after the departure of the German Far East Squadron under Admiral Maximilian von Spee. Yap, however, was the nexus of the German information system in the Pacific. Cables from Shanghai and the Dutch East Indies connected at Yap, and a third cable linked to Guam and the Pacific cable to the United States. Its radio station tied together the scattered German possessions in the Pacific. Linking these islands with the global cable network and thus to Germany, Yap served as the main relay point for Admiral Spee's squadron. If the allies could seize Yap or destroy its radio station, then the squadron would lose contact with home and intelligence about the Allies from the German islands. On August 12, Admiral Martyn Jerram's naval force accompanying the HMS *Triumph* arrived at Yap and destroyed the station by naval bombardment. After eight weeks, all of the remaining small stations scattered through the German Pacific colonies had been destroyed or captured by other Australian or New Zealand forces. Allied control of the Pacific meant continued control of information as well.[46]

In addition to this coordinated offensive, the Admiralty implemented a system to monitor, decipher, and analyze the radio traffic to and from the central station at Nauen. The purpose was to use the intelligence gathered from these messages as an additional weapon, to direct imperial naval forces as rapidly as possible against German commerce raiders. This strategic imperial listening-service made use of various commercial and government radio stations in Britain to monitor Nauen's transmissions on wavelengths over two thousand meters, which were used over very long distances to work with the various overseas German radio stations.[47] Set up by the Director of Naval Intelligence, Rear Admiral Henry Oliver, who appointed Sir Alfred Ewing, the Director of Naval Education, to oversee its operation, this institution became known as Room 40, for the part of the old Admiralty building in which it later had its offices.

From August to November the staff of Room 40 concentrated almost exclusively on the transmissions to and from Nauen, although as overseas stations went off the air one by one, the load reduced to traffic only with stations in the United States and Spain. As a result, many of the Room 40 group began to work with their counterparts in the War Office on intercepted tactical radio traffic from the front or returned to their previous assignments. The arrival of a captured German naval codebook, the SKM, on October 17 and the use of this in the decryption of intercepted orders to German submarines on November 5 led to the reunion of the Room 40 staff and a new focus on German tactical naval communications. Given the importance of the material acquired, the First Lord of the Admiralty, Winston Churchill, ordered that Room 40's work be kept secret and its distribution very limited. Room 40 now came under the direction of Captain Reginald "Blinker" Hall, and he took advantage of his organization's abilities and its growing importance to seek out new sources of traffic.

Under Hall's leadership, Room 40 moved beyond simply analyzing intercepted German tactical naval communications to examining commercial, diplomatic, and military traffic of every kind. Hall arranged to acquire copies of the intercepted mails and cable messages that the Home and War Offices had been examining since the beginning of the war, even though the Admiralty was not permitted to have access to either of these. Called before Reginald McKenna, the Home Secretary, to explain his actions, Hall pled his case well enough that Prime Minister Herbert Asquith approved the creation of the joint War Trade Intelligence Department to monitor all aspects of embargo-related communications to and from Germany. By May 1915, Room 40 had received a number of important messages that were held by the War Office but never utilized, including a great many dispatches from German naval attachés in South America that related to the movements of Spee's squadron before and after the Battle of Coronel. Hall had realized that more could be gained from surreptitiously monitoring selected traffic than by shutting off communications altogether. Henceforth,

Room 40 maintained a close watch over all forms of communications that passed through Britain or over its cable lines.[48]

Britain, with French help, now turned to closing down the remaining routes that Germany might still use for overseas communications but that were beyond Britain's direct control. This information blockade would allow Britain to control Germany's financial and economic contacts abroad. It also would prevent pro-German news from reaching influential neutrals and would hamper German efforts to coordinate espionage and sabotage operations abroad. Britain increased the diplomatic pressure on those neutrals who had German cable or radio stations in their territories to close them down.

Following the interruption of the cables in the English Channel, Germany had relied on its high-power radio station at Nauen and a few remaining cables to route information through the Iberian Peninsula and directly to the Americas. The Nauen station exchanged traffic with several interned ships in Spanish and Portuguese ports using their shipboard wireless sets. From there German embassy officials were able to arrange traffic to the Americas along two routes. The first was through Portugal and over the Azores to the remaining German cable to New York. The other was by Spanish government cable to Tenerife in the Canary Islands. From there German cables went to Liberia and on into South America. In North America, the German station at Sayville worked with Nauen directly and could relay signals to South American stations under German influence or to German warships off the Atlantic coast. From Washington or several South American capitals, German diplomats could also pass information out over U.S.-controlled cables in the Americas. For particularly sensitive messages, German diplomats arranged to send their traffic under the diplomatic cover of friendly neutrals, particularly Sweden.

The German information network through neutral territory presented Britain with a difficult situation. Under existing international treaties, cables between neutrals were inviolate from attack, regardless of ownership. The neutral powers had an obligation to ensure that the cables and radio stations were not being used in direct support of any belligerent's military actions, but their use for diplomatic or economic contact was a gray area. Shortly after the outbreak of war, British diplomats had pressured the United States and other countries with German cable or radio stations to seal the stations and prohibit further work by any German company. The United States implemented censorship on all radio stations but not on the cables. After much delay, the Colombian government claimed to have shut down the Telefunken stations in their territory and the sets aboard interned German ships. Efforts to shut down the German operations in Liberia meanwhile proved ineffective. The Liberians did not have sufficient numbers of qualified personnel to ensure that the stations were following neutrality regulations. Instead, the Liberian government ordered both the German and French radio stations to take down their aerials and seal their equipment on October 12, 1914. Here, as in the United States, the German cable remained in operation.[49]

Despite this diplomatic pressure, sympathetic Portuguese and Spanish officials overlooked German indiscretions and permitted the traffic to continue through their territories. After the Royal Navy intercepted several coded messages sent by German and Austrian consular officials using a private radio set in the Canary Islands, British authorities brought pressure on Spain to tighten regulations on the use of radio.[50] Britain realized that it could not rely on Spanish censorship to stop the flow of information to the German cable at the Canary Islands. Wartime necessity had to outweigh the rights of neutrals. The Royal Navy then cut the German cable between Tenerife and Monrovia, Liberia, in November 1914.[51]

The German cables from the Azores to New York also remained a persistent concern. The Portuguese government was reluctant to close them down for fear of having to pay heavy compensation to the German company for breach of landing license. After dissembling, under pressure, they eventually shut the cables. At British insistence, Portuguese authorities added guards at the German cable station in the Azores and placed caps on the termini of the cables at the end of March 1915. This was still not enough. An increase in submarine attacks appeared to correspond to a spike in wireless traffic between Nauen and Spain in early 1915, and the Admiralty came to worry that improvements in submarine range would allow German submarines to operate more effectively in the South Atlantic and possibly the Pacific. Indeed, Spee's squadron had been able to remain in contact with Germany through agents in Chile, using the cables when the squadron operated off the South American coast in late November 1914.[52] Control of cable and wireless access to the Americas would therefore be "of the utmost importance." In the Admiralty's view, nothing could be left to chance. The Royal Navy had the two Azores–New York cables cut on April 9 and May 17, 1915, some fifty miles out from Fayal.[53]

The cable between Liberia and Brazil was the final target of importance, but here the attitude of the United States and Brazil were important. After the United States made it clear that the French cable between Dakar and Monrovia would be sufficient for the necessary continued contact with Liberia, the British cable ship *Transmitter* cut the German cable to Brazil some twenty-six miles off Monrovia on September 13, 1915.[54] Her cables cut and her radio network eviscerated, Germany was now almost completely dependent upon secret messages through Allied cables and her radio stations in the United States.

Germany carried out similar operations to wreck Allied communications, but as these proved to be less successful than those of Great Britain, the effects of the German operations have correspondingly received minimal attention from historians. Still, like that of the British, the effort appears to have been centrally directed, well organized, and sophisticated in its approach. The effects of this campaign would also have important implications for the efforts of the United States to develop its own network. It is difficult to evaluate the impact a total cable isolation of Britain might have had on the war effort, but it would not have been insignificant. A tremendous percentage of regular governmental and military traffic—and all urgent confidential messages—went by cable during the war. British fears of attacks by German raiding parties or saboteurs on cable landings had prompted the deployment of infantry for guard duty throughout Ireland and Great Britain as early as July 31, 1914. Germany, however, preferred to attack at sea.[55]

The first phase of German anticable operations appear to have aimed at splitting Russia from its western allies. The first strikes were against the Great Northern Telegraph Company's cables in the Baltic linking Russia with France and Britain. Seven cables ran across the North Sea from Britain, two to Norway, two to Sweden, and three to Denmark. From there, messages went by a combination of government landlines and Great Northern cables across Scandinavia and the Baltic to Russia. Between September 29 and November 30, 1914, German warships made a series of strikes against the cables that connected Denmark to the Russian ports of Libau and Saint Petersburg. To the south, the German battlecruiser *Goeben* cut the cable between Sevastopol in the Crimea and Varna, Bulgaria, in the Black Sea on November 1.[56] Together these attacks left Russia without a direct cable connection to her allies in the west, and it was usually difficult to repair cables in the wintertime.

For Russia to communicate with Britain and France, messages now had to go either by one of two wireless circuits, which were unreliable, interruptible and always vulnerable to interception, or by the extremely roundabout course by cable from Siberia to Europe around the globe.[57] Britain and Russia had begun negotiations shortly after the outbreak of war to lay a new cable between the two countries as an alternate, safe route. The cable attacks made this plan imperative. By January 1915, after an extremely hazardous cable-laying operation, the British had added a direct cable around Norway to the extreme northeast tip of Russia.[58] This cable quickly reached capacity by the middle of February, and the Russian government appealed for yet another. Adequate stocks for such a lengthy cable required six months additional production, however, and the British government had to reject the plan. After turning down the request again in late 1916, the British government managed to construct a small extension cable to speed up the heavy traffic relating to munitions and supplies.[59]

The widespread redundancy of Britain's cable connections throughout the world and the stockpiled cable supplies and repair-ship capabilities helped to limit the effectiveness of the German attacks, particularly where the Royal Navy retained command of the sea. This was most evident in the Far East. In the Pacific, the German cruiser *Nürnberg* attacked the cable station at Fanning Island, part of the Imperial Pacific Cable from Vancouver to New Zealand and Australia, on September 7, 1914. The German raiders wrecked the cable equipment and cut the two cables coming ashore. Similarly, the cruiser *Emden* disabled the cable junction at Cocos Island in the eastern Indian Ocean on November 9, 1914. Cocos was an important location, where British cables from Africa, the East Indies, and Australia converged.[60] Neither of these attacks carried any lasting damage to the imperial network or cut Britain off from her allies for any considerable length of time.[61]

Shortly afterwards cable ships, pre-positioned according to the company's needs and the requirements of the Imperial Cable Report of 1911, were able to make the needed repairs and bring these cables back into operation. The absence of German cruisers in the Pacific and Indian oceans after the destruction of Spee's cruiser squadron at the Falklands ensured that further attacks against the cables were unlikely.

Where command of the sea was still in dispute, Germany could launch further attacks on the cables. The second phase of Germany's attacks against Allied cables came between May 1915 and April 1917, in the North and Baltic seas. During this time, German naval units systematically cut every cable that went out from Great Britain except the transatlantic ones. This included cables to Iceland, Norway, Sweden, Denmark, and the Netherlands and those between France and Denmark, some of them being cut repeatedly.[62] In one of the more humorous instances, Norwegian cable engineers repairing one of the severed Anglo-Norwegian cables discovered a hidden message left for them. The German raiders had attached a device designed to give a false electrical reading on the cable, which would mislead the engineers to a different distance along the cable when searching for the damaged portion. Inside the capsule holding the device they found a scrap of paper with a simple exhortation: "No more Reuter war-lies on this line! Kindest regards from a 'Hun' and a 'Sea-Pirate.'"[63] Even the supposedly secret cable between Britain and Russia was vulnerable: a German ship cut it on November 5, 1915. At the request of Sweden, Denmark, and Norway, now all suffering the depredations of the "Hunnish" cable pirates, the British government issued a series of "non-interference" guarantees that the Royal Navy would not interrupt the repair operations by neutral cable ships. Both the neutrals and Britain tried to secure similar guarantees from the German government, to no avail. The Norwegian government was particularly apprehensive. When the Norwegian telegraph authority repaired one of the two cables across the North Sea to Britain, its director asked the British government to keep secret the fact that it was operational, lest it become a target again. Gradually the Danish, Norwegian, and British authorities repaired each of these cables. The cumulative effect was mostly one of harassment than lasting destruction of British communications, for

Britain retained the supplies and ships needed to maintain the network.[64]

The time-consuming and difficult job of locating, raising, and then cutting a cable limited action by German surface vessels to only those cables near the European coast.[65] For cables farther out at sea, the German navy began in mid 1915 to use submarines in a coordinated campaign. Very little is known about these U-boat raids, and even less on how exactly they carried out their work. It appears that the U-boats attacked while submerged. Cuts by U-boats could be made only on cables that lay in depths of up to forty fathoms, or about 240 feet. Several crews in both the North Sea and Adriatic carried out training for this type of work, which seems to have been a normal part of the attack mission for more than a few U-boats.[66] Using equipment specially mounted on the ship's deck for the task, the crew of a U-boat could run out a grappling hook attached to one of two motor-driven winches on capstans controlled from inside the vessel.[67] The U-boat cruised back and forth across the field of seabed where a cable was known to lie. An engineer on board would monitor the strain on the wire rope that held the grapple, and the tension on the ship's engines to determine when the grappling hook had acquired the heavy cable. The next step was to sever the cable by using the shears built into the grapple.[68] Such an operation was tricky even for experienced cable crewmen on board a stationary vessel on the surface, but for the crew of a submerged U-boat it must be considered extraordinary. Not every operation was a success. Several U-boats reported the loss of their only grapples in these attempts, which in turn prevented still further cable attacks. Research on cable cutting continued throughout the war, and when the United States entered the war, Germany extended its attacks to U.S. cables as well.[69]

Despite the sophistication of these cable cuts, it was the threat of submarine attacks on the cable ships themselves that did the greatest damage over the long term. Submarine telegraph cables required regular maintenance to repair damage from ships' anchors, sea worms, electrical defects, gradual deterioration of weakened armor, or even seaquakes, which bent or broke cables. The regular minesweeping of the English Channel and other regions around the coast periodically fouled the cables as well and prompted further repair missions. Because grappling, retrieving, and repairing a cable were techniques that required the cable ship to move extremely slowly through the water or to remain motionless for extended periods of time, these ships were particularly vulnerable to attack by submarine. Protecting these ships required the diversion of destroyers and other surface craft to patrol the adjacent waters. Consequently, the General Post Office and the Admiralty had to restrict cable-repair operations to only the most necessary and immediate requirements, to which the cable companies could scarcely object.

One strategy that might have greatly served Germany would have been to destroy Britain's communications by targeting her cable ships before turning to the cables. Britain had a limited number of cable ships capable of operating in deep water, most of which were scattered throughout the empire to service the various strategic cable routes.[70] Fitting out new ships would have involved custom construction and specialized equipment, which would have been a difficult diversion of manpower and tonnage the country could have ill afforded. Indeed, Britain lost two important cable ships in European waters during the early part of the war, the *Monarch* to a mine off the straits of Dover in 1915, and the *Dacia* to a U-boat off Madeira as the ship returned from cable work in 1916. With British cable ships gone or seriously depleted, German raids on the remaining cables would have had more lasting effect. Britain's radio circuits with her allies at the time were completely unable to carry the load of traffic going by cable. Still, on routes with more than one cable, such as on the transatlantic routes, the shadow threat of German U-boat attack did more to disrupt British imperial communications than the actual attacks.[71]

The strategic information war on cables and radios, though not as desperate as fighting in Flanders or at the Masurian Lakes, was a crucial but overlooked aspect of the First World War. Both Great Britain and Germany had given careful consideration to the vital importance a global network held for their military and economic connections around the world. The United States, on the periphery of this network, found itself drawn into the conflict unexpectedly. The effects of Britain's campaign to isolate Germany showed both government officials and private businessmen in the United States the importance of having a cable network free from British control. Germany's war against Britain's cables and the Germans' use of high-power radio to circumvent Britain's information blockade revealed for many proponents of radio the great need for a similar network of radio stations that would supplement—but not replace—an independent cable network. It is to the effects of this information war and the initial attempts by a neutral United States to rectify the imbalance that we now turn.

TWO

✦ ✦ ✦

Neutrality and Vulnerability

IMAGINE FOR A MOMENT two merchants, one in London and one in a small town in Ohio. Cousins, the two built up a regular trade in wax candles and other products of industrious rural Ohio bees. Amid his other duties, the London merchant acted as the agent for his cousin's flourishing business in Britain. In order for the cousin in Ohio to know what to send to London, the two men had to maintain regular contact by cable. Suppose, then, that once a week a cable arrived from London to the factory in Ohio, with the latest orders for specialty candles and wax goods. Similarly, a message passed back to London with a list of what had been shipped and inquiries as to other possible contracts. To the untrained eye, the cryptic collection of numbers and abbreviated words in the cable meant absolutely nothing. Between the two cousins, however, the short messages unlocked a wealth of information about the growing popularity for these sturdy Ohio candles in Oxfordshire or the Pennines. To save on the size of the messages and thus their cost, the cousins used a personal code that referred to the company catalog and shipping details.

Good fortune favored these cousins and their correspondence for several years until war intervened. The cousin in London was then obliged to set aside the personal code and send his weekly message in plain language. Without the codes, the size of every message increased. With the extra girth of the daily volume of traffic, the transatlantic cables began to slow down. The Ohioan had come to expect his cousin's message on Friday mornings, perhaps two hours after the merchant in

London had stepped out to the cable office down the street. Over a matter of weeks, however, the messages took longer and longer to arrive. Some did not arrive until Saturday morning. Occasionally the delay stretched across the weekend. Ordinarily this might have been tolerable; working with bees required patience. The order would still have taken time to fill, and speed was not of the essence. What complicated the matter was the growing cost to send these longer messages, which began to cut into the otherwise handsome profit on fine beeswax candles.

After several months, the Ohioan then did not receive any cabled messages for nearly four weeks. Only when a letter arrived in the mail did he learn what had happened. Apparently his cousin had been sending orders repeatedly. Receiving no reply but learning of no bad news from Ohio, he had assumed something was amiss with the cables. When asked, an overworked cable company clerk had shrugged his shoulders, sighed, and referred the merchant to the regulations about censorship that stated messages might be suppressed. If it appeared that the information in the cable was somehow suspicious, the censors might freely hold on to the message. There was no obligation to inform the sender that this had occurred. Regrettably, there was nothing the cable companies could do, although they did apologize profusely. The London cousin concluded his letter with the warning that a British competitor had lately beaten the Ohioan out on the two otherwise secret contracts he had mentioned in his last message. How the British firms had learned of the bid from the Ohioan candle maker he could not fathom. Between the cable delays, the mounting costs, and this danger of suppression, the Londoner offered that it might be best to exchange coded letters instead. The Ohioan, dismayed at these latest complications to his international businesses, could only shrug his shoulders and return to his bees.

Though just a fable, the story of the two cousins hints at some of the immediate effects of the war on the United States. Nearly all American cable traffic with Europe as well as eastern South America had to pass through Canada, Newfoundland, or the Azores. In all three areas traffic came under direct or indirect British control.[1] Volume on all of these cables rose exponentially as traffic relating to the war jumped. Diplomats and military attachés on all sides dispatched urgent messages between Europe and the Americas. Trading and banking houses scrambled to rearrange commercial deals and financial transactions. Anxious Americans sent repeated inquiries as to the fate of loved ones caught behind the lines. Complicating all of this was the imposition of censorship. British authorities informed the American owners of cables landing in Britain and Ireland that all traffic would henceforth have to be in plain English or French, not in any sort of code. Every civilian message sent or received, regardless of its origin or destination, would be subject to official scrutiny. France (and some neutral European countries) also applied this rule less stringently to their cable and domestic telegraph networks. Before the war it had taken as little as forty minutes to exchange the most important messages between London and New York. By December 1914 it took seven hours.[2]

Britain did little to alleviate the situation, particularly in relation to the important routes to South America. Two German cables were still active between New York and the Azores. These provided an important additional route for commercial traffic with Brazil and Argentina. Because the cables connected two neutral powers (Portugal and the United States), Britain was at first very reluctant to cut them. The pariah treatment was more effective. British cable companies quickly canceled all prewar commercial agreements and refused to exchange any traffic. Because of the interrelated nature of the cable networks, this left the German cables isolated and nearly useless. The American company that relied on these cables, Commercial Cable, now scrambled to work out a new arrangement to pass traffic through the Azores. They could not find anyone at the New York office of the German cable company with the authority to make any changes to the contracts and were fearful of reprisals from the British companies. Within days, however, officials at the Eastern Telegraph group of British cable companies had to relax their draconian position on the Azores. The complaints from Commercial and the interference with U.S.–Brazilian communications raised the danger that the British companies might be driving their customers to rival U.S. cable companies. Equally important, the interference might hurt Anglo–Brazilian relations and ruin the chances that the British cable company could renew its valuable cable concessions in Brazil. In a compromise, the British cable companies agreed to accept from the German cables at the Azores only

U.S.–South American cable traffic. That traffic bound for Europe would be rejected. For the American cabling public, it was a temporary concession. The British government, increasingly concerned about the danger that Germany could communicate through these cables, pressured the Portuguese government into closing them on December 9, 1914.[3]

The overall effect of the cable cutting, imposition of censorship, and boom in war-related traffic was akin to pinching a water hose while twisting the spigot to increase the pressure. The result was chaos for American businesspeople, diplomats, and private citizens. Before the war the German cables to the United States alone had carried some 826,000 messages annually. Most of these messages rerouted to the British cables. Official traffic relating to the war effort quickly became so heavy that civilian messages had to be suspended at night and over the weekends. In addition, deliberate attacks on cables or deferred regular maintenance caused disruptions to the regular cable routes to Russia, India, and the Far East. This led to a general rearrangement of traffic through the entire Western Hemisphere. Consequently, it placed additional burdens on the two woefully inadequate transpacific cables. The cable companies might have been able to handle the additional volume were it not for the requirement that all messages be in open, plain language. This ballooned the average length of a message from eight to twenty-two words. Costs more than doubled, and the regular capacity of the Western Union and Commercial Cable Company transatlantic cables was cut in half. Compounding the problem was the lack of available additional cable supplies. Because the British government considered cables to be war munitions and therefore a restricted export, it was not possible for U.S. companies to lay additional cables in hopes of easing the congestion.[4]

The largest initial complaint centered around the prohibition of encoding. The use of cable codes had been extensive before the war as a cost-saving device and as a rudimentary way of hiding the contents of a message from the casual observer. Thus, before the war, an American commercial agent in Berlin might have cabled this message back to his firm in New York:

> The war is evidently about to commence. The cable between New York and Berlin has been cut. Expect the war to continue for some time.

He could, however, have saved a lot of time and money by simply sending this message, at a discounted rate of five words rather than twenty-five:

WANGSPIER CABESTROS BICHOSO BETTLEREI WANGGUNST.

Though the cable company might have been aware of the fact that the two parties were in contact, no one could have read the message without considerable time and effort spent locating the specific commercial code book and translating the words.[5] For personal, routine subjects, especially proper names, firms had used extra unassigned code words usually located at the end of code books.[6] In addition, regular cable users registered special cable addresses with the cable companies to reduce costs. Thus a firm like the British Lamp Manufacturing Company at 14 Newhall Street, London, might simply have substituted the single word "Britlamp" or a similarly short word to save its cable correspondents time and money.[7] Britain and France feared that such simple messages and confusing words could easily hide secret instructions based on prearranged procedures. Indeed, there were instances when a secret message was simply the name of the intended recipient of a message sent to a registered cable address of a fake company. The prohibition on coded messages and registered cable addresses extended both to private codes, financial codes used by banks, and commercial codes often prepared by the cable companies themselves for use by the ordinary businessman.

Americans and other neutrals also chafed greatly at the practice of suppression, which involved not notifying either the sender or the intended recipient of a message that the censors had stopped a cablegram. To censor cable traffic in wartime under the regulations of the International Telegraph Convention, the British government had only to issue a notice through the International Telegraph Bureau in Berne, Switzerland. All messages passed at the sender's own risk as an "act of grace" over British territory or cables.[8] The British government itself bore no burden for any reimbursement to either party for delays or stoppage of questionable cables. Indeed, Britain did not need to notify the sender or recipient that any such action had occurred.[9] This was precisely the point of censorship. Instead, the message merely vanished into the files of the War Office for later review and languished in the sent-cables files of the cable company, among the millions of other messages. If an interested party wished to check on the progress of a message, he or she had to pay for an additional message to the intended recipient, to inquire after the previous one. This too might be suppressed. In the case of garbled messages, the cable companies had as a matter of courtesy routinely corrected errors in transmission with a follow-up cable at the company's expense. British censors ended this practice as well. Because the additional messages from individuals trying to learn what had become of their earlier cables only generated additional revenue, it soon became an embarrassing situation for the cable companies. Western Union officials were loath to see these policies continued and pressed Secretary of State William Jennings Bryan to seek quick relief from the British.[10]

British censorship affected cable traffic globally. The British government had long required that any company landing a cable on any British territory agree to a provision in the required license that would permit the government to control cable operation and to implement censorship in an emergency. This applied from London to Sydney and all points in between. It existed informally at British cable stations in neutral territory as well. From Ascension Island in the South Atlantic, where cables from South Africa, Brazil, and Argentina joined, the British government maintained a close watch over cable traffic to and from South America. Where one important Western Telegraph cable landed at Pernambuco, Brazil, the British consul had a standing arrangement with the local cable manager to examine traffic when necessary.[11] From Valparaiso, the managers of the West Coast of America cable company, another subsidiary of the Eastern Telegraph group, regularly passed to British military attachés copies of traffic moving between Chile and Peru over their cables.[12] Outside British territory, this practice was necessarily kept very secret. It was made easier by the fact that the majority of cable operators of British and U.S. overseas cables were British citizens. In light of this informal relationship between cable company managers and British consular, diplomatic, or military officials, it is understandable that allegations began to circulate in South America and elsewhere that Britain used cable surveillance for economic gain at the expense of the United States and other neutrals.[13]

Global censorship led to problems for the United States in unexpected areas. Traffic from the United States bound for Puerto Rico, for example, that passed over a British cable through Haiti or Bermuda had to meet the censorship restrictions. The cables also had to contain the complete address (full name and street address) of the recipient. Not surprisingly, this too added to the cost of sending the message. When firms complained strongly to the State Department that this practice halved the capacity of the cables and was an interference to interstate commerce (by virtue of the fact that Puerto Rico was U.S. territory), there was little Secretary Bryan could do to assuage their ire.[14] Western Union took great pains to make it known publicly that it opposed this procedure and did not wish to profit from the public's misfortune. Equally ludicrous in the eyes of cable officials was the broad sweep of these requirements. Companies like Cunard Steamship or Morgan, Grenfell, and Company were so well known (and therefore presumably trustworthy) that the practice was little more than a waste of their money, Western Union's cable capacity, and the British censors' energy to examine their traffic.[15] Most startling of all, sometimes the censorship extended to U.S. diplomatic or military traffic. In two notable instances, British censors, without explanation, blocked instructions to the commander in chief of the U.S. Asiatic Fleet and dispatches to the Philippines from the colonel commanding the China Expedition.[16]

Along with the removal of code words, suppression and the extension of censorship worldwide affected the business opportunities afforded by such rapid exchange of information over the oceans. Banks could not be certain that their transactions with other banks were properly recorded. Financial speculators could not engage as easily in arbitrage, while quick-footed importers could no longer count on beating out their competition.[17] Ships might arrive before a telegram alerting an importer that his goods were on board. Though the British intended their control of the cables to be an important weapon in the economic war against Germany, it affected the course of the entire global economy.

The only possible alternative to the cables for swift transatlantic messages was to send them by high-power radio. Here the United States faced a different problem: the best stations were those of German companies, and Great Britain clamored for their closure. Even before Britain joined the war against Germany, the British chargé d'affaires in

Washington, Colville Barclay, presented to Secretary Bryan a request from the Foreign Office that the United States respect its role as a neutral by prohibiting Germany from operating the station at Sayville as well as another under construction at Tuckerton, New Jersey. The British view was that the German government had subsidized these two stations as "intelligence bureaux" and that the Germans had already relayed instructions from Berlin to the German warships *Dresden* and *Karlsruhe* off the Atlantic coast. The Admiralty warned the naval attaché at the U.S. embassy in London that instructions to head to neutral ports to evade British warships had gone out via Sayville to German merchant ships. This improper use of the stations confirmed U.S. Navy officers' suspicions about the secret purpose of these stations.[18] British officials feared that these unneutral transmissions might persist if not stopped. They asked that either a censor be in place at the stations to ensure "equal treatment as between the belligerents" or that the stations close.[19]

To answer the British and make the U.S. position clear, President Woodrow Wilson issued on August 5 a neutrality proclamation on the use of wireless in the United States. He forbade the operators of all radio stations within the United States and its territories from sending or receiving unneutral messages or providing any unneutral service to the belligerents during hostilities. All radio messages were to be in clear or unencoded form. The secretary of the navy was to carry out whatever action was necessary to enforce compliance.[20] Because Britain and France could still use their cables to send coded messages relating to military affairs, this put Germany at a disadvantage. Bryan, mindful of the disparity, sought an equitable solution to place all belligerents on an equal footing. One proposal was to permit both sides to send messages through Tuckerton and Sayville, provided that the U.S. censors there had copies of the codes and ciphers used. Similarly, Germany would be permitted to use the British and French cables to send traffic between the German Foreign Office and its embassy in Washington.[21] The duties of the United States in this situation were unclear under international law. State Department Counselor Robert Lansing, who considered the matter closely, concluded that the United States needed to maintain "an impartial neutrality to prevent communication between a belligerent . . . and its agents on neutral territory when such communications are of an unneutral character unless both belligerents possess equal opportunities of communication."[22] Under the circumstances, without cutting off all radio and cable contact, the United States could no longer achieve true neutrality.

Lansing's suggestion did not mollify either Britain or France. Both powers objected to the fact that German citizens continued to operate these two stations. They reiterated their demand that the United States shut them down immediately. For its part, the German government maintained a strenuous denial of any direct or indirect connection to the stations or the companies that operated them. The Justice and Navy departments, however, had strong reason to believe that there were in fact links between the German government and the Sayville station.[23] As a stopgap measure, Wilson allowed that the U.S. government would send diplomatic messages via Sayville to Germany, and the German chargé d'affaires would pass his dispatches through the State Department. The German government then agreed to provide the United States with three copies of its codebook, in order that the United States could safeguard its neutrality. By executive order on September 5, Wilson instructed Secretary of the Navy Josephus Daniels to take over one of the transatlantic stations for official U.S. use.[24]

The U.S. Navy selected the high-power radio station nearly completed at Tuckerton, New Jersey. Ownership and the right to operate this station was a matter of dispute. A German company, the Hochfrequenz-Machinen Aktiengesellschaft für Drahtlose Telegraphie (HOMAG) had constructed the station and installed its equipment on contract to a French firm, the Compagnie Universelle de Télégraphie et Téléphonie (CUTT) but had not yet turned it over when the war broke out. On purely technical grounds the Commerce Department informed HOMAG in late August 1914 that the station did not have the proper license to operate, and shut the station down.[25] On September 9, the navy took control of Tuckerton from HOMAG under Wilson's executive order and set about preparing it to work with the companion station at Eilvese, Germany, under government administration.[26] Unexpectedly, the generator for the main transmitter burned out six days later, but when HOMAG officials requested that the U.S. Navy permit the transportation of the generator to Germany for repair, the navy demurred. In October naval personnel replaced the German equipment with a 60 kw arc transmitter manufactured by the Federal Telegraph Company, which had built similar arc stations elsewhere for the navy.

Though powerful, the arc was barely capable of throwing a signal all the way across the Atlantic.[27] Meanwhile, the French refused permission for any ship carrying the new generator from Germany through the blockade.[28]

Like Tuckerton, the station at Sayville was still a work in progress. Built in 1904, its equipment was powerful, but its operation was neither continuous nor thoroughly reliable. The station worked under an experimental license from the Department of Commerce.[29] Still, its operators, the Atlantic Communication Company (ACC), carried out regular commercial exchanges with Nauen in Germany and with Cartagena, Colombia. This alarmed the British government, for it meant Sayville could relay instructions from Germany to German cruisers in the Atlantic or in the Caribbean. In fact, this is what happened. Several weeks after the outbreak of war Captain Guy Gaunt, the naval attaché at the British Embassy in Washington, passed to Robert Lansing copies of transmissions from Sayville to German cruisers off the U.S. coast, actions impermissible under the rules of neutrality.[30] The British Embassy also pushed the United States to monitor transmissions from Sayville to Cartagena, where several interned German merchant ships might be using their shipboard wireless sets to relay messages. The navy maintained that its censors at Sayville would catch or deter any unneutral messages and downplayed the significance of subsequent reported transmissions to ships at sea.[31]

Neutrality requires that neither belligerent side in a conflict be favored, and radio stations under apparent British control in the United States came in for just as much scrutiny. The predominant radio firm in the United States at the time was the Marconi Wireless Telegraph Company of America, an independent subsidiary with a majority share owned by its British parent. Like the ACC, the U.S. Navy suspected that American Marconi was not entirely free to chart its own course and therefore should not be considered an "American" firm. In addition to two nearly finished high-power transatlantic stations near New York and Boston, American Marconi maintained the most extensive chain of ship-shore stations along the Atlantic coast.[32] When Wilson issued his neutrality proclamation and the Navy sent censors out to the foreign-owned radio stations, those of American Marconi were on the list.[33]

Allegations of neutrality violations surfaced almost immediately. Belligerent warships were to seal their radio sets upon entering a neutral port, but it had become customary for ships of all flags to contact a coastal radio station to exchange general news and information as they approached the harbor. In early September, the British cruiser *Suffolk* allegedly sent an unneutral message through the American Marconi station at Siasconsett on Nantucket to New York. This prompted a rebuke from the State Department and the attorney general about the company's responsibility to prevent violations of neutrality. American Marconi officials countered that the censorship and allegations that the company was British were unfair. As punishment, Secretary of the Navy Josephus Daniels then ordered that the Siasconsett station be closed down. Although it was a very important station, it remained shuttered until mid-January.[34] After a similar incident at an American Marconi coastal station in Hawaii, Assistant Secretary of the Navy Franklin Roosevelt ordered the commandant of the naval district there to shut that station down as well if an explanation and an apology were not forthcoming. Chastened, American Marconi officials promised to take great care in avoiding similar incidents in the future. Despite the palliation, the experiences did not diminish the belief among many in the U.S. Navy that American Marconi was, underneath a thin veneer, a British operation.[35]

Because the German radio stations were neither continually operable or thoroughly reliable, those Americans wishing to send messages to Europe still needed to suffer the difficulties of the cables. From August to October 1914, the U.S. ambassador in London, Walter Hines Page, protested repeatedly about these censorship restrictions to the British foreign minister, Sir Edward Grey. Grey held firmly to the position that Britain could not deviate from the requirement for full names and addresses, the prohibition on commercial codes, and the use of plain languages, as these messages were the only way to expedite the work of the censors. There would be no notification that cable messages had been suppressed, for this would undo the very point of censorship. Of course, it would appear unfair to those who messages were inadvertently stopped or delayed, but this could not be helped. The British government would not alter these rules, even for the United States.

The cable censorship and information control served as a potent weapon for Britain as it intensified its economic war against Germany.

The cable censorship was not only about blocking war news and forestalling espionage. It was about removing Germany from the international economy by systematically blocking the financial and commercial transactions that the cable connections had made possible. U.S. firms trading with Germany and lending it money through neutral countries became a major focus of the effort. By targeting commercial cables that were "detrimental to British interests" and suppressing them, Britain extended into the realm of the cable an information blockade that, in its effectiveness, would come to rival the one at sea.[36]

Bryan rejected Grey's explanation that nothing could be done to limit the impact of this blockade on the United States. He instructed Page to pursue a compromise offer of placing copies of leading codebooks with the British authorities and to emphasize repeatedly the great burden that this situation had put on U.S. firms. Page continued to press the Foreign Office along these lines through the fall. By mid-October he had won an initial compromise. The British government would let pass all commercial messages between the United States and other neutral countries, even though it appeared that some of these messages, though thinly disguised, related to trade with Germany. Toward the end of October, British censors again relaxed the rules. This time they permitted private individuals to send messages to previously registered (and therefore abbreviated) cable addresses in Britain. Senders could also use a first initial with a full last name. Still, no notice of delay or suppression could be made under any circumstances. Bryan and Robert Lansing continued to press the notification issue but found themselves reduced to the slightly ridiculous suggestion that permitting notification would be courteous and just.[37]

By November, the initial concessions that Page had won contributed to a noticeable decline in complaints to the State Department. At the same time, the cable censors in Britain had begun to centralize operations and improve their work.[38] This did little to remove the strong distaste for censorship and its effects on international commerce. The Swiss government then approached the United States to propose a joint protest. Banks in Switzerland had reported that it was becoming nearly impossible to carry on financial and commercial relations with the United States amid the delays. In fact, some cables concerning Swiss governmental purchases of U.S. grain had never reached the United States.[39] The Italian government, similarly inconvenienced, proposed a similar joint démarche in December. Bryan received complaints from U.S. diplomats in Copenhagen, Rome, and Madrid about interference to commercial cables to and from the United States. In London, Page received repeated instructions to protest the matter with Sir Edward Grey. At the same time, Ambassador Myron T. Herrick in France and Page were to work with the Swiss ministers in London and Paris to make joint petitions against further censorship.[40]

After this round of protests, it was France's turn to relent. The French government agreed to permit the use on their cables of five widely available commercial codes, provided the sender also brought a translation of the message to file as well. In Britain, Grey stood fast. Pleading ignorant of the particulars of cable censorship, he held to the line that no notification or explanation of suppression would be made unless the State Department cited the specific cable in question. Given the fact that some fifty thousand neutral messages passed through British hands each day, such a formality was nearly impossible. Page reported to Bryan that similar discontent over censorship was widespread in Britain, and Page was certain that commercial considerations on behalf of British firms played no part in the operation of censorship. Still, Page could go no farther with Grey without the specific date, time, and sender of every cable in question. Official diplomacy apparently exhausted, Western Union officials discussed with the British how the French now permitted the use of code books. To Western Union, it appeared that this move was an attempt to divert cable traffic to the inefficient and unpopular French line. The company was anxious to secure the same privileges from Britain, but such an outcome was unlikely.[41]

By early December 1914, the U.S. cotton trade with Germany had become a major target, and cable censorship was a key weapon. Although Britain still permitted the shipment of cotton to German ports, reports came from Berlin, Galveston, New Orleans, and Memphis of unexplained delays or disappearances of cables related to cotton and cottonseed trade with neutral countries. Outraged cotton brokers and merchants seeking relief quickly put pressure on the U.S. government. Various cotton exchanges as well as the United States Chamber of Commerce petitioned Bryan directly for help, while others routed their complaints through their representatives or senators. From London, Page sent the usual declarations from Grey that it was not Britain's intention to harm U.S. or other neutral trade, that notification of suppression continued to be impossible, and that only with precise information about the particular blocked message could any explanation be given. Despite a hint from Grey that Britain was considering the allowance of one or more commercial code books, an exasperated Page reported his conviction that the cable censors simply had not yet learned their job.[42]

Page's persistence and his joint protests with his Danish, Swiss, Italian, and Spanish colleagues in Britain seemed to be successful. According to Grey, the cable censors were inclined to permit the use of some seven different standard commercial code books. Page then began to receive from the chief British cable censor the daily report of stopped cables headed for the United States, a secret privilege afforded to no other country. Still, there was no progress on the notification issue, and the use of these commercial code books would not apply to messages about certain war-related industries, such as mining, oil, and rubber. While it was not an end to the hated censorship, the concessions that Page had won were significant. In Washington, Bryan was optimistic that the French government might be induced to match this progress.[43]

Hoping to widen the concessions still further, Page pressed forward in early 1915 on several different angles. One matter of particular importance was the use of arcane language by cotton brokers and other merchants. Technical trade terms used in describing agricultural or bulk industrial goods were among the more restricted, because the actual message was difficult for the uninitiated to understand. Page took the position that commercial code words were innocent and that it was up to the censorship officials to learn the details of the trade messages in advance. This backfired when a U.S. Navy censor stopped a message at the Miami radio station bound for the Bahamas sent by the Lever Brothers soap company. When the navy requested a plain-language explanation of the trade words in the message, they turned out to be merely brand names and quality levels of ordinary soap. Page sourly concluded that the department would have to yield on the matter of trade words, but Bryan urged him to emphasize the distinction that censorship on radio necessarily had to be stricter than that on cables.[44]

By this point the nature of the complaints received in Washington had shifted. The information blockade around Germany was effectively complete, and the angry voices were of those whose words could not longer reach Germany. At a loss for any other ideas, Page recommended that in future any messages sent to Germany or via neutrals should go by non-British cables. Such a choice of routes, however, had become impossible. The importance of cable control as a weapon in economic warfare meant that there was little chance Britain would relax the censorship further.[45] Even after Ambassador William G. Sharp in Paris won the coveted prize of notification from French authorities, Grey and the resolute cable censors in Britain remained noncommittal. All that Page could win was the right for cotton brokers to use standard codes in certain restricted instances.

Page became very pessimistic about any further progress. While a three-day sample of traffic passing through the chief censor's office showed Page that the censors stopped 14 percent of all U.S. cable traffic with the Netherlands but only 3 percent of that with Scandinavia, the sheer number of specific claims he would have to file would be impossible for anyone to cope with. It would take, the War Office informed him some time later, two men an entire year to comb through all the records to respond to the complaints he had been forwarding. Further complicating Page's work, not every complaint proved to be a valid one. Of the 350 he provided in early January, the censor's office could find that only three of the first sixty or seventy had in fact been stopped by British censors. Confronted by this persistent bureaucratic stonewalling, Page could only report the obvious to Bryan: the United States would need its own direct cables to Scandinavia, Holland, or Italy to avoid the nightmare of British and French censorship and the infringement on neutral trade.[46]

Exasperated, Bryan and other department officials decided upon a drastic measure. In late January, consuls in Sweden had reported that messages expected from U.S. firms were not arriving and that the situation was particularly egregious in Göteborg. This port city was an important transshipment point for American cotton into Europe as well as a major exporter of wood pulp. The firms handling cotton and wood pulp from Göteborg were not getting their cabled instructions from the United States.[47] To ensure delivery, Bryan authorized consul Emil Sauer to transmit plain-language commercial messages within the cover and codes of a diplomatic message. This was a flagrant abuse of international telegraph regulations.[48] Evidently Bryan extended this instruction to several other consuls and legations elsewhere in Europe as well. Such a practice was generally frowned upon as cheating, because all government messages received priority on the cables over regular private and commercial messages.[49] Still, when the minister in Sweden, Ira Nelson Morris, reported on March 4 that several larger U.S.-Swedish trading firms had received no messages for as long as two weeks, Morris included messages from one Swedish cotton dealer to his U.S. clients in the cabled dispatch.

To the disappointment of many, this measure backfired. Several days after Morris's message, Grey presented to Page a curt memorandum on the matter. He reminded the United States that the previous November Britain had warned the United States about not sending commercial traffic under diplomatic cover. Subsequently, eight more messages of this sort had been intercepted from American diplomats in Norway, Germany, Denmark, Italy, the Netherlands, and Switzerland. Grey did not inform Page of precisely how Britain had come to know that this was happening, but it is likely that the Admiralty's Room 40 was behind the discovery of this ruse. British officials had "a good deal of suppressed indignation" at this behavior, Page reported. They even quietly threatened to withdraw the privilege of diplomatic cables from the United States entirely if the practice continued. On March 16, Bryan conceded the point. He instructed all diplomatic and consular officials to stop the inclusion of commercial messages in diplomatic dispatches. By this point it now must have been very clear to senior State Department officials that no governmental message could be considered safe if it went over non-U.S. cables.[50]

By the summer of 1915, Page believed that the British had yielded as much as they were willing on the censorship issue. Accepting the information blockade as well as the new maritime one, he despaired to Bryan of further progress. Page even refused to forward any more copies of stopped messages to the cable censor for explanations. "I do not know what to say or how to try to go further than I have gone," he lamented, even as department counselor Robert Lansing encouraged him to keep up the pressure. Private groups also tried to mediate but to no avail. The Netherlands Overseas Trust offered to set up its own clearinghouse for cable messages that they would paraphrase or translate into another language in order to foil secret messages or codes. Secretary Bryan enthusiastically instructed Page in London and Minister Henry van Dyke in the Hague to support this measure. Predictably, however, British authorities refused to grant any special waivers or privileges to the trust and the plan collapsed.[51]

As Britain expanded the blockade in mid-1915, cable censorship became a much more potent weapon. To this point British authorities had used cable traffic in a largely passive manner, suppressing those messages that appeared suspicious and tracking trading relationships in support of the maritime blockade. In the summer of 1915, Britain struck against Germany's overseas financial relationships. By completely denying cable privileges to selected banks in neutral countries, British officials were able to extract from them promises to end any relationships with Germany or its allies. To make an example, the censors first selected the prominent Irving Bank of New York and sent letters to its partners in Britain, warning them that the bank's messages would be held up repeatedly. After a few weeks, the bank capitulated and in October signed an agreement to abide by the British demands. With the cables and the legal right on the British side, there was little that the State Department could do for the Irving Bank. As Britain widened its economic war against Germany through 1915, it created both a public and a confidential blacklist of firms or individuals all across the world whose relationships with Germany or its allies condemned them. These firms were forbidden to use British cables, shipping, or banking facilities anywhere, even in neutral countries. Consequently, Britain and its allies were able to reshape the entire structure of global trade in such a way as to drive Germany out virtually altogether.[52] It cannot be overemphasized that Britain's control of the cable network and the information coursing through it was key to the effectiveness of the entire operation, a fact that U.S. officials would appreciate more fully once they too joined the war on Britain's side. Lacking a direct cable to Germany and being dependent upon Britain for cable access to the whole world, United States could do little but acquiesce. The British information blockade remained in place for the rest of the war, with the United States at its mercy.[53]

While the experience of the United States with British cable-domination revealed that this situation conferred the power to control the information passing over the cables, German high-power radio stations in the western Hemisphere showed a different danger. Allowing a foreign firm to build radio stations on U.S. territory potentially threatened

U.S. neutrality and security. In April 1915, the Atlantic Communication Company, the operators of Sayville, finished upgrading the station. They had replaced its weaker 35 kw spark transmitter with a new 100 kw Telefunken double frequency alternator and had constructed a huge new antenna array of three five-hundred-foot towers. This made Sayville one of the most powerful radio stations in the world, on par with the U.S. Navy's new station in the Canal Zone.[54] In peacetime, this would have been welcome news in the United States, but the Commerce Department, which held the power of licensing stations, had reservations. ACC was primarily owned by the Telefunken Company of America, which in turn was a joint venture of Allegemeine Elektrizitats Gesselschaft, and Siemens and Halske, the two leading electrical firms in Germany. Dr. Karl Georg Frank, the secretary and treasurer of the ACC, was also the New York representative for Siemens. Within Germany, the stations that Sayville communicated with (primarily Nauen) were dually owned by the German Imperial Post Office and the army. The U.S. Navy had learned that a Professor J. Zenneck, attached to the station now as an experimental engineer, was also a captain in the German marines. The British offered similar allegations about another engineer at the station. With the recurring claims from British officials about the relay of unneutral messages through Sayville, these issues had raised serious doubts among many senior U.S. naval officers about the true purpose of the station.

Whatever uncertainty that remained, however, vanished after the revelations by a curious engineer for the American Marconi Company. In his spare time, Charles Apgar had taken to recording the Sayville station signal from his home on newly available wax discs. Between June 15 and June 22, 1915, he recorded the high-speed transmissions from Sayville, which he then played back at lower speed to listen to the operator's technique. As he listened to the recordings, he realized that something was not right. An operator working manually would stop his transmission if he made an error, send a word indicating the error, and retransmit the word correctly. Sayville used high-speed automatic transmitting, which allowed for more signals to be sent. To do this required typing out the message beforehand and then running it through the transmitter at a faster rate than the human ear could discern. At the other end, the receiving station would record the signal on tape and the operators would read it later. This method was error free, because any incorrect portion of the tape could be cut out and a new, corrected section inserted before transmission. Apgar noticed that the Sayville operators were leaving in the errors. In fact, the errors and corrections appeared in a curiously repetitive pattern. Apgar collected more than 175 Edison wax disc recordings and then turned over his findings to the government. A review of the messages against the originals, which had been filed with the navy censors, revealed still more secrets. Some of the messages filed did not correspond to the actual signals sent, some of the errors were not reasonable ones to commit, and some of the messages had simply been made up.[55] These findings fueled rumors among many in the navy that Sayville had played some role in providing departure information on transatlantic ships. If true, Sayville's operations could have contributed to the recent sinking of the *Lusitania* on May 7, with the loss of 128 American lives, and perhaps the loss of the *Armenia* on June 30 as well. At any rate, Sayville was not as innocent as its backers had insisted.

Apgar's recordings led to Sayville's seizure. At the end of June, naval secretary Daniels convened the Neutrality Board of cabinet officials to review the recordings. Convinced by what they heard, Daniels, Secretary of State Lansing, Secretary of Commerce William C. Redfield and assistant naval secretary Franklin D. Roosevelt agreed to recommend to Wilson that Sayville be turned over to the navy. The pretext would be the ACC's application for a new operating license for its improved station. Secretary Redfield concluded that granting such a license would be engaging in an unneutral act. The commercial utility of such a station was too great for it to be shut down. Rather, the Navy would operate it in trust for the duration of the war. Wilson agreed. On July 8, the U.S. Navy took control of Sayville's operations and shortly thereafter, following several further incidents, ejected the German staff and took over operations completely. As if to offer final proof of Sayville's real purpose, the naval attaché in Berlin reported back to Washington in October that the seizure of the station had caused great consternation among German naval officers.[56]

The boom for the United States in international financial and commercial trade spawned by the war steadily stretched the existing cable and radio connections to their limits. Growing numbers of complaints from the merchants and financiers made it apparent to officials, if they had not understood before, the great inadequacies of the existing networks serving the country. Before August 1914, the United States had been in the bottom of a business cycle that had been the worst depression seen since the 1890s. The outbreak of the war had initially aggravated the situation. Cotton and other export sectors suffered from the disruption of trading patterns and the isolation of traditional partners like Germany and Austria-Hungary. The growing demand for supplies from other neutrals and the Anglo-French alliance, however, sparked an economic acceleration in 1915 that continued through the 1920s. "For Woodrow Wilson and the men in the State Department who advised him," historian Arthur Link has concluded, "the primary objective in foreign policy once the war in Europe had begun was to win the largest possible freedom of trade with all belligerents for American citizens, within the bounds of neutrality."[57] In order to trade, one needed to be able to communicate easily.

Besides Europe and the belligerents hungry for war supplies, South America had also become of particular economic and financial importance to the United States. Before the war, European countries, particularly Britain, had provided markets, secondary goods, and investment capital as well as banking, transportation, and communications services to Brazil, Argentina, and other nations. The withdrawal of European funds and the diversion of European shipping had consequently paralyzed many economies in the region. In desperation, Brazil and others turned to the United States.[58] Over the thirty-three months of U.S. neutrality, trade and investment with South America increased 100 percent. Finally permitted by the Federal Reserve Act of 1913 to establish foreign branches, the leading U.S. banks steadily opened offices in the major cities of Brazil, Argentina, Uruguay, and Chile. Likewise, U.S. merchant houses increased their imports of South American goods, particularly coffee, while developing new markets for industrial and consumer goods in the region. Permanent expanded trade and investment with South America would not be possible, however, without greater cable and radio connections and an augmented merchant marine.[59]

Vital organs in the body of international trade, the United States and the countries of South America lacked essential arteries to let circulate between them the oxygenated blood of information and goods. The existing infrastructure of international trade and investment did not favor the United States: The vast majority of hemispheric commerce moved between U.S. and Latin American ports in European-owned ships. The war had thrown the regular shipping schedules into disarray. There were few U.S.-owned ships available to take up the shortfall. Likewise, no direct cable or radio connection existed between the United States and the principal markets of Brazil, Argentina, or Uruguay. Indirectly, U.S. merchants could send messages via London or the Azores on British cables, but messages now suffered from censorship, delays, and high rates.

The only American firm serving Latin America was James Scrymser's Central and South American Telegraph Company. Launched in the late nineteenth century, its cable network reached from New York and Texas down through Central America to the west coast of South Amer-

Principal South American cables, 1914

ica as far as Chile. Landlines connected with Argentina, but no cables had yet reached the most important markets on the east coast.[60] Either way, the high costs of sending messages restricted cable use to the most essential traffic or the most eager merchants. Axiomatically, more cables would lead to cheaper rates, which would in turn make banking, investment, and shipping much easier for businesses in both the United States and South America. As trade with Latin America accelerated under the pressure of the war, so too did the clamor from leading businesses and public officials for improved communications throughout the hemisphere.

The Wilson administration supported the drive for such improvements publicly but could do little to alter the situation rapidly. President Wilson had personally decried the situation to Latin America delegates attending the first Pan American Financial Conference in May 1915. Expanded cables and shipping connections, he declared, were "absolutely necessary" for "true commercial relations": "We cannot deal [with each other] unless we communicate with each other." Later in the proceedings, Commerce Secretary Redfield, echoing Wilson, called explicitly for improved cable connections, lower rates, better news services, and generally cheaper contact with the major cities of South America. Behind the scenes, Treasury Secretary William G. McAdoo, organizer of the conference, exhorted Western Union officials to explore the problem and seize the opportunity.[61] In an era when state intervention was rare, Wilson and his advisors expected private firms to redress the imbalance on their own initiative.

Motivated as much by economic opportunity as presidential encouragement, American telegraph companies attempted to improve hemispheric cable connections, but significant problems stood in their way. Foremost was the Western Telegraph Company. This British firm had acquired in the late nineteenth century a set of restrictive licenses that blocked other companies from operating cables in Brazil, Argentina, and Uruguay. The prize market was Brazil. Here Western Telegraph held a twenty-year monopoly concession for cables connecting to Argentina and Uruguay and for cables touching at more than one Brazilian port. Compounding this, Western Telegraph held a fifty-year monopoly over all of Uruguay's external cable links. For Scrymser's Central and South American Telegraph Company, which had just entered Argentina via landlines over the Andes, this license meant it was impossible to run cables northwards to Brazil. The only other route, down from the north, lay in the arthritic hands of the French Telegraph Cable Company. Its obsolete lines ran from northern Brazil to New York over a series of regularly interrupted cables.[62] To go by land was to rely on inefficient state telegraph monopolies and roundabout routes. Western Telegraph, it seemed, sat astride the easiest path and had barred the route to its competitors.

Still, Scrymser's agents found a way through. Western Telegraph's monopoly concession for cables from Brazil to Argentina and Uruguay had expired in June 1913. Scrymser focused his attention on winning the right to lay new cables between Argentina and Brazil. Because Western Telegraph retained the concession on cables between Brazilian ports until 1933, he would be able to lay only a single cable between Argentina and Brazil. The monopoly in Uruguay would expire in July 1917, and if Scrymser could beat Western Telegraph there too, he would be able to lay another cable from Uruguay to Brazil. This would double his connections. Shortly after the war broke out, Scrymser requested diplomatic support in his efforts to win a concession to land a cable in Argentina. The United States had long needed such a cable to Brazil, he pointed out to the State Department. Now the spike in war-related traffic, the imposition of censorship, and the severance of the German cables made it all the more necessary. Correspondingly, the ambassador in Brazil and minister in Argentina received instructions to lend all support. Secretary of State Bryan informed Minister F. J. Stimson that he was to impress discreetly upon the Argentine government that the United States sought an "all-American cable connection with Brazil via Argentina, in every way independent of British control." No British cable, Bryan stressed, could meet the diplomatic and commercial needs of the country.[63]

Western Telegraph had no intention of allowing Scrymser to gain the slightest foothold in their territory. Cable traffic between the United States and Brazil was lucrative: eighty-five cents a word, with the average length of a coded message around eight to ten words. The cabling public had the right to select the company and the route that their message took, known as the "via," but Western Telegraph took steps to make it much more expensive for American businessmen to send their cables "via Colón" and over Scrymser's cables. Western Telegraph tacked a special fee of forty-one cents per word onto any message that went through their Uruguay cables (thus, between Brazil and

Argentina) destined for the United States. This was a hefty fee—an additional $4.10 for an average-sized message. Thus it became faster and cheaper to send messages for the United States through London than up the Pacific coast. Scrymser's company had little choice but to pass this special fee on to its customers—both businessmen as well as U.S. diplomats. In order to avoid Western Telegraph, a businessman could route the message deliberately over Uruguay and Brazil's landlines, but this was not a good idea. Diplomatic traffic sent from Washington to Rio through these lines took up to three days instead of the expected half hour. The special fee was an underhanded maneuver, particularly in light of the overcrowding and delays on the British cables. Both Scrymser's company and the government of Uruguay tried to get the Brazilians to force Western Telegraph to stop.[64] Still, the only effective outcome would be a new American cable. That required concessions.

Brazil was the first target. Because of the web of interrelating concessions, Frank Carney, Central's agent in South America, had to defeat Western Telegraph's Brazilian monopolies before he could turn his attention to Uruguay or Argentina. Until the Brazilian government made an offer to another company, Western Telegraph's expired concessions remained in force. Western Telegraph also had the right of first refusal. When Carney applied for new concessions, Western Telegraph representatives promptly objected and took the matter to the Brazilian courts. The Brazilian federal court found initially for Western Telegraph in September 1914. The court granted the company an injunction stopping Central from winning the concession and ordered the entire matter into arbitration. A delaying tactic welcomed by the British firm, this decision provided Western Telegraph officials a chance to gain political support within the Brazilian government against Scrymser's company.[65]

Meanwhile, the boom in U.S.–South American trade and suspicions over Britain's control of the cables steadily increased traffic on Central's lines. By November 1915, Minister Stimson reported from Buenos Aires that the New York–Rio traffic over the Scrymser company lines had increased substantially. "Owing to the censorship [in Britain]," he reported, "many merchants are unwilling to send their cables by the English Co., independent of the delays caused by it." This was the case even though Western Telegraph had levied highly discriminatory rates on the Argentina-Brazil route. The Brazilian government had unsuccessfully appealed to the International Bureau of the International Telegraph Union (ITU) in Switzerland to force Western Telegraph to relent. At the end of 1915, Stimson was working on a new joint appeal to the ITU by the ministers of Argentina, Brazil, and Uruguay in Switzerland. The only alternative—routing messages through Paraguay—remained impracticable.[66] Despite these problems, Scrymser's company continued to pursue new customers and gained still more traffic. Wester Telegraph Company officials in London became concerned in late 1915 when they learned that Central was advertising the complications of British censorship and the absence of such restrictions on its own lines. There was no way for Western Telegraph to reduce the delays any more than it had and still meet the censorship rules. Western Telegraph officials in Buenos Aires and Rio worried that the longer censorship remained in place, the greater the incentive the public had to switch to Scrymser's lines, particularly if Central finally reached Brazil. In fact, through the entire period, cable use on the British lines actually declined.[67]

The legal battles in Brazil were lengthy, but by mid-1916 Scrymser believed that the tide had turned for his company even though Western Telegraph had managed a two-year delay. In November 1916, after further appeals, the Brazilian courts found in Central's favor. Three months later Carney then asked the Brazilian government to reconsider his company's application for a cable-operating concession.[68] Scrymser predicted that once Western Telegraph saw defeat in Brazil, it would move to block Central's efforts in Argentina. This might not be a problem. To U.S. diplomats in Buenos Aires it appeared that the Argentine director general of telegraphs was generally receptive to Central's proposed cable extension, although Stimson had become worried that further delay in Brazil would lead to problems with the Argentines.

Further adding to the confusion, the Western Telegraph monopoly over Uruguay's cable connections was set to expire in July 1917. Company officials had already begun to renegotiate the monopoly. The draft language in the concession included an exclusive license for Western Telegraph, which would have been a significant setback for Scrymser. John Merrill, a vice president at Central and the elderly Scrymser's eventual successor, urged a strong diplomatic protest to the Uruguayans. "I am quite sure you appreciate the serious effect such moves would have upon American commerce and American interests if successful," he politely suggested to Lansing. The secretary of state ordered a joint offensive by U.S. diplomats in Buenos Aires, Montevideo, and Rio to bring strong, simultaneous diplomatic pressure on Uruguay. Frank Carney was confident about this, having learned that the director general of the Uruguayan government telegraph system, like his Argentine counterpart, was opposed to renewing the British monopoly.[69] Carney pressed the Argentina and Uruguayan governments in regard to Western Telegraph's discriminatory rate as well. He also had help from the major Argentine paper, *La Prensa*, which relied on the American company for access to news from the United States and the rest of the world. As the nation moved closer toward war with Germany in early 1917, Carney and U.S. diplomats kept up the pressure in South America, with hopes of cracking the Western Telegraph monopolies completely.

Despite Central's apparent triumphs in South America, John Merrill was apprehensive about the prospects of lasting success. For all the great demand to extend cable connections to Latin America or Europe in order to ease the growing traffic burdens, the supply of cable available to U.S. firms was practically nonexistent. Even if the Central and South American Telegraph Company acquired all the concessions it needed in the region, the wartime demand for submarine telegraph cable among the Allied powers in Europe was so great that it would not be possible to extend Central's lines until after the war.[70] Indeed, the British government had already seized two large orders of cable that Central had intended to use in routine maintenance. To manufacture the lengths of cable that Central would need to run from Argentina to Uruguay and Brazil would take months. Merrill had no assurance that Britain might not seize these too.[71]

Beyond supplies of cable, the British dominated all major areas of submarine cable technology: Britain controlled the gutta-percha. Britain had the largest supply of deep-water cable ships with experienced crews. Britain led in cable manufacturing and in technological innovation of cables. British cable firms had long-standing familiarity with all aspects of cable operation. They also had a leading position through restrictive concessions in those markets of particular interest to the United States beyond South America. Concessions might lapse or be thrust aside in favor of greater competition. Yet without a cable industry of its own—with research laboratories, equipment, and cable-manufacturing plants, more cable ships, and adequate supplies of gutta-percha—the United States would continue to remain dependent upon Britain and its cable network for the foreseeable future.

The experiences of being a neutral in the war so far had shown U.S. businessmen and officials in the Wilson administration that such a prospect of cable dependence upon Britain was not a particularly good one for the United States. The prohibition on encoding, the suppression of cables without notification, the rising costs of operation, and delays served to show that censorship had a profoundly negative effect on the commerce and standing of the United States as a neutral. Whoever controlled the cables controlled the information. In the modern international economy, control of the cables was a potent weapon in peace as well as war. Across the Atlantic, where the cables were ostensibly plentiful, the number of messages already far outstripped the system's capacity to handle them. To regions indirectly connected to the United States, the situation had gone from inadequate to intolerable. The only solution would be to create a rival cable network to serve directly the needs of the United States. Such a system would take considerable time to implement. Without it, however, the nation could only expect continued disadvantages in the future.

And what of the high-power radios that promised to connect distant lands just as easily as the cables? The few stations in the United States built to work with Europe by 1914 were scarcely up to the task. The American Marconi stations sat idle, their companion stations in Britain and Norway silenced by the war or under construction. The German stations had passed into U.S. Navy control, but neither Tuckerton nor Sayville were continual or reliable enough in their operations to handle the additional loads expected of these stations. While the experience with British domination over the cables had revealed to the United States that this control conferred power over the information passing through them, the problems with the German and American Marconi stations showed how allowing foreign firms to meet the needs of the United States for radio stations on U.S. territory endangered neutrality. Parallel to the efforts of the State Department to confront the diplomatic problems associated with cable connections to Europe and South America, farsighted officers in the Navy Department had at the same time tackled concerns about neutrality and security in the new art of radio.

THREE

❖ ❖ ❖

Security and Radios

IN THE LATE SPRING of 1913, young naval lieutenant Stanford C. Hooper drafted a note that within days rocketed all the way to the desks of the secretary of the navy and the most senior admirals in the U.S. Navy. Serving as the fleet radio officer with the Atlantic Fleet, Hooper had become concerned about the newly opened radio station of the Atlantic Communications Company (ACC) at Sayville, Long Island. In his confidential missive to his superior, Commander in Chief of the Atlantic Fleet Rear Admiral Charles J. Badger, Hooper warned that the station was well positioned to monitor the fleet's radio traffic.[1] The ACC was a subsidiary of the German Telefunken company. If there were German naval radio officers at Sayville, Hooper confided, it was entirely possible that they were learning the U.S. Navy's radio procedures by listening in to the fleet's radio traffic. In the event of war, it might be possible for the station to transmit fake or disruptive messages to the navy as it moved along the coast. If this were the case, it would not be possible to change the navy's codes in time. Hooper believed that the U.S. Navy should have an officer stationed at Sayville to keep watch as a censor. Somehow the company ought to be required to have only American citizens as operators. Perhaps the United States should open its own station in Germany to monitor the German navy in the same way. What prompted this concern from Hooper over a commercial radio station? Because Sayville did "little commercial work," Hooper concluded that "its value" lay in "other purposes than financial return."[2]

Within days, the confidential note landed on the desk of Secretary of the Navy Josephus Daniels, who circulated it among senior officers for answers. All expressed considerable concern over the danger posed by a secret German listening station outside New York, but they quickly discovered that there was nothing the government could do to stop the ACC from operating its station at Sayville. Admiral Robert Griffin, whose naval bureau oversaw radio, pointed out that there was no law requiring civilian radio operators to be U.S. citizens. That said, his bureau was firmly convinced that Telefunken, the parent of ACC, had strong ties to the German government. If German agents were at Sayville, then the United States should have a similar station in Germany if at all possible. The naval attaché in London reported that the British had dealt with a similar situation by surreptitiously monitoring the German station to master its techniques before closing it down.[3] Lieutenant Commander S. W. Bryant, the acting head of the Naval Radio Service, and Assistant Secretary Franklin D. Roosevelt tried to initiate an immediate investigation of Sayville by the Department of Commerce and Labor, which oversaw radio stations.[4] With few federal laws governing how radio stations could operate or who could own them, however, the Navy could do little. There was no way to shut down the station merely on suspicion that a foreign power subsidized its operations. Though all appreciated the seriousness of Hooper's warning, little else could be done.

Hooper's note highlighted one of the many problems that had arisen from the rapid spread of the new technology of radio in the first years of the twentieth century. The pace of change had quickly exceeded the ability of the government to keep up. The most recent legislation on radio, the 1912 Radio Act, did not dictate the citizenship of station owners. Theoretically, any government could open a radio station in the United States or subsidize a trusted company to act on its behalf. From such a lodgment, a station could monitor the navy's operations or jam its signals, while to all outward appearances remaining a legitimate commercial firm. By early 1914, the General Board of senior naval officers concluded that, to counter this danger, the United States should have stronger powers to restrict radio licenses, control the emplacement of radio stations, monitor operations at major radio stations owned or operated by foreigners, and require all operators to be U.S. citizens. Most importantly, the U.S. Navy should open its stations to commercial service and offer lower rates. This would strip the veneer of commercial service from those stations surviving only by foreign subsidy. As Admiral Griffin and others believed at the time, "radio is a natural monopoly." There was chaos in the new field of radio, but service seemed to be most efficient if under a single authority. That single authority, in the view of the U.S. Navy, ought to be the U.S. government. The security of the country compelled it.[5]

Matching the anxiety over foreign radio stations in the U.S. were simultaneous concerns about how effectively the navy could use radio. Over the previous years the use of radio communications in the navy had grown considerably, in large part to the efforts of young officers like Lieutenant Hooper. The actions of the U.S. Atlantic Fleet during the crisis with Mexico in April 1914, however, brought to light serious logistical and operational problems involving radio. When President Wilson ordered parts of the Atlantic Fleet to take up position off Veracruz and Tampico, the navy had to use the USS *Birmingham* to serve as a radio relay between Key West and the two squadrons of ships off Mexico. Existing shipboard equipment could not transmit across the distance. But static interference endemic to the Tropics, human error, interference from other stations, difficulties with transmitters, and inadequate prioritizing of messages all caused significant delays. As messages backed up, the navy had to take over the cable station at Veracruz to send the most important messages back to Washington. The experience led senior naval officers to question the navy's ability to handle the levels of radio traffic expected in a significant naval operation or a war. Inadequate national regulation and problems associated with the adoption of radio technology then spurred the navy to reconsider radio policy.[6]

The outbreak of war in August 1914 and the experiences of neutrality sharply altered the direction of the navy's subsequent reevaluation of radio. This in turn had consequences for the growing efforts to eliminate dependence upon foreign communications. Wilson's proclamations of neutrality had included a mandate to Secretary Daniels that the navy should ensure radio stations in the United States followed the neutrality requirements. As events had shown, Hooper's warnings about Sayville had been prescient. The navy took steps to be certain that other stations suspected of foreign control could not harm the United States. At the same time, naval officials had begun to study seriously the use of radio for strategic and operational control of the fleet at sea. The navy's General Board, mindful of the Mexican intervention, ordered in late 1914 the creation of a board to consider the rearrangement of naval communications and the centralization of radio's administration to correct the problems. The objective was to make the navy's communications at all levels, from individual ships to the headquarters in Washington, "continuous, reliable and rapid." There would also be the construction of a giant chain of powerful stations to link Washington directly with Panama, Hawaii, and the Philippines and with the fleet at sea.[7]

In 1914–1915 the concern for neutrality and the reconsideration of radio in the navy in light of the war then led to a general policy that had three main components. These were the establishment of an improved regional radio network to link all areas of strategic importance outside the United States, the revision of national radio policy to codify complete government control over operations, and the extension of radio regulation throughout the hemisphere into U.S. or at least non-European or Asian hands. What is significant in the formation of these policies is that organizational changes and technical decisions about the use of radio by the U.S. Navy and concerns about manufacturing, wavelength distribution, and national security all played a role in shaping U.S. policy toward the hemisphere and, ultimately, the world. The evolution and the effects of this policy, though mixed, demonstrate how the experience of war and the changing perception of the role of the United States in the world were inherently linked to the growing understanding of the strategic importance of communications.

From time to time the course of affairs turns on the actions of a single individual, and the work of Hooper as assistant naval attaché to London was one such instance. As a junior officer, Hooper had played a prominent role in the development of radio in the U.S. Navy. As Fleet Radio Officer, he accompanied the expedition to Veracruz and experienced the problems with radio there firsthand. Ordered to London shortly after the outbreak of war, he used his time in London to learn as much as possible about the use of radio in war by both sides. His observations and conclusions directly influenced the direction the U.S. Navy's use of radio would take.

Hooper arrived in London in mid-September and, remaining in Europe through early January, traveled widely through Britain, Belgium, France, and Holland. While in Britain, Hooper inspected the Marconi station at Carnarvon. It was the companion to the New York station of American Marconi and had been under government operation from the outbreak of the war. Here Hooper learned about the technique of distant control, which allowed for two stations to transmit and receive simultaneously on two different frequencies and was a method the navy did not use. Landlines connected together the antennae and transmitters, otherwise located physically well apart, to form a single station. From London, he listened to both the German and British fleets at night. He learned of the British network of listening stations that had been set up along the coast to intercept German long-distance transmissions. The reduction of the German overseas network should also have registered with Hooper, and it is not unreasonable to conclude that he would have appreciated both the vulnerabilities as well as the advantages of the scattered German stations. He then traveled to Holland and, after the fall of Antwerp, behind the German lines. From all of this he concluded that in its development and use of radio the United States was very much on par with the belligerents. He shared his work with the military attaché at London, Colonel George O. Squier, the army's leading authority on radio. Squier forwarded Hooper's reports back to the U.S. Army with great interest. Hooper came away from his experiences encouraged by the state of radio usage in the U.S. Navy. He was also full of ideas as to how to improve the planned network of high-power radio stations that was to serve the navy in the Pacific and Caribbean.[8]

Several aspects of British and German use of radio during the war in particular had caught Hooper's attention. Most significant appeared to have been the distant-control, "duplex" operation at Carnarvon. Radio operation on U.S. stations functioned somewhat as telephone conversations do: only one party at a time could send a message, and if more than one tried to do so at the same time, the result was unintelligible noise. In places where the number of users would be great, such as the entrance to a busy harbor, radio work was always on the edge of chaos. Between two stations set up to work with one another over long distances, each station would have to spend up to half the time receiving. If the sending and receiving was done on separate wavelengths, the power of the transmitter physically so close to the receiving antenna was still so great that its signal would bleed over and overwhelm the weaker signal from afar. The duplex method placed the transmitter and receiver far apart from one another but linked them together by landline into the same control station. This way a single operator could maintain simultaneous transmitting and receiving and make more efficient use of the station. Compared to the U.S. Navy's existing method of relaying messages, it was an important operational innovation.[9]

Hooper made additional observations. He noted the highly intricate methods that the Royal Navy used to handle traffic for the fleet and Admiralty headquarters. Using a well-trained staff, the Royal Navy allowed for an expedited information flow that minimized unimportant messages and signal interference—both problems that the U.S. Navy had encountered at Veracruz. This meant that the Admiralty could control the fleet from ashore by sending orders out through one high-power station, and the fleet or scattered parts of it could respond on a different wavelength with less power to a smaller coastal station close by. Thus ships were not tethered to the distance they could send messages back to the high-power station but just to the local ship-shore station. Information then became independent of the route to be used. This allowed a greater operational flexibility. The Royal Navy had designed this system to work in the waters around Great Britain, the eastern Atlantic, and the Mediterranean, over a comparatively short range. Hooper saw that this system could also work for the United States, but the distances to be covered would be far greater. Though Hooper may not have realized it at the time, developing a U.S. naval network scattered throughout the Western Hemisphere and across the Pacific would require not only serious consideration of design and technology but also deeper questions of strategy and foreign policy.[10]

Hooper's return set in motion a chain of events that significantly shaped the future of naval radio and the involvement of the United States in the expansion of radio communications throughout the hemisphere. When he arrived back in Washington, Hooper was appointed to head the Radio Division of the Bureau of Steam Engineering, under Admiral Robert Griffin. Hooper then drafted a final report on his tour in Europe for the Naval Radio Service, the Bureau of Steam Engineering, and the Office of Naval Intelligence. He recommended operational, procedural, and technical changes to make the system more responsive to the needs of the fleet at sea. Hooper's report led Secretary Daniels to convene the previously planned Board on Organization to reconsider naval radio policy, with Hooper as one of the four members. Hooper then wrote most of the board's report.[11]

The board proposed sweeping changes. First and foremost, they decided that the navy should acquire total operational control over radio in peacetime as well as wartime. The limited wavelengths available for communicating with commercial shipping and the continual problems of interference on these wavelengths threatened the effective use of radio for naval command and control and, ultimately, for defense of the United States. The solution to this problem required a single governing body over radio. Because of its role in the defense of the country, it had to be the U.S. Navy. The board would have the navy purchase all existing commercial ship-to-shore stations. This would completely eliminate the dangers posed by stations operated by foreign firms like that at Sayville. In order to keep the skills of naval operators at their peak, the board continued, the navy should handle commercial traffic. Wavelengths would be organized so that all commercial ship-shore traffic would be on the internationally accepted six-hundred-meter wavelength and below, while the navy would transmit signals to its warships using wavelengths between six hundred and twenty-four hundred meters.[12]

The report also heralded a significant change in organizational thinking. Hooper insisted that authority over the radio stations no longer rest with commanding officers at various naval yards, who often had little understanding or interest in radio. Instead, there would be special district radio officers to oversee stations; these officers would report directly to the head of the naval radio service. This centralized administration would ensure continual, widespread development of radio across the navy for the first time. So important was this change that the following year the naval communications service and its head came under the direct authority of the new chief of naval operations.[13]

The Board on Organization also recommended an extremely ambitious extension of the naval radio network. It would cover the areas of principal strategic concern for the U.S. Navy: the U.S. continental coast, the approaches to the Panama Canal, and the scattered islands in the Pacific. In addition to the existing ship-shore stations, Hooper and the board envisioned three tiers of radio stations to handle strategic communications over the long distances between the United States and its scattered overseas interests. Up to this point, important messages passed along the navy's coastal chain in a relay. This method rendered the system as vulnerable as the equipment on the weakest station. Its signals could not reach out to the Panama Canal or across to the Philippines. Hooper and the board envisioned eliminating these gaps in the new network with new high-powered stations that could transmit farther. The network would thereby reduce the danger of depending on cables, as Admiral Dewey had experienced in the Far East in 1898 and the Atlantic Fleet had at Veracruz the previous year. The network would also minimize the vulnerabilities of a relay chain to the loss of a single station, as Germany had seen in Africa in 1914.

The network was innovative. The "primary" system would consist of several high-power stations. The backbone of the navy's network, they would transmit signals on a wavelength between five thousand and ten thousand meters, with an anticipated range of several thousand miles. These stations would include the existing ones at Arlington, Virginia, and the Panama Canal and the new ones at San Diego, Honolulu, and Cavite in the Philippines. The "secondary" system would consist of medium-power stations with a smaller range (to a maximum of three thousand miles), working wavelengths between two thousand and three thousand meters. These would include stations in Washington, Alaska, California, Guam, and American Samoa.[14] Should the need for transcontinental or even transoceanic work develop, the navy would use wavelengths of over ten thousand meters with what stations it acquired. Because of the maximum lengths of shipboard antennae, only the secondary system and the existing low-power ship-shore stations could exchange traffic with the fleet at sea. All flagships and battleships would now carry powerful arc transmitters with ranges of up to eight hundred miles. The naval radio network would support fleet operations beyond the continental shelf, around the strategic points of the Caribbean, and across the Pacific. The placement of these primary and secondary stations at places already well defended would help to minimize the vulnerabilities of the network. It was an productive use of technology to solve the problem of naval communications. At the same time, the network did so without succumbing to the operationally dangerous solution of plugging every important location into the same overburdened relay chain. Grand and ambitious, the only problem with the envisioned network was that the technology necessary to build it did not yet exist.

Hooper and the Board on Organization had created the basis for significant changes in naval communications. It would not only link U.S.

naval and military forces overseas directly to the center for the first time but would also lead to significant changes in how the United States viewed its cable and radio connections with the world. Secretary Daniels approved the board's confidential conclusions on February 20, 1915.[15] Far from simply reordering how the navy used radio, the program that the board's report set in motion had three important tracks. The first was the expansion of the navy's radio network to meet the U.S. Navy's growing operational needs. The second was the pursuit of government ownership of all radio in the United States in order to rationalize the use of limited wavelengths and compel adoption of the latest technologies. The third and most extensive track was the navy's joint initiative with the State Department to eliminate European influence over radio throughout the Americas.

The extension of the navy's radio network was the most immediate and challenging project. The initial appropriations for high-power radio in the navy, the trunk primary system, predated the war. To build long-distance naval radio stations in the United States and its overseas territories, Congress had budgeted in 1913 a total of one million dollars, with the first disbursement to be $400,000. The hub of the network was to be the navy's station at Arlington, Virginia. A landline would link this station directly to headquarters in Washington, D.C. The navy had originally installed a large spark transmitter at Arlington, but subsequent testing showed it be less efficient than the new arc transmitters provided by the Federal Telegraph Company of Palo Alto, California. Spark transmitters were noisy, impossible to tune to a specific wavelength, slow to use, and unsuitable for voice transmissions. The arc transmitter, however, produced a more refined signal, was more accurate over a greater range, and could send signals farther. Tests carried about between Arlington and the USS *Salem* in early 1913 demonstrated that the warship could receive signals from the arc transmitter at Arlington as far away as Gibraltar. Consequently, the first contract for the rest of the stations went to the Federal Telegraph Company in June 1913 to build a 100 kw power arc station at Darién in the Canal Zone.[16]

The costs of building the stations proved to be more than everyone had anticipated. The Canal Zone station unexpectedly ate up 40 percent of the total appropriation. The planned stations for the transpacific network would have to share the remaining $600,000. This would make them all much smaller in power and range than the Darién station and require them to relay traffic across the Pacific. Hooper's view, shared by the board and by senior naval officers, was that smaller stations would be inefficient and strategically vulnerable. Guam in particular was neither fortified nor protected. A single determined raiding party could therefore disrupt the entire network. The alternative was to have fewer stations but boost their power.[17]

Without the relays, the distances that the proposed stations would have to cover were fantastic. It was fifty-three hundred miles between the naval station at Cavite in the Philippines and Hawaii, and seventy-eight hundred miles between Cavite and San Diego. The farthest regular transmissions to date had been in the range of three thousand miles, across the Atlantic or between Berlin and Kamina, Togoland. Hooper and the board proposed to double the reliable range. Compounding the problem were the little-understood phenomena of static interference and signal fading associated with sending radio signals through the Tropics. The latest thinking on radio was that higher transmission power, blasting through with more kilowatts, would overcome these static and distance problems. The leading manufacturers of radio equipment in the United States, Federal Telegraph and General Electric, doubted that transmitters of the power and size Hooper envisioned were at all feasible. These distances simply exceeded the real or imagined capabilities of radio technology to that point.[18]

To overcome the atmospheric problems, strategic limitations, and the budgetary constraints, the board reduced the plan to just the San Diego, Hawaii, and Cavite stations. Guam and Samoa would be given 30 kw medium-power stations similar to those of the other secondary network stations working with Hawaii or ships at sea. Hooper, now the head of the Radio Division of the Bureau of Steam Engineering, was in charge of the development of these high-power stations. He planned on installing a 200 kw transmitter at San Diego, and 350 kw ones at Hawaii and Cavite. He at first intended to try out a variety of transmitters from U.S. and German companies, but only the Federal Telegraph Company was able to take up the contract. Although their engineers blanched at the thought of such powerful stations after the 100 kw Darién station had already taxed their knowledge and experience to the limit, Hooper's decision to use Federal Telegraph's arcs pushed the

United States to the very edge of radio technology for long-distance communications.[19]

After much delay for investigation and research, the navy in February 1916 issued contracts to Federal Telegraph to construct these powerful stations. Hooper's ambitious requirements led not only to a new class of high-power radio stations but also a new field of antennae, insulators, and related radio equipment that also had to be designed from scratch. None of the stations would be complete before the United States entered the war. San Diego came online in July 1917, followed by Pearl Harbor in September and Cavite in December. Additionally, there would be a high-power station in Puerto Rico to provide coverage in the Caribbean. Beyond this high-power network, Federal Telegraph's arcs would equip the myriad of smaller secondary and ship-shore stations envisioned by the Board on Organizations. By May 1916 Federal Telegraph had already supplied more than forty-six smaller arc sets for battleships, scouting vessels and flagships. Indeed, the U.S. Navy intended arc technology to spread throughout all areas where the navy might have to cruise.[20]

The planning for this strategic radio network, based on the use of high-power arc transmitters, partly addressed a deeper problem that the U.S. Navy confronted in adopting radio technology before World War I. This was the steady transition toward the more efficient "continuous wave" method of operation and the corresponding effort to ensure that the most advanced continuous wave equipment was available to the United States.[21] Naval secretary Daniels and many naval officers had come to believe that only through government control of all radio operations in the country could the navy secure the orderly use of the limited number of wavelengths available and the steady adoption of the latest and most advanced radio technology throughout the United States and the world. The unsuccessful pursuit of this control came in part from a widely held perception that foreign firms held a dangerously large influence over radio in the United States.

Though the field of radio technology was in a period of great innovation, the standard radio transmitters in use at the time were those known as "spark" sets. A controlled, periodic spark of electricity across a gap between two charged plates created an electromagnetic impulse that then traveled out from an antenna. Other antennae tuned to the same wavelength could detect this emission, which a receiver converted into recognizable signals for an operator to read. The spark gap had first been popularized by Guglielmo Marconi at the turn of the century. Since then, it had found widespread commercial and military use. In the United States, for example, successive legislation following the 1909 *Republic* and 1912 *Titanic* disasters required that all ships of certain sizes carrying passengers also carry sufficient radio equipment and operators to maintain continual watch for distress signals. At the third International Radiotelegraphic Conference in London, in June 1912, the participants recommended that all signatories adopt similar requirements as a measure to improve safety at sea.[22] The Marconi Company leased radio sets and fully trained operators to shipping firms and provided access to a growing international chain of ship-shore coastal radio stations in the Americas and Europe. Spurred by disasters and legislation, demand for radio sets reinforced Marconi's position at the forefront of the industry.[23]

At the same time, however, those at the leading edge of radio research had concluded that radio transmitting and receiving based on the spark was inefficient. Transmission speeds were slow. The signals given off by the intermittent spark were stronger at the beginning of the transmission than at the end, as the spark faded away. The transmission blanketed a broad slice of the spectrum on either side of the principal wavelength. Without refinements to equipment, it appeared likely to many informed observers that the available spectrum of wavelengths in use might soon become full. This was particularly a problem at busy ports such as New York, where a powerful signal from an irresponsible amateur might easily jam the transmissions of commercial vessels or naval warships. Even with the initial regulation of the available wavelengths and efficient practices on the part of radio operators, the growth in numbers of radio sets foreshadowed significant future problems.[24]

Only signals given off by continuous wave transmitters offered a solution. Operating in a tighter wavelength, such signals were refined enough to carry voice transmissions effectively and could cover the ranges necessary for truly continual and reliable long-distance radio communications. The most refined continuous wave–emitting device available by 1914 was the arc transmitter, initially developed by the

Danish inventor Valdemar Poulsen. The Federal Telegraph Company of Palo Alto, California, held the license to manufacture and use the Poulsen arc in the United States. Its chief engineer, Leonard Fuller, had made important modifications to the original designs that made very-high-power arc transmitters technically possible. The navy had already begun in 1913 to adopt the arc for use on its leading battleships as well as for the new navy radio network. The navy's commitment to

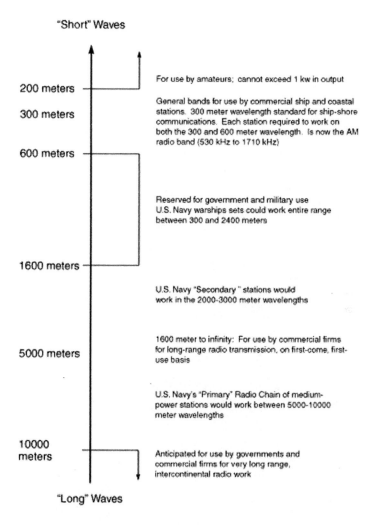

United States wavelength allocations, 1912–1916, based on Radio Act of 1912

the arc and the continuous wave raised the likelihood of a conflict with the Marconi firm and its reliance upon the spark.[25]

The problem of moving to continuous wave was that the spark and the arc were incompatible. The receivers in use at Marconi shore stations and on board spark-equipped ships were not sensitive enough to pick up the more closely attenuated arc signal. This created a frustrating situation for start-up radio companies that wanted to push the new arc transmitters. To make money, they would have to enter the market for ship-shore radio. But potential competitors to American Marconi could not challenge the firm's coastal radio monopoly unless they made a tremendous investment in their own chain of stations. Neither American Marconi nor its British parent exhibited any interest in adopting the new arc technology, despite the fact that British Marconi held the patent rights for using the arc in much of the world. The spark was less efficient, but the firm's predominance in ship-shore work had locked in most civilian users to sparks. Ship owners, required to by law or by their insurers to carry radios, could not invest in the arc system without losing the ability to work with spark-based shore stations, and purchasing both systems was costly and impracticable. As American Marconi rented out both the shipboard radio sets and the services of operators, many merchant shippers had little reason to care about the distinction between arcs and sparks.[26]

The United States Navy, however, did care about the use of arc-based sets. During the 1914 Veracruz operation, one of the problems the navy had coped with was interference from commercial stations employing spark transmitters.[27] If U.S.-flagged shipping remained locked in to the outdated Marconi spark equipment, then the U.S. Navy's warships or shore stations using arc sets would not be able to intercommunicate with civilian shipping or shore stations at times of crisis. Under existing legislation, there was no way to compel American Marconi or any commercial shippers to adopt the continuous wave. Left unattended, the situation would lead to the development of two incompatible, potentially interfering radio networks in American waters. At the same time, without a large client base, firms working on arc technology would have fewer funds for research and development in the field. Correspondingly, the navy would lose a domestic base for acquiring the latest in radio technology for its own uses. Replacing the spark and committing to the continuous wave method of radio technology appeared to naval radio officers to be crucial for national defense.

From the point of view of the navy, the most appealing solution to this problem was to centralize operational control over radio in the navy's hands. If the U.S. Navy ran all ship-shore radio stations and equipped them with arc-based systems, then commercial shipping would have to adopt the arc. Government interest in the latest advancements in radio technology, unlike that of the stolid American Marconi, would stimulate continued research and development into the art. Furthermore, government control over radio operations would allow for the most efficient use of the apparently limited wavelengths available for ship-shore and long-distance communications. Interference between stations or from irresponsible radio operators, as the navy had already experienced during its operations off Veracruz in early 1914, would cease. Finally, government control would also eliminate the concern that Hooper had raised in 1913 over the nationality and ownership of radio stations built in the United States. Thus Hooper and the Board on Organization concluded in their report of February 1915 that it was "of paramount importance that the [navy] control radiotelegraphy in peace as well as war times for purposes of national defense, as this is the sole means of successfully solving the many problems of interference and friction connected therewith."[28]

Winning such authority required persuading a skeptical or indifferent Congress. Outright nationalization of the industry was unlikely. Existing station owners might sell out if there were legislation limiting the construction of new commercial stations. Should Congress balk at such a sweeping measure, Secretary Daniels and other senior naval officials believed that opening up the existing naval radio stations to handle commercial traffic might be more palatable. Under the 1912 Radio Act, the naval radio stations had to refuse commercial traffic if they were within one hundred nautical miles of a commercial station. With competition, the navy could use its lower rates to drive the spark stations out of business and compel shippers to adopt arc technology.[29] While many naval radio officers approved of the idea of government control simply as a way to solve technical and strategic problems, to Secretary Daniels the Progressive idea of government control over this public utility became an end in and of itself. His resilience on this point would, over time, leave him isolated and make him an obstacle to other, more innovative efforts by lower officials in the navy and State Department.

To win the necessary legislation from Congress, Secretary Daniels organized an interdepartmental effort in the spring of 1915, and used his own authority to block commercial firms from expanding into Panama and the Pacific territories. Despite its affection for Federal Telegraph's arc transmitter, the navy turned down repeated requests to construct high-power commercial stations across the Pacific. Federal Telegraph sought to compete with the slow Commercial Pacific cable. It had already built stations in San Francisco and Hawaii. But Daniels could not agree to the project without contradicting the goal of government ownership, and so he repeatedly blocked requests for permission to build stations at Guam and the Philippines. Lengthy pleas from company officials went unanswered, even when in desperation they offered to turn the stations over entirely to the navy after only five years of commercial operation. Despite the growing need for improved Pacific communications, Federal Telegraph's desire for business, and the navy's lack of direct radio contact with the Philippines or Asia, principle trumped expediency. Daniels remained steadfastly opposed to any further commercial radio development in the Pacific.[30]

Meanwhile, the interdepartmental board charted the treacherous waters of drafting legislation to give control over the nation's radio to the U.S. Navy. Captain W. H. G. Bullard, the Superintendent of the Naval Radio Service, oversaw deliberations by participants from the U.S. Army to the U.S. Post Office to the Department of Agriculture. Half the members believed that the proposed legislation went too far, while the other half felt that it did not go far enough. Bullard spent December 1915 and much of 1916 trying to build support for a policy that would, in effect, drive legitimate firms out of business.[31] Within the navy, support remained strong. Hooper and the other members of the Board on Organization, updating their earlier report in July 1916, concluded, "Experiences of the present war have shown that radio is a natural monopoly, which must be exercised by the Government in wartime, and . . . [in] neutrality . . . The experiences of this war have also shown us conclusively that we must exercise this monopoly in peacetime if we desire to do so effectively in wartime."[32] To head off anticipated criticism, Bullard invited various radio companies and interest groups to appear before the committee to discuss the bill. Bullard used the hearings to gauge the level of opposition and prepare responses to arguments that opponents would use before Congress. Finished in November 1916, the bill covered much of the navy's concerns. It would have allowed the navy to handle commercial traffic and to purchase private stations. Strengthened licensing regulations would enable the government to close down stations using sparks. The government would also have the power to inspect all records—including copies of traffic—at a radio station. Finally, the president would have the power to shut down stations at his discretion, not just in wartime. The outcry from American Marconi, smaller radio operators, and the Institute of Radio Engineers was strident but less than what Captain D. W. Todd, who took over from Bullard, had anticipated. In fact, Todd expected support from shipping companies and American Marconi's rivals when the bill finally reached Congress.[33]

Captain Todd felt the bill was a start but did not go far enough. This was particularly the case with the "very serious problem" of high-power, long-distance stations. These were the stations that would send signals out above the sixteen-hundred-meter wavelengths but that could disrupt the working of the new navy high-power chain under construction. Though only eight such stations troubled the navy, there would undoubtedly be more in the future. American Marconi's stations in Hawaii, Boston, and New York were already starting to cause interference to the navy. Federal Telegraph proposed to build a massive high-power station near New Haven, Connecticut, to work with South America. Naval radio officers worried that the proliferation of stations could lock the navy into a small corner of the long-distance part of the spectrum. Interference would only continue, Todd noted, "Unless all existing high power stations are brought to equal efficiency with our own or to greater efficiency by some new discovery or development." But unlike Daniels, Todd believed that commercial competition would be enough to force the private stations to upgrade their equipment and operate more efficiently. On this issue Todd and other naval radio officers had a vision of technical policy very different in sentiment and understanding from Congress or the public. It would be hard to convince either of the need to impose a particular order on the vaguely understood radio spectrum. To do so before many of the radio stations expected to use that part of the spectrum had even been constructed would be harder still.[34]

Congress began to consider the bill at the end of 1916. In case they rejected it, Todd planned to have key provisions of the bill attached as amendments to the naval appropriations bill if necessary.[35] Secretary Daniels wrote to the bill's backers repeatedly. He stressed the urgency with which he viewed the question of government ownership and the importance of radio regulation to the navy. In Daniels' view, as the largest single user of radio in the country the navy was in the position to make the best recommendations about the development of the industry and manufacturing of radio. With more stations than wavelengths available, only a government monopoly could restore order. Congress, he urged forcefully, would have to give the U.S. Navy that power.[36]

Senior State Department officials shared Daniels's views on the necessity of government ownership, for broader reasons. "It is not only necessary for military reasons to control all high-powered stations as a part of national preparedness," wrote one senior advisor, Leland Harrison, in late January,

> but it is also desirable in times of peace to be in a position to supervise the news items distributed to foreign governments through such stations. Their possession will insure expeditious handling of all Government messages. Absolute control under one authority, which can be only the Federal Government, is the sole safeguard against general interference and what is called "fighting for the air."
>
> Our national safety demands that the Government control high-powered stations and the sooner we get that the better. The present tendency is all toward Government control and the acquisition of these high-powered stations will be far less expensive now than say ten years hence.[37]

As evidence, Harrison cited the proliferation of stations under foreign control in the United States, as well as the earlier neutrality troubles with the Telefunken station at Cartagena, Colombia. Using similar language, Secretary of State Lansing wrote to one key member of Congress several days later to urge passage of the bill. Protection of the national interest in neutrality or belligerency, he argued, required better controls than the existing legislation provided. Lansing concluded that he could not "too strongly endorse this bill to regulate radio communications nor too strongly emphasize" the necessity for its earliest enactment.[38]

Congress did not oblige. The core problem of regulating the radio spectrum was lost behind the more ominous bugbear of government ownership and operation. Congress heard testimony throughout January from department secretaries, government radio experts, and officials of every major radio company in the country. Bill opponents stressed that navy operational control would stifle innovation and the progression of the radio art. The proximity between development and operation in the commercial firms and their research laboratories, in the opponents' view, provided a more fertile testing ground for ideas. Even within the navy, some found Daniels' position too extreme. Captain Bullard and Lieutenant Hooper firmly believed that the navy should acquire only the coastal radio stations and not the high-power ones. By late January 1917, it became apparent to Daniels that support was too weak for the bill to go anywhere. The Senate even refused to consider tacking the commercial operation provision to the naval appropriations bill as an alternative. Amid the larger events of the winter of 1917, the bill and the dangers it addressed seemed less and less urgent. The break in diplomatic relations with Germany on February 4, 1917, prompted the navy to remove all German citizens from the Tuckerton and Sayville stations. The prospect of war raised the possibility that the navy would soon acquire the control it sought anyway. Consequently, the bill died quietly in committee.[39]

The navy's prewar hunt for control over radio operations in the United States was unsuccessful, but it stemmed from realistic concerns about the strategic importance of radio. It came from a recognized need to encourage the adoption of the latest radio technology among civilian users while at the same time preserving the research and development of new radio technologies whose inventions would benefit the navy. The existing firms were unwilling or unable to adopt the latest technologies, particularly those based on continuous wave principles. At the same time, the navy's construction of high-power radio stations that would work on the same wavelengths as those used by international commercial radio companies raised concerns about the apparently inevitable interference that would result. The lack of regulatory controls for the government to stop foreign firms from operating radio stations in the United States also was an important factor. For these reasons, the navy believed that radio control needed to be in the hands of the government, as it was in many European countries. Despite the disinclination of Congress to act on this argument, Secretary Daniels, Captain Todd, and other senior officials firmly maintained their belief that government ownership, in some form, was necessary and inevitable. Without action, the problem would only grow more pressing and, in their view, imperil U.S. security. Captain Bullard, Lieutenant Hooper, and their allies, meanwhile, remained personally opposed to the broad sweep of the plan but could do little to challenge it overtly. This internal navy division over how to deal with high-power long-distance stations and the growing desire of commercial firms to set up such stations in the United States would have important consequences for the course of naval radio policy and, ultimately, for the pursuit of an international radio network centered in the United States.

The third part of the U.S. Navy's radio policy was to eliminate the danger of European influence over radio in the Western Hemisphere south of the United States. An ambitious goal, it stemmed from the inability of radio waves to respect political borders. Just as along the United States coast, unregulated stations operated by Europeans in the Caribbean basin or South America could interfere with U.S. Navy radio communications or violate the neutrality of the host country. As naval officials saw it, there were two solutions Latin American governments could take that would help the United States. The first was to nationalize all radio operations. The other was to grant concessions for stations to reliable U.S. companies. Either way, these stations would then use the most advanced equipment and operating procedures. This would make them compatible with one another and, most importantly, with the United States Navy.

The proliferation of radio south of the United States in the years before World War I had been slow but not inconsiderable. German, British, American, and French radio firms had all enthusiastically marketed their equipment in the region. In the Caribbean basin, most stations were under the control of mining or agricultural companies. The most expansive of these was the United Fruit Company. The company's own radio network allowed continual contact among the plantations, the ships at sea, and American ports. Given the fluctuation of market demand and the danger of fruit cargo spoiling quickly, this system improved the efficiency of the company's operations and cut costs substantially. From two initial stations built in 1903 in Panama and Costa Rica, United Fruit steadily built installations at major fruit ports along the east coast of Central America. At the same time, the company acquired a small radio firm and its patents. In 1913 the company converted the radio network into a wholly owned subsidiary, the Tropical Radio Company. Continuing to serve the internal communications needs of United Fruit, by 1914 Tropical Radio's network extended from Colombia to Louisiana and offered service to the general public as well.[40]

Elsewhere in the Caribbean, only the German Telefunken company enjoyed much success. Telefunken and its U.S. subsidiary, the Atlantic Communications Company, had initially planned a network of powerful radio stations to cover the entire Caribbean basin. Though never completed, it would have included two stations in Cuba, one at Veracruz, Mexico, and others at Cartagena, Caracas, Lima, and as far south as Paramaribo and Pará in Brazil. The Cartagena station had been operational since 1912. The Lima station opened shortly before war broke out.[41] The Colombian government had purchased a Telefunken station for the island of San Andres (Saint Andrews) off the Nicaraguan coast. Telefunken agents were also bidding on similar projects in Venezuela and throughout Central America. In Mexico, the revolutionary government had turned to Telefunken for parts and equipment after General Electric and Westinghouse halted their sales to the country. Had the war not intervened, Telefunken might well have gained a strong position in the Caribbean.

In South America, particularly in Brazil, the use of radio was more widespread. The Brazilian telegraph administration operated a dozen coastal stations and twenty inland stations by August 1914. Much of Brazil's early development had come at the hands of private firms. In 1911 the Brazilian government withdrew permission to operate from the largest, the Amazon Wireless Telephone and Telegraph Company, in favor of a new plan for a national radio network. After a protracted legal fight, the Brazilians bought out Amazon Wireless. Legislation passed the following year cemented plans for the domestic radio network and required that any station working with other countries be owned and operated by a Brazilian firm. Federal control over radio in

Brazil allowed the central government greater influence over both state governments and foreign companies. Like U.S. Navy officers, Brazilian officials observing the war in Europe became convinced of the military importance of radio and the great need for it to be under government control. Though several firms, including Marconi, had hoped to build high-power stations in Brazil, the new legislation threw their plans awry.[42]

Across South America, many countries found it less expensive to rely on medium-power radio stations rather than delicate telegraph wires for internal communications through jungles or across mountains. To do so, they turned to Marconi and Telefunken for the necessary equipment and expertise. In nearly all cases, there were few local engineers with the necessary skills to operate the stations. To compensate, governments often acquired experts from the companies to manage the station and operate its equipment. Under this arrangement, Telefunken or one of its partners, Siemens and Halske, built stations in Chile, Ecuador, Peru, Bolivia, Paraguay, Uruguay, and Argentina before 1914. Marconi had built similar stations in the region as well, but most of its efforts were in securing concessions in Brazil and Argentina for a high-power international network to link with the United States and the rest of the world. While most of the stations in South America were nominally under government control, the foreign equipment and staff often gave them a more European character.[43]

The spread of Telefunken's influence through Central and South America alarmed British officials at the outbreak of war. Where stations using German equipment were in operation, British diplomats pressured governments to respect neutrality regulations. In Colombia, the government shut the Cartagena station only briefly in mid-September 1914 and allowed the Telefunken engineers to remain. Ordered to investigate the danger of radio assistance to German commerce raiders, Captain Guy Gaunt, the British naval attaché in Washington, discovered that the stations had not been closed or censored. The British and French ambassadors in Washington then jointly warned the United States that if Colombia would not act to close the stations, the Allies would. Britain and France would have to "adopt such measures as might seem to them appropriate" to protect British and French interests in the region. The British chargé d'affaires in Bogotá spared Secretary of State Bryan any cause for alarm, however, by thanking the Colombian government for their efforts at censorship. This wholly unauthorized expression of goodwill undermined the Foreign Office's maneuver to force the Colombians to shut down the station. Alerted by this to the danger of losing Telefunken's influence in the region, the German minister to Colombia then secured a guarantee from the company that it would not seek damages if its station closed. The Colombian government, now under close scrutiny, shuttered these stations in early December.[44]

British fears over German stations in neutral territory were not without foundation. Radio had played a leading part in the cat-and-mouse game with the German East Asian Squadron in late 1914. When the force reached the west coast of South America after fleeing from Asian waters, Vice Admiral Maximilian von Spee found willing ears at many radio stations in Peru and Chile. Telefunken had built these stations before the war and supplied engineers to help operate them. German diplomats and naval attachés routed information on shipping and supplies to the squadron through these stations, often with the tacit acceptance of local officials. This gave Spee, while still at sea, advance knowledge of the movement from the South Atlantic of the British naval force under Admiral Christopher Cradock. Beyond the range of the small station at the Falklands, Cradock could not make use of the Chilean or Argentine stations himself. This left him out of touch for extended periods of time with the Admiralty in London as well as Britain's own network of agents on shore in South America. When the Admiralty dispatched a force of battle cruisers to redress Cradock's subsequent destruction, they took steps to integrate these ships into the worldwide communications network. One of the two warships had a high-power arc transmitter on board, while a third ship with an arc transmitter took up position near the cable station at Ascension Island. This relay allowed word of Spee's defeat to flash to London immediately.[45] Though this was the end of the German cruisers problem, Britain did not overlook how the German admiral's use of the coastal radio stations in neutral territory had arguably prolonged his survival and success. Consequently, British diplomats maintained an uneasy watch over Germany's efforts to expand its radio network in neutral countries for the rest of the war.[46]

The United States also worried about the spread of foreign-controlled radio stations in Latin America, although for different reasons. The spread of radio to the region had introduced a new variable in the calculus of national security. Over the previous two decades, the

United States had gradually expanded its strategic outlook to include the sweep of the Caribbean as well as the waters of the western Atlantic and the Pacific. The opening of the canal in Panama in 1914 increased the importance of the Caribbean. It changed how the navy intended to position its forces to defend the nation. Naval strategists at the time, citing the Suez Canal as an example, believed that the Panama Canal's importance to global shipping would make it a prime target for those seeking a preponderance of regional or global power. To meet the threat to the canal as well as any bid to gain control of the waters around the continent, the navy intended to fight with a combined fleet of all its battleships, a doctrine promulgated most forcefully by Captain Alfred T. Mahan. Such a plan to combine the fleet in crisis or at the outbreak of war required assurance that the canal would be continuously available to the United States. While the army constructed fortifications on both ends of the canal, one of the navy's priorities became to defend the canal and its approaches in the Caribbean. This preoccupation with the security of the canal, linked as it was to the defense of the country, led to constant concern that foreign powers might acquire naval bases or inordinate political influence in the region. Preventing this from happening had been one of the motivations behind the Caribbean interventions of the early years of the twentieth century. At the same time, the idea that any European power might build a radio station near the approaches to the canal had also become anathema to the navy.[47]

Uncontrolled expansion of radio stations in the Caribbean basin, in the view of the navy, threatened the use of radio for the strategic, operational, or tactical control of the fleet. Several different scenarios were possible. Commercial radio operators across the region could, through careless behavior or outdated equipment, unintentionally jam the navy's signals. Stations operated by German or British firms could also function as outposts should the United States go to war with either country. Nominally located in neutral countries, the European operators could intentionally transmit signals to disrupt the navy's radios at key moments. The stations could also function as quiet listening posts for tracking the movements of the navy. Even more dangerous, these radio stations could help to coordinate an initial enemy naval strike during the crucial first phases of a war, before the fleet could unite or the United States force the neutral stations to shut down. Even if such stations could be closed, the operators and engineers might scatter, taking their expertise, equipment, and influence elsewhere in the region. As events had shown, none of these ideas were particularly far-fetched.

In a broader sense, and one less well understood by historians, there were also fears about the limited number of wavelengths available. By 1914 the existing international agreement governing radio—the third International Radiotelegraph Convention of 1912—was outdated on this point. It had not addressed the incompatibilities between the "interrupted wave" emitted by spark transmitters and the "continuous wave" signal that the U.S. Navy had begun to champion. Nor had it specified how neighboring countries might agree on sharing wavelengths that they—and others—wished to use for medium- and long-range transmissions. Furthermore, not all Latin American countries had adhered to this convention, and their radio stations did not yet consistently follow the basic, accepted operating procedures. There had been plans to hold another international convention in 1917, but it had been postponed indefinitely after the outbreak of war. From the perspective of the U.S. Navy, any future development of radio networks in the Caribbean basin would have to be done with efficiency and cooperation. Because stations built in Colombia or Nicaragua might easily interfere with those in Panama or Cuba, such arrangements would also have to be done in such ways that did not adversely affect the U.S. Navy's radio network. Thus, regional governments would have to take an active role with the United States in controlling the spread of radio by European firms. If the governments did not, these companies would apportion the wavelengths according to their own needs. This would be at the expense of the United States, which had the most widespread radio interests in the region. The conclusions from this line of thinking were that the presence of European radio technicians and the haphazard construction of radio stations around the Caribbean basin represented potential, indirect, yet nonetheless critical threats to the defense of the United States.

The first focus of the navy was on Panama itself. In 1913, at the behest of the navy, the State Department had begun negotiations with the Panamanian government to grant total control over radio communications to the United States. As justification, the United States cited rights reserved to it to protect the canal and defend Panamanian independence laid down in the Hay-Bunau-Varilla Treaty of 1903 and the Panama Canal Act of 1912. Secretary Daniels noted, "To fulfill these obligations it is militarily essential that the United States shall have actual physical control of all radio stations . . . at a time when the independence of Panama may be in jeopardy or the United States may be at war or threatened with war."[48] By July 1914 the negotiations had reached the point where the United States had offered to build a chain of small stations for domestic communications, in exchange for authority over all radio across the country.

After the outbreak of war in Europe, the radio control issue in Panama became more urgent. Setting aside negotiations, the United States asked for and received total control unreservedly for the duration of the crisis. The implications of this at the time were minimal. Three of the four stations operational in Panama were those of the U.S. Navy and the fourth was that of Tropical Radio. Yet the Panamanians lost the promise that the United States would build a network of small stations to connect the country's interior. The matter remained a point of contention between the two countries through the war, but there was little the government of Panama could do.[49] For the navy, concerned with radio across the entire region, this move was only the first step. From the initial concern over radio security at the Panama Canal itself, the navy's focus of attention gradually expanded to include the entire Caribbean and Latin American region.

Though the State Department held the responsibility for carrying out foreign policy, the navy exercised a virtual veto over matters relating to radio. Because few diplomats grasped the technical details of the new technology or the navy's arguments about the relationship between radio and security, policy was largely ad hoc, reactive, and dependent upon the navy's initiative.[50] One of the few State Department officials who did understand was Boaz Long, head of the Latin American Division in 1913–1914 and later minister to Salvador. When the United States learned in late 1914 that a Telefunken agent was in Central America to sell radio equipment, Long headed an effort to convince governments in the area not to sign any contracts and to consider U.S. manufacturers instead. This effort likely came at the navy's suggestion, but Long on his own could not persuade his superiors to treat other proposals as seriously. When Guatemala sought out the assistance of the United States to build a government radio station in late

1914, the State Department took months to arrange the purchase and installation. Tiny El Salvador forwarded a similar request to the United States in 1915. More senior officials in the State Department rejected Long's endorsement of this request, "lest that small country become involved in questions of neutrality" that it presumably could not handle. As Long would complain in 1919, it was only when the navy became directly involved that any effort at a coherent policy could be made.[51]

Within the navy, however, there was not unanimity as to what the hemispheric radio policy ought to be. There was universal agreement on the need to ensure that U.S. Navy tactical and strategic radio communications would not encounter interference and that countries in the region not harbor unneutral foreign stations. Secretary Daniels hoped that all countries within the hemisphere would accede to the same idea of government ownership and operations that he proposed for the United States. Daniels remained consistently firm on this position, despite pressure from Treasury Secretary William G. McAdoo and others who wanted to encourage U.S. radio companies to expand abroad. Simply put, Daniels's view was that the efficiency and security of radio operations necessary for the defense of the canal and the country required government control over operations both in the United States and all countries to the south.[52] Senior naval officers, including Captain Bullard, the naval communications director, and Admiral William S. Benson, the chief of naval operations, as well as Assistant Secretary Franklin D. Roosevelt, were more willing to support private efforts by U.S. firms when they could accomplish the same goal more quickly and securely. At times, Bullard, Benson, Roosevelt, and their supporters quietly encouraged U.S. companies even when Daniels publicly opposed their plans. The complex relationship between the United States and the various Latin American countries, the uneven spread of radio technology in the region, and the divergent views over the question of radio control led to an awkward, conflicting mix of initiatives from the navy.

The first of these initiatives was that the United States would persuade as many countries as possible to commit to the idea of government control. Daniels warned Secretary Lansing in June 1915 of the "great menace to [U.S.] government forces" if the United States became engaged in war with a country controlling radio stations in the Caribbean or Latin America. To mitigate this threat to neutrality,

Daniels thought the United States should push a hemisphere-wide policy of government control over radio while also encouraging the latest radio technology. They should consider U.S. radio manufacturers before awarding contracts to Europeans. To sweeten the deal, the United States could offer traffic-exchange agreements with U.S.-based stations or merchant ships, which the secretary anticipated would soon come under government control. Daniels's concern stemmed less from desire to expand the influence of U.S. radio manufacturers than from genuine if exaggerated fears about neutrality, technology, and national security.[53]

Within the State Department, responsibility for drafting such a policy fell upon the shoulders of Boaz Long. The chief of the Latin American Division, however, did not hold Daniels's extreme position on government ownership. Long hoped to build on the earlier diplomatic offensive against Telefunken by supporting U.S. commercial radio firms. He instructed U.S. diplomats throughout the region to recommend only that ownership and control of radio stations should "not pass beyond this Hemisphere . . . into European or Asiatic hands." Long believed this approach would discourage countries from nationalizing existing stations like those of Tropical Radio, while still encouraging the purchase of U.S. radio equipment over that of European firms. Diplomats were to extend an invitation to discuss questions of radio and regional security during the upcoming Pan-American Scientific Conference, convening in late December.[54] President Wilson had already expressed his hopes for the greater economic and political integration of the hemisphere. Cast in terms of this Pan-American program, the proposal for hemispheric control over radio would be, in the view of the Department, another important step toward this unity in the Americas.[55] At the same time, each chargé d'affaires, minister, or ambassador was to report back information on all aspects of radio that they could gather discreetly from their posting.[56]

The hemispheric plan went nowhere in 1916. On January 7, the navy secretary himself made the first pitch. Diplomats from Latin America already in Washington for the scientific conference assembled informally at the State Department. Daniels's address to the delegates echoed the language he had used with Congress. He hoped that Latin American countries would consider placing all operations under government control. At the same time, he urged that they consider U.S. radio equipment before granting concessions or building new government stations with the help of Europeans. Awkwardly, Captain Bullard then added that the United States did not intend this line of thinking to keep U.S. companies from operating radio stations in the area. The participants agreed only to several vague recommendations and the need to consult their respective governments.[57]

Following the conference, the navy then proposed in March an ambitious and far-reaching proposal to link all the countries of the hemi-

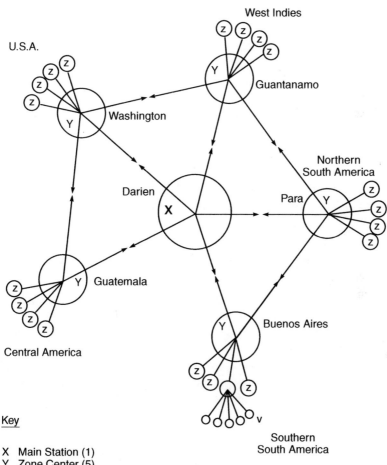

Key

X Main Station (1)
Y Zone Center (5)
Z Government Center Stations (Distributing)
V Local Stations necessary for each country

U.S. Navy Proposal for hemispheric radio network, 1916. *Source:* Navy Memorandum, *Foreign Relations of the United States*, 1916, p. 9

sphere together in a massive radio network. This would align radio equipment, operating procedures, and wavelengths throughout the Caribbean and Latin America with that of the United States at the leading edge of the technology. If successful, the network would minimize or eliminate European involvement, ensure radio neutrality in times of crisis, and serve the growing radio requirements of each country.

To accomplish this, the navy envisioned a Pan-American radio organization to administer the network, handle traffic regulation, assign wavelengths, and standardize equipment use. The hemisphere would be divided into five zones to handle international traffic. Anchored around the navy's new high-powered station in the Canal Zone, the network would link five proposed regional stations in the United States, Cuba, Guatemala, Brazil, and Argentina. These regional stations would link with individual stations in each the hemisphere. At the core, the network would require government ownership of all stations in each country, from small coastal ones to large international ones. The navy cited its own experience in high-power work as an example of what could be accomplished and what expertise the navy could share other countries. Each government was invited to consider the matter further, in advance of a proposed hemispheric conference to finalize the plan. For the rest of the year, U.S. diplomats from Cuba to Chile pushed the proposal with their hosts, with little success.[58]

At the same time, the second navy initiative was to assume direct control over radio stations where possible, as had been done in Panama. "The subject of the extension of our communications system to the southward," Assistant Secretary Roosevelt noted to Lansing in 1916, "is of considerable importance and one which our Government... greatly desires to promote."[59] Given the tremendous costs involved, not every nation could afford radio stations. Some countries without technical experience or personnel, Roosevelt argued, might invite the United States in to provide this for them. The U.S. Navy itself could "build, control, administer and operate" stations if the navy thought it best to do so. Such stations would provide an "undeniable advantage" in wartime.[60] Captain Bullard noted to Secretary Daniels, "The advantages from a military point of view of controlling as many radio stations in foreign countries in a time of war must be apparent as it simply extends our lines of communication to that extent, with the added feeling of security that they never could be used to our own disadvantage."[61] In late

1916, the United States gained such a lodgment in the Dominican Republic. While U.S. Marines occupied the country to restore order and ensure its financial stability, a radio station concession became available. Captain Bullard pushed the idea of winning the concession as a means to fulfill "a long felt want from a military point of view" and stressed its utility as a relay point for radio traffic with South America. Though woefully inadequate at first for the tasks expected of it, the station became an important part of the navy's Caribbean communications system through the 1920s.[62]

However advantageous it was to have navy radio stations in foreign countries, there were limits to these benefits if the methods were underhanded. In late 1915 the navy learned that the Tropical Radio Company had the opportunity to construct a station at San Juan Bautista in the southeastern Mexican state of Tabasco. Tropical Radio had no need for a station there and would likely lose money on its operation. The navy, however, did have tremendous need for such a station. Between Texas and Panama lay a large gap in the western Caribbean and Gulf of Mexico, where the navy had regular difficulty in keeping direct contact with warships. Captain Bullard, deeming the prospective station of "inestimable value" at the outset of a war, quietly recommended that the navy subsidize the construction for Tropical Radio. Roosevelt found the plan appealing as well. He endorsed it to the officers of the General Board. The "important strides" that were "being made at present in the development of radio," he argued, "and . . . the lessons already learned from the European war" made it desirable to have such a station.

The head of the General Board, the distinguished Admiral George Dewey, blasted this idea of secret control. It was dangerous, he countered, for the United States government to join in a private commercial venture when its only value to the nation would be in wartime. It would be contradictory for the nation to obtain such a station under conditions that it had, in the case of the German station at Sayville, already condemned on its own territory. Indeed, in the midst of a serious campaign to block the foreign control of radio in the country and in the hemisphere, it would be poor form for the U.S. government to engage in the practice itself. Dewey also questioned the strategic utility of the station to the navy for operations. The only way the navy could use the station was if its subsidy of Tropical Fruit remained a secret, but in the United States such secrets were nearly impossible to keep. Unless the United States controlled the territory where such a station might be built, it was not possible to have anything but local government control or private U.S. commercial involvement. Unlike the station in the Dominican Republic, obtained in a legitimate manner, secret and surreptitious control over radio stations would not be permitted. Neither the navy nor Tropical Radio ever built a station in Mexico. Bullard meanwhile reached a quiet yet important agreement with Tropical Radio to use its existing stations elsewhere in the region.[63]

Although the navy encouraged U.S. firms to build stations in the Caribbean or Latin America, certain areas remained off limits. Secretary Daniels was so wedded to the idea of government control that he held to the policy even when it went against the deeper needs of the United States for improved communications abroad. When cable supplies became all but impossible to acquire, the cable companies explored the possibility of using radio but quickly ran afoul of the navy. James Scrymser's Central and South American Telegraph Company sought a radio relay through Panama to ease the congestion on its vital Panama-Colombia cables, while Newcomb Carlton of Western Union inquired about setting up a radio network of stations based in Cuba to bridge the gap to South America across the Caribbean. Daniels strongly opposed both proposals. Just as it had rejected Federal Telegraph's request to build stations at Guam and the Philippines, the navy would block any move by commercial firms into areas under its authority. There could be no challenge to the ultimate goal of government control over radio in the United States and its territories.[64]

If private companies could expand their radio networks in areas where the United States did not have direct strategic interests, the navy would encourage this expansion even if secret subsidies were out of the question. In the Caribbean basin, the favored company was Tropical Radio. To boost the need for ship-shore communications in the Caribbean, the Board on Organization had recommended that an agreement be reached with United Fruit to take over their stations in Central America "as a branch of the Naval Communication Service" in wartime. This was relatively easy to do, as the Tropical Radio stations already worked on protocols similar to the navy, had a great many former navy radio men on their staffs, and were located, from the position of the navy, in strategic locations between Louisiana and Colombia.[65]

To South American officials, the firm to be supported was Federal Telegraph. The company that had been building the arc transmitters for the U.S. Navy also operated commercial radio stations. In 1915 Federal Telegraph looked to expand into Latin America. Federal Telegraph representative Chauncy Eldridge toured several Latin American countries that spring, to pursue concessions. The intention was to build a powerful station in one or more countries that could work directly or in relay with a corresponding station in the United States. "[If the] plans of this company can only be carried out," Eldridge promised Lansing, "one of the most important steps will have been taken toward cementing the diplomatic, financial, and commercial relations of the countries of the Northern and Southern Hemispheres."[66] As this project promised to be an important step in the extension of international radio links, the State Department instructed diplomats in Chile, Peru, Argentina, Brazil, and Uruguay to lend every support to Eldridge. When the navy learned that rivals Marconi and Telefunken were preparing to bid on concessions in Venezuela, the State Department passed this information along as well to Federal Telegraph. In late September, Eldridge won an important concession from the Argentine government to build and operate a station in Buenos Aires. By January 1916, he had gained a similar concession in Uruguay, and negotiations in Brazil looked promising as well. News of these concessions excited officials in Venezuela, who then invited Federal Telegraph to bid on a similar station there too. By the summer of 1916, it appeared as if the Federal Company had a strong position in Latin America.[67]

Though initially promising, Eldridge's work did not lead to success for Federal Telegraph. The first hint of problems came when the State Department floated the Daniels plan of government control. In Montevideo, Uruguayan officials halted negotiations "suddenly and unexpectedly" in late December, despite the fact that the two sides had almost finished the concession.[68] Eldridge reported to Lansing that he believed a similar collapse was likely in Brazil as well.[69] By October 1916, the Brazilian government had passed a law that placed all control of radio in the country in the hands of the government. This effectively eliminated any chance that Federal Telegraph would build a private station there.[70] In the spring of 1917, after many months of negotiations, the Venezuelan government rejected Federal Telegraph's bid as too high. As Telefunken and Marconi prepared their own bids, the American minister in Caracas repeatedly urged the State and Commerce departments to press any American radio company to bid and win the contract. "I presume Venezuela is the only country in the world," he lamented to Lansing, "which has no wireless communication."[71] Though a favorite of the navy and well served by the newly won concessions, Federal Telegraph proved curiously unable to capitalize on its gains. The reasons for this have never been clear, but the implications would be important for the course of radio policy and the efforts to promote an independent, global radio network for the United States.

The fourth initiative on the part of the U.S. Navy was to stop foreign radio firms from gaining any further ground in Latin America. The State Department had already made efforts to stop Telefunken's agents from landing contracts in Central America. From his new assignment in El Salvador, Minister Boaz Long continued to do this. It was equally important, in the eyes of the navy, to stop the Marconi Wireless Telegraph Company (British Marconi) from increasing its hold in the area as well. The navy had long been suspicious of the perceived ties between Marconi and the British Admiralty, as well as of the firm's restrictive practices and its adherence to the outdated spark system. Unfortunately for the Marconi Wireless Telegraph Company of America (American Marconi), the child carried the stigma of the parent. When company president E. J. Nally sought to expand his company's operations into South America to take advantage of the demand for improved service and to make use of the idle Belmar, New Jersey, station, he ran into difficulties with the navy.

These difficulties occurred because it appeared to the navy that American Marconi's expansion into South America was in support of British Marconi. In mid-1915, Nally had requested State Department assistance in pursuing concessions in Latin America. The main objective was Brazil, where British Marconi had acquired a concession in August 1913. At the same time, the Brazilian representative of British Marconi requested help from U.S. Ambassador Edwin Morgan in Rio. The Brazilian authorities had already abruptly canceled negotiations with British Marconi when they learned that Federal Telegraph would be making a similar offer. On the navy's advice, the State Department politely rebuffed the requests. In Rio, Morgan was to refer the Brazilian representative to the British minister and support Federal Telegraph instead. Lansing informed Nally, meanwhile, that the U.S. government believed his company to be British in nature. No help would be forthcoming for American Marconi.[72]

Undeterred by the initial snubs, Nally bravely made repeated representations to convince the State Department of his firm's autonomy and loyalty. It would be American Marconi, not its British parent, that would apply for the concession in Brazil. His firm could be trusted to keep American interests in mind.[73] When Lansing checked again with the Navy Department, the negative reply was more forceful. The company used outdated spark technology and would apparently employ it at the new stations. As for the company, it was apparently not very "American." Several members of the board of directors were not U.S. citizens and were on Marconi boards in Canada, Britain, Russia, and France. The British parent company held the majority of the stock in the American firm. Most damning, British Marconi had announced that it would be the one to build the stations. This announcement led senior officials from Captain Bullard up through Secretary Daniels to conclude that there was no practicable difference between the two. "It cannot be a moment doubted," Daniels warned Lansing, "but that if [American Marconi] obtained concessions for the erection of radio stations in South America, the apparatus would be of a foreign manufacture and under foreign patents, and installed by foreign personnel, and finally operated in the interests of foreign capital."[74]

Nally's appeals could not overcome the navy's two basic concerns: the American branch's uncertain relationship with the British parent and the incompatibility between the spark and the continuous wave systems. The State Department deferred to the navy's advice. Nally learned in December 1915 that further appeals would be useless. Aware of precisely who was behind the opposition, Nally finally wrote directly to Captain Bullard to press his case. Pleading that he desired to cooperate with the navy and the U.S. government in any way, he offered the entire resources of his company for use in a crisis as a pledge of his firm's loyalty. Unmoved, Bullard and the navy would not take Nally at his word. The navy could endorse only reliable companies with entirely American financial backing and utilizing wholly American-manufactured equipment. Such threads were not woven into American Marconi's cloak.[75]

At the same time that Nally's plans were met by the navy's intransigence, Sir Godfrey Isaacs, the aggressive head of British Marconi, attempted from London to regain the initiative in Latin America. If Federal Telegraph was to be the favored instrument for the United States, then perhaps British Marconi could acquire control of the company and its valuable patented improvements to the arc system. Marconi had similarly acquired control over local rivals in other countries in the past. The only hindrance to the plan was a paucity of investment capital during the war. If Isaacs could make the case that the acquisition was in Britain's interest, he might secure a government loan.

To win financial support from a wartime government for a project of this sort required considerable gall and not a little subterfuge. In December 1915, just as Nally was making his final futile appeal to the State Department, Isaacs wrote to the Foreign Office to warn them that he had learned there was the strong possibility that Telefunken, through its ACC subsidiary in New York, intended to acquire Federal Telegraph. He claimed that this was to be part of a larger attempt by Telefunken to reinvigorate the German international radio network. Telefunken had recently won a contract to build a medium-power station in Sweden, had approached the Norwegians about taking over the idle Marconi station at Stavanger, and apparently had an agent in China about to land a contract for a high-power station.[76] If Telefunken could win Federal Telegraph, then Germany would have a way into Latin America through the company's new concessions there. Should the Marconi companies acquire Federal Telegraph instead, they could stop this German plan and help the war effort.[77] His company would only need about £100,000 from the British treasury. Isaacs then began to pressure the government with claims of a rapidly closing window of opportunity. Delay would only increase the price of Federal Telegraph, and he needed a commitment quickly. Isaacs had, deliberately or otherwise, conflated negotiations between the ACC and Federal Telegraph to share certain patents and the wild idea that Telefunken's purchase of Federal Telegraph was imminent. From Washington, Ambassador Spring-Rice then reported the true situation of the Marconi Company's rising difficulties in South America and the proposed Pan-American radio network. Isaacs did not win his £100,000. As one Foreign Office official perceptively pointed out, it was unlikely that the United States government would ever permit the consolidation of its national radio industry under a single foreign firm, British or German.[78]

By the beginning of 1917, the navy's hemispheric radio policy had been only mildly successful. Like so many blades of grass, antennae for naval radio stations had sprouted at the Panama Canal, Puerto Rico, the Dominican Republic, and Cuba and along the southern coast of the United States from Key West to the Mexican border. Tropical Radio had improved its own network of stations from Honduras to Colombia. In line with the navy's wishes, Tropical Radio employed the latest equipment and operating procedures, and an agreement had been signed to allow the navy tacit use of these stations in wartime.[79] Neither Telefunken nor Marconi had expanded its influence in the area, in large part because of timely U.S. diplomatic pressure. The Division of Latin American Affairs in the State Department had even prepared draft treaties for negotiations with Guatemala, Salvador, Honduras, Nicaragua, and Costa Rica to turn over to the United States control over radio operations in those countries. Yet none of the governments whose representative had attended the Washington conference in January 1916 had offered to join the navy's proposed network. There was no common hemispheric policy on radio, nor was there much evident movement by South American governments to improve control over radio in ways that would limit foreign involvement. Federal Telegraph had not yet managed to develop a commercial network in the region, which meant that Marconi or Telefunken might still win a foothold. Despite all of the efforts that had been made to that point, Boaz Long later concluded, the hemispheric radio policy had collapsed as a failure.[80]

By the outbreak of war, the U.S. Navy had initiated a significance transformation of the nation's use of radio. With Hooper's encouragement, the Federal Telegraph Company had pushed the limits of radio design, to create arc transmitters of extremely high power that were capable of blasting signals thousands of miles reliably and continuously. Using this technology, the navy had begun construction of a massive network of stations from the Philippines to Puerto Rico. The espousal of the arc and the related continuous wave method of transmitting signals, however, had brought to the fore crucial questions about the ability of the United States government to regulate radio. The growing use of this technology for marine and long-distance communications threatened to create an increasingly chaotic storm of interference. There was no regulatory way for the navy to compel civilian adoption of continuous wave technology or other measures to improve the situation. The situation unchanged, increasing interference from stations using outdated equipment and overcrowding of the air would make it more difficult for the U.S. Navy to use radio effectively with its ships at sea. Moreover, the tremendous lead that the United States enjoyed in the development of radio technology would not last, as researchers in other countries discovered further important advances in this new field. At the same time, commercial companies faced few restrictions in their operations and might easily open a radio station anywhere in the country. Stations operated by foreign firms might violate the neutrality of the country or serve as secret outposts for monitoring naval communications. For these interrelated technical and security reasons, many in the navy concluded that the problems had to be dealt with sooner rather than later. Moreover, because of the great range of radio transmissions, the problem also had to be confronted throughout the entire hemisphere. Should these conditions persist, so the logic went, the safety of the Panama Canal and the defense of the country might ultimately be in jeopardy. At a minimum, a looming diplomatic problem, simultaneously obscure and yet central, would have to be dealt with on a hemispheric or international basis, regardless of the present wartime difficulties. It was not a problem that, left alone, would go away.

In the months that followed, the crucial issue became who should have authority over long-distance radio communications. Daniels and Todd believed devoutly that governments alone ought to control all forms of radio communications. Indeed, they sought actively to persuade as many governments as possible in the hemisphere, including their own, to adhere to this idea. Wrapped up in the internal logic of radio and security that had developed over the past four years, Daniels and his supporters were unable to understand that this policy was too rigid for the subtleties of U.S–Latin American relations or the nuances of commercial radio operations. Those in the State Department who might have understood these things, however, deferred to the navy on matters of radio and backed the plan without reservation. The single individual in the State Department with the best understanding of the issue, Boaz Long, was unable to shape the debate from his office in El Salvador. Throughout this entire period, the pursuit of government control over long-distance radio operations in the hemisphere remained the avowed policy of the U.S. Navy and therefore of the United States.

What supporters of this plan did not understand was that this policy would relegate U.S. radio companies to being simply equipment suppliers, not strong operating firms capable of challenging Marconi or Telefunken in Latin America. The real long-term prospects of revenue for radio companies like Federal Telegraph, however, came not from equipment contracts with the navy but from handling international commercial traffic. This would generate the revenue necessary to support further research, which the navy desired, and the continuing expansion of the networks. As Chauncy Eldridge and others at Federal Telegraph hoped, the extension into Latin America would bring just this sort of return. Federal Telegraph now was the only company in the world that made the high-power transmitters—developed at Hooper's behest—that would work effectively over the great distances involved. This meant Federal Telegraph could provide a valuable alternative to the British cables, open up Brazil and Argentina to direct U.S. contact, and make it more difficult for Marconi or Telefunken to establish a presence in the region. But because the radio technology was still in a period of great development, Federal Telegraph's advantage was only temporary. Yet the paradoxical dual diplomatic support for government control and Federal Telegraph ultimately wrecked the company's plans in Latin America. The navy's opposition to a commercial long-distance station in the United States gave the appearance that Federal Telegraph would never be able to establish direct two-way commercial contact to the south. This uncertainty soured efforts to raise the necessary investment capital and political support needed to build the initial stations in Argentina and elsewhere in Latin America.

Through the efforts of Hooper and Bullard and the attention to these matters from Daniels and Roosevelt, the U.S. Navy had come to hold a large stake in the development of the country's foreign radio connections. Unlike its role in the field of cables, the United States was now at the leading edge of radio technology. As Hooper had discovered in 1914, the United States was equal to or ahead of Britain, France, and Germany in the use of radio. Though apparent to only a few, radio offered a way to bypass British control over cable communications in the world. As the United States plunged into war in April 1917, few in the Wilson administration could have anticipated the tremendous role that radio and cables would come to play.

FOUR

✦ ✦ ✦

At War in Europe

AFTER SITTING ON the sidelines through thirty-two months of carnage in Europe, the United States joined the war against Germany in April 1917. President Woodrow Wilson, seeing in Germany's resumption of unrestricted submarine warfare the evaporation of any further chance at peace, had resolved to ask Congress for a declaration of war. On the night of April 2, 1917, a motorcar, flanked by cavalry, carried the president up Capitol Hill, past the crowds of people and through the slow drizzle of rain to the covered carriageway by the House of Representatives. After first composing himself in an antechamber, Wilson delivered his most important speech to Congress on the subject of the war in Europe. It was now no longer possible, he informed the assembled congressmen and dignitaries, to remain simply armed neutrals in the face of a threat to maritime commerce. By engaging, without warnings, in submarine attacks on neutral ships, he argued, Germany had chosen war and thrust belligerency upon the United States. The question before Congress now was how the United States would make use of its power and resources to bring Germany to terms, end the war, and make the world safe for democracy. A speech stirring to the ears of many in the House chamber that night, its significance left Wilson overwhelmed. Later that evening his personal secretary, Joseph Tumulty, found him in the empty Cabinet Room in the White House. Acknowledging to Tumulty that this presidential call for war effectively meant the deaths of many young Americans in the months to come, Wilson wept at the weight of the moment. After strident debate in the days that followed, the Senate voted eighty-two to six to approve the war resolution. On April 5, Good Friday, the House of Representatives passed the measure 373 to 50. The next day the joint war resolution arrived at the White House for Wilson's signature. Upon the moment of Wilson's inscription, a naval aide signaled across the lawn to the Navy Department. The message went out by radio: the country was at war.

Relations between the United States and Germany had steadily deteriorated through the winter of 1917. Wilson's successive efforts to curb the horrors of the European war had proven fruitless. Desperate to isolate Britain by cutting off her overseas trade and thus the lifeline of food and war matériel, German officials had decided in mid-January to resume the controversial practice of unrestricted submarine warfare. Any ships, whether neutral or belligerent, would be fair targets for attack by U-boats in Allied-controlled waters. The result, the Germans hoped, would be a counterblockade of Britain that would shatter her economy, starve her people, and end the war. Germany had attempted this strategy the previous February, but Wilson's threat then to break diplomatic relations with Germany over this issue brought the campaign to an abrupt halt. This time, the German high command believed that an end to the war was close enough to be worth the risk of American anger. On the last day of January, Germany revealed to the United States that the submarines would be unleashed once more the following day. True to his earlier threat, Wilson then broke off diplomatic relations with Germany on February 3. Explaining his actions before Congress, Wilson asked that there be a state of "armed neutrality" with Germany and that American merchant ships be equipped with weapons for their own protection.

In the weeks that followed the breach, further events aggravated the tense situation. Fearful of submarines, merchant shippers kept their vessels in harbor rather than chance a cold, watery grave. Ships and immobilized cargo soon clogged ports along the Atlantic. On February 25, Wilson asked Congress for the authority to arm the nation's merchant ships, but senators anxious to preserve the peace stopped the measure. Meanwhile, British intelligence had passed to the United States the astonishing contents of an intercepted German diplomatic message calling on Mexico to join in an alliance against the United States in exchange for Texas, Arizona, and New Mexico. The Wilson administration released the text of the Zimmermann telegram, as it became known, to the public on March 1. Not surprisingly, it generated tremendous public indignation and undercut the arguments of many who urged peace.

As German torpedoes took American ships, pressure grew for defense. On March 12, Wilson ordered that merchant ships passing through the war zone be armed. A critical moment then came on March 18, when three U.S. ships sank under torpedo attack. Convening his cabinet two days later to discuss the matter, Wilson found unanimous conviction that war was at hand. Congress having been recalled already, Wilson arranged to ask for the declaration of war on April 2.

The experience of the war that followed, like that of neutrality before it, demonstrated firsthand to the United States the tremendous importance of continuous, reliable communications with the rest of the world. In all previous U.S. military engagements, the country had not had to consider the question of rapid contact on a global scale. As U.S. officials soon learned, the situation in 1917 was worse than they could have imagined. Scarcely adequate in the months after August 1914, the North Atlantic cable network had deteriorated as the threat of U-boat attacks deterred cable companies from all but the most essential work. Radio contact over the Atlantic was still in its infancy and could carry but a fraction of the traffic passing over the cables. The additional military, diplomatic, press, and commercial traffic that the country would generate as a belligerent—compounding the existing problems with censorship and the ban on commercial coding—might well overwhelm the cable and radio networks entirely. Like a hand parting a curtain behind which had been hidden the true workings of the world, the war unveiled the limitations of the existing networks in a moment of supreme crisis. What had begun as largely a commercial concern now metamorphosed into an important strategic problem for the United States.

Overall, the senior government officials who confronted the issue pursued several solutions to the shortcomings they identified. They encouraged the profligate use of the latest radio technology, seeing a current and long-term political and commercial advantage in its employment. From Vladivostok to Constantinople, the U.S. Navy subsequently built up the most powerful and wide-ranging radio system in the world. In Latin America, the U.S. fought to block the extension of British and German radio stations and to break apart British cable concessions. Understanding that control over the cable and radio networks conferred power over the information flowing through them, U.S. officials established a rudimentary intelligence operation in tandem with cable and radio censorship. These efforts set the stage for postwar programs intended to remove U.S. dependence upon Britain's global network. This goal would involve establishing a new cable industry to serve the anticipated future needs of U.S. cable companies. It also included establishing non-European, U.S.-controlled companies operating the latest radio technology and building stations in Latin America. Begun as a result of the war, these programs demonstrated the transformation of U.S. strategic understanding of global communications in war and peace.

Britain's control over the transatlantic cables played a prominent supporting role in bringing the United States into the war. The systematic destruction of the German cable network in 1914 had forced Germany to seek other ways of escaping the information blockade. Since the outbreak of war, the British Admiralty's Room 40 code-breaking group had been monitoring cable and radio traffic to catch this running of the blockade. On January 16, 1917, Room 40's net ensnared an astonishing message. The German foreign minister, Dr. Arthur Zimmermann, had dispatched special instructions to the German minister at Mexico City, Heinrich von Eckhardt, through Count Bernstorff in Washington. Eckhardt was to invite Mexico to join Germany in war against the United States should it declare war on Germany over the upcoming resumption of unrestricted submarine warfare. In offering this alliance, Germany promised Texas, New Mexico, and Arizona as spoils to Mexico at the end of the war, as well as financial assistance. Eckhardt was also to suggest that the Mexican president offer enticements to Japan to switch sides as well. Of all the messages British intelligence had intercepted, this one was certain to fan the flames of anti-German sentiment in the United States if revealed.[1]

Britain chose to share with the United States the contents of Zimmermann's telegram amid the atmosphere of anger and dismay following Germany's resumption of submarine warfare and the breach in relations. The discovery of the message had put Admiral "Blinker" Hall, the head of Room 40, in a quandary. Though America's distress would serve Britain's interests, the release of the message might reveal that Britain was reading neutral diplomatic traffic—including that of the United States. Room 40, it now appears, had in fact discovered the message by reading U.S. diplomatic traffic. However, a copy conveniently acquired in Mexico City provided an alternate source that Hall could share with the U.S. Embassy intelligence liaison, Edward Bell. Foreign Secretary Arthur Balfour then presented it formally to Ambassador Page, who hurriedly cabled this disquieting revelation back to Washington. When shown the message by counselor Frank Polk on February 24, Wilson exploded and threatened to make the matter public without delay. Polk and then Lansing, upon his return to Washington on February 27, convinced Wilson to wait until they could verify the message's authenticity.

Particularly damning was the method by which Zimmermann's message had reached Eckhardt in Mexico City. The Germans had available three different routes to get the message through. The first was to send it by high-power radio from Nauen to the station at Sayville, despite the danger that U.S. Navy censors might read it. The second was under cover of Swedish diplomatic traffic, sent from Stockholm to Buenos Aires over the British cables and then up over Central's lines to Mexico. It was the third method that, when revealed, proved most duplicitous. Count Bernstorff, the German ambassador at Washington, had earlier persuaded Wilson that unfettered communications between the United States and Germany would help peace efforts. But the cutting of the German cables and the Allied information blockade had left Germany without a protected way of communicating secretly. In hopes that it would accelerate the peaceful settlement of the war, Wilson had granted Bernstorff the exceptional privilege of sending German diplomatic messages under cover of U.S. diplomatic messages cabled to Berlin. As a courtesy, the State Department allowed German diplomats to use a code without providing a copy of the key. Thus U.S. officials, believing that neither Bernstorff nor his superiors would abuse this trust, had unwittingly protected the transmission of a coded message that ultimately might harm the United States. Under strong pressure from Lansing, Western Union reluctantly yielded a copy of the message. This copy went to Bell in London, who had Room 40 staff decode it in his presence to confirm it was real. Shaken by this breach of trust as well as by Germany's inflammatory invitation to Mexico, Wilson could withhold the revelation no longer. The text of the message became public on March 1. Two days later, Zimmermann himself acknowledged that it was authentic; it was not an Allied fabrication.²

How important was the Zimmermann telegram? Alone it did not bring the United States into the war. Instead, its revelation angered Wilson, undermined those seeking peace, and solidified support in Congress and the public at large for intervention. Wilson had been reluctant to push the country forward into war without the domestic support necessary to sustain the war effort. When he severed diplomatic relations with Germany in response to unrestricted submarine warfare, Wilson had been willing to go as far as a quasi war, with the arming of merchant ships. To have convinced the rest of the country—parts of which cared little for the abstract concept of maritime rights or which felt that the United States had no stake in the outcome of the war in Europe—that such risks were worth taking would have been very difficult for Wilson. It was the revelation of Zimmermann's offer, with its promise to hand over parts of the American Southwest and the hint at Japanese involvement as well, that inflamed otherwise lukewarm passions. Outrage and indignation drove out doubt and antipathy in the minds of many. Without the telegram, Wilson's efforts to convince the country to go to war in April would have been much harder, if not impossible. More significantly, behind all of this lay Britain's control of strategic communications, the informational blockade Britain supported, and the intelligence it could glean. This fact and the lessons of how Britain had really acquired the telegram and used the cable network to its advantage were not lost on administration officials as they guided the nation through war.

Once President Wilson made the decision to commit U.S. forces to a French expedition, the U.S. Army General Staff began to contemplate the tremendous personnel, transportation, and logistical requirements of raising an army, moving it into the Western Front, and supplying it. The task of managing the strategic communications between France and the United States fell to the Signal Corps. General George O. Squier, recalled from London to be the chief signal officer of the army, and Colonel Edgar Russel, who would hold a similar position in the new American Expeditionary Force (AEF), quickly surveyed the anticipated needs of the army in the field. They realized that the task of providing continual contact between the War Department in Washington, D.C., and the AEF in Europe, entailing the rapid handling of millions of messages, over a distance of thirty-eight hundred miles, "presented many problems unique in the history of warfare." Initially they assumed that the existing cable networks would be adequate. This was hopelessly optimistic.[3] Already the State Department had noticed its own cable traffic had increased precipitously: in June the department sent and received more messages daily than during any week before March 1917. The army simply had no experience upon which to gauge its needs.[4]

Further complicating the situation, Germany's submarines threatened allied communications as well as allied shipping beyond European waters. Both directly by breaking the cables and indirectly by endangering the repair work, German submarines had already disrupted interallied cable contact. Since the first months of the war, they had continued to attack cables in deep water. During the nights of February 10 to 12, 1917, for example, the cruiser submarine *U-155* cut a series of cables linking Britain, Portugal, Gibraltar, and the Azores, greatly upsetting British communications to the Mediterranean and the rest of the world until a cable ship could be brought in for repairs.[5] The extended range of German submarines meant that cables along the North American or African coast were vulnerable to attack as well.

The implicit danger of submarines also affected the cables by deterring the cable companies from carrying out routine maintenance. Be-

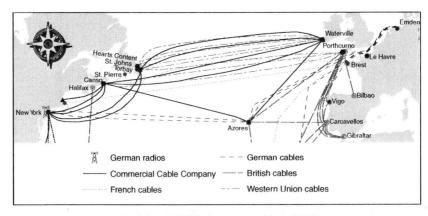

Principal North Atlantic cables, 1914

fore the war there had been seventeen operational cables of varying degrees of reliability between North America and Europe. By 1917, with the two German cables to New York cut, the remaining fifteen had suffered from lack of maintenance. Whether from seaquake, an errant anchor, or simply manufacturing defects, faults on the several-thousand-mile-long cables were not unusual. The danger of easy submarine attack against a slow-moving or motionless cable ship, however, had nearly halted the usual summertime repair missions. Neither the U.S. Navy nor Allied naval forces had been willing to spare the warships needed to protect a single exposed cable ship positioned above a cable break for several hours. Ordinarily, the companies anticipated having one or two cables out of service at any given time. The excess capacity on the rest of the cables distributed the burden without noticeable delays until the cable could be repaired. Without regular maintenance, the entire network slowly deteriorated and threatened to break down entirely as the number of usable cables declined.

Before departing for France, Colonel Russel received a sobering briefing from the three major cable companies' experts on the commercial capacity available to the army. The engineers revealed to Russel the delicate situation of the North Atlantic cables. The cable companies had long feared that German submarines would mount an attack on the transatlantic cables off the Canadian coast.[6] Russel learned that Germany certainly had the ability to damage or completely interrupt these cables and that such attacks had in fact already occurred. Western Union's vice president, J. C. Willever, expressed to Russel his worries that Germany might actively target the North Atlantic cables once the United States tightened censorship. If this happened, making repairs in the face of the submarine threat would not be possible. Willever believed that the radio stations, now under navy control, ought to be put into operation as soon as possible.[7]

With that warning of the cables' vulnerability in his mind, Colonel Russel sailed on May 28 with the rest of General Pershing's staff for Europe. Visiting Britain briefly, they arrived in France on June 13. Over the following days, they began laying out the foundations of the expeditionary force and planning the logistical, transportation, and communications requirements for maintaining the AEF over three thousand miles from the United States. Russel soon met with Colonel Gustave Ferrié, principal radio officer for the French army, and Colonel François Cartier, the chief of the French military cryptologic bureau, to discuss the question of how to relieve some of the pressure on the cables. Ferrié outlined for Russel a proposal to make use of the existing high-power long-distance stations to form a transatlantic network that would provide at least a minimal amount of communications.[8]

This idea of a high-power interallied radio network had first emerged shortly after the United States had entered the war. It was not a particularly great concern for the navy, which oversaw national radio policy but had little need of regular radio contact with the Allied powers. There was already in place the Interallied Radio Commission (IARC), formed earlier in the war to coordinate operating procedures and allocate wavelengths among the allies. Meeting in Paris, the commission included representatives from the major allies as well as from Serbia, Romania, and Japan. Within days of the declaration of war, the U.S. military and naval attachés at the U.S. Embassy in Paris had joined the proceedings as well. It was important to adjust the existing Allied radio schedules to incorporate the stations operated by the United States and thereby to ensure that there would be no interference. Arranging a regular schedule for the exchange of traffic between the United States and Europe was feasible, but many problems still remained.[9]

For reasons of war as well as geography, development of high-power long-distance radio in Europe had not kept pace with development in the United States. Because the majority of radio communications in Europe passed over short distances, military and naval radio users relied largely on lower-power transmitters and shorter wavelengths. For long-distance communications, the plethora of cables served well. Still, each of the major powers had radio stations capable of exchanging signals across the Atlantic. Nauen, in Germany, was already hard at work. In Britain, the Royal Navy had taken over operation of the Marconi station at Carnarvon, Wales, which had been designed to work with the American Marconi station at New Brunswick, New Jersey. The French had high-power stations in Lyon and at the Eiffel Tower in Paris. These used arc transmitters installed by C. F. Elwell, the engineer who had helped to found the Federal Telegraph Company in the United States. The Italians had a similar station outside Pisa, originally built by Marconi well before the war. With Elwell's assistance, in the spring of 1917 the Italians had begun construction of a large arc transmitting station near Rome.[10]

These five stations all varied in quality and reliability, but only the Lyon signal could reliably reach the United States. Transmissions from the Americas, meanwhile, could be heard with some regularity; the Eiffel Tower station had even been able to hear transmissions from the U.S. Navy station in the Canal Zone, nearly fifty-four hundred miles distant. None of the European high-power stations, however, could handle messages sent at a high rate of speed or offset any intentional jamming from Nauen. More problematical for the United States, none of the stations had the organizational capacity or infrastructure to receive and distribute by telegraph lines any large volume of traffic.[11]

The Interallied Radio Commission formally asked the United States to make the Sayville station available for communication with France on April 13, 1917. The navy began to carry out tests six days later. Soon the powers had worked out a process for routing traffic from Sayville to France. Colonel Cartier then proposed that the United States assign different stations to handle traffic with Britain, France, and Italy. With only two commercial high-power stations available, the U.S. Navy offered a preliminary arrangement. Tuckerton would exchange regular traffic with Carnarvon in Britain and Pisa in Italy.[12] Sayville would work with the Eiffel Tower and Lyon. To prevent interference, the IARC then laid out a plan of frequencies used by each station and the times of day during which each would transmit its signals and listen for other stations. At this point, the intention was still just to have regular radio contact rather than to use the radio stations as the primary or exclusive method for interallied communications or contact with the expeditionary force.[13]

The French appear to have been very serious about improved radio contact with the Western Hemisphere. Intending to construct a new high-power station specifically for contact with the United States, French officials asked the United States to assign one of its stations for permanent postwar radio contact with France. A visiting French delegation even offered to construct such a station for the United States if it were not able to do so, an offer that their navy hosts firmly rejected.[14] Prepared to use either Sayville or Tuckerton for this U.S.-France connection during the war, the navy would not commit to postwar plans until Congress had decided to grant national radio operations to the navy.[15] The French were also in discussions with the Brazilian government about a similar arrangement, a development that the U.S. Navy welcomed so long as the Brazilian station was not under European control.[16]

By the summer the cable situation in the North Atlantic had become precarious, but few officials in Washington were aware of the extent of the danger. Only ten of the prewar seventeen cables were operational and company officials believed that further deterioration was a certainty. In June Western Union requested a U.S. Navy escort to accompany a cable-repair ship urgently needed to work on two different breaks. The navy refused. "All available vessels," Secretary Daniels informed company president Newcomb Carlton, were "being actively employed in important military service," and there were no submarines reported in the vicinity of the cable breaks.[17]

From France, Colonel Russel warned that strategic transatlantic communications were far more vulnerable than military officials or the administration back in Washington understood. As he emphasized to Commander W. L. Sayles, the U.S. Navy attaché in Paris, the relative importance of cable communications to the United States was continually increasing: "There may come a time when the enemy will find it worthwhile to forgo his own benefit [from the cables] . . . in order that he may do us the far greater harm by interrupting the communications."[18] To General Pershing, Russel stressed, "There is no question of the grave situation in which we may find ourselves as a result of the extensive cable cutting, which, in the belief of all [whom] I have consulted, may be easily effected by the enemy. The enormous importance of immediate provision of reliable and extensive transatlantic radiotelegraph service is therefore evident."[19] Reinforcing this warning was the earlier revelation from British officials that German submarines had sunk so much British shipping that there were not enough remaining ships to bring over the entire AEF or keep it regularly supplied without drastic action.[20] Whether electrical or waterborne, the lines of communication were under threat.

Russel's warnings and Colonel Ferrié's proposal filtered back to Washington, D.C., in mid-August.[21] General Pershing then fired off his own urgent dispatch to Washington on August 29, ordering that everything be done to ensure continual transatlantic communications. He demanded that there be some arrangement with the French and British governments to ensure the use of transatlantic radio if necessary in the face of cable disruption.[22]

Back in Washington, General Squier received more news from cable companies about the steady deterioration of the network. In early September, G. M. Yorke, the chief engineer for Western Union, informed him that yet another cable had failed. Now only half of the company's entire eight-cable system was functioning. Three of the breaks were in water so deep that repair work would be impossible before the summer months. The fourth break was on the cable with the greatest capacity but in a region well within the German submarine danger zone. Because the British government had rejected a request to send a cable ship out, Yorke hoped that perhaps the Signal Corps could impress upon the British the urgency of the situation.[23] By early October, the number of usable cables had fallen to just nine, while traffic demands continued to increase. The time for safe repair work in midocean was rapidly passing. Newcomb Carlton, president of Western Union, confided to one British official that despite the difficulties and dangers of midwinter repair, the work "should be proceeded with at all hazards" to vessels and crews.[24] The United States simply did not have the redundancy that the British Empire had built into its cable network, and any further disruption to the cables could not be overlooked.

The core problem was that there simply was too much traffic for the existing cable network to handle and little room for more wartime messages. By October the average load passing each way over the working transatlantic cables became 970,000 words per week, out of a total capacity of 1.2 million. This included all diplomatic, military, commercial, press, and private messages. The ban on codes ballooned the size of messages in the latter three groups. The delays reached four and a half to nearly eight hours, and the loss of another cable would lengthen this time to thirty hours, even with further restrictions on message size and priority. An additional margin of just 230,000 words each way remained if the cable equipment and private company personnel operated at maximum efficiency with little or no interruption. Signal Corps officers, however, estimated that the AEF alone would generate five hundred thousand words per week, only if the AEF maintained extremely tight traffic management over its cables.[25] Never having carried out such a massive operation before, however, the Signal Corps estimates were barely realistic. Had more of the cables been cut or broken, by now a distinct possibility, the United States would have to reroute some of its traffic via an alternate route, either through South

America or across the Pacific. Yet there was no direct cable to Brazil, where the British transatlantic cables landed. The transpacific cable was notoriously slow and periodically broken. The concept of routing orders for Pershing in France through Brazil, Japan, or China was scarcely imaginable. To U.S. commanders, neither alternative was acceptable in the slightest for maintaining continual contact with an expeditionary army.

Squier reassured Pershing, saying, "This office fully realizes the gravity of the situation." To ensure that a modicum of continual contact remained even if all cables fell silent, Squier decided to push the navy to expand its high-power long-distance network. He then sent Colonel J. J. Carty, peacetime chief engineer of AT&T, to work out details with the navy.[26] In mid-October, the United States and Britain finally began to discuss repair work on the transatlantic cables. From London, the Admiralty coordinated with the General Post Office to direct cable ships to the breaks and increase stockpiles of spare cable. The U.S. Navy now backed the idea of convoys to protect cable ships. Admiral Benson, the chief of naval operations, responded favorably to the Commercial Cable's request for a naval escort for the company's next repair mission. The State Department instructed the embassy in London to line up support from the Royal Navy. In Britain, the Admiralty was equally anxious to repair the cables, but senior officials worried that a slow cable ship would present an "easy mark." Because the breaks on the cables were closer to Britain than to North America, the British would send out their own convoy and requested that Commercial Cable's ship, the *Mackay-Bennett*, remain safely close to Halifax. The Foreign Office then reassured Ambassador Page that any delays would be due to the submarine situation and not any lack of cable ships. The Commercial cable was fixed by the end of October. Plans were also underway to dispatch two British cable ships to repair the Western Union cables in December.[27] For all these efforts, however, the cable situation continued to decline. By the spring of 1918, only seven cables were usable (with another available one way only). Hard work in the face of greatly reduced supplies of fresh cable enabled the companies to bring this number up eventually to eleven by July 1918. At the same time, the navy worked feverishly to develop a transatlantic radio network as a backup system for the cables.[28]

War brought the U.S. Navy control over the largest radio network in the world. Besides the unfinished high-power chain, there was also an intricate system of ship-to-shore and district radio stations scattered along the continental coastline. The navy also had operational control over the former German radio stations at Tuckerton and Sayville near New York City. Following the declaration of war, President Wilson had placed all radio operations in the country under navy control. The navy shut down those commercial stations, mostly those of American Marconi, which duplicated existing navy stations or caused interference.[29] Among the high-power stations passing into navy hands were those of American Marconi in Massachusetts, New York, California, and Hawaii, as well as those of Federal Telegraph along the Pacific coast.[30]

The U.S. Navy had given only selective attention to intercontinental radio transmissions prior to 1917. The radio reorganization board in 1915 had formulated a plan to create a three-tiered system of stations. The lower two tiers linked ships at sea and naval districts in the Caribbean, western Atlantic, and Pacific. The top tier was for strategic communications, to tie the United States to the Canal Zone and the Philippines. Almost as an afterthought, the board noted that should the need arise in war to connect with Asia or Europe, the navy would simply supplement the cables with the existing commercial stations. There had been no serious estimation of the volume of traffic expected in wartime or of the network's real capacity. In fact, the prewar commercial radio stations that the navy intended to use were neither continuous in service nor reliable. Atmospheric disturbances regularly interrupted transmission. None of the stations used the latest in arc transmitter technology. The navy had initially recognized this while operating the German radio stations near New York. Still, senior officials in both the U.S. Navy as well as the Army Signal Corps assumed that the United States would simply make tremendous use of the cables. As they had learned over the summer of 1917, the deteriorating conditions of the cables and the technical inadequacies of the radio stations meant that neither were capable of handling the prolix correspondence of modern war.[31]

It was not until the first week of October that the two services finally worked out the details on using navy-commandeered commercial high-power radios to serve as a dependable complement to the cables. Colonel Carty and Lieutenant Commander Stanford Hooper, now head of the Radio Division in the Bureau of Steam Engineering, met with French representatives and civilian radio experts to devise a plan for the U.S. Navy to operate four complete stations along the eastern seaboard of the United States. These would provide continual, reliable radio contact with the Allied stations in Europe, and one powerful station would maintain a connection with France at all times. Recognizing that Germany might attempt to jam the signal or physically disable the stations, the U.S. and French officials agreed to formulate contingency plans as well.[32]

The navy was going to have to press existing commercial stations into service and build new ones to meet its half of the agreement. In peacetime, the radio businesses had been able to depend on using the cables as a backup in an emergency. During the war and under government control, the situation was now reversed. With a growing naval force operating in European waters and convoys heading across the Atlantic in the face of submarines, the U.S. Navy faced something well beyond anything the Radio Board in 1915 could have envisioned. To work with shipping along the Atlantic coast, the navy used its main station at Arlington, Virginia. In November, work began on a new high-power station in Puerto Rico, to extend the range to ships in the Caribbean and central Atlantic. For contact with Europe, the navy had already assigned Tuckerton and Sayville. The equipment soon failed to handle the volume of traffic or to provide operating consistency needed. At the navy's request, Federal Telegraph began construction on yet another high-power arc transmitter for installation at Tuckerton. In the meantime, the navy began to rely more and more on the third station in the transatlantic network, the American Marconi station at New Brunswick, New Jersey.[33]

In taking over New Brunswick, the navy learned to handle a more advanced transmitter than Federal Telegraph's arcs. In March 1917, shortly before the final collapse of U.S.-German relations, General Electric had installed an experimental 50 kw alternator built by company engineer E. W. F. Alexanderson. The alternator worked by spinning a large iron core inside a metal housing. The resulting electromagnetic current provided a signal much more refined and continuous than that produced by existing transmitters. Though not as powerful as the latest arcs, this alternator was more efficient in its operation. A problem with arcs was that they emitted harmonics parallel to the primary wavelength, and it was difficult to keep the frequency of the signal steady. As a result, they transmitted a broader-than-necessary signal, which tended to crowd the already limited number of wavelengths available for long-distance transmission. Alexanderson's invention produced a signal in a far tighter wavelength, refined enough for transmitting even the human voice. Although it could work only on a single fixed wavelength, this made it ideal for use with point-to-point transmissions over long-distances. Still in its initial stages, the alternator represented the next important advancement in radio technology. At New Brunswick, naval radio engineers tested the alternator against the latest tuning and receiving equipment, all of which worked smoothly under the extreme pressures of wartime.[34]

To meet its transatlantic commitment, the navy also began to build a new high-power station at Annapolis, Maryland. In late 1917, Federal Telegraph built a massive five-hundred-kilowatt arc transmitter, its largest to date, which would enable the station to blast a signal through any amount of atmospheric disturbances during the daytime. Until the new station was finished in August 1918, the navy had to depend on Sayville, Tuckerton, and, most importantly, New Brunswick.[35] Telegraph lines leased from Western Union connected all of the stations together, and it was possible to send and receive messages directly from the navy building in Washington or the fleet radio station across the river in Arlington.[36]

As winter approached, the United States pressed the Allied powers to expand and improve their high-power radio stations. The French agreed to construct near Bordeaux a massive long-distance station, designed to be the central transatlantic station in Europe. The United States Navy arranged for Federal Telegraph to construct 700 kw arc transmitters, so powerful that they would be able to blast through any atmospheric static, for this new station. Navy engineers estimated that the sizable project would take eight months to finish. In the meantime, the navy continued to maintain regular contact with Paris and Lyon through Sayville.[37]

Beyond providing assurance of continued contact with the AEF in France, the transatlantic radio network also became a conduit for sharing news with the rest of the world. The Committee on Public Information (CPI), responsible for disseminating U.S. news to countries around the world by every medium possible, had learned that the German station at Nauen regularly monitored cable transmissions from the United States. In a bid to bypass British and French attempts to censor news coming from the United States, the CPI arranged for a regular news service to U.S. forces in Europe to go by radio rather than cable. This way the United States could avoid Allied filters and send news directly to Germany. One of the most important of these broadcasts was of President Wilson's Fourteen Points speech, sent January 8, 1918. U.S. officials concluded from this news service that, in the future, with an effective global radio network, the country could bypass attempts to control the news and information coming from the United States.

Despite all the efforts to improve transatlantic communications, however, the situation remained tenuous through the winter and spring. The number of operational cables continued to decline despite the repair missions, and eventually by July only seven were available (with an eighth cable usable in one direction only).[38] At the height of a particularly bitter winter, powerful ice storms in New England shut down all but the New Brunswick station. The ability of the General Electric alternator at New Brunswick to handle the additional traffic—including the telegraphed text of President Wilson's Fourteen Points speech—impressed the naval radio officers in charge. Though only fifty kilowatts in power, the alternator was still capable of throwing a signal four thousand miles to the receiving station at Nauen, Germany. The future development of long-distance radio work, many concluded, would require the alternator. Because the prototype's small size did not work consistently well at the ranges the navy required of it, General Electric made plans to install a two-hundred-kilowatt alternator, which was under construction. In the meantime, the older German transmitter at Sayville burned out. With construction continuing at Annapolis, by April the U.S. Navy could depend only upon Tuckerton.[39] Despite fluctuations in service, the Navy continued to send some thirty thousand words and receive twenty-five thousand words of diplomatic, military, and press traffic a day through the Atlantic chain.[40] The U.S. Army, meanwhile, had increased its estimates of how much daily traffic it would need to support the AEF if cable messages were to be limited to ten thousand plain-text words a day. By the summer of 1918, the estimates would go up again to twenty-one thousand words a day, with future projections of thirty thousand for the fall of 1918 and forty-five thousand for the summer of 1919.[41] To handle the possibility of increased traffic and the unresolved threat of German attacks on Allied communications, the navy contemplated the construction of a fifth high-power station in late 1918.

The danger to allied communications in the winter of 1917–1918 was greater than U.S. officials realized. With the intention of bringing the war to the United States and isolating it from the other powers, Germany specifically targeted interallied communications networks in early 1918. Unsuccessful and complicated, this early campaign in information warfare has escaped historical notice.

Following the declaration of war by the United States, German naval officials had decided that the transatlantic cables were now legitimate targets. The German High Seas Fleet staff had objected to the use of submarines in cable attacks as a feat technically too difficult and as a diversion of resources from the economic war against merchant shipping. The German Admiralty removed the cruiser U-boats from the High Seas Fleet's control and endorsed the idea.[42]

Planning began in the summer of 1917 on how and where to make the attacks. The Germans had already made earlier successful submarine raids on cables in the English Channel, North Sea, and Baltic Sea and along the Atlantic coast. Taking this fight to the other side of the Atlantic required adapting the longer-range cruiser submarines to carry cable-cutting equipment. This would include both specially fitted machinery on board the submarine and specialized grapples, newly forged, capable of seizing, raising, and cutting a cable. The cruiser U-boats were to make these raids in addition to their regular attacks on Allied shipping in the U-boat's target areas. The intention was to hit every major Allied cable in the Atlantic at the relatively few points where several cables came close together, such as off New York or near the Azores. Corvette Captain E. Winkler, who formulated the initial list of targets, suggested that only a small number of boats would be necessary to cut most or all of the cables.[43] The cruiser U-boats were to attack within a narrow window of time in mid-January 1918. If successful, the U-boats would silence each cable at both ends, compounding the difficulties of locating and repairing the cuts. The resulting near-simultaneous disruption to transatlantic communications would interfere for weeks on end with everything from routine financial transactions to arrangements for shipping munitions and U.S. soldiers to interallied diplomatic negotiations.

No one had ever attempted such an ambitious program before. The British destruction of the German cable network had taken the better part of a year, had involved experienced cable crews aboard properly equipped cable ships, and had occurred in areas where Britain largely controlled the seas. The German operation was intended to be completed within a few days, from submerged submarines, with crews largely unfamiliar with the intricacies of submarine cable repair, and in waters potentially filled with hostile surface vessels. It was the logical complement to the British attacks on the German system at the outbreak of the war and built upon the earlier effort to split Russia from Britain and France. Audacious, sophisticated, and daring, the operation was fraught with risk but promised significant chaos for the Allies if successful.

Many of the attacks appear to have succeeded. British intelligence reported to the United States Navy in the last week of April that German submarines had attacked four cables off the Iberian and African coasts within the last six weeks and that a new phase in cable operations might be expected. Indeed, three U-boats had damaged British and French cables to the Mediterranean, Africa, and the Americas at critical points off Lisbon and Sierra Leone.[44] There was little that the United States could do to protect the cables at sea, but the navy increased its defenses at the cable landings and the radio stations against raiders or saboteurs.[45] On May 28, the German submarine *U-151*, trolling the waters off Sandy Hook, New Jersey, managed to sever two cables just miles from New York Harbor. Although these cuts, on cables to Europe and Central America, did not do much lasting damage, it surprisingly took nearly a month to repair the first cable and six weeks to repair the second.[46] In June the German Admiralty staff could report that seven different cruiser U-boats had struck at cables near the Azores, Lisbon, Gibraltar, Dakar, and Freetown and off the coast of North America. Cruiser U-boats continued to make sporadic attacks on the transatlantic cables through the last months of the war and as late as mid-September hit British cables off the Portuguese coast.[47]

In the end, the German campaign failed to achieve its objective. Though U-boats damaged or broke many cables, the attacks were not widespread enough nor coordinated enough to overwhelm the entire network in a brief period of time. One problem was simply learning whether the attacks had succeeded. Because the attack occurred underwater and several hundred feet behind and below the submarine, it was impossible for the submarine captain to ascertain whether he had severed the cable, damaged it, or simply moved it. In early January 1918, the German Admiralty instructed naval attachés from Spain to Scandinavia to forward immediately any information that they received on the disruption of the transatlantic cables. Because of censorship and the secretive nature of cable work, the attachés found it all but impossible to learn anything.[48] Without a method for assessing the damage rapidly, the German navy was unable to redirect U-boats back to unsuccessful strikes and complete the overall campaign in a timely manner. Technical problems also plagued the project. German Admiralty documents indicate that in several of these raids the specialized grappling anchor broke under stress from the weight of the cable and the roughness of the ocean floor. The loss of both grapples to the bad seafloor off the Azores, for example, stopped *U-157*'s anticable mission.[49] The Germany navy could not acquire more of these specialized cable grapples quickly enough to refit those submarines that had lost theirs. With the attacks scattered across several weeks rather than concentrated in a short span of time, the individual disruptions could not overwhelm the overall cohesion of the international cable system or the ability of the British and U.S. cable ships to make repairs.[50]

German attacks on Allied communications were not limited to the submarine cables. On at least one occasion, the operators at Nauen transmitted signals in such a way as to jam Tuckerton. "Although it has not been renewed," one naval officer reported later, "[the attack] proves that the Germans have thought of the possibility of interrupting our communications . . . and have organized effective methods for this purpose."[51] Some U.S. officials suggested a counterjamming of Nauen, but Colonel Carty and other senior radio officers were reluctant to initiate a radio fight of this sort, preferring instead to read the German traffic and apply the information to the war effort.[52]

The threat of further German jamming or cable attacks spurred the U.S. Navy to begin a fifth high-power stations along the eastern seaboard. "If the [threat of German attacks] is true," minuted one radio officer, "we should get behind the Alexanderson [alternator] radio barrage immediately and also push completion of transatlantic stations... We will need a new high-power... station in the South." Mindful of the sleet storm that had shut down three of the four stations in the winter, the navy located the station near Charlotte, North Carolina, well beneath the "sleet line" and far removed from the threat of coastal bombardment.[53] This new station would be the most powerful yet built, equipped with twin one-thousand-kilowatt arc transmitters. This would exceed the size and scale of anything Federal Telegraph, or any radio company, had built to that point. Daniels hoped that it would also serve after the war as the primary government station for handling traffic with South America and Europe. Its completion would bolster his efforts to convince Congress to approve the navy's control over all radio operation in the country. However, the end of the war removed the urgency driving the project. The station was never built.[54]

Meanwhile, in France the construction of the new high-power transatlantic station had not gone well. By February 1918 the French had selected the location at Croix d'Hins, Gironde, and begun work. Wartime shortages of skilled labor and key supplies, however, compounded by a lack of support from local officials, had slowed progress considerably. U.S. Navy officials, inspecting in the late spring, found no electrical power available and only two of the eight concrete foundations for the 820-foot-high towers in place. The navy assigned Lieutenant Commander George Sweet, an officer who had overseen the construction of the Annapolis station, to handle the completion of this new station. When Sweet finally arrived in August 1918, he was shocked to find there had been no progress at all since May, even though the arcs were ready for shipment from the United States and the need for an operational station was still very great. At this point U.S. Navy personnel, with Federal Telegraph engineers, took over the project from the French, but they completed it only after the war had ended.[55]

The tremendous challenge of ensuring continual contact between the United States and France during the war was unlike anything that the government had confronted before. U.S. officials learned that they could not assume that the existing prewar commercial cable capability would be adequate for the pressures of wartime. It was also apparent that the danger of attacks on cables were now sufficiently real that complete disruption was no longer unthinkable. This threat to cables, and the joint efforts of the army and navy in the face of this ominous possibility, drove the creation of the transatlantic radio network. Like much of the planning for the First World War, from the expansion of the army to the intense economic mobilization required by a nation in modern war, the consideration of the nation's international communications connections were something that neither armed service nor the civilian leadership had ever seriously had reason to consider. Though the transatlantic radio network was impressive, its capacity was scarcely adequate to have carried the most essential traffic should the German campaign against Allied communications have succeeded. That it did not does not diminish the significance of the lesson learned by senior U.S. officials: in the future the more global role of the United States would necessitate an expanded international cable and radio network to ensure adequate contact abroad. The country's simultaneous experiences with the censoring of the cable traffic passing through U.S. hands and with the development of an intelligence operation to glean information from this traffic further underscored this conclusion.

As warriors have known for millennia, it is of immense value to be able to read the traffic of your enemies in war. To do so, you must ensure that your enemies send their messages through routes that you can monitor, and you must block those routes that you cannot. This had been the underlying principal of the British information war against Germany since 1914, but no one had ever before attempted it with the geographic spread or quantity of intercepted traffic that Britain now could control. By silencing the German cables and restricting the ways in which Germany could pass messages elsewhere, Britain was able to listen in on the transmissions from Nauen and capture copies of German messages buried in neutral diplomatic traffic. The global reach of Britain's cable network increased the likelihood that if an opponent were to send a message, it would go over British cables or through British territory and thus be available to Britain's scrupulous censoring. With the widening of the war in 1917, U.S. officials learned firsthand of this important relationship between control over communications networks and access to the valuable intelligence passing over them.

U.S. monitoring of cable traffic actually began informally several weeks before Congress declared war. In mid-March, the State Department counselor, Frank Polk, confidentially requested copies of diplomatic cable traffic from Clarence Mackay, head of the Commercial Cable and Commercial Pacific Cable companies. Because of the implicit trust the public put in the cable companies and various laws enshrining this client-business relationship, Mackay was naturally reluctant to do as Polk asked. Should word leak out that he was passing traffic to the State Department, regardless of the honorable intentions of the government and the business, the company's reputation and possibly its balance sheets would suffer. Polk assuaged Mackay's fears by giving him a letter thanking him for "any assistance that [his] company [could] give . . . in connection with the secret service work of the government."[56] It may well be that Polk's close personal friendship with Mackay alone allowed the State Department access to these messages, for Secretary Lansing faced extreme opposition from Western Union when he asked for a copy of the Zimmermann telegram in late February.

At Polk's suggestion, Mackay arranged a conduit for passing the copies of cable traffic to the State Department. Mackay and William J. Flynn, the chief of the U.S. Secret Service, decided that G. M. Foote, the Postal Telegraph manager in Washington, would turn over to Flynn whatever was needed. Among the targets were cables sent by Count Bernstorff, the German ambassador, to Haiti, Cuba, Guatemala, and various South American countries in January and February 1917. Flynn would then bring these copies the Bureau of Secret Intelligence, established in April 1916, overseen by Polk, and managed by Polk's assistant, Leland Harrison.[57] The bureau was responsible for coordinating the accumulation and dissemination of intelligence at the State Department with the FBI and Secret Service.[58] Because the United States did not have the ability to read the German diplomatic codes at this point, Harrison then forwarded the copies of cable traffic via Edward Bell, the second secretary at the U.S. Embassy in London, to Room 40 at the Admiralty for decryption. The results would then filter back to Washington for use by the State Department.[59]

Once the United States entered the war, President Wilson issued a series of executive orders that gave the government tremendous power over the nation's cables and radios. On April 25, the heads of the cable companies met with Secretary of the Navy Josephus Daniels; Commander D. W. Todd, navy communications chief; and George Creel, the journalist Wilson had appointed to oversee censorship generally. The cable executives assented to any executive order on telegraphic censorship Wilson might put forth. Three days later, Wilson instructed the navy to take over censorship of all cable traffic entering and exiting the country. Responsibility for carrying out censorship fell to Commander Todd, who became the chief cable censor in addition to head of the national radio network. Todd and his office thus became masters of the information routes between the United States and the rest of the world.[60]

In neither the Civil War nor the war with Spain in 1898 had the United States implemented censorship on the scale or scope that it did in the spring of 1917.[61] This censorship began at Galveston on April 28, on the cables to Mexico, the Caribbean, and South America. British officials had prevailed upon the United States to monitor this South America traffic, which lay beyond Britain's reach, as quickly as possible. In turn, Britain reimposed censorship on the traffic between the United States and South America via Western Telegraph's cables, which had been in abeyance since 1914. General censorship everywhere except the transatlantic cables went into effect on May 1. Navy censors took up positions at Key West, New Orleans, and San Francisco. In the Pacific, additional censors operated at Honolulu and Guam along the Pacific cable. In the Caribbean, censors worked in Puerto Rico, the Canal Zone, Guantánamo Bay in Cuba, the Dominican Republic, and Haiti and at Saint Thomas and Saint Croix in the newly acquired Virgin Islands. After further discussions with British and French officials, the U.S. Navy began to censor the transatlantic cables on July 17. Because of the large number of cables landing there and the presence of the three cable company headquarters, New York City soon had the largest censorship operation.[62] The imposition of censorship by the United States became a significant problem for Germany. Almost immediately, British cable censors intercepted complaints from German diplomats about the difficulties in communicating covertly with Germany or one another.[63]

Censorship in the United States was haphazard and chaotic at first. Little thought had been given to its administrative and operational problems before the war. Todd was ill prepared to take on the work of being chief cable censor as well as director of naval communications. Consequently, the work devolved to temporary or retired naval officers brought back from civilian life, a program that caused its own problems. In Washington, Todd assigned a temporary lieutenant to manage operations, but in New York City a retired naval commander, A. B. Hoff, was put in charge. With New York handling on average one hundred thousand messages a week and eventually having a staff of fifty-five officers and 695 enlisted and clerical personnel (40 percent of whom were women), Hoff was mindful of how, in importance and technical rank, he outweighed Todd's deputy.[64] Amid the urgency of the situation such confusion occurred.

New to their jobs, the censors were very stringent. Like their British counterparts in 1914–1915, they prohibited confusing or unclear words such as might be found in commercial and financial transactions. After the censors realized the true volume of traffic and certain patterns emerged, Todd relaxed some of the rules. By November, for example, banks could use special code words to confirm the legitimacy of transactions.[65] Officially the navy maintained that censorship added only fifty minutes to the transmission time, but in practice the steadily increasing volume of traffic associated with the war clogged up the cables, and the delays were greater. In particular, the closure of the commercial radio network in the Pacific, which had carried nearly 50 percent of U.S.-Japanese traffic, added serious burdens to the cables when combined with the censorship. In large part, the censors bore the responsibility for these delays.[66] To help bring the U.S. system in synch with Britain's, the Admiralty dispatched a liaison officer, Captain J. H. Trye, to New York. By April 1918, with some help from Trye, the censors had developed a daily report for limited circulation, a method that the British had used since the beginning of the war.[67]

The United States also had to develop from scratch a proper system for decrypting, translating, and analyzing the censored cable traffic as well as intercepted radio signals. This duty fell to the army, which had been interested in establishing such an operation from early 1917.[68] Suspect cable messages and radio traffic (including diplomatic messages) intercepted by the army and the navy passed to the Communications Section of the army's Military Intelligence Division, known by its abbreviation, MI-8.[69] Established in the late spring of 1917, MI-8 came under the responsibility of Herbert Yardley, a young State Department code clerk hurriedly commissioned as a first lieutenant.[70] The unit's job included developing new codes and ciphers for the army, translating foreign messages written in shorthand, revealing invisible ink messages, and breaking intercepted coded messages.[71] Inexperienced in the actual art of code breaking and deciphering, MI-8 regularly passed certain suspect traffic, particularly that of German diplomats within the Americas, to the British for processing. MI-8 routed these messages through Leland Harrison, the liaison at the State Department, to Edward Bell at the U.S. Embassy in London, who in turn provided them to Room 40. Bell, Harrison, and Yardley all tried in vain to gain assistance from Admiral Hall, the director of British naval intelligence, to build up the U.S. cryptological unit. It was not until August 1918 that MI-8 had the size and experience to handle messages on its own, having broken the diplomatic codes of Germany, Spain, and several Latin American countries.[72] Information gleaned from the cables as well as other sources allowed MI-8 to contribute to the economic war against Germany as well as to counterintelligence efforts against German spies in the United States.

Relations between the navy and the cable companies, which had initially offered unconditional support, became uneasy. With censorship an official wartime measure, the companies no longer needed to worry about violating their customers' privacy rights. Still, censorship generated delays, which angered customers to no end. Sometimes the cable companies had to rearrange their normal operations to meet the navy's requirements. Cable traffic from New England, for example, previously had gone straight to the cable stations in Canada, but Western Union now had to send messages first to New York, in the other direction, for censorship. Secrecy and trust had been two hallmarks of cable operations in the past, but the new guild of naval censors insisted on setting these values aside in order to read every message passing through the system.

Not all firms remained at odds with the government, however. John Merrill provided the total assistance of his firm to the Wilson administration early on.[73] Naval officials came to believe that the Central and South American Telegraph Company could be "thoroughly trusted to help [the United States] loyally."[74] Merrill made available the use of his company's agents abroad. Unlike Clarence Mackay of Commercial Cable or Newcomb Carlton of Western Union, Merrill freely arranged with Secretary Lansing to provide to the State Department copies of all traffic involving Germans across Central and South America, even though these were beyond the range or the purview of naval censors. Merrill eventually volunteered copies of traffic that dated back through 1914. It was no surprise, then, that as early as October the Department of State had made Merrill a special agent, a title that may have held little beyond decorative value but that reflected how Central, with offices from Mexico to Buenos Aires, had become an intelligence-gathering extension of the United States government. This relationship was little different from that between the British cable companies and the British government.[75]

The imposition of censorship in the Unites States and through it to the rest of the Americas was a significant boon to Britain in its information blockade of Germany. As the Zimmermann telegram had shown, the control Britain had over the cables allowed her to use the information traveling over them as a weapon against Germany. Several months after the United States joined the war, Britain attempted a similar maneuver against Germany in Latin America. Room 40 officials provided the United States in late August with copies of four revealing dispatches from Count Luxborg, German minister to Argentina. They had gone under the "Swedish roundabout," encoded under cover of Swedish diplomatic traffic and sent out over the British cables. Admiral Hall, the head of Room 40, now revealed to the United States how this system worked and how his office had acquired the Zimmermann telegram. Presumably this also meant revealing that Britain had been monitoring neutral diplomatic traffic. With Hall's blessings, Secretary Lansing made public the text of the Luxborg telegrams to Argentina.

As with the Zimmermann telegram, the German minister's messages were damning and the effect of their release significant. Luxborg had explicitly encouraged the sinking of Argentine ships "without a trace" by German submarines. To make the matter worse, he had also insulted the character of the Argentines generally. Hall intended that the messages precipitate a break in relations, which, given the general pro-German sentiment in Argentina and the sizable German-speaking population there, would have been a considerable achievement. Predictably, the Luxborg telegrams sparked a tremendous outcry in Argentina. Count Luxborg quickly found himself a persona non grata, and the government expelled him from the country. Though Argentina did not declare war, Germany was in an awkward position.[76]

Brazil's declaration of war against Germany on October 26, 1917, effectively sealed the Western Hemisphere off from the Germans. Relations between Brazil and Germany had steadily cooled since April, but it had still been possible for Germany to circumvent the British information blockade via the cables that landed at the major station of Pernambuco in the north.[77] This was the only landing point in South America for cables from Portuguese territory (from Saint Vincent, in the Cape Verde Islands). Throughout the war, the Portuguese had been reluctant to extend censorship where cables landed on their territory. Because of this, Germany had risked passing coded information out from Spain and Portugal over the British and French cables touching at Lisbon, the Azores, and Saint Vincent.[78] The declaration of war ended this practice. At the invitation of the Brazilian government, the United States and Britain supplied censors to monitor traffic at Pernambuco. With censorship across the hemisphere no messages entering the Western Hemisphere escaped scrutiny.

At the same time, concern grew in the United States that somehow Britain abused censorship and monitored U.S. cable traffic for her own gain. The claims were that either the British government's censors or the cable companies themselves were deliberately interfering with commercial messages from U.S. firms. The State Department received complaints of three different kinds. The first was that the contents of commercial messages had ended up in the hands of a British rival. The second was that important messages had been suppressed, during which time a British rival had gained a temporal advantage. In the third kind of complaints, merchants complained that only key data, such as prices or the size of an order, had been garbled in an otherwise correct message in order to create confusion and head off a potential transaction. From the documentary evidence that remains, it appears that no one in the United States government ever had the complete picture, but a variety of diplomats, military officials, and merchants came to suspect that the number of coincidences simply were too great to be anything but deliberate.

Amid the swirl of wartime censorship and the interallied confusion over wartime economic cooperation, such claims were particularly hard to verify. American officials had a difficult time separating the grain of legitimate complaints from the chaff of expected wartime misunderstandings. In two instances, for example, the Russian representative of U.S. Steel complained that his commercial orders were not arriving in the United States, a complaint also made by the Colt Firearms Company about its negotiations with the Greek government. Upon investigation, it turned out that the United States and Britain had already agreed that any messages relating to munitions, regardless of the sender or intended recipient, were being held up unless they passed through official diplomatic channels. Delays might also stem from unintended similarities between a sender, an address, or a message and items on the blacklist of firms believed to be trading with Germany. At times Britain even practiced wholesale information blackout, as it did between Holland and the Dutch East Indies for a period of time in late 1917. U.S. messages caught up in this action were not any more targets than those of everyone else. Still, some of the claims may very well have been correct. The limited evidence that percolated up to the attention of senior State Department and Navy Department officials suggests that many believed deliberate interference to be the case.[79]

Many of the complaints related to commercial traffic passing to and from South America. In August and December 1917, for example, the U.S. consul general in Buenos Aires, W. Henry Robertson, reported to Washington that copies of traffic from U.S. businessmen in Argentina were ending up in British hands. In one instance, the local manager for the Barber shipping line, A. C. McCarthy, had sent over six days several important cables regarding a possible contract with the Argentine government to arrange monthly shipments of several thousand bales of wool to the United States. He never received replies. Sir Reginald Tower, the British minister, then began working on the same deal three or four days later for the Lamport and Holt line of British steamers. According to McCarthy, there was no way that Tower could have learned of the deal except by having read the cables. Robertson passed on similar cases involving other American merchants dealing in animal products and hides: "It seems more than a coincidence that Sir Reginald Tower should have learned of the case in question, especially since the exporter of the wool appeared quite as anxious as [McCarthy] to keep the prospective transaction entirely secret." Complicating the matter, McCarthy apparently had used Central's lines to send his messages, which suggested that someone within the American company was giving out the cables.[80]

Similar complaints of British cable espionage reached the State Department from the navy. The naval attaché in Rio de Janeiro had learned from a number of American merchants that Western Telegraph was somehow interfering with their messages. In some instances, "interested English firms [were] furnished copies of cablegrams of American competitors," while in other instances commercial messages were suppressed. Most damning of all, however, was the attaché's own experience. On several occasions the British naval attaché had shared copies of messages that a contact in the Western Telegraph office had provided. "He had daily records," the attaché attested, "consisting of a dozen or more sheets furnished him, containing messages which were thought might be useful. If these had contained only military or naval information, or were for such use, it would have been justified, but as a matter of fact, they were mostly commercial."[81] In response, Assistant Secretary William Philips instructed Ambassador Morgan in Rio de Janeiro to corroborate the allegations in order for the State Department to prepare a formal complaint to the British. Tellingly, the dispatch went by surface mail rather than by cable through the hands of those under investigation. This was a much slower route, but the United States had no other option if it wished to keep the matter quiet.[82]

Complaints abounded, but evidence did not. Morgan investigated the allegations yet found little firm proof. Still, he could not dismiss their larger significance. In each instance, it was possible that others may have had access to the information, and he could not be certain the cable company was at fault. Sharing information between a cable company and the British naval attaché might well be thought of as a normal relationship between a government and a private firm. That such allegations had surfaced, however, demonstrated to Morgan the supreme importance of having direct cable contact between the United States and its important overseas markets. "Until we have control of cable communications," he informed the State Department, "we are at the mercy of our competitors of whatever nature they may be and dependent upon them for the receipt and communication of news which is necessary for the maintenance of our political position and the retention and expansion of our commerce." Morgan had worried even about the cooperative censorship that the United States and

Britain operated at the cable station in Pernambuco. In early 1918 he demanded that the U.S. Navy send a sufficiently senior naval officer to this assignment in order to outrank the British censors who were there. Pleading to the department, Morgan made it clear that he could "imagine few situations less advantageous to [U.S.] commercial interests than British control of censorship" at a time when allegations swirled that the British were using their control of the cable censorship to extract commercial gain.[83]

U.S. cable company officials could only agree with Morgan's assessment. John Merrill, the president of Central, passed on to Secretary Lansing complaints that his own agents had uncovered. To bring this kind of practice to an end, Merrill urged Lansing to continue supporting Central's efforts to challenge the British cables in the region. In testimony before the Senate some years later, Western Union president Newcomb Carlton indicated that his firm had similar suspicions of cable espionage. "I believe that all foreign countries used the censorship during the war to enlighten merchants," he testified, "and that the merchants profited thereby . . . As a result . . . there were some unfair advantages gained abroad." Although Merrill and Carlton had their suspicions, without clear evidence that was otherwise hard to come by, no one could prove such espionage had occurred.[84]

An important part of the problem was the extensive number of British citizens who worked for the Central and South American Telegraph Company and the other U.S. cable firms. "In the commercial war that has already begun," Consul Robertson warned, "it seems like business suicide to keep British subjects in practically sole control of all the cable offices . . . down the west coast of South America. Our country has already suffered the disastrous effects of having to deal abroad through British and German banks, and even greater betrayal of American business secrets in Latin America is possible under the foreign administration of an American cable company." In Robertson's view, it was impossible to prove where the leaks occurred, but that they did could not be doubted. He believed the problem to be one of "the most serious questions now confronting" American trade with South America.[85] In the absence of any firm proof of this espionage, however, all the State Department could do was to note the claims as they came in. At a minimum, the allegations reinforced the growing conviction that the United States would need its own communications network to ensure the security of its messages abroad. As Robertson had pointed out, if the United States was to create its own network, it would also have to train its own cable operators.

If the United States could rely on the integrity of its cable operators, would that alone be enough to ensure the complete security of its messages? Interested in improving the speed of cable operations, the Army Signal Corps examined this question with care. Government and cable company experts had long thought oceanic cables to be the most secure method of sending information electrically. On land, enemy agents could tap telegraph wires without either party being aware of the intrusion. Anyone using the proper receiver and antenna could pick up information sent by radio. To protect the contents of messages sent by telegraph or radio, therefore, governments and armed forces had largely adopted the use of codes and ciphers. The use of these methods to disguise messages was cumbersome. It took time on both ends of an exchange to convert the message in and out of its secure form. Cables, however, appeared to be immune to such monitoring. The armored coating, insulation, and great depths at which a cable lay effectively prevented anyone from tapping it easily or unnoticed. Cable engineers understood at the time that any effort to cut or tap the cable would cause disturbances in the signal strength. This would be sufficient to attract the attention of the engineers on either end. So long as the personnel handling the traffic were trustworthy, the secrecy of the messages could be assured. If the U.S. Army could be certain that it was not possible to tap a submarine telegraph cable secretly, then it could hope to maximize space on the available cables and improve the speed of communications between the AEF and Washington by dispensing with the use of codes on the slowest link in the electrical chain between Washington and Europe.

The Army Signal Corps set out in the late summer of 1917 to test this logic. General Squier, the chief signal officer, appointed Colonel J. J. Carty, lately the chief engineer at AT&T, to head up a special board of engineers and cable operators. After considering the matter further and consulting with engineers at AT&T and General Electric, Carty concluded that it was in fact technically possible to tap the cables.[86] Doing so would require some method of electrical induction and the use of high-power amplifiers to boost the faint signal. If done correctly, this would not physically disturb the cable but would allow whoever ran the tap to monitor the signal in real time and record it.

Intrigued by the theory, Carty's board then set out to prove it. The engineering department of AT&T created a rough prototype of a tapping device for the army. It would allow someone to tap a cable several miles offshore without the operators on either end becoming aware of the tap's presence. The device resembled an iron jacket similar to that a plumber might use to seal off a leaky pipe and had copper wires wound around the inside with which to capture the electrical impulse of the cable. This then connected by a small cable to an amplifier and additional equipment aboard ship, all designed to capture and record the signal. To use it, one would raise a cable and then place it within the hollow cylindrical core of the device. Able to split into two parts lengthwise, it was insulated against water pressure.

The device did not actually have to touch the center of the cable to obtain the signal. In the practice of submarine telegraphy, the electrical signal in a cable has a "return" current that flows through the armor wire. This complements the main signal, forms a complete electrical circuit, and allows the cable to operate efficiently. The large part of this current dissipates in the water around the cable. The idea behind the tapping device was that some of the return current given off by the cable could be captured by the copper coil contained in the iron jacket. As the return current passed around the conjoined cable and coil, it would create a magnetic flux in the core of the coil, which would be a very small voltage. With a very sensitive vacuum tube amplifier, the "energy of the impulses in the coil winding is very greatly increased, and the current from the amplifier can then be used to record easily legible signals on an undulator or similar recording apparatus."[87] Carty's team designed an amplifier using five vacuum tubes arranged in a line to boost the signal sequentially. Such an operation would have to be done relatively near the shore, as the signal strength dissipated the farther along it went. Recording of the signals need not even occur at the point of tapping, but with sufficient amplification the operators of the tap could direct the signal down another cable to another location. With the proper equipment, Carty reasoned, a ship might operate a cable tap up to three hundred miles from shore.[88]

With the help of Western Electric and Western Union, Carty then conducted experiments to verify that the device would work. On March 16, 1918, Carty went out on the Western Union cable tug *Robert C. Clowry* with an engineering crew and an observer from the U.S. Navy. About four miles out from New York City, where the depth was only forty feet, they raised a Western Union cable from New York City to Canso, Nova Scotia, up to the boat. Carty's team bolted together the tap around the dripping cable. Activating the amplifier, they intercepted messages and recorded what they had done. At no point did the operators of the cables discover that Carty's crew was tapping the cable. To make the experiment as authentic as possible, they listened in on the cable's ordinary traffic. Having recorded and deciphered the messages, they later compared them with the ones at the Western Union offices and found that they matched with about 20 percent mutilation of the signals (attributed to interference on the cable from some electrical power supply on shore that affected the tap's ability to "read" the cable signal). Carty believed that they could run a one-hundred mile cable from the site of the tap to the amplifier and the signal recorder aboard ship. With the right equipment and practice, those tapping the cable would not need to remain very close to land at all.

The Signal Corps shared Carty's results with the navy as well as with Britain and France. It was, in fact, possible to tap a submarine telegraph cable and not have the operators be aware of the activity at all. The United States now had to assume that it was not beyond the means of Germany to carry out such taps. Indeed, the tap need not occur directly above the cable, for Carty had worked out that it was possible to run a small cable from the tap over a hundred miles or to a small station on the shore or a small vessel. "It demonstrated that it would be unsafe to attempt to send plain English messages through the ocean cables," the Signal Corps later summarized. "Until some new discovery was made, the ultimate protection of the secrecy of messages must be found in the use of code or cipher."[89] Carty's invention even led some to suspect that the reason that the Germans had not yet attacked the transatlantic cables was because they were somehow tapping them to read the traffic passing through them.[90] Though exceedingly clever, Carty's invention was useless against Germany's already cut cables. Still, his warnings about cable security were lasting. To this day, the United

States has continued to operate under the principle that even ordinary cable lines at the bottom of the sea can be tapped and that government messages must pass over American-controlled routes when possible and be encoded for security at all times.[91]

Prior to April 1917, the concern of the United States government over cable connections to Europe, Latin America, or Asia had centered around their commercial importance to the nation. The navy's concern for radio had focused on domestic and hemispheric communications, at the level of command control of the nation's warships, rather than on the potential need for long-distance contact with allies across the globe. Never having considered a war on the scope that they eventually would confront during the First World War, officials assumed that the existing commercial infrastructure was adequate to the nation's potential needs in wartime, despite the inconveniences of censorship imposed by other powers.

State, Navy, and War department officials discovered over the course of the war, however, unanticipated requirements that showed how the departments' initial assumptions had been very much off the mark. The transatlantic cable system turned out to be barely adequate for the demands placed upon it, even without the danger of further disruption. Had the United States needed to field a large force in Latin America or Asia at the same time, the resulting complications stemming from the paucity of cable connections and the vast volume of traffic would have been overwhelming. Nor was the concern limited to military communications. The State Department, which fought assiduously to ensure that all cable traffic from civilian government agencies passed under its cover, had its cable traffic rise precipitously and its cable expenses grow from $185,000 in 1914 to $975,000 by 1919, or roughly from $3.45 million to $12 million in 2005 dollars.[92]

For all the limitations of the cable networks, however, it was the threat from German submarines to the cables and regular maintenance more than anything else that spurred the creation of the transatlantic radio network. Because the U.S. Navy had to ensure the reliability of these stations, they operated with the very best equipment and placed the United States at the very forefront of radio technology by the end of the war. At the same time, the imposition of censorship, the parallel creation of the intelligence operation for reading intercepted traffic, and the growing concerns about the security of U.S. diplomatic traffic all taught U.S. officials about the great power that control of the cables could convey. It also made them aware, if they had not been before, of the latent power that Britain exercised with its tremendous influence at the center of global cable and radio networks. Thus the future quality and reliability of cable and long-distance radio connections available to the United States became a matter of serious military and diplomatic importance as never before. Mindful of the overall need for better lines of communication with all regions of the world, the navy and the State Department were at the same time hard at work improving cable and radio connections to Latin America and Asia. Little could President Wilson have realized how much his call for war before Congress on April 2, 1917, would set in motion far-reaching efforts to place the United States at the center of world affairs for the century to come.

FIVE

✦ ✦ ✦

In Pursuit of Cables to Asia and the Americas

FOR THE UNITED STATES, like the principal European powers, the war became more than just an event in northern France. Along the Western Front, growing numbers of doughboys from Maine to California steadily joined the lines alongside British, French, Belgian, and other forces. In the Atlantic, the Mediterranean, and the chill waters off Great Britain and Ireland, U.S. Navy warships patrolled against German submarines. Farther afield, a different, shadow campaign also raged as the United States joined the Allies in driving German interests out of the Americas and Asia. The objective was to eliminate German economic and political influence and to confound any financial or economic support that might pass surreptitiously back to Germany. At the same time, the mobilization of the nation's resources to form a modern industrialized army required complex adjustments to the country's economy as had never before been attempted. This included not only the careful alignment of agriculture, industry, labor, and financial means but also the painstaking adjustment of foreign trade as U.S. firms met the continuing demand from abroad. Just as Pershing's expeditionary force in Europe required reliable and continuous contact with the United States, so too did U.S. diplomats and merchants reaching out to Europe, Latin America, and Asia need a greater cable network to handle the expanding telegraphic traffic spawned by this growing American presence in the world.

For the past three years, State Department officials addressing the cable situation had largely concerned themselves with the Allied disruptions to the existing networks and the expansion of new U.S. cables throughout Latin America. Censorship and the cutting of the German cables interrupted the regular lines just as economic ties between the United States and other countries had grown dramatically. The extensive efforts by Western Union and Central and South American Telegraph to expand their cables in the face of British competition in Argentina, Uruguay, and Brazil had not yielded results yet. These experiences in neutrality had unveiled the importance for the United States of rapid, unimpeded communications across great distances. Belligerency and intensified military, diplomatic, and commercial contact with areas other than northern France made the matter all the more urgent.

During eighteen months of war, public officials and cable executives discovered that despite the growing need for cables, a variety of obstacles so hampered further private development that government intervention might be the only solution. In South America, both Western Union and Central had gained the concessions they sought, but global cable supply shortages prevented the companies from laying and operating the new lines quickly. State Department officials realized also the even greater problems with in transpacific communications. Domestic and international complaints prompted Assistant Secretary of State Breckinridge Long to lead an interdepartmental effort to correct the existing problems. Developing the first comprehensive understanding of the larger picture, Long also planned a more sweeping project to end the nation's dependence upon foreign cable companies and manufacturers. Though unfinished by the end of the war, Long's ambitious project was one important result of America's five-year experience with cables in war and peace.

Motivated as much by economic as by political and security concerns, the United States continued to pursue the extension of submarine telegraph cables around South America during the war years. On behalf of anxious cable company officials, Robert Lansing's diplomats applied pressure to governments in Brazil, Argentina, and Uruguay to grant necessary cable concessions. The principal obstacles had been Western Telegraph's own exclusionary concessions and its discriminatory practices. The ferocity of the commercial fight offered by the British company in all three countries was impressive. The diplomatic, legal, and administrative maneuvers arranged by Western Telegraph revealed the determination with which the British would fight to protect their interests in Latin America. Ultimately, Western Telegraph's efforts proved unsuccessful. Both Central and Western Union secured concessions that could permit inexpensive, more direct contact with Brazil. Like mountains approached over a long plain, however, the goal of American-controlled cables throughout Latin America remained tantalizingly distant. Cable companies soon realized that wartime shortages of cable supplies, which were controlled by Britain, would leave them hard pressed to act quickly on their hard-fought gains. Even if the United States obtained the right to land cables everywhere in the world, the nation was still dependent upon others for supplies of the needed cable.

Western Telegraph's strategy in 1917 was to continue attacking its American rivals on every front with the full arsenal of weapons at its disposal. The victory by Central in the Brazilian courts the previous year had broken wide open Western Telegraph's monopoly there. "Every legal impediment has now been removed," reported the chargé d'affaires in Rio, Alexander Benson. Blocked in the courts and forced to forward traffic to Central's lines, Western Telegraph would still "leave no stone unturned" in its effort to stop Central.[1] The Brazilian public works department then unexpectedly imposed a special rate of three francs per word on any telegram going to Buenos Aires but destined for the United States. Compared to previous rates, this was a 71 percent increase in the cost of sending messages from the southern half of Brazil, where 80 percent of foreign cable traffic originated. The new rate thus selectively harassed only those senders of messages that were not going by British cables. Lansing ordered Benson to protest this to the Brazilians immediately. The demand for an explanation, passed off from official to official, languished in the Brazilian bureaucracy for months. The rate remained an unchecked canker for the cabling public through 1918. It also compounded the cost of the similar discriminatory rate that Western Telegraph's subsidiary in Uruguay had leveraged the previous year. Giving one more blow, the office of Western Telegraph in Buenos Aires at the end of April simply stopped accepting any messages from Central Telegraph destined for Uruguay or Brazil. This policy forced Central Telegraph into an awkward decision. It could pass traffic over the sluggish government landlines, with considerable delay and cost. Alternately, it could route U.S. commercial and diplomatic traffic more swiftly over the little-known and still very operational German cable from Buenos Aires to Montevideo.[2]

What had been a simple commercial fight between rivals suddenly escalated into an awkward diplomatic crisis. In the midst of a war in which the two companies were now ostensibly on the same side, a British firm had put its American competitor in the nonsensical position of having to pass information through German hands. Not surprisingly, calmer heads on both sides swiftly intervened. State Department officials in Washington took up the matter directly with the British ambassador. The British chambers of commerce in Buenos Aires and Montevideo, alarmed that sensitive commercial messages were available to the enemy, both strongly urged the two companies to reach some accord. Adding to the confusion, a main Western Telegraph cable in the South Atlantic between Ascension Island and Buenos Aires had become damaged in May. Central then had to make available its cables as a detour for some of Western Telegraph's traffic. Only at this point did Western Telegraph officials relent slightly. In mid-July they began accepting U.S. diplomatic messages for Uruguay and Brazil from Central.[3]

Despite the pressure to play fairly, Western Telegraph continued to block traffic at very inopportune times. In late July, the U.S. Navy Department telegraphed orders to Rear Admiral William B. Caperton, whose armored cruiser squadron had just arrived at Brazil to carry out war patrols in the South Atlantic.[4] When the cabled messages arrived at Buenos Aires, Western Telegraph refused to accept them for further transit. Consequently, Central arranged for them to pass over the German cable, as it was the other fastest available method. Because cable companies routinely kept a copy of a message in case of error, it became possible that U.S. Navy codes and orders relating to the war patrol were in German hands. Within a half hour of a meeting between an incensed Ambassador Stimson and the British minister in Argentina, the Western Telegraph subsidiary in Buenos Aires agreed to handle further military cable traffic for the United States without delay.[5] Not until November 1917 did Western Telegraph agreed to accept inbound messages to Montevideo and Brazil at the normal rate. They insisted on keeping in place the discriminatory higher rate for messages traveling outbound.[6] In spite of the ambassador's intervention, the problem still continued intermittently. As late as April 1918, the Office of Naval Intelligence was complaining that sensitive information still passed over the German cables at Uruguay from time to time because of Western Telegraph.[7]

Merrill and the Central company stubbornly pressed ahead despite Western Telegraph's counterattacks. Worried about the availability of cable supplies, Merrill had decided to concentrate first on the direct Argentina–Brazil cable, which was of greatest importance to the firm.[8] From Rio, Ambassador Morgan continued to warn of rumors that Western Telegraph would now try "by what [Morgan could not] consider but underhand and unjustifiable means" to stop any concession. Yet, according to the consul general, public sentiment in Brazil held that competition among the cable companies would only be to Brazil's benefit. Bolstered by Morgan's efforts, Central agent Frank Carney secured an important permission from the minister of public works in August. Then, on October 27, 1917, Carney finally won the full authority to bring two cables ashore. Almost a year after the court decision and three years after the company's initial moves in Brazil, Central had secured the chance to land one cable at Rio de Janeiro and another at São Paulo's port city of Santos. Both would link to Buenos Aires. There, they would join the rest of Central' network. If Argentina and Uruguay granted permission as well, Brazil and the United States would have a direct, American-controlled connection. Ambassador Morgan informed Washington, "The establishment of all-American cable communications between the United States and Brazil . . . will be an event of considerable international importance, both because it will break the British monopoly . . . and because it is the beginning of that free telegraphic interchange between Brazil and the United States which it is hoped will be extended and developed in the future." Morgan's mood improved still further with the arrival of Western Union in late 1917.[9] The domestic telegraph giant had made clear, shortly after Wilson's call for improved connections in 1915, its own intentions to expand service to Brazil. Now that Central had cleared the way, Western Union's representative was free to join the tumult. To informed observers, it appeared as though the firm handle on the largest Latin American market had slipped from Western Telegraph's grasp.

Merrill turned next to Uruguay and Argentina. With Carney having opened Brazil, Merrill dispatched a new agent to the region that October. James J. Shirley's first responsibility was to acquire in Uruguay the right to land a Montevideo–Buenos Aires cable. There was reason to believe this would be an easy task, as the Uruguayan government had refused the Western Telegraph subsidiary the right to renew its concession upon expiration in July. At Merrill's request, Lansing instructed the minister at Montevideo, Robert E. Jeffery, to block diplomatically any British application for a new concession or attempts to purchase the German cable company. Apparently successful in Uruguay, Shirley then went to Argentina the following February. With Stimson's diplomatic support, he renewed an existing application to land the proposed cable from Brazil. President Hipólito Irigoyen opposed Western Telegraph's holding a monopoly over Argentina's external communications and so welcomed Central's efforts. The Uruguayan government, equally interested in cable competition, made its own diplomatic overtures to the Argentines in support of Central's plans. The combined efforts of Stimson, Shirley, and the Uruguayans yielded success. On August 1, 1918, President Irigoyen granted Central the right to land a cable from Uruguay in Argentina. Shortly thereafter, Uruguay awarded reciprocal permission to land a cable from Argentina.[10] Following nearly four years of effort, Central held the right to extend its network from Buenos Aires to both Uruguay and Brazil. Once constructed, this intricate web of cables would provide the United States a secure network among the principal countries of the Western Hemisphere.

In addition to diplomatic support, the State Department provided assistance in safeguarding Central's messages against corporate espionage. Worried that a single word might reveal the scope of his plans, Merrill had actually requested that the department not even mention Shirley's name or that of the Central company in their dispatches to Uruguay. Central company officials suspected that Western Telegraph had read some of Central's traffic in the past when British cables were moved over between Buenos Aires and Montevideo. Consequently, Merrill did not wish to take any chances.[11] Merrill's apprehension about the security of his messages were not baseless. Censorship rules in place in most countries across the region required that all messages, except those of diplomats, be in plain English or Spanish. This made it very easy for company officials to read the contents of what passed over their lines, despite the traditions of discretion and secrecy that prevailed in the industry. Appreciating Merrill's concerns, Lansing granted Stimson the authority to send Central's messages between Buenos Aires and Rio de Janeiro—over the British cables—under diplomatic cover.[12] Later experience demonstrated that this was a wise precaution. In one instance several months later, Ambassador Morgan, while away in New York, had sent a message to Frank Carney via Central's cable network. Upon the telegram's arrival in Buenos Aires, the Central agent forwarded it to Rio over the British cables but signed it as if Morgan were in Buenos Aires, not New York. Some time later, "a discussion occurred at the Club in Rio as to the whereabouts of Mr. Morgan and one of the Western's representatives insisted that Mr. Morgan was in Buenos Aires and proved [the] same on the following day by showing the telegram [Merrill had] sent from Buenos Aires."[13] Because of the high stakes for Western Telegraph's future in the region, Merrill had every reason to be worried about his rival seeing his hand too early.

The fight between the U.S. and British cable companies then expanded to a northeastern front. Far from giving way to upstart competitors, Western Telegraph officials formulated plans to deepen the regional network's influence with two new cables. The first would run from Brazil to Nova Scotia via the British islands of Barbados and Bermuda. The second would run to Ascension Island, a major cable hub in the South Atlantic, to duplicate the existing line.[14] Together these new cables would increase Western Telegraph's traffic capacity with Latin America, allow lower rates to lure customers away from Central's lines, and bolster Western Telegraph's threatened position. As the first step in this plan, the British company won a concession on October 25, 1917, to lay a cable northwards from Brazil to the British island of Barbados.

Anticipating that Central or others would pursue this route as well, Western Telegraph had already formulated a plan to divide and conquer. The general superintendent in South America, W. S. Robertson, had suggested earlier that year to his superiors in London a tacit arrangement with Western Union. It would allow the British company to play the two American cable companies against one another. If Western Union and Central could be made to compete for a concession in Brazil, it might create a deadlock. Robertson wrote, "[The deadlock] may be made to last just as long as we choose to go on discussing terms with the Western Union Co." In fact, Western Union had previously offered a deal to the British company. Western Telegraph would drop its opposition to Western Union's entry to Brazil in exchange for that company's support on Western Telegraph's proposed cable to Ascension. Robertson believed that if his firm could keep Western Union interested in a southern approach into Brazil from Argentina—where it would compete with Central—this would suit Western Telegraph's interests. "On no account, if we can prevent it," he advised, "should they be allowed to come in to Brazil from the North." Central was only a threat to the south, but if Western Union tried to come in from the north or make a deal with the existing inadequate French cable, the British firm would be in serious trouble on two fronts.[15]

The Western Telegraph plan to lay cables from Brazil to British North America seriously worried Ambassador Morgan. Bypassing the United States for landings farther north in Canada or Newfoundland, Western Telegraph cables would have the effect of drawing U.S. traffic up into British territory and undercutting further the Central cables.[16] He predicted opposition from the French Telegraph Cable Company, which currently held the monopoly concession granting the company the sole right to Brazil–North American communications along this route. Its cable network, however, was old and frequently interrupted.[17] Morgan concluded that Western Union would have good reason to align with Western Telegraph against the stubborn French company, to eviscerate the monopoly concession. The uncertainty over the proper interpretation of the various concessions and the likely objections from Western, Western Union, and the French Telegraph Cable Company to any proposed Central cable in the area would only delay the opening of any such line for several years.[18]

The implications of a British-controlled line northwards from Brazil troubled John Merrill greatly as well. Having considered the plan, he concluded that the only way Western Telegraph could make its proposed Brazil–Canada cable profitable was with a spur to the United States at some point along the line. He feared, as he confided to Secretary Lansing, that if an American company contracted with Western Telegraph to provide this link, it "would be a decidedly objectionable proposition to [Lansing] and to the American Merchant." The reasons were as much political as they were commercial: "American cablegrams handed over to a British-owned and British-controlled cable would not be conducive to the promotion of American commercial supremacy in Brazil." It was Merrill's belief that the British Admiralty lay behind much of this effort to expand the British cable lines and the desperate fight in Brazil to block Central.[19]

To meet the British offensive head-on, Merrill envisioned that Central would wire the Americas. His company would create its own new network along the northern coast of South America. Cables would land at each of the major ports in Guiana, Venezuela, and Colombia before joining with the existing lines landing in Panama. Once complete, the network would form a single great telegraphic ring around the continent, all in the hands of one American company and free from the danger of European influence. Another cable would go north from Brazil to Saint Thomas in the newly acquired Virgin Islands. From there the cable would continue on to Guantánamo Bay, Cuba, and then up to the United States.[20] With continuing diplomatic support from a department anxious to see the extension of American-controlled cable lines, Frank Carney fought for a new concession to lay a cable from Brazil to Cuba. By November 1918, this too was in hand.[21] Simultaneously, Western Union leapt into the scrum. Nelson O'Shaughnessy, the company's agent in Brazil, won rights to lay cables south to Argentina and northwards to a group of the Netherlands Antilles. The three competing cable concessions offered a tremendous opportunity for Brazil but raised for others the specter of a difficult fight to come.

Western Telegraph officials worked feverishly to contain quickly Central and Western Union on these new projects. British diplomatic and political pressure on the Brazilian government reduced Western Union's new concession to only half of what the firm had originally sought. The Brazilian senate also attached amendments to the proposed agreement, amendments that might hamper the operation of the cable. Reporting this to Washington, Ambassador Morgan held out some hope that the next Brazilian government, which was to take office in November 1918, would view the situation differently. Many of the incoming officials were from the São Paulo area and had long been on record as wishing to benefit from improved direct connections to the United States.[22]

Until Central could actually lay its own submarine cables between Argentina, Uruguay, and Brazil, it remained at the mercy of Western Telegraph's discriminatory rate practices. U.S. diplomats in these three countries all fought against these tactics through 1918. In addition to the previously enacted predatory charges, Western Telegraph's subsidiary in Argentina managed to have a special new one on traffic going from North America to Brazil imposed at Buenos Aires in March 1918. Pressing the Brazilian government repeatedly for explanations of the earlier rates, Morgan in Rio received only vague apologies and claims that the rates were less than what Western Telegraph had requested. In his dispatches to Washington, Morgan decried the effect of these practices, which forced senders to route their messages through British territory "where they [were] subject to British censorship with its diverse inconveniences for American interests." Morgan's reports and Merrill's repeated protestations led Lansing and other officials to impress upon the Brazilian ambassador in Washington, Domicio da Gama, their true concerns. Soon to become minister for foreign affairs, Gama was receptive to his hosts' worries and agreed that the rates were discriminatory. Lansing instructed Morgan to hold off further work on the rates until Gama could return to Rio to take up his duties in November. Although diplomacy might well bring relief in time, it was apparent to Merrill that the only solution was to lay the new cables as swiftly as possible.[23]

Unbeknownst to Central or the United States, Sir John Denison Pender, head of the Eastern Telegraph group of cable companies, had also undertaken to minimize the delays to messages bound for South America over the British cables. The previous November, Pender had arranged personally with the War Office and the British censors to allow Western Telegraph to wait a day before handing over copies of messages for inspection. Because the United States Navy now censored Central's cable traffic at Galveston and New York, Central Telegraph had begun to suffer the same delays that had plagued the British cables since August 1914. Pender's arrangement had the effect of making Central's cables at last appear comparatively slower and more expensive than those of Western Telegraph. In this way, he managed to undercut Central's principal selling point with the public without unduly undermining the war effort.[24]

The ferocity of the cable fight in South America impressed diplomats and businessmen alike, but it was the conviction that eventually Central would be able to lay the cables that sustained Central's senior officials. By mid-1918, however, with the cable concessions still not finalized, Merrill had come to question whether there actually would be adequate supplies of cable to meet the growing global demand. Already two earlier sections of cables ordered by Central had been appropriated by the British government for wartime use, and it was clear that the British cable companies had made their own plans for laying many new cables. Even obtaining short lengths of repair cable proved difficult. In July the Telegraph Construction and Maintenance Company, citing shortages of copper and steel and the need to secure permission from the British government, placed on hold indefinitely a March 1918 order from Central for 590 nautical miles of cable. Merrill and other Central officials became particularly concerned that they would never obtain the 4,765 nautical miles of cable required for the new South American concessions—or the anticipated 12,325 miles of cable needed for Merrill's ambitious cable ring—from British suppliers or anyone else.[25] The United States did not have a cable industry of its own, and Central was extremely dependent upon British manufacturing and engineering expertise if it wished to capitalize quickly on Central's newly won concessions. With a view to anticipating future demand and the likelihood of obtaining adequate supplies, senior Central officials then spent the summer of 1918 analyzing the cable industry. Their conclusions, that the United States would have to develop its own industry and secure its own access to raw material supplies like gutta-percha if it wished to have available enough cable to meet Central's needs, were not that different from what previous experts had advised over the past two decades. These deficiencies, however, would become all the more stark in light of the simultaneous problems with Pacific communications during wartime.

Though the attention of Washington was for the greatest part focused on Europe and the desperate state of the transatlantic cables needed by Pershing's expeditionary force, by far the worst situation was in the Pacific. The world war had complicated transpacific communications nearly beyond measure. The disruptions reinvigorated long-standing public demands for better cable and radio connections to Asia. The problem centered around the woeful inadequacies of Commercial Pacific's single cable. Laid in 1902–1903, it ran from San Francisco to Manila and Shanghai by way of Hawaii, Midway, and Guam. Ever since the fall of 1914, war-related traffic had overwhelmed its meager capabilities. The introduction of censorship and the imposition of new radio regulations in April 1917 threw cable operations into total confusion. As in South America, the shortage of cable supplies, the lack of a U.S. cable industry, and the enormous costs involved in laying cables prevented any commercial firm from rectifying the situation on its own. As a consequence, forward-looking officials in the Wilson administration intervened to apply the powers and resources of the government. Their aim, developed in the final months of the war, was not just to acquire a few new cables to suit U.S. needs. Instead, it was to free the United States entirely from dependence upon Britain for cables. To do so, officials realized, would require the creation of a domestic cable industry, the discovery of a new source of gutta-percha, and the effective creation of an artificial replacement for insulating wrap. If successful, the program would enable the United States to wire the world in ways that would make possible the greater commercial and political role Wilson and his advisors anticipated the United States would play after the war.

Before April 1917, it had been possible for a merchant in the United States to exchange information swiftly with Japan by either of two principal ways. His dispatch would first go from California to Hawaii by commercial cable or radio. There an American Marconi long-distance station traded traffic with a Japanese government station. Or, if the message was not urgent, the merchant might send the telegram by cable to Guam, where it could then pass over another cable to Japan. To reach China, the merchant's messages could go to Japan and then by cable to China, or pass over the Commercial Pacific cable to Hong Kong or Shanghai via the Philippines. On a good day, the merchant could expect this to take at most an hour or two, but disruptions were not uncommon. The Pacific cable frequently broke on the hard coral bottom of the San Bernardino Strait in the Philippines. When this happened, transpacific traffic for the Philippines and China stopped at Guam. There it passed onto the Guam–Japan cable and went through Japan and into China and back down into the Philippines. Even at the best of times, these were delays costly in time, money, and message security. The alternative was to send the message through the very slow cable from British Columbia to Australia, or clear around the world in the other direction, through Europe.

Following the outbreak of war, however, the situation changed remarkably. The U.S. Navy instituted censorship down the length of Pacific cable, banned the use of commercial codes, and took control of the private radio stations in Hawaii and San Francisco. Shortly thereafter the navy closed those stations operated by American Marconi and absorbed Federal Telegraph's into the navy radio chain. The American Marconi stations employed powerful spark transmitters, the signals of which frequently interfered with the workings of radio transmitters for a radius of one thousand miles.[26] The shuttering of these stations, however, meant the closure of the only commercial radio link to Japan. At the same time, as part of its censorship policy, the navy stopped the handling of any commercial messages by radio. Meanwhile, the transpacific radio chain was not yet operational. The San Diego station would not open until July, and the Cavite station in the Philippines was not ready until December. Consequently, beyond Hawaii all government and military traffic had to pass by way of the cable. Altogether this threw an additional load of traffic onto the single, expensive, and now extremely slow Commercial Pacific cable.

Then a great outcry arose from those whose livelihood depended upon transpacific trade and rapid communications. Cable rates for traffic to the Philippines, Japan, and China from the United States were already three times higher than traffic to Europe. The ban on commercial and private codes doubled the length (and cost) of messages, and these larger messages slowed the cable still further. High costs and added delays became an unwelcome burden to merchants taking advantage of the ever-growing trade between the U.S. and Pacific Rim markets. Exports to Japan from the United States between 1913 and 1917, for example, had grown by 66 percent, while imports of Japanese goods to the United States had increased by 61 percent. Overall U.S. trade with the Pacific Rim had grown by more than 50 percent in the same period. As President Wilson had noted publicly in 1915 (with South America in mind), the tremendous growth in trade required an equally strong growth in rapid communications. More than two-thirds of business transactions with the Far East during the war years involved sending information by cable.[27] U.S.-Japanese cable traffic in particular had jumped incredibly: over one million telegrams in 1914 became three million telegrams in 1917 and grew, despite the cable problems, to well over five million in 1918. Over half of the Commercial Pacific Cable Company traffic was with Japan.[28] Given this incredible demand for communications, it was not surprising that the chorus of complaints from merchants over cable delays reached a magnificent crescendo by the summer of 1917.[29] The American Philippine Company and other large firms with interests across the Pacific at first complained fruitlessly to the Commercial Pacific company. Some suggested that the navy's radio chain might provide relief. Because laying a new cable would take months and the navy's stations were not complete, there could be no quick solutions from either the cable company or the government.

The sorry state of cable ties between Japan and the United States soon became a diplomatic concern as well. In mid-July the Japanese government petitioned to have Japanese commercial messages exempted from censorship. Acknowledging that this alone might be too sweeping a proposal, Japan suggested compromises. One was that the United States allow this exemption in only the four cities where Japanese business interests were greatest: New York, Seattle, San Francisco, and Honolulu. Another suggestion was that Japanese consuls in those cities could file certified translations of the coded messages with the navy's censors. The issue was as much practical as it was technical. Japanese merchants suffered disproportionally more from the ban on codes than their counterparts who used Western languages. Those sending messages in Japanese had to translate them into English in order to pass through the censors and over the cables. Upon arrival in Japan, the messages passed back into Japanese again for domestic transmission. The privilege of coding had reduced the time and expense of this cumbersome process by substituting abbreviated words for regular phrases, but the navy now forbade codes. Finding this argument compelling, Assistant Secretary of State Breckinridge Long, whose brief included Asian affairs, promised the Japanese Embassy that he would pursue the issue with the navy.[30]

Many wondered why the U.S. Navy could not route some of this commercial traffic through radios to relieve the pressure on the cable. There were several reasons, but few sated an outraged public that did not understand the restrictions the navy faced. The first was that the navy actually did not have statutory authority to handle commercial radio traffic, even in wartime, in addition to government and military traffic. Several members of Congress, with active encouragement from

Secretary Daniels, introduced legislation in an attempt to correct this. In addition, the naval radio chain was not yet complete. Though the Marconi stations had been shut down, the United States government could not automatically take over American Marconi's traffic agreement with the Japanese government. Nor would the addition of the naval chain alone solve the problem. The growing traffic load between the United States and Asia had simply exceeded the total available cable and radio bandwidth. Because cables could carry more traffic than radios, only a new cable would solve the problem. Another reason the navy could not route commercial traffic by radio was that senior naval officials understood that Germany could monitor transmissions from the Pacific area radio stations. If these stations handled commercial messages for the general public, it would be possible for German agents to pass messages back to Germany around the censors. Thus traffic would have to remain on the cable and under close scrutiny.

Less attuned to the nuances of wartime diplomacy or the particulars of Pacific trade, Secretary Daniels was not willing to do anything to weaken the effectiveness of cable censorship. He was reluctant to permit the use of Japanese phrases for standard commercial expressions or for staple product names in cable traffic. At first he contemplated granting this privilege as a favor to the Japanese government, but between August and October he became firmly opposed to even this idea. By November Long had to tell the Japanese that there would be no special arrangements for commercial traffic with Japan. Even when Japan offered to provide telegraphers trained to work with Japanese messages, as they had for the British, Long remained pessimistic that the navy would change its view.[31]

The sclerotic conditions of transpacific communications also complicated the efforts of the Wilson administration to spread American news to Asia. To convince the American people of the need to go to war and bolster their morale through the great challenge, Wilson had sanctioned the creation of the Committee on Public Information. Established on April 13, 1917, with the secretaries of state, navy and war as members, the committee had as its head the progressive journalist George Creel. Creel aimed first at the home front but gradually expanded the committee's scope overseas. The idea was to convey positive views of the United States and its ideals to every corner of the world. By doing so, the United States could counter skewed propaganda of both the Allies and the Central powers with U.S. war aims while building support for Wilson's hopeful plans for peace and a new international order. An important part of this task was to send great quantities of U.S. news stories into Europe, Latin America, and Asia. But making propaganda and effectively disseminating it are two entirely different operations. Prewar agreements among the major British, French, and German press agencies and the concomitant unfavorable cable situation had seriously minimized both the quantity and quality of U.S. news that regularly reached the rest of the world.[32]

Surveying the international cable and news scene for the committee in June upon his return from Asia, Walter S. Rogers glumly concluded that cable and radio links between the United States and Asia were scarcely adequate for the wartime demands of diplomacy and trade. Rogers, former assistant to Wilson advisor and industrialist Charles R. Crane, would go on to head the Wireless-Cable Bureau within the foreign section of the Creel committee, where his responsibility would be the dissemination of U.S. news across the world.[33] While he was traveling in Asia, newspaper editors there had complained repeatedly to him about the high rates for press messages sent by cable. For example, United Press was able to send only 150 words per day of news to Japan, an amount that was not really able to convey anything important at all. Important stories and government announcements, Rogers found, reached Asian newspapers as crude condensations, and "because of the lack of news, friendly relations based on mutual understandings [were] impossible under present conditions." Rogers continued, "There is at present always the danger that sensational or garbled accounts of important events will so arouse the public that a government may be forced into drastic action."[34] Rogers had found also that senior officials in China, Japan, and Russia were willing to discuss with the United States ways to improve transpacific communications. He had also lined up support from the Associated Press and the United Press, as well as the Kokusai press agency in Japan, to back any effort at improving dispersal of U.S. news into the Far East. "Present war emergencies demand quick attention to better news service to the Orient," Rogers advised Frank Polk. Rogers even suggested that after the war an international conference be held to address the problem of unequal press rates. He wrote, "America will be in a better position if she attacks these problems at once and shows by her activity her interest and realization of their importance."[35]

The quickest practical solution was to press the navy's radio chain into service to carry government-sanctioned news across the Pacific until new cables became available. Rogers briefed President Wilson on this in late June.[36] Though the U.S. Navy was not authorized to send commercial traffic between the United States and the Philippines, China, or Japan, there was a way around this ban with press transmissions. The navy already received from the United Press a daily news report, which it then broadcast as a naval digest to U.S. warships at sea. Handling the news in this way was a legitimate use of the navy's radios. Once the station at Manila opened, it would be possible to send this daily digest via Manila to the navy receiving station at Peking. There the United Press could redistribute it throughout China.[37] Rogers pointed out that with the right formal agreements the navy could also use its Alaskan radio stations, which legally could handle commercial traffic, to send news via Russian stations in Siberia down into China. Though Rogers eventually arranged for routing news from the Manila station to a French station at Shanghai, the radio alternative could be only a temporary solution. The transmission speeds for radio were still a fraction of that of the cables, and it was by cable that the bulk of traffic continued to cross the Pacific.[38]

As Pacific communications deteriorated throughout the summer of 1917, the need for a new cable became extreme. In late August, the Pacific cable failed completely. Navy censors reported that before it did, the backlog of governmental and commercial traffic had reached three to five days. The navy had opened its high-power station in San Diego, but the station in Hawaii was still being tested. To handle government traffic through to Hawaii and Japan, the navy still had to rely on the commandeered commercial stations. The Manila station would not be ready until December. As a result, the broken cable meant that for a period of time there was no direct, two-way link to the Philippines or the Far East from the United States at the height of the war.[39]

For the long term, naval officials recommended a second cable along either of two routes. The first was to duplicate the existing cable to the Philippines but to land the cable on the eastern side of Luzon, away from the rough bottom of the San Bernardino Strait, where much of the damage occurred. The other was to run a new cable from Seattle to Japan via the Aleutians. The navy's Alaskan radio stations could back up this cable in case of interruption. The navy preferred this second option. Such a northern cable "would be of great military value in connection with the strategy on the Pacific Ocean." This northern route might also permit a branch cable to Siberia for connection to the Russian telegraph network. Whether the cable went via the Philippines or Alaska, the U.S. Navy clearly understood the tremendous commercial, political, and military benefits the additional cable would bring.[40]

It now began to dawn on U.S. officials that solutions could be neither swift nor easy. "It does not seem as if early relief, other than that which may be afforded by the transpacific radio circuit, is probable without concerted Government effort," noted Daniels in a missive to the secretary of state.[41] As John Merrill had already learned, it was virtually impossible to obtain new cable from British suppliers because of wartime shortages and exorbitant costs. Yet even if sufficient supplies were at hand, landing a new cable in Asia was not without difficulty. More than a decade earlier, China had granted a confusing set of concessions to British and Danish cable companies, concessions that effectively blocked other companies from landing cables in China.[42] Like the United States, Japan had gradually become very sensitive about foreign control over cables landing on its islands. There were restrictions on the nationality of cable operators and the ownership of companies that would control cables landing in Japan. In the case of wireless, Japan had governmental control over operations, to prevent foreign firms from working there. Japan also exercised a virtual veto over new foreign radio ventures in China. Should the United States wish to extend radio and cable connections with Japan and China, doing so would involve considerable investments as well as significant diplomatic and commercial negotiations.[43]

Temporary relief came only at the very end of 1917. The Pearl Harbor station opened in September, but the Cavite station was ready only in December. At last the high-power radio network that Hooper had envisioned was complete. At last there was reliable, continuous, and redundant communications between the United States and the Philippines. Through the smaller stations at Guam and American Samoa, there was constant contact with warships in much of the western Pacific. By relay through the Cavite station, Washington could remain in contact with American forces at Shanghai and the navy receiving station at the legation in Peking. Through the Alaskan stations, it was also possible to exchange traffic with Japan and Siberia.[44] No longer dependent upon the commercial stations if the cable broke, the U.S. Navy could for the first time ever command and control its forces all across the Pacific.[45] The great challenge of bridging the vast distances of the Pacific Ocean had led to the development of new technology. The arc transmitters built by Federal Telegraph for Cavite and San Diego were ten times more powerful than those it had built before the war. The new transmitters could throw a signal well over seventy-four hundred miles, a distance scarcely imaginable even three years earlier. For all this accomplishment, however, the demand for more cables across the Pacific remained unsated.

The State Department had meanwhile learned of another reason to improve the transpacific cable situation immediately. The single direct line between the United States and China had failed at a crucial moment in Sino-American diplomacy. In the late summer of 1917, the government of China contemplated the weighty decision to declare war on Germany. Its officials had been unable to secure promises from Britain and France that should China join them in the war, these two powers would recognize China's sovereignty at any peace conference. Chinese officials then approached Dr. Paul Reinsch, the U.S. minister to China, to obtain explicit guarantees from the United States, which had already interceded against Japan's "Twenty-one Demands" on China in 1915. With such promises China would enter the war on the Allied side. Reinsch needed State Department approval for what he believed to be the right course of action. The negotiations required secrecy as well as celerity. Reinsch's communications would have to go by the American cable. At the critical moment, however, Reinsch found that the cable had broken. He could not provide such an important guarantee without the approval of his superiors a continent and an ocean away, but he could not entrust such sensitive diplomatic messages to non-American hands. The cable's failure had paralyzed, however briefly, the practice of diplomacy and the course of international affairs.[46]

Meanwhile, the Japanese continued to complain about the great harm inadequate cable contact was doing to economic relations with the United States. The absence of any combat or key support operations in the Far East and Pacific prior to 1918 meant that there was no pressing need for the United States and Japan to reach a radio agreement as the United States had with the Allied powers in Europe. Compounding this situation was the navy's continued prohibition on sending commercial messages over the Pacific radio service. Still, Japanese diplomats petitioned Assistant Secretary Long repeatedly in January, March, and May 1918 for the easing of censorship regulations or the laying of new cables. Viscount Ishii, the Japanese special envoy, had even brought the problem up personally with Secretary of State Lansing when the two met in late 1917. When a U.S.-Japanese radio circuit finally opened at the end of May, the navy restricted its use to government messages from Washington, San Francisco, and Hawaii. This exiled private and commercial traffic to the overburdened cables and perpetuated an already exasperating situation. With the State Department unable itself to do anything directly, the Japanese asked for official pressure on Commercial Pacific either to open negotiations for a second cable or to lower rates with the Japanese department of communications.[47]

When senior State Department officials finally engaged the problem, they found Commercial Pacific surprisingly unwilling to lend assistance. Chief Engineer George Ward advised Frank Polk in April 1918 that the company believed the wartime congestion to be a temporary phenomenon, which would ease after the war. Any reduction in rates, as they saw it, would affect the profitability of the cable once the load dropped to peacetime levels. At the end of June, Assistant Secretary Long met with Ward to discuss the chances that the company might soon lay additional cables to Japan for the war effort. Like Polk, Long found Ward dismissive of any need to be concerned about the current congestion and delays. He was uninterested in creating the suggested cable extensions to Japan from the army's cable to Alaska or in duplicating the existing route. Ward reiterated his belief that the cable and its stations would be sufficient to handle postwar traffic. Ward's views were unusual. The cost of cables admittedly was great, but demand had been high in the region before the war. It was logical, therefore, to conclude that a second cable and lower rates would spur increased demand that would generate enough revenue to cover the investment, as had frequently occurred with other cables elsewhere in the world. Either the company was in serious financial trouble and could not invest in a new cable, or it had other reasons for retarding the development of transpacific cables.[48]

Commercial Pacific actually had a vested interest in seeing Pacific communications not improve, a fact that Long and Polk likely did not know. The firm was a joint venture by the Commercial Cable Company, the American firm operating cables in the Atlantic, with the British Eastern Extension and the Danish Great Northern Telegraph companies, which already had restrictive concessions in China and the Far East. By forming Commercial Pacific with the help of Mackay's Atlantic company, which controlled only 25 percent of the new company, Eastern Extension and Great Northern created a prohibitive price structure that diverted Western Hemisphere cable traffic for Asia eastward via Europe and thus over their own cables. Should Commercial Pacific lower its rates or add a second cable, the traffic flow into these cables westward, away from the existing British and Danish cables, would cost Eastern Extension and Great Northern money. Mackay, perhaps at Polk's personal appeal, agreed to reduce the rates by about 20 percent in August, but this would not be enough for the State Department. Amid Commercial Pacific's reluctance and reports of fresh breaks on the cable, Breckinridge Long seized the initiative. His subsequent efforts in spite of Commercial Pacific's interests laid the groundwork for lasting changes to the strategic communications of the United States in the twentieth century.[49]

Assistant Secretary of State Breckinridge Long organized at the end of June a joint committee of the State, War, and Navy departments to consider the transpacific communications problem and formulate solutions. As he informed the participants, the need for improved Pacific communications was of "great importance, politically, militarily, commercially, and in the matter of providing for a more complete exchange of public opinion between the United States and the Far East." From the navy came Captain D. W. Todd, the director of naval communications. Major General George Squier, the army's chief signal officer, joined as well. Walter S. Rogers came to represent the press and information interests of the Committee on Public Information.

Dr. Paul Reinsch, who had returned from his post in China, as well as Philip Patchin, the foreign intelligence division chief at the State Department, rounded out the group.[50]

Long's committee was the first assembly of the different parts of the government that had an interest and ability to formulate a central foreign policy to address the international communications needs of the country. The participants worked actively from August to December. During that time they came to appreciate the need to protect the existing cable and radio connections against further degradation as well as the great importance of extending the network centered in the United States as rapidly as possible. Doing so, it was now clear, would yield not only political or military advantages but also economic, cultural, and even intelligence benefits in the years to come, as the United States assumed a greater role in the world. With that in mind, Long directed the committee to consider not just the Pacific but the larger question of international communications around the whole world, with a view to providing information and recommendations for the upcoming peace conference.[51]

If the committee was the first serious joint consideration of cable and radio problems, then it was also the first time that senior-level officials realized how difficult it would be to achieve any independence in strategic communications. Long asked for reports on the political, military, naval, and press aspects of the problem from each of the members.[52] The initial proposals advanced by Todd, Squier, and Rogers included obtaining several thousand miles of new cable, diverting existing cables, constructing new high-power stations in China and Siberia, and legislating that radio and cable operations be placed into the hands of the military. They also suggested that Commercial Pacific's cable was too essential to be left in private hands and should be under federal control. Walter Rogers wrote, "[The] importance of the transpacific communication far transcends profit making considerations," and he proposed that the cable should be taken from its owners. The proposals envisioned significant, long-term changes to the cable network, not just cosmetic improvements for relief of wartime congestion.[53]

The initial solutions put forward by the committee members, however, were not at all feasible in the short term. Nor did they address the more fundamental issue of U.S. dependence upon other powers. Squier's proposed duplication of the transpacific cable, for example, required buying many miles of cable while also diverting German or British cables onto the proposed route. But Reinsch, the minister to China, warned that Japan was uninterested in improving U.S.-Chinese ties at Japan's expense and would resist any calls from the United States to divert the captured German cable connecting with Shanghai from Yap to Guam.[54] Nor would the British be particularly excited about redirecting their strategic Pacific cable to touch on non-British territory, such as the Hawaiian Islands, when the original purpose had been to keep the cable landings on imperial soil only. There were also few guaranteed supplies of cable available in the next few years. As John Merrill had already learned, postwar production had been largely earmarked for the use of British firms, and there might not be any available to serve existing U.S. orders for South America. The current lack of a U.S. cable industry and the continued high demand for cable by Europeans made laying a completely new Pacific cable unlikely anytime soon. To add new radio stations was another possibility, but radio stations were expensive operations and military liabilities, and they were hardly able to handle the load of traffic on the cables. Transferring commercial operation of cables or radio permanently to the military after the war was unlikely to be popular with Congress or the private firms, even if this would bring the improvements that the public demanded.[55]

Long and the others eventually settled on two courses of action. The first was intensive research into technical improvements to boost the efficiency of cable operations on the existing cables as a short-term solution. Long now understood that Commercial Pacific would not be willing to carry out this research on its own. The federal government would have to do this instead. Since Congress had recently granted President Wilson the power to nationalize cable operations in wartime, federal funded research was an easier prospect. The second, longer, and more difficult course of action was the creation of a new cable industry in the United States almost entirely from scratch. It would have to be done as quickly as possible in order to end the dependence upon the British cable industry. General Squier had been an advocate of both ideas since the Spanish-American War. On Squier's advice, Long first organized an expert panel of electrical engineers to research improvements to cable operations and equipment before investigating the cable industry itself.

The importance attached to the project was apparent from the prominence of the experts accepting Squier's nomination. Gano Dunn, the expert committee's chair, was the president of the J. G. White Engineering Corporation of New York, a major engineering and construction company at the time. Also on board were Dr. Arthur Kennelly, professor at Harvard University and director of the research division of the Department of Electrical Engineering at MIT; Colonel F. B. Jewett, the chief engineer of General Electric; and Bancroft Gherardi, an electrical engineer with AT&T. Technical experts from the navy and the army assisted the committee as well. The laboratories of Western Electric were made directly available to the committee for research and development.[56]

Dunn and the other experts looked first at improving the efficiency of cable operations. One idea was to change the very nature of how information passed through the cable. The traditional method had been the abrupt on-off pulse of electricity, controlled by the telegraph operator on one end of the cable. The resultant switch in polarity between positive and negative on the other end caused a finely balanced glass tube filled with ink to slide left and right, with one side representing dots and the other dashes. A key problem, however, was that the strength of the electrical signal in a submarine cable dissipated over distance. The longer a cable, the weaker the signal became and the slower transmission had to be in order to keep the clarity of each pulse. Squier himself had suggested before the war an alternate idea known as continuous sine-wave signaling. In this system, an unceasing alternate current passed steadily through the cable. Variations in the amplitude of the signal, rather than its interruption, represented dots, dashes, and spaces. British tests of this theory in May 1916 had shown that such a method could yield a speed increase of around 20 percent.[57] Working throughout the fall, Dunn's committee collaborated with Western Electric to examine the technique. Dunn was even able to bring A. B. Crossman, the chief engineer at Muirhead and Company, to the United States for several months to advise the committee. In the end, the sine wave system proved less reliable than mechanical devices such as signal amplifiers and repeaters, which the committee ultimately selected.[58] With Long's backing, Dunn was also able to coax highly proprietary information about operations and equipment from the three cable companies.[59] As the war came to a close and delays on the Pacific cable reached two weeks, the Dunn expert committee kept at its research.

The second course of action Long's committee investigated was the creation of a cable industry in the United States. They envisioned the construction of a one or more plants capable of producing several thousand miles of deep-water submarine telegraph cable each year and the development of a fleet of cable-laying ships large enough for long-distance ocean work. With such a capability, it would be possible for the cable companies to lay enough cables to keep up with the increasing demand for international telegraphy. There was no reason why the United States should not have its own cable industry. The country already had in abundance much of the materials needed for making submarine cables, particularly steel wire and jute. Copper, though in short supply during the war, could be expected to be plentiful shortly. There was also industrial experience and the physical plant necessary to support spinning large wires used in bridge building or electrical wiring. Several metal wire firms in the United States had limited experience in constructing submarine cable for the U.S. Army Signal Corps' Alaskan cable.

U.S. cable companies had become increasingly conservative and complacent in the years before the war, however, and this had impeded the creation of such an industry. Western Union, Central and South American and Postal Telegraph, the parent company of the Commercial Cable companies, had not developed any significant research laboratories of their own. They relied instead upon the advances of Muirhead and Company, Telegraph Construction and Maintenance or the British cable firms. The equipment used in 1918 for transmitting and receiving signals was essential the same as had existed at the turn of the century.[60] Happy to continue purchasing cable and equipment from British manufacturers, these firms had eschewed the efforts of the U.S. manufacturers, who lacked the capacity or experience to offset British competitors.[61] More vitally, the key component the United States lacked in the era before mass production of polyurethane and plastics was the gutta-percha latex wrap that most efficiently insulated the electrical signal in the submerged cable. Control of the world's supply was largely in British hands. For a U.S. cable manufacturer to succeed, it would have to ensure continual access to such supplies as it needed, but such an effort was only worthwhile if the U.S. cable companies were interested in purchasing U.S. cable. The general manager of the United Press Association concluded, after examining the situation, "All authorities seem to agree that submarine cable could be successfully produced in this country if the government determined to produce it. It is equally certain that it will not be produced unless the government orders it."[62]

The Long committee learned in September the extent to which the United States was at the mercy of Britain in expanding the cable network. John Merrill forwarded a copy of a Central and South American report that was completed earlier that summer. After Merrill and others had become concerned about the future supply of cable, the company board of directors had investigated the state of the industry. The conclusion was that the shortage of cable would lead to an awkward situation. Besides winning monopoly-free concessions in Latin America, the company would need to create a cable-manufacturing facility, establish a research laboratory, and investigate the potentials of alternate materials in constructing cables.[63]

The report identified in particular two key factors: Britain's predominant role in manufacturing cables and the relative shortfall in supplies of the key gutta-percha insulator. After the war Great Britain and the United States alone would require some thirty-seven thousand nautical miles of cable for planned expansion. Of the twelve cable plants in the world, Britain's six were capable of producing about twenty-seven nautical miles of cable per year. It was to be expected, however, that all of these plants were under government contract through the foreseeable future.[64] Compounding this situation was the war-driven inflation of the costs to manufacture cable. In 1906 a single nautical mile of one type of deep-water cable cost $350 from a British firm. The German cable company offered the same for only $300 in 1913. By 1916, however, the cost in Britain was $610, to rise later to $775 in March 1918. This doubled the cost of the three cables Merrill had to obtain for the new South American concessions to six million dollars. A significant issue here was also the supply of gutta-percha. There were only about thirty-five tons of the latex available on the market in the summer of 1918. Central's engineers estimated that they needed, for the two new cables between Buenos Aires and Brazil and a supplemental spur between Ecuador and Chile, 380 tons of gutta-percha for 4,765 nautical miles of cable. Central's larger plans for encircling South America and linking it to the United States required 12,325 nautical miles of cable—and more than a thousand tons of gutta-percha.[65]

Creating an independent ability to manufacture cables was thus a two-part process. Central's board concluded that there should be at least one cable-manufacturing plant in the Unites States. Construction would take fifteen to eighteen months, they estimated, and would cost about five million dollars. But the increase in demand for gutta-percha driven by this new cable plant would throw the international market out of whack. Either the price would rise precipitously or, as Central's report glumly assumed, the British brokers would restrict the supply to the point that there would not be enough for the United States. The only alternative, it seemed to Central's board, was that it should search out its own supply of gutta-percha or even discover a replacement, artificial or natural, for it, to allow the company to bypass the British completely.[66]

Central's survey of the international cable industry, focused as it was on Latin America, resonated with what Long's committee had considered in relation to Pacific communications. The problems of cable supply were the same in both instances, and unless the industry shifted, the additional demand for a transpacific cable would aggravate the situation still further. If these issues could be overcome, however, the potential benefits for the country were great. The Central report concluded, "The nation at the close of the war that has the money available for submarine construction, the cable works of the largest capacity, the control of the raw materials required, the special ships for the storage, transportation, laying and maintenance of its cables, and a fleet of modern freight carriers, will be able to at once appropriate and expand a considerable portion of the disturbed trade in foreign countries and eventually come to dominate the commerce of the world."[67] Long's committee would have found little to disagree with, except to add that an international cable network would also confer political, military, and intelligence benefits as well. Work on this project began in earnest in early 1919, but the direction and scope of the Wilson administration's efforts were very similar to those recommended by Merrill and the Central and South American Telegraph Company in the summer of 1918. Now that the United States government had become directly involved, thanks to Breckinridge Long, there was the chance that the country would secure a major presence in the international communications field. Able to meet the strategic and commercial interests of the United States in the world, this new industry would have eliminated the nation's dependence upon the British cable-manufacturing and -operating companies. Once established, the cable-manufacturing industry would allow the operating companies to capitalize quickly on the concessions that the diplomatic efforts of the State Department had underwritten. Carried to fruition, these plans might well have been as significant a development as the formation of the Radio Corporation of America the following year: an independent ability to control the flow and route of information to and from the United States.[68]

By the end of the First World War, there were some 273,600 nautical miles of submarine telegraph cable in the world. This included all manner of cable, from small interport sections to vast lengths across the largest oceans. Of these, Great Britain and her companies controlled some 51 percent. The combined lines of France, Germany, Denmark, the Netherlands, Spain, Japan, and Italy accounted for roughly another 24 percent. The remaining quarter was under United States influence. Perhaps half of these cables served the transatlantic route. The rest were all those in the Caribbean and Central and South America and across the Pacific.[69] Though in sheer mileage and on paper the United States was a significant cable power, growing American demand had filled its network's capacity. New conversations of diplomacy, trade, news, and ordinary human affairs had opened with countries connected only by foreign lines. From the country's experience first in uneasy peace and then in aggrieved war, the United States had learned that it would need to expand its cable connections to meet its growing international interests but that there were considerable barriers obstructing this path.

Encouraged by the Wilson administration, whose officials had come to understand how commercial and national interest now coincided, Central and South American Telegraph Company and Western Union had confronted the problem with plans to lay new cables. Part of the desire was to widen the capacity over existing lines, whose deficiencies the war had made glaringly apparent. In the last six months of the war, the transatlantic cables had operated continuously at never less than

91 percent capacity, and frequently cable traffic backed up for days. Four days after the armistice, Western Union ceased to accept any new commercial traffic for three days in order to clear the immense quantity of government traffic that had piled up.[70] The cable companies also expanded into new markets. In South America, Central and Western Union had raised a substantial challenge to Western Telegraph. Ambitious plans foretold of cables encircling the continent along with long-desired direct cables to Brazil. Western Union intended to reach out with a new cable to Scandinavia and Russia as well.[71] But these fast-moving hopes skidded to a halt. Cable and its vital gutta-percha ingredient, both in short supply, might become all but impossible to acquire in the years to come, as British companies drew first on the limited output.

What appeared at first a commercial problem then transformed into a government concern as Breckinridge Long pulled the State Department into the matter. The limited resources of the cable companies would compel them to accept the existing situation as the least risky alternative. Shortages of cable would simply mean less ambitious plans and favorable agreements with British and other cable companies. The federal government, however, unbound by financial risks and alert now to the larger strategic issues stemming from cable networks, would take a different path. In the final years of the Wilson administration, officials crafted ambitious plans at home and abroad to draw upon the lessons of the past five years and continue the wartime efforts of Long's cable committee.

SIX

Radio, the Navy, and Latin America

"ANY SUFFICIENTLY ADVANCED technology," the author Arthur C. Clarke once wrote, "is indistinguishable from magic."[1] Though the technology of radio was nearly two decades old, to many in the late 1910s the sending of radio signals through the clear blue sky must have appeared somewhat magical. In 1915 AT&T and the U.S. Navy transmitted the spoken word from the United States to Paris and Hawaii. Marconigrams and other radio-transmitted telegrams carried the printed word across continents and oceans. All the while, the medium by which these messages traveled was invisible. It was the thin air itself, or as the more romantically inclined described it, the ether. Faith in science convinced people that it was neither magic nor fraud but a new amazing facet of human existence.

For all the wonderment at this method of communications, since 1914 the United States had fervently and consistently tried to keep European companies from building and operating radio stations in Central and South America. The improvement of rapid electrical contact between the Latin America and the United States had become a matter of commercial, political, and military importance to the nation by 1917. But as the largest user of radio in the government, the U.S. Navy was very reluctant to permit Europeans to meet the growing demand. Anxious to avoid the danger of interference and concerned for the neutrality and security of the hemisphere, the navy sought instead to guide hemispheric radio development, to keep it in line with the latest technical and operating standards and with U.S. interests. To carry this out, the navy had tried several approaches but had accomplished little, other than blocking further European incursions.

After April 1917, U.S. policy on radio proliferation transformed. The principal aims remained the same: keeping European companies out and pushing radio development, either publicly or privately, in ways that were friendly to U.S. interests. But now the most immediate concern became the spread of German radio stations, which could be used directly against the United States. The strength of British Marconi and its anticipated influence after the war was also a concern but called for a more circumspect approach toward a wartime ally. United States officials worked hard to check both German and British radio companies. Through the course of the war, the United States was largely successful at stopping these companies but failed to offer an alternative that could meet the great political and economic demand for radio that had attracted the companies in the first place. Internal divisions within the U.S. Navy over both foreign and domestic radio policy prevented it from developing a viable program for high-power long-distance radio, stopped U.S. companies from constructing a strategic radio network in the Western Hemisphere, and hindered the overall effort to develop independent lines of communication with other regions of the world. The experience, so frustrating for many officials, would have important implications for the development of radio after the war.

The clouds of war darkened all German activity, legitimate or otherwise, in Latin America after April 1917. Because of their myriad uses, radio stations in the area with German ties came under particular scrutiny. The outbreak of hostilities intensified U.S. efforts to gather information on the activities of Telefunken and other firms in the area. Reports arrived in Washington of radio transmissions in German near the Panama Canal and of Germans involved in radio matters in Mexico. Radio equipment of German origin surfaced in El Salvador and Costa Rica as gifts of the Mexican government. Representatives of German radio interests bid on concessions in Venezuela. Some State Department officials feared that Telefunken stations already in place across South America were being used to communicate with German ships in the area or possibly even with Germany itself.[2] Though it was not entirely clear in Washington what exactly was going on, naval officers and diplomats had already resolved to eliminate any such German influence as swiftly as possible.

It is now clear in retrospect that in 1916 German authorities attempted to redevelop a global radio network. Allied officials had only the barest hints of the plan. Two of the three major stations were to be located in the Western Hemisphere. Mexico, Colombia, Venezuela, Suriname, Ecuador, Peru, Chile, Argentina, Uruguay, and Brazil were all to have stations. Looking beyond the eventual end of the war, German officials envisioned that the stations would also help to revitalize trade and spread German political influence by replacing the now-destroyed cable system. Anchoring the network would be a new high-power station in Mexico City, to replace the ones in New York. Noting with approval the request from the German minister in Mexico for the station, the Foreign Office in Berlin understood that it "would make [Germany] independent" of U.S. goodwill and the stations in New York. Though not as successful as the German planners had originally intended, the radio network eventually constructed was still extensive. Based in neutral countries, it lay largely beyond the direct reach of Britain and the United States.[3]

Planning for the Mexico City station and the larger network occurred between mid-1916 and early 1917. After some debate over the costs and utility of the network, German officials decided by July 22, 1916, to upgrade an existing station at Mexico City with new equipment from Telefunken. Because of the allied blockade, the transmitter and receiver could not be shipped directly from Germany. Instead, an individual not connected with the ACC or Telefunken would have to obtain this equipment in the United States. As relations between Germany and the United States soured in the winter of 1916–1917, German officials approached the Mexican government to obtain a concession to build a high-power radio station capable of working with the high-power station at Nauen. The new, improved station in Mexico City would allow for censor-free coded messages to pass freely between Germany and her agents in the Western Hemisphere. A German interdepartmental committee concluded in early 1917, "We have urgent need of direct cable and telegraph links with certain lands, with whom we could previously communicate only by cables under foreign control. Without this radio and telegraph link, Germany would be cut off from world commerce for some time."[4]

Construction on this first part of the network began in early 1917. Telefunken secretly dispatched equipment to Mexico in February. The first step was to build a receiving station to pick up Nauen's transmissions. The new receiving station was in the Mexico City suburb of Ixtapalapa. By March the station was operational. By mid-April it regularly received signals from Nauen, approximately six thousand miles away. From the transmitting station in the suburb of Chapultepec, two smaller transmitters allowed the German engineers to work with stations in Mexico and Central America.[5] Radio engineers who had fled from the United States assisted the Mexican technicians in the construction and running of the station as well as in the operation of fifteen to twenty smaller stations across Mexico. At night, these Germans took over operations to handle the messages from Germany. At the request of the Mexican government, neither Nauen nor Mexico City identified themselves on air when working this Mexican connection.[6]

Representatives of Telefunken pursued the construction of similar stations elsewhere around the Caribbean basin. The Mexican government, probably on German advice, gave small radio stations using Telefunken equipment as gifts to the governments of El Salvador and Costa Rica in early 1917. These stations were capable of receiving the transmissions from the new high-power Mexico City station and in turn working with similar stations in Colombia. German agents also unsuccessfully pursued a powerful station in Venezuela. Telefunken representatives had beaten out British Marconi and Federal Telegraph on the contract to build the national radio network there. Operational oversight would come from the Atlantic Communications Company, which had worked in New York and still operated the station at Cartagena, Colombia. But the entry of the United States into the war complicated matters. It prevented ACC and Telefunken from sending to Venezuela a promised transmitter that could reach North America and Africa as well as a smaller one for working between ship and shore. The project came to a halt, and ACC requested postponement. A thinly veiled substitute, the New York Patents Exploitation Company, tried in vain to revive the contract, to no avail. Despite this setback, however, Telefunken had still reinforced its influence from Mexico to Colombia.[7]

At the same time, Germany expanded its radio network through South America and pursued another large station. Only rudimentary information about this filtered back to Washington. The navy learned that while Ecuador, Peru, Bolivia, Paraguay, and Uruguay all were using Telefunken equipment at their stations, these operations were apparently under firm government control. Chile had about twelve stations in private hands, several of which were Telefunken.[8] Besides the elusive Venezuelan station, Telefunken agents pursued a massive facility in Argentina. There had been a strong German presence in the radio field in Argentina before the war, with some twenty commercial and eight government stations all using Telefunken equipment. German or German-trained operators staffed these smaller stations. In April 1917 the United States learned that German agents had acquired a concession to construct a large receiving station outside of Buenos Aires. By late July, the German station neared completion, and German engineers began to test the reception of Nauen's signal. From Mexico City to Buenos Aires, the antennae of German long-distance radio stations had sprouted quickly.

Germany used the radio network to coordinate propaganda, intelligence, and economic activities across Latin America.[9] The transmitting station at Chapultepec had a range of one thousand miles, which enabled it to reach any of fifteen local stations within Mexico as well as the Telefunken stations in El Salvador and at San José, Costa Rica.[10] From San Salvador or San José, information passed down to the station at Cartagena, Colombia, and went through this station to Ecuador, Peru, or Chile.[11] In a matter of hours, information from Nauen in Germany could reach the smaller stations in Latin America and pass through national telegraph networks to agents across the continent. With the principal cable connections throughout the Americas in the hands of either British or the United States companies, the radio network offered a valuable alternative for Germany. "These plants operate at will," Boaz Long later warned Secretary of State Robert Lansing, "and the propaganda they spread is favorable to our enemies."[12]

The prospect of these German long-distance receiving stations was unsettling to U.S. officials. Closing them became an important objective. As early as April, senior U.S. officials had learned that the Mexico City station was sending coded messages in German, but it was not entirely clear who was receiving these transmissions. Only as naval attachés and diplomats reported in from across the continent did an adequate picture of the network take shape. Because Germany had located the stations in neutral countries, the United States could use little more than diplomatic protests and interception of equipment. U.S. diplomats in Mexico and Panama kept watch for unauthorized shipments of radio equipment. Meanwhile, Ambassador Stimson in Buenos Aires kept up hopes that Federal Telegraph could finish its station and supplant Telefunken's. By July 25, the German receiving station was nearly complete, however, and there had been little progress from Federal. Under intense pressure from the United States, the Argentine navy made arrangements to seal the station as soon as it was completely operational.[13]

Such steps were soon not necessary. In July Secretary Lansing publicly released intercepted diplomatic cables by the German minister to Argentina. Their embarrassing contents quickly damaged German-Argentina relations. Days after the German minister had to leave the country in disgrace, Stimson could report to Washington that the nascent German station had been dismantled even before it was completely operational.[14] The station would not be resurrected for the rest of the war, although German agents tried to reopen it in 1918. Several pro-German Argentines also traveled to Spain to train in operating a receiving station and returned with instructions to procure equipment from Spanish suppliers. U.S. officials, alerted to the danger, now kept close watch over these matters.[15]

If the stations could not be shut down, then the next best thing was to monitor the transmissions for intelligence. The United States and Britain created a network of listening posts for this purpose. With the U.S. Army's mobile stations along the Mexican border, the U.S. Navy's intercept station in Maine, and the Royal Navy's listening posts in Britain, the two countries were able to record much of the traffic heading along the chain from Nauen to Mexico City and beyond. The British Admiralty handled most of the decryption, and the messages quickly confirmed that German propaganda and disguised commercial traffic was passing by radio. Meanwhile, the U.S. Navy worried that clandestine stations might jam naval traffic or direct U-boats against shipping near the canal. Although several U.S. searches for such stations proved fruitless, the claims may not have been without foundation. On one occasion a British agent learned that a German team was heading for the coast with a small radio set for ship-shore work. After he spread the rumor that the men were carrying diamonds, the team disappeared. German radio stations in the hemisphere alone would not have changed the balance of the war, but the network's existence confirmed long-standing fears about German influence in the region and the strategic threat that could not be ignored.[16]

Only clandestine direct action against the stations was possible. Here the British, not the United States, had more success. Mexico City was the critical node. Only it had the massive antenna array and amplification equipment that could reach into the wavelengths where Nauen transmitted its signals. Mexico's unsettled politics and pro-German neutral position ruled out diplomatic pressure. In the view of the British intelligence officers, the only possible action was some sort of secret operation to shut the station down and silence the entire network.

It fell to A. E. W. Mason, a member of the Royal Marines and an experienced intelligence agent, to carry out just such a mission. In November 1917, Room 40 ordered Mason to Mexico to investigate the radio chain. From telegraphed purchase orders intercepted in Spain, British intelligence had learned that German radio engineers in Mexico City were using the newly developed vacuum tubes to amplify the faint signals from Nauen. These tubes became essential pieces of the station's receiver but were obtainable only in Britain and the United States. Mason's job was to discover how and where the five dozen requested vacuum tubes were to be used in Mexico. Passing himself off as a lepidopterist, although he knew nothing about butterflies, Mason developed a network of operatives. They soon discovered for him that, indeed, Mexico City did receive signals from Nauen regularly. Every night at 11:00 PM, German radio engineers from commercial ships interned at Veracruz took over operations and handled this secret traffic.[17]

Returning briefly to Britain to share what he had learned, Mason then moved cautiously but deliberately to silence this network. First, he purchased all eleven remaining vacuum tubes available in Mexico. After more Odyssean subterfuge, Mason arranged for one of his agents to tour the Ixtapalapa station under escort of the captain of the guard. From this he learned that the receiving equipment used thirteen vacuum tubes, with two spares on hand. Mason himself held all the remaining tubes in Mexico. "It was now clear," he later recalled, "that the destruction of the [vacuum tubes] in that receiving station would . . . preserve the neutrality of Mexico during the Great War with a more scrupulous precision than her government was prepared to observe." Mason organized a distraction for several days later (a drunken brawl among the guards), during which his agent managed to smash almost all the tubes. German agents, suspecting Mason's involvement, then invited him to the station for dinner several days later. They plied him with alcohol in an effort to make him slip his cover. Mason, feigning the need to vomit, managed to slip away, smash the remaining vacuum tube, and survive the remainder of the evening without revealing his identity or what he had just done. Mexican and German officials never learned who had really carried out the sabotage but cast much blame toward the United States. Mason's operation rendered the Mexico City station unable to receive transmissions from Nauen effectively for much of the rest of the war. By dealing a crippling blow to German communications across Latin America, he performed a very effective if secret operation.[18]

For all the excitement of Mason's mission, removing German radio influence from Latin America during the war was a complex task. The demand for improved cable and radio communications across the region had grown considerably, and the Germans had effectively tapped into that need. Unless the Allied powers could offer a viable alternative, many of the governments across the region had little incentive to reject the otherwise beneficial services of German radio experts or commercial stations. Because the stations that these Germans operated or equipped were not clandestine but rather legitimate operations, stopping them required both removing the direct influence (the engineers and equipment) and supplanting it with assistance from Allied powers. U.S. officials, however, were just as suspicious about the long-term implications of allowing British companies to fill this void, for precisely the same security and technical reasons that underlay U.S. wartime opposition to the German stations. The only effective way to safeguard the area, in these officials' view, was to oppose British radio ventures while championing those of American firms.

Like Germany, the British Marconi company also pursued a hemispheric radio network despite the war and the temporary seizure of its companion stations in the United States. If completed quickly enough, the proposed stations in Latin America would link the region with Britain and Europe via the American Marconi stations in the United States. British Marconi's radio network would then be a valuable conduit for postwar British economic and political influence throughout the Americas. At the same time, by filling what was seen as a limited market, it would have the additional effect of locking out U.S. competitors completely.[19] The anchors of this proposed network were to be at least two high-power stations in Central and South America.

Developing these leads was J. J. Almonte, the Latin American representative for both British and American Marconi. Almonte had already crisscrossed the area to pitch Marconi equipment. In the spring of 1917, the government of El Salvador requested British Marconi's involvement. Desirous of a direct connection to the United States, El Salvador had not been able to secure a station powerful enough to cover that distance. The 1915 request to the United States had been rejected out of fear that the station would imperil El Salvador's neutrality, while the 5 kw station given by Mexico was powerful enough to reach only Mexico City. Almonte offered the high-power station that El Salvador wanted. By the end of May, he had secured a contract to build it. If completed, it would be a major node of Marconi's proposed Latin American network.[20]

As it had before April 1917, the United States continued to challenge the extension of British radio into the Americas. While opposition to Germany's radio network was caused by the war, it was the long-term technical concerns about Marconi's use of the outdated spark transmitters and their disruptive signals that led the U.S. Navy to check a wartime ally. Navy officials monitoring Almonte urged that he be stopped; his station was "highly undesirable" to the navy: Its spark signals would generate interference in the Caribbean. Its operations would require a companion commercial station in the United States, undermining the goal of government ownership of high-power stations. It would also be "an extension of the British Marconi worldwide wireless scheme." Daniels offered that if there were to be a station, it should be U.S. built and compatible with the navy's standards.[21]

Boaz Long, the U.S. minister in El Salvador, who was versed in radio policy, blocked Almonte. Long asserted to the Salvadorian government that a U.S. representative would soon offer a competing bid. At the same time, Long intervened directly with Guatemala's President Cabrera to stop Almonte's negotiations there too. The State and Navy departments drew up a sample contract with Tropical Radio, later forwarding it to Long in October. Though no representatives from U.S. companies offered a competing bid, British Marconi had been stopped momentarily.[22]

In the face of the U.S. opposition, in early 1917 Sir Godfrey Isaacs, head of British Marconi, renewed his pressure on the British government for financial support. In Brazil, Guatemala, and now El Salvador, his firm had spent a great deal of money and was on the eve of completing agreements but for these U.S. countermoves. Several factors constrained Isaacs's planning. The first was that many governments in the region needed British Marconi to finance the construction of the stations. Repayment would come from the operating revenues. Another was that some governments had already given out concessions, particularly to cable companies, that included radio-operating rights. Not mentioned was that British Marconi no longer had the most-advanced transmitters. These were in the hands of Federal Telegraph, whose patented Fuller improvements to the original Poulsen arc were beyond American Marconi's reach.

To jump financial, legal, and technical hurdles, Isaacs estimated a necessary initial investment of around one million pounds. It would be nearly impossible to raise that money privately in Great Britain now. Isaacs informed the British government in February that he had lined up two backers in the United States, but that as a condition of the investment the firm carrying out the operation would have to be "American" in character. This was not an issue for Isaacs, for the Marconi Company had long exercised control through locally owned subsidiaries. Still, he wrote, "[In the] national interest . . . we can conceive that it is desirable that such a Company should be British and under British control and management." For Isaacs to forgo the American investors, however, he urgently need an advance of £500,000 from the British government.[23]

Isaacs had presented a difficult proposition to the British government. On the one hand, the construction of high-power stations in the region would strengthen British control over radio operations throughout Latin America, with all the commercial and strategic benefits that would accrue. On the other hand, the narrow financial straits that Britain found itself in at the height of a war for which it had already borrowed vast amounts made it hard to justify large investments in private ventures yielding benefits only after the war. Arthur Balfour, the foreign secretary, indicated that he was reluctant to support what seemed to be just a commercial venture, even though he understood the Admiralty's interest in maximizing British radio influence in the region. Keeping up the pressure through the summer, Isaacs even suggested a trade deal: British purchases of Brazilian coffee in exchange for a monopoly concession in international radio. Though Isaacs had support in both the Admiralty and the Foreign Office for these schemes in principle, officials simply could not overcome his hefty demand for money. "I think we ought to do all we can for the Co. for naval reasons," minuted one Foreign Office clerk, "[but] all the coffee schemes never seem to materialize." By July the Treasury rejected the Marconi proposal. The head of the American section of the Foreign Office then suggested that the proposal be dropped, which it was.[24]

Undeterred, Isaacs upped the pressure on the British government in late August as the situation appeared to reach a critical point. From New York, American Marconi head Edward Nally had made clear how much the U.S. Navy wanted British Marconi out of the picture. Writing to Isaacs, he had passed on a threat from Commander Hooper to use the Monroe Doctrine to drive British Marconi from Latin America. Isaacs presented a desperate situation. Without British government financing, Isaacs would have to give up not only the Latin American prospects but also quite possibly the American Marconi Company as well. "We are now threatened," he warned the Foreign Office, "with not only the determined opposition of the United States Government to all our negotiations with the Central and South American Republics, but also with the application of the Monroe Doctrine . . . It seems to me to be a very far-reaching menace." Isaacs believed that the company's strong position on patents could change rapidly as technology advanced. He pleaded to know whether the government's earlier decision was final or not. "It behooves my Company to act very quickly," he added. If there could be no financial help, then he would be forced to accede to the U.S. requirements, reduce the investment in American Marconi to 25 percent, and turn over its patents to a new American radio company.[25]

Isaacs agonized as officials debated his offer into the fall. The Foreign Office accepted his view of the situation. In view of the danger of losing influence, the Admiralty backed either a loan or a subsidy for the Marconi Company, provided it could win the objectives Isaacs claimed it could. Isaacs met Foreign Office, Treasury, Admiralty, and General Post Office officials on September 3 to make one last pitch. He reiterated his company's fervent desires, his opponents' determined resistance, and his great need for a large government loan. Remarkably, he suggested that the loan should be surreptitious, to conceal from American competitors his plans. Isaacs threatened that without this financial support, he would be forced to spin off the American Marconi subsidiary and lose any chance at control over radio in Latin America. Government officials were not convinced. The Treasury's representative pointedly remarked that the required parliamentary vote on funding would reveal the secret plans. When the meeting broke up without resolving Issacs's request, it was clear to Isaacs that there was nothing else that the British government would do.[26]

All avenues in London exhausted, a Marconi representative sailed within days for New York, to preside over the apparent capitulation. Sydney Steadman's job was to negotiate a new combination, formed of the American Marconi company and its principal competitor, Federal Telegraph, that could enter Latin America while remaining friendly to British interests. British Marconi would transfer to this new combination all of the long-distance stations in the United States under British Marconi's control, as well as its rights and patents in Latin America, as related to communications with the United States. British Marconi would not then compete with this new company. Even though this new company would have a U.S. character, the British Marconi company would retain some investments in it and the American Marconi subsidiary. Convinced by Isaacs that it still might be possible to retain some concessions in Latin America, the Foreign Office instructed all British diplomats in the area to support this latest Marconi plan. With proper negotiations, Steadman might yet salvage, with the new combination, some influence for British Marconi.[27]

Between Federal Telegraph's earlier marketing in South America and Boaz Long's efforts in Central America, the United States had effectively kept British Marconi from establishing high-power radio stations in Latin America by the autumn of 1917. Isaacs could not gather together the necessary investors outside of U.S. capital markets to finance an effective challenge. At the same time, the U.S. Navy's pressure on American Marconi had complicated the situation further for Isaacs. The net result was that Isaacs found himself left with the possibility of having British Marconi enter Latin America only through American Marconi. Yet all was not lost. With proper negotiations, it might be possible to contain the U.S. radio companies in the new subsidiary, retain control over the direction of this consortium, and obtain access to the latest radio patents held by Federal Telegraph. Meanwhile, the United States would be able to keep British Marconi at bay only if the country could offer up the elusive alternative that could meet the growing demand for service with Latin America.

For all of Boaz Long's efforts, diplomatic maneuvers would not keep determined German and British radio interests out of Latin America. The demand for improved hemispheric radio contact was too great. Since 1915 the official U.S. position had been to encourage governments to own their stations. If the local government did not have the ability, either the navy itself or U.S. companies would build, equip, maintain, or even operate stations for each country. Holding overall control, governments, rather than foreign radio companies, could then collectively decide the optimal use of the limited radio spectrum. Governments would also ensure that neutral stations across the hemisphere could not pose a danger to the United States. Despite Secretary Daniels's enthusiasm, Latin American governments had politely ignored his proposed Pan-American radio network of high-power stations. At the same time, the confusing variety of methods the navy encouraged—from outright U.S. control in Panama to private commercial operations in Uruguay or Costa Rica—made the official policy appear inconsistent. Despite these setbacks, Daniels retained his belief in total government control over all aspects of radio operations. The State Department, deferring to the U.S. Navy, maintained this official position as well.

After April 1917, U.S. Navy and State Department officials intensified their pursuit of U.S. radio influence in Central and South America. "The endeavors of any purely American company, as the Federal Company is believed to be," advised Secretary Daniels in April, "should be encouraged, in order that the needs of Venezuela be met before German and English companies can act in the matter." From Caracas and Bogotá, the U.S. ministers strenuously urged that U.S. firms bid on available contracts as soon as possible. Despite these opportunities and government encouragement, Federal Telegraph curiously failed to pursue them. Meanwhile, the repeated calls for government control finally won over some converts. Several South American countries formalized this control, at least in name only, although the degree and significance of these declarations varied from place to place. In Brazil, the country with the greatest progress in radio before the war, an executive decree of July 17 brought all radio stations under national authority. Foreign firms wishing to build a station for international work had to operate through a local subsidiary, and only three concessions would be available.[28] In Guatemala, the U.S. Navy supplied the necessary equipment for the government's Guatemala City station. Working with the Port Isabel naval radio station in Texas, the station provided continual radio contact with the United States.[29] Meanwhile, in Haiti the navy negotiated a concession to build and operate a radio station to communicate with the navy's station in Santo Domingo and with vessels in the surrounding waters.[30] Though more by public means than private, U.S. radio influence in the region had grown.

To fill in gaps in the existing naval network, the navy drafted Tropical Radio into wartime service. Having taken over the company's U.S. stations, the navy also quietly integrated the overseas stations as a secret auxiliary. Naval censors allowed United Fruit to handle commercial and private traffic through this network and back into the United States via the company's stations and ship-based sets.[31] At the same time, however, a naval officer took charge of handling all traffic at the Swan Island station in the Yucatán Channel, the main relay point between the United States and the stations in Central America and Colombia.[32] The senior operator at Bocas del Toro in Panama joined the U.S. Naval Reserve and received operating instructions from the naval communications officer of the Canal Zone. The reason for all this activity was that the State Department and the Office of Naval Intelligence used the system to transmit confidential information to and from Central and South America. Some of the traffic had to be relayed via the United Fruit Company ships, and the masters of those ships were permitted to handle the traffic themselves. "You might say," confided one naval radio officer, "that the United Fruit Company are practically Government agents in this matter." This arrangement made the Tropical Radio Company's network "practically an extension of the Naval communications service along the eastern shores of the Caribbean."[33]

Tropical Radio's prominent position along the Caribbean coast from Texas to Colombia made it an attractive proxy for extending U.S. radio influence. Boaz Long urged that Tropical Radio counterbid on the looming Marconi contract in El Salvador, with the aim that a Tropical Radio station would also drive the Telefunken station out of operation. Long interceded with the government of El Salvador to suspend the Marconi deal, pending Tropical Radio's offer. Then officials from the Latin American Division at the State Department and the Radio Division in the Bureau of Steam Engineering drafted a sample contract for Tropical Radio's representatives. Urging a federal subvention, Long recommended that the State Department advance $25,000 to Tropical to purchase the existing Telefunken station and start work on its own quickly. Starting construction quickly was important, he argued: "It will be instrumental in *promoting the interest of the United States* and will serve as a war measure necessary to destroy German propaganda, and bring wireless communications in Salvador into American hands." Long remained convinced that this project should be the first of many such federal projects.[34] Ambitious dreams and rich patrons cannot always bring success, however. Despite Long's efforts, Tropical Radio officials and the government of El Salvador were unable to reach an acceptable agreement. The company was not profitable, for its real purpose was to provide internal communications for the United Fruit Company. Losing between $50,000 and $80,000 on the overall radio venture, United Fruit could not easily afford the costs of buying a new station in El Salvador. The plan stalled. Through the winter of 1917, the German station at San Salvador continued to operate unhindered, much to the dismay of Long and others. Long mounted a fresh effort the following February, but despite Tropical Radio's willingness to build such a station, Long's pleas for funding met with an awkward silence. For all the interdepartmental discussion and the mounting evidence of Britain's and Germany's influence in the region, there was still no general policy toward radio that could shape a response. "Our deliberations . . . have run on from month to month," an exasperated Long finally complained to Herbert Stabler, head of the Division of Latin American Affairs. Concluding that it was "of the most vital importance" that the United States acquire the Telefunken station in El Salvador, thereby "destroying an easy means for German propaganda," Stabler recommended to Lansing the subvention to Tropical Radio.[35]

This proposal appealed to some in the navy. The Communications Division recommended to the chief of naval operations, Admiral Benson, that the plan go forward quickly. Breaking with the official line from Daniels, the division even suggested that relying on local governments to control radio might no longer be advisable at all. Government stations might still interfere with one another around the region, while hostile governments might let their stations be used for "secret/enemy use" or intentional jamming. Communications Division officers recognized that it was unlikely the United States government would obtain direct or overt control over the station in El Salvador or anywhere else in the region (as it had in Panama, Haiti, and the Dominican Republic). Instead, these officers suggested that the United States would have to rely upon private firms. They appear to have convinced Benson.[36]

Secretary Daniels signed off on Long's plan on March 11. The next day, Admiral Benson laid out the rationale for acting quickly. In his view, the policy of government construction and ownership was, in effect, dead. Under the circumstances, it was not likely that the United States would obtain direct control over any other country's radio stations. It was not likely that governments in the region could obtain the needed capital to build the stations themselves. If the U.S. companies did not meet this demand, then the British and German companies were already at work on meeting it. Because British Marconi and German Telefunken operated with the support of their governments, Britain or Germany would gain influence in the region through those stations. Benson believed that the current arrangement with Tropical Radio—the Long plan—provided a model for what might be possible elsewhere. Ultimately, the overall extension of these high-power stations would help the expansion of commerce and regional goodwill, "to say nothing of the fact that such stations [were] American agents and [were] the best channels in the world for American propaganda." It would take federal money to have Tropical Radio and other U.S. companies expand their networks to suit U.S. needs.[37]

Secretary Daniels, Frank Polk, and Admiral Benson then all urged President Wilson to approve the Long plan during the cabinet meeting on March 12, 1918. Wilson was not interested at all. He "would not be party to getting concessions for private companies," as Daniels recorded in his diary that night. Wilson particularly objected to the fact that United Fruit and its Tropical Radio subsidiary was not primarily in the business of commercial radio.[38] It was a repeat of the Tabasco station fiasco of three years before, when Captain Bullard attempted to have Tropical Radio secure a concession in Mexico, and the General Board rejected summarily it. The U.S. government would not pay to have private companies operate radio stations secretly for the United States.

Despite Wilson's rejection, Long and his supporters continued their efforts in hopes that the president might change his mind. Casting their gaze ambitiously, Long and naval radio officers believed that the most promising places for Tropical Radio were Honduras, Panama, Colombia, Brazil, Ecuador, Paraguay, and Venezuela. Long remained concerned about Central America. He believed action was immediately necessary in El Salvador and Honduras, where he had hints that Mexico intended to give to both of these countries another Telefunken radio station.[39]

Long appealed once again to Lansing on April 20. Long argued that it was essential to remove the Telefunken station from San Salvador: "It scatters unfavorable [German] propaganda which cannot be checked until the plant is done away with." The U.S. had failed to accomplish his original proposal for the "unification of wireless" into "sympathetic hands" in 1916 and 1917. By 1918 in South America alone the majority of stations in operation had been manufactured by Telefunken, with a few by Marconi. Only one was that of an American firm. In Central America the United States had a greater presence, but the Telefunken stations there were "annoying," and those operated by the Mexican government were "a menace to [U.S.] interests." Long repeated many of the usual arguments: High costs for constructing stations and the scarcity of well-trained local engineers were difficulties for government, difficulties that made the prospect of local ownership unlikely. Allowing European radio engineers into the region posed a threat to local neutrality. Hostile governments could knowingly allow their stations to be used against the United States. The disorganized development of radio in the hemisphere would lead to interference with stations the nation needed for its defense.

Long remained convinced that the most desirable plan was to support two companies, Tropical Radio and the new Pan-American firm, rather than nineteen separate nations. Representatives of these two companies, he believed, should meet with the State Department to divide up territory in the Western Hemisphere in the best interests of the United States. In Central America alone, Long argued that five more stations were necessary: one in Guatemala and one in each capital of El Salvador, Honduras, Nicaragua, and Costa Rica. Further delay would only hurt the United States. "The vast importance of radio to our future commercial development cannot safely be ignored, nor can we afford to delay . . . in the thought of giving effect to a Eutopian [*sic*] plan [of hemispheric government ownership]." Unless some greater power gave assistance to South American countries, they were not likely to develop the extensive radio network the United States hoped would emerge.[40]

Long drafted a final plea for Lansing to send to President Wilson. The revised plan was to give Tropical Radio an assurance of $25,000. Once that guarantee had been given, the company would spend $132,000 of its own money to build the San Salvador station. Long recommended the construction of more stations near the political centers of each Central American country. These proposed stations would "be secretly directed by the navy during the war." The newly organized Pan-American firm would then work with the navy to build more stations in South America and offset the existing Telefunken and Marconi ones. "Many years might be consumed in endeavoring to have the Latin American Governments co-laborate in this regard," Long wrote, "whereas a much shorter period should suffice to see the American wireless system an accomplished fact if the responsibility for accomplishing this end rested upon but two American radio companies working sympathetically for our Government."[41] Long's plan was unlike anything that the United States had carried out before. Whether the letter reached Wilson's desk is not known, but this second attempt also failed. Lansing told Long and Captain Todd that he would deliver the letter personally to Wilson. Before this occurred, Daniels himself interceded with Wilson in late April to stop the plan, to Long's deep, lasting regret. Daniels's motivation is not clear, but in any event this was the final step. Long's plan was now dead. However urgent the situation appeared, the United States would not solve the problems of its strategic communications by directly subsidizing private companies the way that Britain and Germany had done in other places.[42]

Not everyone in the U.S. Navy agreed that the hemispheric radio problems were best solved by government ownership or secret subsidies. As head of the Radio Division of the Bureau of Steam Engineering, Commander Hooper had continued to think about the growing differences between high-power international and coastal ship-to-shore radio operations. While preparing for testimony before Congress on the government radio bill in January 1917, he had concluded that there should in fact be two separate policies. By that summer, Hooper had committed to this position entirely. He believed that coastal stations should all come under the navy's control but that high-power stations should remain in the hands of private, entirely American-owned companies. Hooper benefited from the support and protection of his superior, Rear Admiral Robert Griffin, head of the Bureau of Steam Engineering, while beginning to act on this heretical conclusion.[43]

The arch of Hooper's argument rested on two pillars. First, he firmly believed that only private commercial operation of the high-power stations would provide the best competition against the cables. This arrangement would force both cable and radio companies to lower the cost and maximize the services available, to the overall benefit of the country. The second argument arose from the first. Competitive high-power radio would drive the cable and radio companies to research, develop, and manufacture the latest equipment. As a byproduct, the navy would be able to draw upon the very latest radio technology. In the past, Hooper believed, government direction of research, hampered by fluctuating annual budgets, had proven ineffectual. Government direction could not be trusted to provide the most up-to-date advances in radio technology that a modern navy continually required. Only the private sector could do this. Commercially motivated, the radio companies would ensure that the United States never fell behind another country in the development of radio technology.

Committing to private control of high-power international radio would also end the ambiguity that had plagued radio policy since 1914. Hooper laid out this argument to Captain Todd, the director of naval communications, in the summer of 1917. If the navy publicly backed away from the pursuit of postwar government ownership over high-power stations, then the radio companies could woo investors to finance the extension of American-controlled radio stations in Central and South America. There would be no danger that the navy would expropriate the companion stations in the United States. Unless the navy clarified this point, Hooper warned, U.S. firms would never expand into the region, and European firms would continue to take advantage of U.S. inactivity. Consequently, there was a great need of pursuing, as he put it, "the Monroe Doctrine as regards high-power radio stations." Without such progress, he concluded, "[The present situation] bid fair to have no results and to become a noose around our necks." Concerned that any compromise could jeopardize legislation to grant government control of radio to the navy, Todd would not back Hooper's proposal.[44]

Hooper did not require Todd's approval or support, however. By controlling the navy's purchase of radio equipment, Hooper held sway over the industry. He used this power during the war to advance his bifurcated radio policy, in spite of the fact that it was at odds with the official line from the secretary's office. To drive commercial firms out of ship-shore work, over which the Marconi interests held the greatest influence, Hooper worked out a deal with the U.S. Shipping Board. This body had been formed in early 1917 to expand the U.S. merchant fleet and operate the existing tonnage brought under government control. At Hooper's request, the Shipping Board agreed to lease and then buy outright from the navy all radio sets required aboard its ships. The navy would supply, maintain, and operate the radio sets. By doing this, Hooper at last pulled the U.S. merchant fleet into line with the U.S. Navy's technical and operational requirements. Even if Congress did not grant ship-shore radio control to the navy, at the least the shore station companies like American Marconi would now have to adopt the latest technology or risk being unable to communicate with any U.S.-flagged vessel. So successful was this strategy that when Hooper returned from sea duty in August 1918, he could open negotiations with American Marconi for the navy to acquire the company's forty-five coastal radio stations as well as the 330 ship-board sets they maintained.[45] It's a critical point, however, that Hooper was interested not in destroying American Marconi but in transforming it into a key manufacturing and research firm to support the navy's continued involvement in radio.

Navy control over radio in the United States shaped the evolution of the industry. From small radio sets to high-power stations to the developing field of radiotelephony and cutting-edge innovations in vacuum tubes, the U.S. Navy's centralized control over research, purchasing, and operations led to a standardization of equipment and expansion of production that was significant and had far-reaching effects after the war. The expansion of wartime demand required the army and navy to cooperate in allocating scarce production capabilities of radio-related equipment. Hooper and General George Squier, the army's chief signal officer, agreed to divide between them the output of U.S. radio equipment manufacturers. AT&T's Western Electric division and General Electric produced equipment mostly for the army, while American Marconi and other existing radio companies devoted their efforts to the navy. Hooper informed the companies that there would be at least two manufacturers for important components and that prices would be fixed in advance.[46]

Though its commercial ship-shore work antagonized the navy, American Marconi's wartime value as an experienced radio firm could not be overlooked. In fact, about 40 percent of the navy's equipment eventually came from the large American Marconi factory at Aldene, New Jersey. By 1914 this factory had been turning out from five to fifty transmitters per year and was the only real radio plant in the country. Hooper had gradually accepted American Marconi, even though he retained his deep suspicions of its British parent. In mid-1916, as the navy checked Nally's efforts to expand into South America, Hooper had met with Nally and stressed to him the importance of building up firms that the U.S. government could rely upon in an emergency. Lacking commercial work and being discouraged about the situation, American Marconi had nearly sold its manufacturing wing to General Electric but decided dependence upon another firm for core equipment would be unwise. Instead, very likely with Hooper's encouragement, Nally doubled the workforce, added new manufacturing equipment, built two additions to the Aldene factory and planned a third. In the process, American Marconi tripled its output of radio production. Starting in April 1916, American Marconi assisted with radio equipment installation aboard naval warships. During the war, Hooper allowed American Marconi an extra 10 percent markup on the equipment it sold to the navy, to cover the costs of this expansion at Aldene. Besides its importance as a manufacturer, American Marconi also had valuable patents that were essential for the operation of high-power long-distance radio stations. Although Hooper would not trust the company because of its ambiguous ties to its British parent, American Marconi's patents and expertise could be a valuable contribution to the sort of international commercial radio firm that Hooper so desperately sought and that Federal Telegraph had failed to become.[47]

Having started to force the commercial companies out of the coastal radio market, Hooper then schemed to create a long-distance commercial firm. Federal Telegraph, the manufacturer of the all-important arc transmitters, may have originally been Hooper's chosen instrument, but two issues had arisen. First, Hooper had lost faith in the company. To E. J. Nally he confided that he was not happy with the company and that its general manager, Howard P. Veeder, had not been entirely forthcoming with him. Among other things, Hooper had been surprised to learn that the Australian government had asked Federal Telegraph to bid on two 1,000 kw arcs for a proposed high-power station—a fact the company had not informed him about in advance. The second issue was that under the patent situation in the United States, no single radio company could own and operate the most-advanced high-power radio station alone. The navy's Otter Cliffs radio receiving station, for example, alone utilized fifty-two patents controlled by eleven different holders. Whoever aspired to operate such stations commercially would have to negotiate through a complex web of patent restrictions.[48]

Overcoming the patent situation commercially was going to be problematic. For the U.S. Navy, however, patents were not an obstacle. Between 1915 and 1918, manufacturers of radio equipment had protection from patent infringement lawsuits while producing under government contract. This allowed the various participants to experiment with each others' proprietary information and led to better equipment for the navy's needs.[49] The construction and operation of a commercial high-power international radio station, however, would require extensive collaboration and delicate negotiations between the leading radio firms. Federal Telegraph had the concessions for high-power stations in Latin America and had planned a circuit from Buenos Aires to New Haven, Connecticut. A lack of funding, however, had stopped any work for over three years. American Marconi had important patents for receiving and antennae equipment, as well as access to financing as an established manufacturer, but the navy had blocked it from entering the international radio market. Under Daniels's continued threats of nationalization, this field had reached an impasse. In the summer of 1917, Hooper then nudged American Marconi and Federal Telegraph into negotiations to resolve the patent and funding issues. He hoped that they would form a combination to deliver the international high-power radio company that he believed could keep the European firms out of Latin America.[50]

Hooper impressed upon Edward Nally his beliefs about postwar high-power radio, the need for a wholly American company to operate in this field, and the place of American Marconi in this vision. The two met several times in Washington over the summer of 1917 to discuss the company's efforts for the navy. Hooper made it clear that he wanted to apply the Monroe Doctrine to the field of radio, in order to keep foreign firms out of Central and South America. The U.S. firm that he wanted to handle international radio traffic with the region would have to have entirely American financing. American Marconi, bearing the stigma of its British parent, could not immediately fill this role. For American Marconi to remain in existence as an operating company, it would have to move into long-distance work. This entailed shedding the company's traditional coastal radio network and driving out the British Marconi investment. Only then would the U.S. government (through the navy and thus through Hooper) support its efforts to win overseas concessions. "It is drastic to a degree," Nally advised Sir Godfrey Isaacs in London, "but from my experience of the past four years and my frequent talks with the different Government officials I feel sure that they consider this the sinequanon [*sic*] for commercial operating companies." At the same time, Isaacs was pleading with the British government for assistance to underwrite British Marconi's efforts in Latin America. "Now that you have the facts [about Hooper and the government's attitude toward American Marconi]," Nally grimly concluded to Isaacs in August, "you are in a position to decide."[51]

Thus Hooper and his supporters were anxious to have American Marconi and Federal Telegraph come together to reach some form of agreement that would allow the United States to extend commercial radio stations throughout Latin America as quickly as possible. This would serve the deeper security and technical concerns of the navy about shaping the spread of radio throughout the Western Hemisphere. It would allow a U.S. company to meet the regional demand for high-power radio that had already attracted British Marconi and Telefunken. It would bring the leading radio patents together into the hands of a firm that could make optimal use of them. Also, the deal would enable American Marconi to remain solvent as a major manufacturer at a time when Hooper was working to take its principal business, commercial ship-to-shore radio, away from it.

Federal Telegraph had its own reasons for opening negotiations with

American Marconi, besides any encouragement from Hooper. There actually were, administratively, two Federal Telegraph companies. The first was the Federal Telegraph Company of Palo Alto, California, the firm that manufactured the arc transmitters and operated commercial radio stations along the West Coast. The second was Federal Holdings Inc., based in New York. Either a subsidiary or a partner company, it had many of the same investors as Federal Telegraph. Its purpose was to acquire the concessions in South America, raise financing in New York, and operate the new stations overseas. The Federal Telegraph Company licensed out the rights to use its equipment and patents to Federal Holdings.

By 1917, however, a problem had developed for the two companies. Federal Telegraph had promised Federal Holdings that it had the full rights to all transmitting and receiving equipment used in the combined radio system it sold. This was not the case. Federal Telegraph had incorporated the Fleming valve, the forerunner to the vacuum tube, into the receivers for signal amplification. This made the company liable to American Marconi, the holder of the U.S. rights to the British invention, for patent infringement. Without clear command of the patents, Federal Telegraph could not guarantee Federal Holdings' investors that the proposed high-power stations would be free of complications if constructed. When William D. Loucks, the attorney for the investors, threatened to sue Federal Telegraph officials for breach of contract, the Federal Telegraph officials came to New York in July to see if some arrangement could be made with American Marconi.

On July 24, 1917, John W. Griggs, American Marconi's president, met with Loucks. The two discussed the possibility of an arrangement between Marconi and the Federal companies for the combined construction and operation of high-power long-distance stations. Loucks made it clear that he represented a collection of investors who were prepared to advance $800,000 for the two stations in Argentina and the United States. Significantly, Loucks informed Griggs that because of the threat of litigation over Federal Telegraph's use of the Fleming valve, Griggs had the California company in a position to do just about whatever he told them to do. Consequently, there would be no obstacles to any agreement between Federal Holdings and American Marconi. Griggs, noncommittal during the meeting, promised only to bring up the matter with his company and with British Marconi. Thereafter the negotiations continued through August into September.⁵² If Hooper had wanted to dictate to American Marconi the terms of its participation in a combination with Federal Telegraph for international radio, Loucks's offer had undercut this. Hooper's own assignment to sea command of the USS *Fairfax* removed him from direct involvement with the negotiations at a critical period. The initiative then passed from the navy to Federal Holdings and British Marconi.

In September the talks in New York expanded. Sydney Steadman of British Marconi joined Nally and Federal Holdings' Loucks at the table, though Steadman was no longer to preside over the British company's capitulation. The initial discussions had concerned only American Marconi and Federal Holdings, not British Marconi, but Nally had kept Isaacs informed of their progress. Steadman understood the importance of Federal Telegraph's arcs to the U.S. government and the strong desire U.S. officials had for a station at Buenos Aires. At the same time, Steadman also recognized that Federal Telegraph needed to use vacuum tubes in its receiving equipment, especially at long-distance stations. The company's own developments in this area were still not as good as the Marconi-controlled Fleming valve. To exploit its concessions in Latin America, Federal Telegraph would need to incorporate the rights to the Fleming valve into the entire radio station equipment package. If the right terms could be found, the Marconi companies would permit this, which in turn would allow the two Federal companies at last to seize a strong position in international radio.⁵³

Steadman and British Marconi then played a complicated game in hopes of containing both the Federal companies and the United States. The trick was to lure Federal Telegraph in with the promise of the Fleming valve patent rights. In exchange, British Marconi would extract from it the rights to the Fuller improvements to the Poulsen arc, which made possible the magnificent high-power transmitters used in the navy's network. A British Marconi subsidiary, the British and Overseas Engineering Syndicate Ltd., already had worldwide rights to the Poulsen arc. These Fuller improvements would allow British Marconi to have the latest high-power transmitter at its disposal for incorporation into its own planned global radio network. Suitably equipped with patents for both sides of the operation, British Marconi could edge out Federal Telegraph in Latin America and any other challengers elsewhere in the world.⁵⁴

The delicate negotiations that followed traversed the confusing realm of business cross-licenses and patent restrictions, where the language was arcane but the implications tremendous. At one point, for example, British Marconi maneuvered to force Federal Telegraph into acknowledging that its original license from the Danish owners of the Poulsen patent prevented the company from exchanging traffic with arc stations outside the United States. Marconi's ploy was meant to force Federal Telegraph to exit the operations business and give up its concessions in Latin America in favor of a partnership with British Marconi, which did not have the restriction. Not to be outflanked, Federal Holdings officials quietly slipped into Denmark and secured a waiver to cover this problem for $100,000, before British Marconi discovered what they were doing.[55] Isaacs and Steadman played a close game in trying to preserve the Marconi position. Surrendering some control of international radio in the United States to a new firm would be an acceptable price to pay, if British Marconi could ensure that it could get the Fuller improvements for use worldwide.

Steadman and the others eventually worked out a deal that would create a new company as a joint venture among the three companies. Federal Telegraph would assign rights to the new firm to use the Poulsen arc and the Fuller improvements with concessions in Latin America, especially Argentina. At the same time, the two Marconi companies would grant to the joint venture all their patent rights and concessions in the Americas except Canada. Federal Telegraph would receive $50,000 in stock, while the two Marconi companies would receive $75,000 in stock. In exchange, Federal Telegraph would receive $100,000 in cash from each of its partners.[56] Neither Marconi nor Federal Telegraph would win the other's patents outright, but the new company would be able to exploit the Latin American concession with use of all the patents necessary. The key issue would then be control of the new company.

Because of the far-reaching implications of this deal with Marconi, Federal Telegraph officials kept the U.S. Navy (but not Hooper) closely informed about the negotiations. Charles W. Waller and H. P. Veeder of Federal Telegraph met with Captain Todd in person on October 7 to brief him on events. They confirmed that Federal Telegraph and American Marconi would be forming a new joint company to exploit the South American concessions. Waller made it clear, however, that the company was to be entirely under American control. Once the new company was in place, he explained, the next step would be to arrange a consolidation of Federal Holdings, which held the concessions, and American Marconi "in such a way that the British Marconi interests would be eliminated, and the patent situation cleared up." When Todd told them that the navy still officially favored the eventual government operation of radio stations in the United States, Waller and Veeder reassured Todd that they understood this.

There was more to the proposed deal, however, than was immediately apparent to all involved. At the conclusion of this meeting, Veeder left, but Waller stayed behind. Waller then confided to Todd that Veeder was not entirely aware of Federal Telegraph's real direction after the negotiations were complete. The company, he revealed, was to have a new president, Washington Dodge, who would come to the Navy Department shortly to meet with Todd personally. Being indirect without being too vague, Waller intimated to Todd that Federal Telegraph would then undergo a reorganization. As part of this, Federal Telegraph would like to sell all of its existing stations to the navy and become strictly a manufacturing firm. To be closer to the navy and financial investors, the company would open a plant on the East Coast. In effect, this deal would allow the new owners to divest themselves of overseas concessions and any ties to the operating half of the business, without arousing the navy's opposition. The new management understood that the navy desired to purchase the stations as part of the push for government control over operations. The only likely buyers of the Latin American concessions, however, were the Marconi companies, and there was zero chance that the U.S. Navy would allow such a sale to go through. The joint venture would allow Federal Holdings and Federal Telegraph to pass off the overseas concessions to the Marconi companies, who appreciated their value, while obtaining access to the elusive Fleming valve rights for sales and manufacturing. Commander Todd appreciated the positive implications of the deal. As he informed Admiral Bullard, "a combination of arc sending and Marconi patents on receiving would be a strong one." Yet it was not entirely clear to what extent the consolidation into a Pan-American company would subsume American Marconi into Federal Telegraph or how "American" the new company might really be.[57]

Pan-American Wireless Telegraph and Telephone Company came

into existence on October 15. A core requirement in the company's articles of incorporation was the firm's "American" character. Nothing the company owned or acquired—property, contracts, or more than three-eighths of the company's stock—could pass to non-Americans or companies not under American control. Indeed, so firm was this rule that proof of citizenship would be required by both parties for an exchange or a transfer of any stock. On the same day, Charles Waller arranged the swap of stocks among Marconi Wireless of America, Marconi Wireless Telegraph Company of Britain, and Federal Telegraph to complete the deal. Each of the Marconi companies received three-eighths of the general voting stock. The final quarter went to Federal Telegraph.[58] In return, Pan-American Wireless received the exclusive right to use, and limited right to manufacture, equipment and patents of the three companies for communication between the United States and countries south of the United States. All of the directors and officers of the company were to be American citizens. Edward J. Nally, president of American Marconi, also became the president of Pan-American Wireless.[59]

On its face, the Pan-American Wireless arrangement appeared to be the best outcome for the companies as well as for the United States. For Nally and American Marconi, it would eliminate opposition to ventures in South America. American Marconi's Western Hemisphere operations would be in the hands of a partly owned subsidiary that was to be, from its inception, American-controlled. For the Federal companies' senior officials, it provided a way to off-load the concessions in Latin America as well as the stations under the navy's wartime control. These transfers would allow the company to concentrate on the more profitable manufacturing business. Yet British Marconi had not been driven out of the United States or the Americas entirely. Some government officials, however, were not entirely reassured. The directors of the company might well be American citizens, State Department lawyers pointed out, but there was no requirement that a controlling interest of voting stock be in American hands.[60] Despite these concerns, though, it appeared that the American child had finally agreed to rein in its British parent.[61]

Ten days later, State Department and U.S. Navy officials granted their blessing after scrutinizing the plan. Herbert Stabler, chief of the Latin American Division at the State Department, warned the companies that the official policy of the government remained the pursuit of total control over radio operations both in the United States and throughout the Western Hemisphere. Official support of the Pan-American Wireless deal by the Wilson administration would not count as a reversal of this policy. Stabler, chief of naval operations Admiral Benson, Assistant Secretary Franklin Roosevelt, and State Department counselor Frank Polk met shortly after this meeting and gave their tentative approval to the deal, provided that there would be proof that American citizens would be in charge of Pan-American Wireless, that no more than three-eighths of the stock, all nonvoting shares, would be in British hands, and that there would be mechanisms to ensure that the company would remain under U.S. control. Steadman, for British Marconi, promised as much in late October. Secretary of State Lansing, warning once more that the official policy remained government control, then accepted Steadman's assurances and granted official blessing to the company.[62]

It now appeared that the Wilson administration would sign off entirely on the project. The offspring of Federal Telegraph's experience and technical improvements and American Marconi's patents and sources of funding would be a powerful new company at the very edge of radio development. Pan-American Wireless would be what the State and Navy departments had looked for initially in Federal Telegraph: It would be of American character and under U.S. control, and the company would be technologically capable of using the most up-to-date equipment. It would be capable of integrating entirely with the navy's radio network. It would have the strength to extend its influence into Latin America or even Europe and Asia. Both Federal Telegraph and American Marconi would remain afloat as strong manufacturing companies able to meet the navy's continuing demand for the latest radio equipment. In the peace to come, the administration thought this new company would be able to meet the commercial, political, and military needs for improved communications abroad by the United States while bypassing British control over international radio. In the view of many, there was much cause for optimism.

Yet when pressed for his blessing of a deal that had originated in the navy, Secretary Daniels balked. He informed the Department of State at the end of November that the navy's official desire remained nationalization: "[The navy] does not desire, directly or indirectly, to change its position . . . or to approve any plan which is in substance a deviation from the principle of Government ownership." He then called for a renewal of the diplomatic effort to persuade other governments in the Americas to adopt this policy.[63] The State Department, the chief of naval operations, and the head of the navy's communications service had all backed the Pan-American Wireless collaboration as an acceptable short-term alternative to the eventual goal of nationalizing radio operations. In the year to come, Secretary Daniels would continue to challenge the company supporters to protect his cherished dream of total government control over radio.

Although Daniels opposed Pan-America Wireless from the top, Nally now received continued encouragement from below. Through the winter of 1917–1918, Pan-American developed a plan to exploit the concessions in Argentina and to open up radio communication as quickly as possible. Nally came to Washington at the end of January to confer with naval radio officers Commander H. P. LeClair and Commander George C. Sweet about Pan-American Wireless's plans and to seek once again the navy's elusive blessing. LeClair was the head of the Radio Division in the Bureau of Steam Engineering during Hooper's absence at sea. Sweet was a retired officer with much experience in radio engineering, which he brought back during the war to oversee construction of the high-power radio stations. Nally intended to coordinate the technical and operational details of the high-power stations with Sweet and LeClair, to bring the company in "closest possible harmony with the wishes and aims of the Government." Nally also pledged the American character and patriotism of Pan-American Wireless in new letters to Daniels.

Without a firm statement of support from Secretary Daniels, Nally could not reassure potential investors that the U.S. government would not arbitrarily appropriate the U.S. station. This put Nally into the same paradox the Federal companies confronted: he had to await a statement from Daniels, a statement that the secretary was opposed to making, before Nally could raise the funds. But Nally received assurances, perhaps improperly given, that he could count on eventual support. After his third letter to Commander Sweet, Nally learned that "the matter was now clear to Secretary Daniels and that there was no obstacle in the way of [Pan-American Wireless's] plans." (This was approximately the time that Boaz Long had been pushing his own plan for surreptitious funding, which Daniels had initially supported). Reassured at last, Nally then set sail for Argentina in April to renew the concession, purchase the necessary land, and follow up favorable leads for other stations in Peru, Chile, Uruguay, and Brazil. He remained in South America through July.[64]

While Nally was away, however, any hope of navy support for Pan-American Wireless evaporated. "Upon my return from Argentina," he explained to the House of Representatives later that year, "I was informed that our Government had undergone a change of heart, that the Pan American Wireless program was in disfavor."[65] The United States Navy had bought out Federal Telegraph in order to block its sale to American Marconi and to ensure that its assets did not end up in the hands of Marconi interests. In the process, Secretary Daniels personally gained the ability to veto any chance that Pan-American Wireless could construct a high-power station in the United States; thus Daniels effectively stopped Nally once again.

In the spring of 1918, Federal Telegraph officials had formally notified the U.S. Navy of their intention to streamline the company. To focus on manufacturing, C. W. Waller and Washington Dodge, the new company president, had prepared plans to sell off the company's stations in several western cities, along the Pacific coast, and in Hawaii. Also up for sale were the operating rights to Federal Telegraph's important patents, such as the Fuller improvements to the arc transmitter. Waller had explained this plan to Captain Todd in the fall. Now that Pan-American Wireless had taken the overseas concessions, it was time for the next phase of divestiture. In light of the navy's steady interest in the arc transmitter and of several lucrative wartime contracts the company acquired to build very-high-power transmitters, it appeared to Federal Telegraph officials that manufacturing would be the best route for the company to follow. Understanding that this move would both protect Federal Telegraph's radio-manufacturing capabilities and eliminate another commercial firm from the domestic radio market, Commander LeClair and Captain Todd paid close attention to the deal.[66]

The deal began on April 5. Waller wrote to Rear Admiral Griffin, head of the Bureau of Steam Engineering, to inform him that Federal Telegraph had prepared an important agreement with American Marconi. In it, Federal Telegraph would sell American Marconi the right to use in the United States the arc patents and Fuller improvements.[67] Such a move would reduce Federal Telegraph's involvement in the Pan-American Wireless venture, giving control over to the Marconi interests. American Marconi would then gain the right to use the arc transmitters on U.S. soil. It, rather than Federal Telegraph, would be the company granting that right to Pan-American Wireless for Latin American radio operations. American Marconi could also transfer those rights to its British parent. Even if transmitter technology changed and new firms emerged with new patents on better equipment, the situation here and now created by the deal would allow Marconi to gain a firm position that any subsequent competitor would find hard to challenge. The U.S. Navy could not accept this situation. If Federal Telegraph were selling out, then the navy would have to prevent American Marconi from acquiring control of the arc rights, the Fuller improvements, and Pan-American Wireless.[68]

Having warned the navy of this imminent development, Waller sent another letter several days later, giving the navy its chance. This letter contained a draft agreement whereby the U.S. government would get the patent rights instead of American Marconi. Waller's motivations—patriotism or profit—are not clear. To the navy, however, the offer seemed too good to pass up. "If we get these rights," one of Hooper's former assistants wrote to him at sea, "it will certainly put us in a very strong position." Six days later, an impatient Waller wrote again to emphasize the need to come to an agreement as quickly as possible. He was himself holding up the negotiations with American Marconi at the personal request of Federal Telegraph president Washington Dodge. Now Dodge was pressing Waller for an answer. Waller offered the navy the curiously low price of only $1.64 million. This made the patent rights and all of the company's stations and equipment a particularly tempting bargain. The letter was a high-pressure sales pitch, with stresses on the cheap price, the company's great need for income to cover debts, and the short deadline. Still, the offer was a remarkably good one. It would give the navy control over the Fuller improvements, keeping the best arc technology in U.S. government hands, and be a major step toward government control over radio operations.[69]

Despite Waller's pressure and with Secretary Daniels away, Assistant Secretary Roosevelt would not be rushed. He informed Waller that although the Department of the Navy approved the offer, the navy first had to wait for Congress to decide on the larger matter of postwar government control of radio. Why Roosevelt stalled the deal is not completely clear, but we can speculate that Roosevelt sided with Hooper's faction in opposition to government control of high-power international radio. He urged Waller and Dodge to continue delaying the negotiations with American Marconi. How naval officials ultimately decided to accept the offer is not clear, but on May 15 the navy's representatives signed the contract and gained control over all eight Federal Telegraph stations and the patents. Federal Telegraph still retained the manufacturing rights to make equipment from these patents, but with the restriction that the secretary of the navy's permission was necessary for making or selling arc transmitters for use in the United States.[70]

This purchase of Federal Telegraph's assets accomplished several things. First, it meant that the navy acquired title to many of the stations that it had already taken over during the war. This removed one more practical barrier to total government control over radio operations in the United States. At the same time, by blocking the sale to American Marconi, the navy prevented the Marconi companies from gaining direct control over the Fuller improvements to the arc transmitter. This indirect control, though not stopping American Marconi from obtaining continuous wave technology, would make it possible for the navy to delay construction of the most advanced high-power network until other U.S. firms had a chance to enter the market too.[71]

The navy was not the only party to gain from the deal, however. It emerged several months later that some of the new members of the board of Federal Telegraph had secured kickbacks on the deal. An intermediary firm, the Valencia Improvement Company, had served as go-between. Although the navy paid to Valencia $1.64 million in Liberty Bonds for the stations and patents, only $1 million passed into Federal Telegraph's bank account. Behind Valencia were Waller, Dodge, Loucks, and several others, a fact concealed from the rest of Federal Telegraph's board of directors and investors. A minor scandal ensued, with Dodge and the rest behind the deal being ejected from the company. The navy's officers, who had acted in good faith on a legitimate deal, remained above the scandal. The deal remained in place.[72]

The evisceration of Federal Telegraph was a major blow for Pan-American Wireless. Nally discovered what had happened only when he returned from South America. The previous ambiguities about navy support or opposition to Pan-American Wireless were now gone. Some of his friends in the Navy Department tried to reassure him that the program was still viable. Others warned him that Daniels remained as firmly opposed to Pan-American Wireless as ever. Daniels, through his control over the Fuller patents, could stop Pan-American Wireless from building its stations in the United States. Nally went to Washington to meet with Daniels, who "positively stated he would not favor" a station built by Pan-American Wireless in the United States. Daniels also denied having ever given his approval of the plan. Nally failed to convince Daniels that private firms could handle international commercial radio better than the U.S. government could. Daniels was willing to see Pan-American Wireless open its station in Argentina, but no stations in the United States. To this, Nally pointed out that unless Pan-American Wireless could be sure of the U.S. anchor, the Argentina station could not be built. Nally later learned from Captain Todd about the proposed superstation at Monroe, North Carolina, and the plan to use this station for postwar communications with South America.

The navy and Pan-American Wireless were at an impasse. Waller pressed the State Department to see if Daniels could be brought around, but there seemed little chance of this. To Frank Polk Herbert Stabler complained "I wish to go on record as believing that the United States has lost an opportunity to get good wireless stations in the Argentine." Polk believed that other countries would soon control the hemispheric radio situation. "In the meantime," Nally complained to the House of Representatives in December 1918, "we are prevented from going ahead with the necessary work at Argentina to enable us to comply with the requirements of that Government's concession, and we have stopped all work on contracts or apparatus, and likewise have called in our representatives [to Latin America]." He concluded, "Really, the greatest loss to private companies is from the uncertainty of the situation. Private enterprise may be trusted not to spend its money recklessly but how is it possible to finance large undertakings when the Government throws its wet blanket of ownership over wireless enterprise." After five years of opposition, Nally's exasperation was deep.[73]

What are we to make of this apparent failure of Pan-American Wireless? On one level, Daniels's and Todd's steadfast devotion to government ownership had checked Hooper's quest for a powerful, U.S.-controlled international radio company. Hooper understood that any commercial operation would require the complicated integration of patents that no single company controlled. Any deal to assemble this commercial operation would have to have government oversight to protect national security interests because of the stakes. Daniels's continued refusal to accede to this path, in the view of Hooper and his supporters, meant costly, possibly dangerous delays in the spread of U.S. influence over radio in the hemisphere.

On another level, the opposition to Pan-American Wireless was an unintentionally wise move for the U.S. Navy. On its face the tripartite deal appeared acceptable, with its restrictions on ownership, but underneath the surface lay cracks. British Marconi was unwilling to abandon its interests in Latin America that easily, and some of the Federal Telegraph officials cared more for personal profit than the national interest. The rock-solid devotion of Daniels, Todd, and others to the idea of government ownership, and the purchase of Federal Telegraph's patents, therefore had the consequence of stopping British Marconi from acquiring a predominant position in Pan-American Wireless and thus in hemispheric radio.

In choosing the principle of government ownership, Daniels, Todd, and their supporters had traded the short-term likelihood that Pan-American Wireless could grasp a strong position in Latin America for the medium-term hope of government ownership and the long-term dream of hemispheric control over radio operations and research. The purchase of Federal Telegraph's patent rights and stations did have the effect of keeping the Fuller improvements to the arc transmitter from British Marconi. In fact, the U.S. Navy now had direct veto power over the manufacture and sale of Federal Telegraph's arcs. This meant that the United States could choose who built the most-advanced radio stations in the Western Hemisphere. The problem was that Congress and the general public were less interested than Daniels in the radical step of government ownership and would therefore not permit such a plan. The result of this conflicted policy was further delay in the expansion abroad of any U.S. commercial radio network that would be designed around the international economic and political needs of the country.

At the same time, the navy's interest in restricting access to the Fuller improvements appears to have been more about safeguarding the

Western Hemisphere than keeping the United States ahead of other powers in radio technology. We should recall that before the United States entered the war, Hooper and other radio officers had been anxious to see U.S. merchant shipping and coastal radio stations adopt the latest radio technology, in order to ensure the interoperability of commercial and military vessels and coastal stations at all times. As the navy's interests in radio communications expanded from the short range to the intercontinental, so too did this desire to see the widespread adoption of the latest radio technology by other powers. If for no other reason, the United States needed to be certain that it could communicate with its forces and allies abroad by radio if the cables fell silent. Compatibility was a matter of national security. The navy's construction in France of Station Lafayette, with its massive arc transmitters, was the foremost example of this policy. As more arc transmitters came online across the world, they would help to push out the older, outdated spark transmitters. This would free up space on the increasingly crowded long-wave end of the spectrum used for long-distance communications. If done in a coordinated fashion, guided by the United States, this adoption of arc technology would make it possible to expand the wartime radio network into a global system of radio stations all using the latest, most efficient technology available. There is some reason to believe that, in the final months of the war, some U.S. naval radio officers began to push this idea and that the Fuller improvements denied to Marconi for Latin America might be freely given for other locations.

In late July 1918, Commander George Sweet, who had recently completed construction of the Annapolis station and was on his way to France to head up the work on Station Lafayette, passed through London. On the last day in July, he met there with Sir Godfrey Isaacs and Sydney Steadman. We do not know what was discussed at the meeting, but the following day Isaacs wrote to Sweet, offering to build the high-power arc stations "world wide" that the U.S. was apparently "desirous of seeing erected." To do this, British Marconi and its subsidiaries would need to secure permission from the governments of Britain, the United States, and France to operate stations in those countries. Also, these three countries would have to lend diplomatic support to Marconi's application for new stations in foreign territories. An agreement between the United States and British Marconi would lay out the number of stations, their locations, equipment, and specified division of revenue. Isaacs made it clear that he knew the navy preferred that such stations use the arc transmitters equipped with the Fuller improvements, the very latest in arc technology, and that his company was willing to use this. However, Federal Telegraph had not provided to British Marconi the Fuller improvements, even though its subsidiary, which held the patent rights to the arc in Britain, claimed a right to them. Necessarily, then, British Marconi would need to acquire the rights to use the improvements everywhere except the United States and Latin America. If the U.S., British, and French governments came to an agreement on a worldwide radio network with arc transmitters, British Marconi and its subsidiaries in the United States and France would be prepared to purchase the Fuller rights from the U.S. Navy.[74]

For all this ambition and complexity, the chronicler of Sweet's strange story is left with a puzzle as to its true purpose. From Washington, Hooper counseled Sweet that it would be unwise to sell the Fuller improvements to British Marconi if the British government might be induced to purchase them instead. Hooper's conversations with various British officials had convinced him that the Royal Navy had little love for the company. Hooper relented his opposition several weeks later, when he learned that British Marconi already held the patent rights to the arc in Britain. This meant that the company could produce these transmitters, if not the most-advanced ones. At any rate, Hooper's reservations indicate that Sweet's plan was not universally accepted within the navy, and quite possibly it was entirely unauthorized. Indeed, this same question occurred to the British government. In early November, the British Embassy in Washington inquired whether Sweet was in fact acting formally as an agent of the United States in negotiations with British Marconi and the government on a worldwide radio plan. The State Department's position was that Sweet was acting alone.[75]

Why would Sweet have entertained the idea of granting this technological advance to British Marconi when he himself had played a role in acquiring these patents from Federal Telegraph to keep them from this same company only a few months earlier? The most plausible explanation is the navy's continued interest in standardizing global radio operations around the continuous wave transmitter, epitomized by the arc rather than the spark. The major powers in Europe had all shifted over to the arc by this time. Allowing British Marconi to build the most powerful arcs would ensure their employment throughout the globe. U.S. firms, as Sweet would have known, did not yet have the commercial reach beyond the Western Hemisphere. But because of the potential interference from high-power stations using outdated technology in Asia and Africa, and the apparent dream of a worldwide network of stations all capable of intercommunications, Sweet must have believed that the U.S. Navy had need of a way to influence the future development of these stations, even if U.S. companies could not be the ones to sell the crucial equipment. Aware of the profit to be won from such sales, Isaacs would have been perfectly willing for British Marconi to serve as the proxy in this arrangement. Nothing came of Sweet's plans in the end. But that he envisioned such an empire by standards rather than by companies and made tentative steps to create it illustrates the growing interest among naval officers in applying the lessons of the war and the potential of this new technology.

As the guns fell silent at the end of the war in November 1918, the United States Navy operated the world's most powerful and expansive radio network. High-power stations in Puerto Rico and Panama and smaller ship-shore stations in Cuba, Haiti, and the Dominican Republic provided continual contact between the United States and its ships from the Central Atlantic to the Panama Canal. In the Pacific, the new radio chain provided uninterrupted strategic contact with the Philippines. Smaller stations in Alaska, Guam, and American Samoa as well as along the continental coast allowed naval headquarters to communicate with warships anywhere at sea. Stations at Peking and Vladivostok allowed for reliable contact with the thousands of soldiers, sailors, and marines sent to protect the nation's interests in China and Siberia. The Sayville, Tuckerton, New Brunswick, and Annapolis stations along the eastern seaboard provided continual if limited contact with Europe and the Near East. By installing the high-power arc transmitter at the former German stations, the U.S. Navy had brought them up to the latest standards. The new 200 kw alternator placed at New Brunswick made it the most advanced station in the world. Only the British could claim to have a similar capability, but the U.S. Navy's radios covered a greater reach and operated over a longer range. The spread of arc and alternator technology placed the United States above any other public or private operator.[76]

For all the accomplishment of the navy's radio officers in constructing such a network, there was always demand for more. Officers afloat in the distant waters of China particularly wanted a regular station at Shanghai, to link them with the Philippines and the United States. The naval force based at Constantinople after the Ottoman surrender forwarded requests for new equipment to maintain radio contact with White Russian forces in southern Russia. Those officers with their eyes aimed to the south hoped for expanded coverage of Latin America and the South Atlantic, with stations in Brazil or Liberia. Concurrent with this expanding attention was a growing public desire for greater radio service throughout the world, to carry ever more American commercial traffic and news.

The United States had been only partially successful in addressing the question of radio development in the Americas during the war. Germany's initial inroads had ended up being relatively minor, due as much to wartime financial and industrial limitations as to any diplomatic or covert operations. British Marconi's efforts had also not been especially rewarding, both for financial reasons as well as U.S. diplomatic pressure. But locking Germany or Britain out of future hemispheric radio developments permanently, as naval officials desired, required the extension of a U.S. radio presence in their place. For most countries in Latin America, the high costs of purchasing equipment and acquiring the technically skilled staff made private commercial radio more appealing than government ownership. An American company that sought to build stations and handle commercial radio with Latin America profitably would have to build a companion station in the United States. But Secretary Daniels unrelentingly pursued a domestic policy of government ownership of all radio operations and remained hostile to the idea of any future high-power commercial stations within the United States. Even when a company had the support of the navy overseas, as both Federal Telegraph and Pan-American Wireless did, the possibility of losing their anchor in the United States proved to be an insurmountable business liability.

Consequently, the failure to craft a concrete radio policy and encourage a privately run hemispheric radio network during the war would make it significantly harder for the United States to build an independent cable and radio network for the nation in the future. The window had begun to close. As soon as Congress declared the war over, the navy would have to return Tuckerton, Sayville, New Brunswick, and the other commercial stations to their rightful owners. American Marconi would then take control of the most advanced station in the world. Neither American Marconi nor Pan-American Wireless would construct more stations or expand commercial radio operations across the Western Hemisphere. Daniels's threats to win federal control over radio operations from Congress, and the navy's ability to block Federal Telegraph from selling the most-advanced arc transmitters, would make this so. This deadlock would leave the field open in Latin America for the return of European radio companies eager to sell their high-power networks to countries anxious to develop their own global communications links. It would also make it harder for the United States to ensure that in the future the nation would be able to communicate with allies or forces abroad.

As the war had made plain, the United States would need commercial long-distance radio stations to augment the navy's high-power stations for critical contact abroad in future conflicts. But the growing use of long-distance radio around the world threatened a crowding of what scientists believed to be a limited number of wavelengths—and thus a finite number of stations—even if everyone used the latest equipment. The United States might find itself closed out from the wavelengths needed for national defense. If there were a limited number of wavelengths that could be used, then the United States would need to be certain that it had available those that worked best for communicating between the United States and places of importance in Latin America, Europe, and Asia. The longer that uncertainty over domestic radio policy continued, the less likely that the United States would be able to establish permanent international radio contact. In the interim, if British, German, or French companies could create all or part of a regional network first, it would be difficult if not impossible for the United States to catch up, because the necessary wavelengths would not be available. Furthermore, as Hooper and others argued, without access to profitable international commercial operations, companies in the United States that provided radio equipment to the navy would have little incentive to continue their research and development into more-advanced radio equipment.

Therefore, the fundamental internal conflict within the U.S. Navy over the future of radio domestic policy threatened not only the chance to create a global radio network aligned with U.S. interests but also the continued presence of the United States at the very forefront of radio technology in the years to come. Without both, the country might never develop the independent cable and radio network that officials now believed vital for the nation's involvement with the world. As attention turned to problems of the coming peace, the questions of the foreign cable and radio interests of the country received their due from the military officials and diplomats who had struggled to correct the glaring problems they had discovered over the past five years.

SEVEN

✦ ✦ ✦

The Quest for Independence

LET US RETURN to the earlier fable of the two cousins, intrepid bees, and the trade in candles. As the news reached the two men in England and Ohio, both shared in the universal rejoicing that accompanied the end at last to the terrible four years of war. On the eleventh hour of the eleventh day of the eleventh month of 1918, the exhausted powers laid down their arms and rested in armistice. The cables had carried the false first news of a peace on November 7; their worldwide reach allowed mass exaltation and then collective dismay within the space of a few hours.[1] But negotiations in the Forest of Compiègne yielded the true armistice on the eleventh. Their joy tempered by sadness at the loss of other cousins in the carnage, the Londoner and the Ohioan nonetheless cheered the welcome end to the horror of the war.

Buoyed by hopes of a swift economic revival, both cousins sought now to resuscitate their trade in beeswax candles. With the war over, the public mistakenly expected censorship to end swiftly. But the end to the war did not bring immediate relief. In the weeks after the armistice, the Ohioan cousin learned from London of continuing congestion and delays on the cables throughout the entire British Empire. Congestion on the Eastern Telegraph Company cables through the Mediterranean, the landlines running over Egypt, and the cables to India aggravated British merchants, who were quick to blame the cable censors for persistent delays approaching ten to fifteen days.[2] All around the world the volume of traffic had grown well beyond all anticipated levels. The cousin's news, meanwhile, jibed with what the Ohioan read in the papers about similar problems on American cables to South America and Asia. Apprehensive about the expense of unencoded messages, disgusted with continuing delay and suppression, and unnerved by hints that competitors were reading their messages, the cousins agreed to wait until the censorship had ended completely before resuming their commerce. Patience, the Ohioan knew, was key when dealing with bees and governments. He had calmly waited since the fall of 1914; he could wait a little longer.

The First World War had laid bare the deeper flaws of the international cable and radio network. In the aftermath of war, public and private officials in the United States intensified their efforts to correct the imbalances as quickly as possible. One of the first issues was censorship and the growing public demand to return the cables to their normal condition in spite of Allied desires. In addition, Wilson and his advisors in Paris fought during the peace negotiations to halt further disruption to the German cable network at the expense of the United States and to make the whole matter of global electrical communications a subject for international scrutiny at the expense of the other great powers. A third issue was an eagerness to reduce the dependence of the United States on foreign suppliers of cables and related equipment. To do so, State Department officials launched an ambitious effort to create virtually from scratch a complete submarine cable industry in the United States and secure technical improvements to existing cables. Ambitious, aggressive, but ultimately unavailing, these initiatives reflected a transformed understanding among a few individuals of the strategic importance of global communications to the nation's changing involvement in world affairs.

Since the outbreak of the war, the United States had been subject to Great Britain's censorship of the worldwide cable network. Whether the cables were those of British companies or merely touched upon British territory, the same provisions had applied: Messages could not be in private codes. Censors could suppress any traffic that they believed might be helpful to the enemy. There would be no notification of message delay or cancellation. When the United States entered the war in April 1917, it soon adopted censorship in concert with the other powers. Though this operation inconvenienced many, the information gleaned from the vast amount of traffic passing through U.S. and British hands—via 75 percent of the world's cables—helped the Allied and associated powers to maintain the massive economic blockade of Germany. This was the most effective way to restrict Germany's ability to import necessary war supplies. Reading cable messages made it possible to determine which companies or individuals around the world were supporting Germany or its allies and to blacklist them. Those unfortunate enough to be blacklisted found it difficult or impossible to send cable messages, conduct financial transactions, or transport goods on Allied merchant ships. But the ban on private codes and the growth of wartime government traffic still caused congestion on the cables and hurt those free of any suspicion. So long as the blockade remained in place, so too would the censorship and the congestion.

Despite the tremendous public demand for an end to censorship and trade restrictions after the armistice, British and U.S. officials initially agreed on the need to maintain censorship. In their view, censorship was the only way to prevent Germany and the Central powers from using the halt to the war to reestablish foreign commerce, find fresh credit abroad, and renew the fight. As the "eyes" of the economic blockade, British and U.S. officials believed, censorship would help to compel Germany to sign the eventual peace treaty.

The United States, bound by its wartime agreements, had to maintain its share of the censorship as long as Britain and France did, but soon the Wilson administration split on the matter. Senior State Department officials agreed with Britain, as did the head of the War Trade Board, Vance McCormick. Frank Polk warned that it would be "most embarrassing to" the United States and might leave the country open to charges of bad faith if the censorship stopped too soon. Navy Secretary Daniels, Postmaster General Albert Burleson, and U.S. Shipping Board head Edward Hurley believed otherwise. Both Burleson and Hurley, understanding the importance of rapid communications to the renewal of trade, wanted to end the practice immediately. Daniels and Secretary of War Newton Baker understood the utility of censorship in stopping German trade in Latin America but nonetheless agreed with Burleson and Hurley.[3]

Vocal opponents of censorship won some relief by the end of the year. At first the U.S. Navy refused to relax any wartime restrictions, despite petitions to pass commercial traffic for Japan by radio and relieve the overburdened transpacific cable. Prompted largely by the Pacific problem, the nascent Council on Foreign Relations convened in New

York on December 17 a meeting of leading manufacturers, bankers, exporters, and news organizations, to formulate a protest on censorship and the ban on codes. The council's Mark Prentiss, already in touch with Long's cable committee, traveled to Washington shortly thereafter to deliver the protest in person to Daniels, Burleson, and other administration officials. At midnight on December 19, Daniels reopened the transpacific radio circuits to Japan and the Philippine to full-rate commercial traffic originating on the West Coast. Censorship on the transpacific cable then ended on December 22. Prentiss returned to New York with promises of similar arrangements on the cables to South America. As it turned out, the interallied agreement on censorship did not actually require the United States to maintain it on the cables to Asia or South America. This gave Daniels some flexibility.[4]

This partial relaxation only intensified the pressure. In January the Merchants' Association publicized the claim from one member that continuing delays of twenty-one to twenty-five days on traffic to South Africa would, if unabated, lead this member to close a plant in New York and fire some three hundred employees. Particularly galling was a practice of double censorship by both the United States and Great Britain. To expedite matters on the U.S. end, the War Trade Board had begun to approve transactions in advance, particularly those with neutral countries in Europe, as U.S. firms renewed their trade links once again. The British, however, frequently ruled that the trade with these neutral countries was not permissible and would not notify the senders of the resulting suppression. Once again allegations surfaced that these delays curiously coincided with successful efforts by British companies for the same deals, but there was little firm proof other than circumstantial evidence. Peace on the battlefield did not yet mean peace on the cables.[5]

The inexorable pressure of public opinion washed away the remaining support for censorship in the United States. With Wilson's encouragement, in early 1919 U.S. representatives in London and Paris reversed course and pressed for the rapid relaxation of censorship. British censors worried that any concessions would lead to an avalanche of similar demands from other countries resentful of the free hand given to U.S. firms in international trade. Bolstered by Wilson's personal requests, War Trade Board head Vance McCormick informed the Blockade Council that the United States would unilaterally lift censorship in the Western Hemisphere on February 28. British officials unsuccessfully fought this action but eventually conceded in early March to a more nuanced and focused censorship of Anglo-American traffic, a policy enacted on April 4.[6]

The end of censorship still took many weeks. From midnight of March 12, all U.S. cable traffic automatically passed unimpeded by British censorship. U.S. Navy censors extended the same privilege to British cable traffic arriving in the United States. The navy then ended censorship over lines to Latin America, the West Indies, and U.S. territories completely on April 18. General cable and radio censorship stopped in principle only on July 23. The steady relaxation of the censorship restrictions by the United States then forced the British authorities to relax theirs as well, until the entire system became untenable, as British officials had originally feared. To the great relief of many but the consternation of a dedicated few, by the end of July censorship on the cables finally ended.[7]

Among those few U.S. officials who supported censorship, its imminent demise raised significant questions about the wartime information-gathering and -processing system that the State and War Departments had developed. Access to the information passing over the cables had yielded important diplomatic and military benefits. If there were a way to maintain this level of access after censorship, these supporters argued, intelligence gleaned from the cables might be invaluable. One important requirement was a new, extralegal relationship between the government and cable companies to maintain access to cable traffic after censorship ended. Another requirement would be increasing the portion of the global cable network under U.S. control. Such a development would ensure that a greater share of the international diplomatic and military cable traffic would come through U.S. rather than British hands. This would also increase the security of U.S. traffic, for the United States had to assume that the British would continue to exploit their preponderance in the global cable network to monitor traffic. While the creation of a domestic cable industry and the support of U.S. firms in their efforts to land new cables abroad would primarily benefit the international economic and political relations of the country, the parallel intelligence windfall could not be overlooked.

The cable companies were understandably nervous about continuing to give the government copies of cable traffic. As early as January,

Frank Polk, now undersecretary, sought their assent to maintaining the wartime relationship. If company officials were so inclined, the department was interested in traffic passing to Mexico. Clarence Mackay, cable company head and close friend of Polk's, demurred. The reading of diplomatic traffic and "the revealing of secrets" were, in Mackay's opinion, "of fundamental importance to a telegraph company." He wrote, "We [feel] morally bound to protect the client." But he offered a way out, if Polk's request came instead from the attorney general. Mackay's companies already had an established program with the Justice Department "under safeguards which . . . [protected] both the Government and [the] company." This program had operated for four years without any leaks or irregular practices. Polk and Mackay had reached an informal agreement in the months before the war. Without clear instructions from the government now, however, Mackay was loath to risk the reputations of his companies without safeguards.[8]

Meanwhile, State Department and army officials made plans to retain as much of the wartime intelligence interpretation structure as possible. Leland Harrison, Frank Polk's assistant in charge of wartime intelligence matters, and others recognized the link between a peacetime diplomatic cryptanalytic unit and the development of a U.S.-controlled international communications network. General Marlborough Churchill, the head of the Military Intelligence Division, had been considering retaining the wartime structure of MI-8, the cryptanalytic section, at a lower level in peacetime. In May 1919, Churchill's staff proposed to the army chief of staff the retention of such a group. Its members would be civilians and would continue to be under the direction of Herbert Yardley, the unit's wartime head. The group would continue to work with and receive funding from both the State and War departments. Frank Polk, as the acting secretary of state, gave his approval on May 17; Chief of Staff Peyton C. Marsh added his signature on May 20. Operations began on July 15. By August 1, the new Cipher Bureau had moved to New York. Ostensibly the law required that the funds be spent outside the District of Columbia, but New York was also the largest cable hub in the country and far away from the prying eyes of curious diplomats.[9]

Once the end of censorship on July 23 stopped the regular flow of traffic to the Cipher Bureau from the three cable companies, Yardley's group obtained traffic under two different arrangements. The first was from a group of listening stations set up by the Military Intelligence

Division during the war to monitor radio traffic to and from Mexico. This involved radio tractors, converted large trucks with radio equipment designed for listening in to smaller regional stations and portable military radios in Mexico. These tractors were based in Texas, Arizona, and New Mexico. The Military Intelligence Division also maintained an operation at the Signal Corps' experimental radio station at Houlton, Maine, to listen in to the signals transmitted by the high-power station at Mexico City to Germany and the rest of the Americas.[10]

The second, more important method of collecting traffic for the Cipher Bureau was under a new arrangement with the cable companies. The plan was for a bureau employee to appear at a cable company's office in Washington each morning. There he would be given a package containing the cables from targeted countries and carry it back to the offices of MI-8 in Washington. Another civilian clerk would copy these messages, and the originals would return to the cable offices in the afternoon. That evening the package would travel by registered mail to Yardley in New York. There Yardley's bureau would decrypt the messages. Western Union was the first to agree to this plan. Negotiations began in April 1919, and by early November the company began regularly providing copies of traffic to Spain and Mexico. By November 20, Postal Telegraph had also agreed, and Yardley recommended that it provide Japanese and Russian diplomatic traffic. Negotiations with the All America Cables Company took somewhat longer, however. It was not until April 14, 1920, that W. E. Roosevelt, a board member who had himself been in military intelligence during the war, met with Yardley in New York and told him flatly, "The Government can have anything it wants." These delicate understandings appear to have been for limited periods of time, rather than being open-ended agreements, and seemed to have worked best when each company knew that it was not the only one under such an obligation.[11]

The decryptions from New York were not ignored by Washington. Yardley passed the completed messages to Military Intelligence and to a liaison in the office of the undersecretary of state. A special group within the State Department now had responsibility for handling more-sensitive diplomatic intelligence. Established in 1919, this organization came under the authority of department counselor, later undersecretary, Frank Polk. At its head was Leland Harrison, who had overseen such work for Polk during the war. Divided into three groups—U-1, U-2, and U-3—the office provided a place for the integration of the decryptions and the classified cables from diplomats abroad for the attention of the undersecretary. U-1 was the central office. U-2 was the apparent recipient of the New York decryptions, the liaison with the Cipher Bureau, and the entity responsible for contact with other government departments interested in secret work, including the Bureau of Investigation at the Justice Department and the Secret Service. U-3 concerned itself with domestic investigations and included work on international issues with the U.S. Post Office through its postal inspectors. The U-system represented an important antecedent to the permanent intelligence bureaucracy created after World War II.

The Cipher Bureau and U-directorate offered a valuable window into the thinking of other governments but was a major departure for the practice of U.S. diplomacy. The creation of these groups revealed the growing interest of senior administration officials in using the cable and radio ties to other countries for new national security needs. The presence of this intelligence system reaffirmed the desire of senior administration officials to expand those ties to new places. The groups' utility required realigning international communications to place the United States at the center. The success of the Cipher Bureau and U-directorate reinforced the need to keep the program secret from the public in order to accomplish what only unpopular censorship had previously made possible.[12]

At Versailles, concern for international telegraphic connections and the fate of Germany's cable network competed for attention with the vast array of other issues arising from the war. Given the tremendous pressures on President Wilson, Secretary of State Lansing, and the other American delegates, it is impressive that they devoted as much to the subject of cables as they did. Despite their limited understanding of the complex matter, Wilson and Lansing strongly challenged Britain, France, and Japan on the disposition of Germany's cables. They also attempted to correct the disparities in the global network by subjecting it to the scrutiny of the international community. In defending their position before others at the peace conference, they drew heavily upon the recommendations of those senior officials who had come to understand the world's cable and radio system and the extent to which it did not favor the United States.

Wilson and Lansing's efforts were initially a success. As part of the Treaty of Versailles, they managed to place Germany's prewar cable network collectively under a temporary international regime, rather than allowing it to become a divided spoil of war. They also won the agreement of other nations to attend an international conference solely on worldwide electrical communications. To be held in Washington, D.C., it would decide the fate of the cables and settle the substantial questions that had arisen about the future evolution of world's informational lifelines. If carried out to their fullest, Wilson and others hoped, these efforts would make it easier for the people of the world to communicate openly and easily with one another, free from the arbitrary censorship imposed by any one country, and enhance the peace that those in Paris so desperately sought to restore.

Over the course of the war, Britain, France, and Japan had not simply severed the German cable network but had largely broken it apart. Some sections were now in entirely different locations. In the Atlantic, the British had realigned one of the two German cables to the Azores and New York. The U.S. end now went to Halifax. The German end now went to Penzance, in Cornwall. This now became an "imperial" government cable linking Britain to Canada and the rest of the empire. When the French Cable Company sought permission from the U.S. government in July 1917 to move the other German cable to their landing site near Coney Island, the Commercial Cable Company strenuously objected. Commercial Cable, one of Mackay's firms, had operated the shore end of the cable before the war and wanted to after the war. They refused to divulge technical details about the location of the cable to the French company.[13] In the central Pacific, Japan had occupied the former German islands and would not allow the United States to use the German cable network centered at Yap to relieve the pressure on the Pacific cable. The United States actually ended the war worse off for cable connections than it had started.

The diplomatic offensive Wilson and Lansing launched at Versailles to correct this situation was the work of Breckinridge Long and Walter S. Rogers. From their efforts on cable issues in the Pacific, in the Committee on Public Information, and in the interdepartmental committee on cable communications, they now understood the subject intimately. Long drafted two important recommendations in the fall of 1918 as he shepherded the cable committee and its technical advisors toward their final report. Rogers, guided by Long's memoranda, the interim report of the cable committee, and President Wilson's own request, provided his own lengthy report in the middle of February.[14] Together they outlined a course of action that would put the United States squarely at odds with Britain, France, and Japan.

Both men emphasized to Wilson the awkward situation the United States faced. Significantly, though, they cast the problem not as one for the United States but rather the entire world. The submarine cable network was inequitable, they argued, arranged in such a way that disproportionally favored some countries over others. The limited cable supplies, the panoply of exclusive landing rights, refusals to exchange traffic, and unfair pricing all hurt those users who had to depend on the cable networks of other powers. The unequal rates and traffic volume quotas for particular countries discriminated against certain cable users and impeded global trade. As Rogers now knew firsthand, restrictive agreements among the three major press agencies—agreements supported by the cable companies—severely limited the amount of news that could travel the world. In the view of Long and Rogers, these existing conditions were unacceptable and required change. Without such an effort, the United States, most other powers, and even the League of Nations would be dependent upon a relatively few countries for global telegraphic movement of information in the years to come. Left unmentioned but obvious was the great vulnerability of cables to disruption in wartime and the corresponding power that naval powers could exercise over the freedom of cable operations in war and peace.[15]

To rectify these problems, Long and Rogers recommended several particular objectives. The issues before the peace conferences were the disposal of Germany's cables, the distribution of German cable ships, the reestablishment of communications with the defeated powers, and the consideration of the former German colonies as cable and radio stations. Rogers suggested a division of the cable ships between the United States and Great Britain. The transatlantic cables should be returned to their original location. If this was not possible, then Britain and France should assist the United States in laying new cables to Europe; cancel exclusive privileges in Britain, France, and the Azores, to allow U.S. companies to land their cables there; and remove any barriers to the equitable operation of the German cable to South America. Whatever ultimately happened to the German Atlantic cables, they should be run without exclusive privileges, operate with due transparency, be run without previous preferential rates or services, and be open to international regulation as necessary.

Of especial significance to Long and Rogers was the fate of the German cables and colonies in the Pacific. For these two officials, the worst possible situation was to have the German cables end up in Japanese hands. Viewing the situation with a wider political and military lens, Long explained that the islands—the Carolines, Marianas, and Samoan groups—were of strategic significance to the United States. He explicitly linked their worth to the need for secure cable communications between the United States and Asia.[16]

Within the Pacific, of greatest importance was the tiny island of Yap. Before the war, it had been Germany's cable hub in the Pacific and was one of two key alternate routes in the event that the Commercial Pacific cable broke. When the Guam-Manila section of the transpacific cable broke, traffic detoured from Guam to Yap and then via Shanghai, China, back to the Philippines. The other alternate route was to go through Japan itself. During the war Japan had occupied Yap and shut down the cables landing there. With Yap and its cables permanently in Japanese hands, Japan would then control the two most direct alternate routes for U.S. diplomatic, military, commercial, and news traffic with the Philippines and China. In the tense period before a war, Japan could cut the main cable and force remaining traffic to pass through its hands. Thus, in Long's view, Yap and the surrounding islands would have to become American territories. Much more specific than the U.S. Navy's general worries about Japanese control of the sea lanes to the Philippines, this warning nonetheless echoed with larger fears about Japanese island imperialism.

Rogers, for his part, argued that the physical barriers to transpacific communications and the dearth of U.S. news reaching Asia required the immediate reactivation of the German cables and a coordinated international program to lay more transpacific cables. "No greater contribution can be made to Japanese-American relations," he promised, "than the making possible of a generous exchange of news between the two countries." Both Long and Rogers concluded that the German Pacific cables first be under international control, or the control of a power other than Japan. If there was no other choice, Japan should be required to open the island for other cables to land and end discriminatory rates. For Rogers and Long, determining the fate of the German cables and islands would be an important first step toward improving the transpacific network, something that they believed to be essential for the United States' continued interests in the Pacific.

Long and Rogers were urging Wilson to use the opportunity of the peace conference to correct larger imbalances in the global system, not just to restore cable access that the United States had enjoyed before the war. Indeed, they were recommending not that the system be redesigned specifically for the benefit of U.S. companies but rather that an open door of economic opportunity would benefit all nations by allowing all of them to add to the network of international cables. The ascendant position that the United States now found itself in, Long proclaimed, allowed it the chance to "generously and graciously take the initiative" in a movement to redress these problems with the whole international community at once. Such a move required aggressive and radical steps. Long even suggested going so far as compelling Great Britain to provide cable supplies to all who needed them and placing all international cables under the control of the League of Nations. "[Equitable] arrangements could be made which would ensure the common use of the world's system for the common good," he explained. Rogers explicitly linked the success of the league to the availability of cable connections for reaching the worldwide public. The league itself, Rogers envisioned, would be the international regulatory body to enforce equitability. The result would be a global dissemination of news and information, for the improvement of peace and trade, which in turn would foster the spread of democracy and the maintenance of international peace. Without such steps to revise the world's network of cables and harness its power for the benefit of all, Rogers and Long implied, the sacrifices of the war would have been for naught.

Reflecting this new perspective, United States officials then pointedly opposed any further Allied attempts to seize sections of the German cable network. The first test of this policy came when France went after the German South Atlantic cable between Liberia and Brazil in the weeks before the Paris Peace Conference convened. French diplomats and cable officials had made repeated requests of Liberia both during and immediately after the war to connect the inactive German cable between Liberia and Brazil to the French station at Monrovia. When Liberian officials rejected this request, the French chargé d'affaires informed Liberian President D. E. Howard and U.S. chargé d'affaires Richard C. Bundy that if Liberia did not give permission, the cable company would remove the cable altogether and relay it to a neighboring French colony instead. Despite a U.S. statement that the cable should remain where it was until the peace conference, the French reiterated their threat. From Monrovia, Bundy sent word of plans to escort the cable ship with a French warship in order to seize this spoil of war. The French were not willing to wait until the conference.[17]

The cables that so energized officials in Liberia also made it possible for wiser heads in Paris and Washington to settle the situation calmly. Alarmed by Bundy's news, acting secretary of state Frank Polk put Stephen Pichon, the French minister of foreign affairs, on notice. Polk stressed the "amazement" of the United States at the dispute, "which [seemed] so wholly inconsistent with the principles of justice and rights of small nations for which the United States and associated governments [had] been contending." Any movement of French warships in support of the cable ship would be a "grave injustice." The French government replied by renouncing the idea of sending a warship but increasing the pressure. If Liberia did not agree to France's demands, the French company would isolate Liberia completely from the world cable network. Polk was insistent, however, and would not budge from the position that the fate of Germany's cables was a subject for the peace conference alone. Judging that the cable was not worth the price of American antagonism just before the peace conference, the French dropped the demand on the Liberians.[18]

The Paris Peace Conference opened on January 18, 1919, but the German cables did not come up for serious discussion until the first week of February. Because the cables had for the most part been cut at sea, the admirals who assembled on February 8 to draft the naval clauses of the peace treaty drew the initial responsibility for the cables' fate. The sentiment of most in attendance was to consider the cables to be prizes of war. For all intents and purposes, the Allied powers had "captured" the cables, just as they had German merchant ships at sea. This approach would give the capturing government the right to dispose of the cables through a prize court, which likely meant that

Britain, France, and Japan alone would keep the sections that they had seized. At this point, Admiral Benson, the chief of naval operations, objected. He insisted that the United States did not wish to treat the cables as common war prizes and demanded that his objection be added to the proposed naval terms.[19]

When the subject came before the Supreme Council of the five leading powers for consideration on March 6, Robert Lansing wedged open the crack that Admiral Benson had left in the naval clauses. Lansing questioned the British and French assertion that the cables, as instruments of war, were subject to capture as war prizes. The U.S. position, he maintained, was that the powers together would have to consider whether Germany could have them back. British Foreign Secretary Arthur Balfour understood Lansing to have raised two different issues: whether one could "take" cables cut in wartime under existing international law and what the powers should do about the cables now that the war was over. He suggested that a special commission should consider the former issue first. At Balfour's invitation, Lansing drafted questions for the special commission: Was it legally right to treat cables as prizes in naval operations? Was it legally right for a government that had taken such cables to keep them as reparations? To what extend did third countries have rights over the fate of such cables that landed on their shores? Further deliberation by the great powers awaited the commission's judgment.[20]

What the statesmen found opaque their judicial advisors strove to clarify. The commissioners were five distinguished international legal experts, including James Brown Scott of the United States, whose job was to draft the actual wording of the treaty itself. The commissioners concluded that the cable cutting could be justified as a military necessity but that the treaty should address their fate. As for the rights of a third country, they held the view that the situation depended upon the particulars of each case but that the belligerents should take these circumstances into account. The committee split on the question of whether cables could be prizes. The British, French, and Japanese legal experts all believed that they could be. Brown and the Italian representative did not. Of particular concern to Brown was that under the circumstances the United States had lost direct access to Germany and central Europe. "Why," Brown asked pointedly, "should the temporary cutting of a cable for military reasons necessarily entail the compulsion . . . thereafter to communicate through Great Britain?" If the United States was out to compete for the world's markets, he continued, it did not "wish to be subject to any Power for transmission." He continued, "Every nation must be equal." He would not accept Britain's being placed as a "toll gate" between the United States and Europe, a move that would only "result in the greatest bitterness."[21] Brown's words did not move the committee any closer to unanimity. Its final report reflected these disagreements.

The Council of Ten considered the judicial committee's findings some two weeks later on March 24. Alfred Balfour pronounced the report not as helpful as it might have been. Setting aside the issue of the future regulation of international cables as a matter to be discussed after the conference, he suggested that Germany had no grounds to complain about the fate of the cables and that the Allies were free to appropriate them as they saw fit. Admiral de Bon, the French naval chief of staff, concurred. Lansing objected. He refused to accept that the act of severance granted the right of assumption. Cables were part of the submarine region, in his view, and like the ocean floor itself could not be owned. Nor should they be considered any one country's property, since they came ashore on the territory of another as well. When Lansing suggested that Allied retention of the cables would further solidify their existing monopolies, Balfour shrewdly pointed out that American companies largely controlled the North Atlantic cables. He went on to note that the United States had already petitioned Great Britain for six hundred miles of the German cables. The U.S. position, it seemed to Balfour, was not entirely consistent.[22]

Wilson, also present, tried to rescue his secretary of state from the heights of morality by withdrawing to the plains of base commercialism. By taking the cables, in Wilson's opinion, the Allied powers had hurt not only Germany but also "the whole commercial world," because the cables were as much instruments of commerce, "indispensable to the pacific intercourse of nations," as they were weapons of war. More practically, Wilson argued that the cables were essential if Germany was to regain its international trade and generate the currency needed for reparations. To the United States, the cables were private property, and private property captured at sea should not be retained after war.[23]

Despite further debate, the assembled leaders were unable to agree.

In part it was the confusion about the international cable system and the anticable operations themselves that was to blame. Wilson had spoken of the cables as though they had been cut in place, while many in fact had been relocated. Balfour proposed a temporary solution. The Allies would keep those parts of the cables they had already taken. Germany would be allowed to repair any cuts, replace any removed sections, and maintain any part of the cables currently under Allied control. This would allow Germany to redevelop its cable network. It was no solution, for it did not say what, when, or how Allied control might end, but this decision held the day. The Council of Ten having approved the measure, the treaty-drafting committee then took up Balfour's compromise.

Wilson would not let the matter rest. Besides the high deliberations of the Supreme Council, representatives of Britain, France, the United States, and Italy met in the Council of Four. During the week of April 15 to 21, Wilson repeatedly brought up the question of Japan's possible control of the German Pacific cables and islands and the great concern with which the United States viewed such an outcome. When Arthur Balfour at the April 15 meeting raised the issue of the interest of the Japanese delegates in purchasing these cables (as a way of settling the international legal question of capturing cables), Wilson made it clear that he would prefer to see Yap, the cable hub in the Pacific, internationalized so that Japan could not influence U.S. communications with the Philippines. Three days later he raised the subject again. Because only the French note taker Paul Mantoux was in attendance on these two days, neither the British nor the United States had record of President Wilson's reservation in what became the official account of the Council of Four's meetings. His full statement is revealing:

> My great concern is to avoid having the essential communications across the Atlantic Ocean, as well as the Pacific Ocean, fall under a monopoly. I have already mentioned the case of the cables seized by the Japanese, which they want to keep. These cables cross at the island of Yap, and if that island remains in the hands of the Japanese, mastery of the telegraphic communications of a great part of the Pacific, especially between the United States and the Philippines, would belong to them. We must see to it that the means of communication across a great ocean are not placed under the control of a single nation.

It was decided the other day that the Germans would have the right to raise and use those of their cables which were cut during the war, but which were not rerouted in other directions. It is interesting to know where they could place these cables. If, for example, all rights of this kind in the Azores were reserved to English companies, the consequence would be that America's communications with Europe and Western Africa could take place only on English cables, which could lead in the future to tension and difficulties.

Wilson made it clear again during a meeting on April 25 his view that Yap should be separate from the Pacific mandates and be under international control so that no one would control the cables landing there, a point that he had explicitly raised with the Japanese delegates earlier that morning and would again later that week. Whatever he thought about the strategic importance of the former German islands in the central Pacific, Wilson cared more for the strategic importance of Yap than the rest of the islands combined. But his failure to put the reservation in writing would vex him later.[24]

The U.S. delegation would not countenance any compromise that vested control in the hands of the few of cables serving many. The draft treaty text, based on Balfour's compromise, came up for discussion before the Council of Foreign Ministers on April 30. Lansing again registered refusal to accept British, French, or Japanese permanent acquisition of Germany's cables. Indeed, the United States would have preferred to see Germany retain the cables, for any other outcome in the Atlantic would hurt the United States—inflicting damage for which the Allies ought to have given compensation. Moreover, Yap Island, Lansing added, needed to be under international control rather than in the hands of the Japanese. Not surprisingly, Lansing's proposed amendments did not find favor among the Allied representatives. Sensing that a final decision was not likely, the secretary of state suggested that the assembled heads of state themselves decide the matter the following day.[25]

The revelation of a fundamental misunderstanding about cables and how they had been cut led Wilson to change his position and open the way for a workable settlement. On the afternoon of May 1, the senior delegates met once more to argue over the Balfour compromise, now part of the draft treaty.[26] Balfour explained how the Allies had actually cut the cables and what this meant for their real location in the oceans. He asked the assembled dignitaries to envision a cable line, running from points A to B to C.

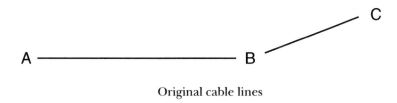

Original cable lines

During the war, the Allied powers had cut the cable at B. They had hauled a severed section from B–C aboard cable ships and then relaid it in a new direction, to point D.

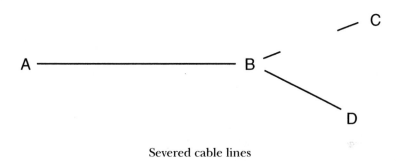

Severed cable lines

This meant that what had been cable line A–B–C was now A–B–D. Though the first section had not moved anywhere, it was still an integral part of the overall cable line and should also be kept by the power that had created the new B–D line. The Balfour compromise covered the entire cable line A–B–C when it defined the cables that the Allies had cut, not just the exact section now at B–D. No one would be returning the B–D section to its original location in B–C.

This was a surprise to Wilson. He had held the mistaken belief that there were cable "trunk lines" to which the Allies had simply attached cables. It was this idea of an existing trunk line that had led him to insist that Germany ought to have access to it after the war. Diverted cables meant that a de facto realignment of the German cable network to suit Allied needs had already occurred, which meant that further U.S.

protest was pointless. Instead, he now suggested that the Allied powers should place all of the cables under international control and that the diverted lines should stay where they now lay. The Allied and associated powers would act as trustees and manage the cables under an international convention pending a future conference to decide their fate. Despite objections from Admiral de Bon that the Liberia–Brazil cable should be the subject of direct U.S.-French talks, the others agreed to consider Wilson's proposals. Wilson's offer, a partial concession to the realities of the situation, had broken through the deadlock.[27]

The great powers settled the issue the following day. The new resolution Wilson and his advisors had drafted would dictate that Germany renounce all claims to the cables, that the powers collectively retain control of the thirteen former German cables jointly, and that the victors convene as quickly as possible an international conference to consider the entire situation of global communications "with a view to providing the entire world with adequate . . . facilities on a fair, equitable basis." Accepting Wilson's compromise, the British delegation remained apprehensive about the fate of a new imperial cable between Cornwall and Halifax. Made from parts of the German cables, it provided a long-sought secure government line across the Atlantic. Balfour requested only to amend the Wilson proposal, to allow for the continuing joint operation of the captured or redirected German cables until their ultimate disposal at the intended conference.[28]

It was a compromise all could agree upon, and the following day the powers approved it before lunch. The final treaty with Germany required Germany to renounce in favor of the Allied and Associated Powers all thirteen cables and whatever rights and privileges had been associated with them. In return, the victors agreed to credit the value of the cables, less depreciation, to the vast reparations bill. A separate protocol among the Allied and Associated Powers secured the joint operation and trusteeship of these cables and identified the need to call an international convention on communications after the Paris Peace Conference. Japan received its mandate over the former German islands in the Pacific north of the equator, but there was no mention of a separate fate for Yap Island. On June 28, 1919, representatives of a defeated Germany signed the treaty.[29]

Had the negotiations at Versailles been a success or a failure? At the time, it appeared to have been more the former than the latter. Rogers and Long had urged Lansing and Wilson to prevent further destruction to Germany's cable network. The two men had also pushed their superiors for changes to the nature of international telegraphy, changes that might improve world communications for peace and prosperity. Couching lofty aims, these proposals were nonetheless about the strategic importance of Germany's cables and the critical island of Yap. But it quickly became apparent to the Americans that restoration of the entire network to its prewar condition was not possible, what with the Atlantic cables cut and Yap given to Japan in the final treaty. This situation left the United States worse off than it had been before the war. Yet Wilson had managed to get the Allied powers to agree to place these cables under international control for the time being and to push the decision on their allocation to a later date. In doing so, he linked their fate with the outcome of a separate international conference that would consider all aspects of global communications, not just the German cables. Winning delay rather than victory, Wilson had succeeded in withdrawing the cable issue from the shadow of the larger treaty. In the process, he had given his diplomats more time to muster for the next offensive.

The situation had clearly become more complicated than many of the participants had first understood it to be, but all sides shared similar desires: There should be more cables linking more parts of the world, with fewer barriers to individuals or governments wanting to use the cables. To this end, then, the great powers agreed to assemble once more to discuss not only the fate of Germany's cables but the larger questions of international communications in the postwar world. After consulting with Admiral Benson, Rogers urged Wilson at the end of May to have the State and Navy departments begin preparations for the conference. By June 4, Lansing had dispatched a joint letter to the foreign ministers of France, Britain, Italy, and Japan, calling for the convocation of this conference in the months to come, which eventually the U.S. would agree to host. In the meantime, back in the United States a concerted effort was underway to redress the imbalances in global communications through other means.[30]

While loosening the fetters of censorship and tightening the claims on the German cables, the United States at the same time pressed forward on its own to improve the cable situation. Public and private leaders—from the postmaster general to leading diplomats, prominent New York financiers, and experienced cable company executives—all had their own ideas about how best this could happen. Some believed that the cables should be nationalized, as part of a comprehensive unification of the nation's communications resources, and that the government should itself lay new cables. Others, opposed to these ideas, believed instead that pressure on the cable firms would yield necessary technical improvements, while deliberate government encouragement could create a private cable industry virtually from scratch. Diplomatic support for cable companies fighting to lay new cables to South America would continue, while the government would actively encourage a new Pacific cable to be laid as quickly as possible. If all of this came to pass as its various adherents hoped, these actions would place the United States at the center of a new network of cables designed around U.S. interests rather than those of Great Britain or other powers. Never again would the country be as dependent upon a foreign power as it had been between 1914 and 1918.

The United States has been the only major power in the world not to have its national communications permanently under government control. Consequently, at the time of World War I no single authority was responsible for overseeing the nation's international communications or coordinating both private and government interests. Understanding the multivariate importance of cables, Breckinridge Long had taken this mantle upon himself and claimed it for the State Department. This clashed with Postmaster General Albert Burleson's pursuit of a domestic policy objective in the consolidation of national communications—telephone, telegraphy, and the postal mail—into a single authority. Burleson and others, such as Theodore Vail of AT&T, believed that such a move toward consolidation would make the national infrastructure more efficient and that it was ultimately necessary for the further economic expansion of the country.[31] Burleson included cables in his ambitious reach, seeing them as an extension of the nation's telegraph network, but his moves alarmed diplomats and military officers, for whom cables were of a different realm.[32]

Burleson's department, the U.S. Post Office, acquired control over the telephones, telegraphs, and cables in 1918. The same spirit of wartime nationalization that had spurred the federal takeover of rail, shipping, and radio guided Congress to grant President Wilson on July 16, 1918, the authority to nationalize any of these systems for the duration of the war. On Wilson's orders, Burleson took over the national telegraph and telephone system on August 1. Significantly, the submarine cable networks were not included. In theory the assumption of government control was to make the national network more efficient and helpful to the war effort. In practice it simply became another layer of administration, and after the war the general sentiment was that it had not been particularly successful.

Emboldened by his domestic success, Burleson hinted that he would duplicate this control on the international cables as well. This prospect horrified State Department and navy officials, who feared that post office control would unnecessarily complicate both the handling of government traffic and the censorship operation. Lansing and Daniels outmaneuvered Burleson within the cabinet, while Captain Todd and other naval officers, with the assistance of the State Department, drafted a counterproposal to put control of the cables in navy hands. Notably, Captain J. H. Trye, the British liaison officer for cable censorship, provided assistance. Trye and his superiors worried that U.S. Post Office cable authority would wreck the navy's censorship operation at a time when its stability was of the utmost importance. Tyre shrewdly urged Todd to limit the navy's offer to the portion of the cables in U.S. territorial waters. The post office's demand included the entire length of each cable to its terminus on foreign soil (and therefore within foreign waters). To finish off Burleson, the State Department then offered its ruling that the U.S. government could not in fact claim ownership over something outside its territorial waters to the extent that Burleson sought. Outflanked on unfamiliar ground, the postmaster general retreated for the moment. After several months, Burleson tried again. This time he interceded with Wilson directly and blocked Lansing and Daniels. To their surprise, the president granted Burleson the authority to take over the cables, effective at midnight on November 2, 1918. But this did not sit well with Daniels, who petitioned Wilson on November 19 to reconsider the decision in favor of the State or Navy departments. But Wilson would not change his mind.[33]

Cabinet secretaries must respect presidential authority; irate company officials have more freedom of expression. To operate the newly combined cable lines, Postmaster General Burleson appointed Western Union's Newcomb Carlton as his designee. The entire situation deeply frustrated Clarence Mackay, who had now lost control of both his domestic telegraph network and his international cable system.

Mackay announced that he was going to sue the government to block this presidential action, which he perceived to be the first step in the eventual, permanent reduction of his company into government hands. When Burleson ordered Mackay to merge his cable operations with Western Union's, he pointedly refused. Burleson then removed Mackay and his senior staff from any control over cable operations and instructed Carlton to integrate everything into a single system under post office oversight.[34]

Burleson then conflated his authority with his influence, to the distraction of State Department and navy officials. In the few months while the U.S. Post Office had control of the cables, Burleson tried to play a role in the international cable discussions. He made clear his desire to shape the deliberations over the German cables, and he dispatched recommendations and newspaper editorials to Wilson. Burleson, or Vail as his advisor, certainly understood the significance of the situation:

> The world system of international electric communication has been built up in order to connect the old world commercial centers . . . A new system should be developed with the United States as a center. This would give the United States business a determined communication with all the trade of the world, and all the countries direct communication with the United States, instead of over the present indirect expensive foreign-controlled lines.

Burleson's influence on international affairs remained minor, however, and the post office's control of the cables ended on July 31, 1919, to the relief of many. Still Burleson's involvement and the idea of integrating the nation's domestic and international communications facilities became a complicating new variable for Long and the State Department.[35]

While Burleson believed in administrative solutions to the existing problems, Breckinridge Long understood that technical improvements to the existing cables and substantive alterations in the very cable manufacturing industry itself were necessary for the United States. Burleson's seizure of the cables and the end of the war spurred Long to action. In the final weeks of 1918 he became anxious to conclude his committee's work and implement its recommendations. "If I can get my report printed in time the State Department can get the benefit of working out a great improvement in the cable service," he wrote in his diary on December 11. "Otherwise, Burleson will beat me to it, and claim the credit."[36] Having at last received Gano Dunn's initial recommendations from New York, Long and Squier dictated the preliminary report on January 25, 1919.

The first course of action was an attempt to impose technical improvements on the slowest of the nation's cables, the Commercial Pacific Cable Company line. Dunn's researchers had concluded that the best way to do this was by adding magnifier equipment at the cable stations in San Francisco, Honolulu, Midway, and Guam. These magnifiers would amplify the weak signal, make it easier for the cable operators to read, and increase the operating speed about 30 percent. Four of these magnifiers were in the country. Western Union had two, while the other two were in the government's control. If possible, the report recommended, the cable should also have an automatic repeater, the Bruce relay, installed at Midway, to minimize the need for new personnel there. The War Department already had one and could easily transfer it. The only difficulty would be continued resistance by Commercial Pacific. But federal control now theoretically meant that Burleson could simply order the company to comply.[37]

Long led the cable company to water, but it would not drink. Burleson received a copy of Long's interim report on January 30; by the end of February Newcomb Carlton, now the federal manager of the cables, had seen it, as had Commercial Pacific officials. Yet despite the urgency, by the time federal control ended in August, the amplifiers were still not in place. Government-sponsored negotiations had begun between AT&T and Western Union, which actually had the amplifiers, and Commercial Pacific, but they never concluded. Apparently Mackay's personality could be so volatile that relations between the three companies were bad. That the recommendations bore the imprimatur of Burleson and Carlton could not have helped matters either. Faced with this outcome, Long dropped the effort to force improvement. Instead, his attention moved to a radical idea: the creation of a cable industry from scratch, which he hoped would meet the national need quickly and provide competitors to Commercial Pacific.[38]

The second course Long pursued was the launching of a cable research and manufacturing industry in the United States. Squier, Long, and officials from Central and South American Telegraph Company had been considering the idea for nearly a year. At first glance the idea might have appeared to be a relatively straightforward matter of enticing existing manufacturers to expand their work to include submarine telegraph cables. But Long's committee had already learned the real problem: the lack of adequate supplies of the gutta-percha insulating latex. Without ready access to this ingredient, it would not be possible for any U.S. company to make cables easily. There would therefore be no investment in cable plants or in cable ships with which to lay these cables in deep water. Nonetheless, Commerce Department officials initiated their investigation in January 1919.[39]

What made the situation urgent in the eyes of U.S. officials was the disturbing possibility that new cable supplies from abroad would not be available for several years. Long had learned that British wartime orders for cable with the six British cable plants—the better part of the world's industrial capacity—topped twenty-four thousand nautical miles. With existing orders, this amount accounted for what was likely three years' worth of output. It would also generate an equally tremendous requirement for gutta-percha. Each mile of cable required several hundred pounds of the insulator. So to manufacture cable, the United States would need not only its own plant but also its own steady source of gutta-percha in the face of rising demand. If the United States could not locate its own new supply, then it would have to discover through scientific research a substitute insulator out of some other material. If the United States could not do this either, then the country would have to go without new cables. There was no other option.[40]

Initial research into the cable industry fell to John Cutter, head of the Commerce Department's Industrial Cooperation Service. Confirming that no submarine telegraph cable was for sale in the country despite the demand, Cutter found three companies able to manufacture cable, with a total capacity of around twenty miles of cable a day. (By contrast, the British company Telegraph Construction and Maintenance could make forty a day.) Labor was a factor: U.S. cable was 30 percent more expensive than foreign-made cable because of labor costs. Cutter estimated that any project would require an investment of $10 million to 15 million, which was not unreasonable given that the British submarine cable industry had a capitalization of $25 million. It would take at least a year to design and build the customized plant and a large, deep-water cable ship. This would require considerable and well compensated expert assistance. Finally, Cutter concluded that there would also be a need to secure a supply of the crucial gutta-percha latex.[41]

The State Department now took up the cable and gutta-percha supply questions in earnest. The Economic Liaison Committee, the high-level interdepartmental body created in 1919 between the State and Commerce departments to coordinate national foreign trade policy, established a new subcommittee specifically devoted to cables. Long urged Wilbur Carr, the director of the consular service, and Julius Lay, the foreign trade advisor, to coordinate acquisition of supplies of gutta-percha from the Malay Peninsula. Long wrote to Lay later, "I do not know how it can be arranged, but it [is] so important to us to be able to extend our cable communications as we desire, and as circumstances may make it expedient or necessary, that I feel we ought to leave no unreasonable step untaken which will put at our disposal gutta-percha in sufficient quantities to enable us to make that quantity of cable which we will need." Long had also learned from Gano Dunn that Western Union and General Electric were willing to start a joint company for manufacturing cable and equipment only so long as a suitable supply of gutta-percha were available. This exotic insulator was now the crux of the matter.[42]

Long also enlisted the Department of Commerce and its Bureau of Standards. By early April, the State and Commerce departments had carved out a three-part approach. The Industrial Cooperation Service, led by Cutter, was to address the problem of cable production and cable ships. The Bureau of Standards was to tackle the research into a gutta-percha substitute. The Bureau of Foreign and Domestic Commerce (BFDC) was to identify alternate sources of gutta-percha free from British influence.[43]

BFDC officials reasoned that the only way to win access to the gutta-percha was simply to outbid the competition. The British did not control the gutta-percha market by virtue of its location within British colonies. Indeed, very little of the gutta-percha actually came from this source. Half the supply, either cultivated or wild, actually came from the Dutch East Indies. Chinese merchants purchased the sap from plantation owners and moved it to the principal market at Singapore. If the United States could offer higher prices, it might well be able to entice these Chinese merchants away from Singapore to a new market at

Manila. "This campaign would require some discreet and energetic efforts on the part of the Government representatives or persons assigned this work," one senior BFDC official advised Secretary Redfield. "It would seem possible," Redfield informed Mark Prentiss of the Council on Foreign Relations, "to purchase what gutta-percha is needed . . . by approaching the Chinese merchants in the proper manner . . . As the supply is limited, there is likely to be sharp competition."[44]

Higher prices for gutta-percha might also spur the discovery of new wild stands of the tree. BFDC officials planned to investigate whether there were such trees in Borneo and in the Philippines, but there was very little information available. "It would be well for the prospective purchasers of cable," the chief of the bureau noted for Secretary Redfield, "to send confidential agents to the Philippines for the purpose of bidding on such supplies as the natives bring in at certain seasons of the year." Cutter recommended encouraging commercial cultivation in the Philippines. In the end, the objective was to divert the gutta-percha market to Manila.[45]

With these ideas in mind, the State and Commerce departments instructed field agents to investigate the supply. Secrecy in the inquiry and the overall cable project was essential. "Any word leaking out . . . would be *fatal* at the present juncture," BFDC chief B. S. Cutler warned a colleague.[46] On July 31 he requested of Wilbur Carr that the consuls stationed across Malaya, Singapore, Indochina, and the Dutch East Indies report on the gutta-percha situation.[47] Meanwhile, the Commerce Department's trade representative at Batavia, John A. Fowler, received similar instructions from BFDC officials. Fowler was to make his own discreet inquiries of the trade at Singapore. Most significantly, he was to transmit his findings to Manila by secure courier, not by submarine telegraph cable, lest word of his mission leak out.[48]

Using the consular and trade representative information, Commerce Department officials made plans to divert the gutta-percha crop away from the British. One important point of contact became the president of the Bank of Java. BFDC officials believed him to be interested in improving U.S.–Dutch East Indies trade and appreciative of the importance of cable communications in this area. Fowler received instructions to meet with the banker and develop further business relationships with a view to setting up a gutta-percha trade route. "It is unnecessary," he was told, "to caution you as to the confidential and delicate nature of the whole investigation." Fowler also received two copies of a confidential circular about the cable situation, which he was to share with local businessmen.[49] At the same time, Fowler was to return to the department as quickly as possible the prices and samples of gutta-percha that he could obtain. "The Bureau is particularly desirous," one BFDC official wrote, "of [pushing ahead] the establishment and location of a market for this commodity other than at Singapore." If the right contact could be made with suppliers, even direct trade was possible.[50]

The significance of this commercial effort was its audacity. Unlike the markets for petroleum, ores, or other strategic materials, to be successful, the United States had to corner the entire market of gutta-percha. A single new transpacific cable would run approximately five thousand to seven thousand miles long. Up to six hundred pounds of gutta-percha per mile was required to insulate properly a submarine cable. All told, the United States would need 3 million to 4.2 million pounds of gutta-percha. *This amount was between 60 and 80 percent of the world's annual production.* At the same time, plans by Central and Western Union for more cables would have taken up the rest of the entire supply. Had the British learned of the effort and its likely impact on their own cable-laying operations, the intense competition for the material would have precipitated a dramatic spike in the price. This most likely would have thrown the cost of cables so high as to make them uneconomical for anyone to manufacture or lay new ones. Still, the urgency was there. BFDC officials learned that British plans for new cables totaled nearly 120,000 miles, or approximately fourteen years' worth of the world's annual supply of gutta-percha. Under such circumstances, a reliable artificial supply or substitute available in great quantities was vital.[51]

Well aware of this, Commerce Department officials had continued their work on encouraging an industry and researching the artificial replacement, but maintaining political and financial support for the project became an issue. At the Industrial Cooperation Service, Cutter had to push for an additional $100,000 in funding, under a supplemental deficiency bill heading to Congress, to support this work, with some of the funds to go toward improving existing cable efficiency. Congressional postwar parsimony now added a new variable to the complicated equation.[52]

Long's actions to induce the business community to take up the burden also appeared successful. Negotiations for a cable-manufacturing plant had begun. A. L. Salt, a vice president at AT&T's manufacturing arm, Western Electric, regularly received updates from the BFDC on the search for gutta-percha in southeast Asia as well as reports from the Bureau of Standards on its research into possible substitutes. Western Electric had even purchased some fifty-two acres of land opposite the Norfolk Navy Yard with the intention of building a deep-water cable plant over the next two years, a fact revealed to the Senate only in executive testimony.[53] At the same time, the nascent Council on Foreign Relations, with the encouragement of the Commerce Department, had also taken up the project. Commerce officials regularly corresponded with the council on acquisition of gutta-percha and the prospects for a substitute.[54] The council then independently contacted leading rubber importers about gutta-percha supplies and prominent shipbuilders about constructing deep-water cable ships. Council members hoped to midwife a venture that would lay a new transpacific cable, provide a market for a U.S. cable manufacturer, and create a reason to build the first deep-water cable ship in the nation.[55] Spurring these public and private efforts was the festering problem of the Pacific cable.

Meanwhile, the pressure for improved transpacific communications had not abated. By early 1919 the U.S. government was itself using 60 percent of Commercial Pacific's cable capacity. Every indication was that the traffic load would increase and cause further delays, even if the cable did not break down.[56] At least eight breaks between February and May interrupted service. The most spectacular break must have been caused by an underwater volcano, whose igneous effusions completely destroyed the cable somewhere between Guam and Manila. The loss of six hundred yards of cable at a depth of forty-one hundred fathoms (roughly 4.6 miles) was an inconvenience. The resulting backlog reached 197 hours at San Francisco and 149 hours at Guam.[57] But neither the proposed technical improvements nor the diversion of some traffic to the navy's Pacific radio chain could provide lasting relief. In the end, the only practical outcome was to have one or more new cables linking the United States to Asia. The additional bandwidth would absorb the growing demand for service, while the redundancy would ensure a continuity of operations.[58]

If American firms were lethargic about building a new Pacific cable, the Japanese were not. Frustrated by the state of affairs, several Japanese firms in 1919 discussed laying their own cable.[59] This culminated in an August tour of the United States by Kakichi Uchida, former vice-director of Japan's Ministry of Communications, to secure private investment and public support. The plan was to create a joint U.S.-Japanese company, capitalize it at $25 million, and lay a new cable between Tokyo and San Francisco.[60] American businesses gave him a warm reception. Long was amenable to the idea with only mild reservations, as was the navy. The War Department, however, recoiled against any idea of a Japanese cable landing on U.S. shores.[61] Some in the State Department feared that a new cable to Asia going via Japan would enable Japan "to inspect [U.S.] messages in transit, to give a preference to Japanese businesses over America," and even to close off Sino-American contact at will.[62] Despite Japanese entreaties, the State Department refused to grant official support to the idea until Congress had considered its own plan.[63]

If Commercial Pacific or other private cable companies could meet the need, the government remained an agent of last resort. At the behest of business, municipal, and regional trade interests, Senator Wesley L. Jones of Washington introduced a bill on June 11, 1919, to construct a government transpacific cable and a Pacific cable commission to manage it. The bill would allocate $500,000 for the initial funding, with a maximum appropriation of only $8 million over several years. So potent was this threat, however, that within eight days of the bill's arrival Commercial Pacific dropped its rates by 20 percent.[64]

Jones's bill was appealing to the Wilson administration, but different departments desired certain changes that would bring the Pacific Northwest interests in line with the larger diplomatic and commercial needs of the country. The greatest difference of opinion was over the cable's route. While the State Department wanted the "southern route" to the Philippines and China, near the existing cable, the Commerce and War departments favored a "northern route." The Signal Corps already operated a cable to Alaska, and this new cable could simply extend from the end of the Alaska line. Running from Alaska to Vladivostok, Yokohama, and possibly Shanghai, it would be two thousand miles shorter, considerably faster, and much cheaper than the existing route of the Commercial Pacific Cable.[65] The Signal Corps' Alaskan radio stations could handle traffic if the cable broke, something illegal for the navy to do.[66] Additional differences surfaced over sources of cable supplies, rates, and the right to purchase private cable assets should the Pacific cable drive the private firms out of business.[67]

All of this talk of another Pacific cable riled the nerves of the Commercial Pacific Cable Company. Mackay's firm lowered its rates 20 percent barely a week after the introduction of the bill, something Long had been unable to get Mackay to do for two years. In September Mackay wrote to the Japanese government with plans for his own new cable. Mackay indicated that this new line would link the United States to Japan, land at Tokyo, and require Japan to grant the special right to the company to have its own office and operators in Tokyo.[68] After hearings on the Jones bill in late September and early November, company vice president George Ward wrote to Senator Jones to reassure him that the new government-backed cable would not be necessary and that Ward himself had gone to Britain to inquire about ordering a new cable. Ward defended the poor performance of the cable by pleading that the wartime traffic was far greater than the original anticipated load and asserted that the company had thoroughly cooperated with the government during the war in trying to install new equipment (which was not entirely true). Eager to denigrate the northern route, he alleged that high tides, great ice, earthquakes, volcanic activity, and a generally bad seabed made the idea terrible. "As a route for cables," he concluded, "the northern route has everything to discredit it in natural and physical properties." Content in their slothfulness, Commercial Pacific's executives feared those more energetic than themselves. Public and private officials were now hard at work trying to remake the country's global communications.[69]

Energized by the wartime experience, U.S. officials in the months after the war did their best to grapple with the enormous aftermath of six years of turmoil. From economic disruption in Latin America to revolution in Russia and imperial collapse in the Middle East and Europe, the world had changed dramatically by 1919. The United States had mobilized millions, transformed its economic might, and projected its military power all across the globe. The looming question the United States now faced was how it would make use of this newfound influence. President Wilson offered his own view, which would keep the

United States involved in the world. His internationalist vision, laid out in his Fourteen Points speech and refined in the months that followed, proposed a new world order to replace that of the exhausted powers in Europe. The League of Nations would form, with its deliberations to be open and shaped by world public opinion rather than by the secret agreements of a relatively few powerful states. The United States would join this body, surrendering some of its sovereignty and the Monroe Doctrine, to pursue the larger goal of a collective security, which would help to safeguard the nation and democracy in the world. A progressive internationalism, this vision ran afoul of those who did not wish to tie the country to such an uncertain future, who were willing to challenge Wilson's dream, and who ultimately defeated the league and the treaty in the Senate.[70]

It was within this vision of a greater role for the United States that government officials and business leaders attempted to realign the nature of world communications in order to move the United States from the periphery to the center of world affairs. This was a bold move. At Versailles, Wilson and Lansing fought further distribution of Germany's cables to the detriment of the United States. They succeeded in freezing the issue, in favor of a multilateral postwar conference aimed at improving global communications for all nations. As Breckinridge Long and Walter Rogers had argued, unimpeded access to these cable and radio networks were essential to the spread of democracy, cooperation, peace, and order that underlay Wilson's dream. If Britain or others would not assist in this multilateral improvement of global communications, then the United States would act independently and create its own cable industry to meet the demand. But these actions were not only altruistic, which broadened their appeal. Such an improved global system with the United States at its center would strengthen U.S. political and military influence in the Western Hemisphere and beyond. This system would broaden U.S. commerce, to reach new and old markets. It would reinforce the placement of the United States as the new financial capital of the world. And it would, with growing access to traffic that a permanent, secret interception and analysis operation could monitor, provide diplomatic and even military benefits in peace and war. The cables and radio network would serve both economic and political ends, to the overall enhancement of American power.

Federal officials on their own, however, could not widen the global web. Given the traditional private ownership of communications in the United States, individual companies would be the ones to meet this demand. Long, Rogers, and others hoped that the proposed international conference on communications would go some distance to leveling the field for firms such as Central and South American Telegraph and Federal Telegraph. Responding to the call for improved communications across the Atlantic, across the Pacific, and to South America, various U.S. companies had so far confronted the challenge with varying degrees of success. What remained to be seen was whether the efforts in the postwar period of the companies involved would be enough and whether their interests coincided with those of the government officials and military officers championing reform. Where these interests did coincide, the results were significant. Where they clashed, the outcomes were surprising.

EIGHT

The Illusion of Success

WORLD WAR I laid bare the deeper flaws of the international cable and radio network. From diplomats to military officers, merchants to journalists, the United States now recognized these problems and their implications for future diplomatic, military, commercial, and cultural interactions with the world. With the greatest part of international cables either being owned by British companies or touching on British territory, Britain appeared to U.S. officials to have tremendous control over the content and use of the global network. Whether for good or ill, this influence reinforced strong Anglophobia among U.S. naval officers and diplomats. In future conflicts, such as a possible one against Britain's ally Japan, the United States might find itself isolated from the world as Germany had been. Structural barriers, such as discriminatory prices and monopolistic cable-landing concessions, made it difficult for U.S. cable companies to compete with the British cable companies from Europe to Asia. Furthermore, the very equipment necessary for having a cable network—cables, cable ships, and specialized operating equipment—was expensive, in great demand, and virtually unavailable in the United States. In the aftermath of war, U.S. officials had intensified their efforts to correct these imbalances as quickly as possible. An international conference on electrical communications would soon convene. Private commercial projects to lay cables to Latin America and Asia intensified. But these initiatives, especially if they involved cooperation with foreign firms, would not always align with the wishes of public officials.

And what of radio? A technology in the midst of rapid transformation, it had become a vital military and commercial tool. To the U.S. Navy, intercontinental radio changed from administrative afterthought in 1915 to essential alternative to the cables in 1918. Though its capacity was not great enough yet to offset more than a fraction of the global cable traffic, radio held great promise. In the United States, this meant that radio would serve alongside cables in challenging British predominance and offering an independent ability to communicate with the world. With the end of the war and in the absence of any action by Congress, however, the high-power stations at the forefront of industry would soon revert to private hands. Naval officers worried about allowing British Marconi access to these stations and permitting General Electric to sell to Marconi its powerful new transmitters, the Alexanderson alternator. In light of the limited number of wavelengths apparently available for long-distance radio, British Marconi's access to the alternator might well extend British strength in international communications into the ether as well. Because of this, naval officers intervened decisively in the commercial radio industry to shape its further development and restrict British access. Though ultimately of mixed success, these ambitious initiatives in the cable and radio industries reflected a transformed understanding among a few individuals of the strategic importance of global communications to the nation's changing involvement in world affairs.

Despite the hopes of President Wilson and Secretary Lansing, the great powers would not agree on a wholesale revision of international communications in the years after the war. From Paris, Lansing had invited Great Britain, France, Italy, and Japan to a preliminary conference in Washington, D.C., to plan the agenda for a full conference for all nations to attend. Originally intended for October 1919, confusion and delay pushed the preliminary conference back to October 1920. The problems that emerged during the preliminary conference and the failure to call the main conference reflected the difficulties within the United States over communications policy, lingering Allied resentments of the wartime experience, and flagging momentum for reform in the aftermath of World War I.

During the year it took to organize the preliminary conference, attitudes on all sides hardened over the fate of the German cables as well as the real purpose and objectives of the general conference. For the British, French, and Japanese delegates, it was important to settle quickly the fate of Germany's cables. The United States had to be convinced not to internationalize the cables but to allow them to go to the powers that had captured them in the war. If the issue festered, these countries feared, the United States might be able to use it to gather supporters for more-substantive changes during the larger congress.[1] The fears of these delegates were not misplaced. U.S. officials saw in these meetings the chance to discuss all aspects of international electrical communications in peace and war, revise the Interallied Radio Protocol of 1919, and settle the future of the International Radio and International Telegraph unions, which set international standards. Private companies, professional organizations, and news organizations in the United States also took particular interest in the conference. They pressed the administration for further diplomatic improvements to the cable system and greater, freer exchange of news and information. Tropical Radio and United Fruit went so far as to hire Robert Lansing, who had resigned from the State Department in February 1920, to lobby on its behalf. Frank Polk, who retired from the department in June 1920, advocated for Commercial Cable from his new position on the board of the Mackay companies. Both private and public officials agreed as the conference opened that the United States needed to continue being a focal point for cable and radio communications in the world.[2]

Growing confusion over who should run international communications policy disrupted U.S. preparations for the conference and reflected the larger exhaustion of attention to these issues. As more departments had become involved, coordination of public and private efforts became ever more difficult to continue. Breckinridge Long, who had played a critical role through the war, made preparations to leave for a Senate bid in Missouri and would retire from the State Department in June 1920. Walter Rogers, who had articulated most clearly the importance of cable and radio connections for world understanding, became little more than a special advisor to the administration. The State Department continued to defer to the navy on radio matters, while the postmaster general continued to eye domestic telegraphy. President Wilson alone had the capability to impose order on the various departments but he did not act before his stroke. The planning for the preliminary conference and the various initiatives for the cable industry coincided with arduous battles between Wilson and the Senate over the Treaty of Versailles. Following Wilson's collapse from a stroke after his western speaking tour in the fall of 1919, his wife Edith Bolling Wilson cloistered him away to protect his health. On December 23, Secretary Lansing advised Wilson that the unorganized state of the governmental policy on cable and radio development and the lack of any clear head to coordinate the interdepartmental response was preventing any coherent reaction to the existing problems and planning for the conference. In Lansing's view, the state of international communications was "one of the most important matters the Government now has to consider." To Lansing's surprise, Edith Wilson replied for her husband and informed the secretary of state that the president shared his concerns and wished to centralize U.S. policy in the hands of the post office. Unusual as this was, Postmaster General Burleson himself conceded by the summer of 1920 that he was ill qualified to lead the delegation, and he became little more than a figurehead behind the State Department. But between disarray over policy direction and personnel changes, momentum had begun to flag for substantive change.[3]

The preliminary conference was of mixed success. The major topics for discussion included the allocation of the German cables, the amalgamation of international conventions, the settlement of the worldwide radio spectrum, the state of cable-landing licenses, improvements to worldwide communications facilities, and protection of cables in time of war.[4] The U.S. position was to use these issues generally to improve global communications and, more specifically, make the United States a key nodal point for cable and radio operations.[5] After a month's negotiations, the five powers reached an impasse over Germany's cables. The British and French believed that the United States deserved none of the cables and would not concede the U.S. demands. All sides soon came to recognize that the Allied powers' refusal to acknowledge that the cable cutting had hurt the United States was poisoning the atmosphere. Allegations began to surface again that Great Britain had not ceased intercepting international communications after the war, and Anglo-American relations soured notably. The French refused to compromise over the cables. Tensions mounted. Indeed, Wilson went so far as to threaten the British and French delegates that should the conference fail, the United States would abandon the League of Nations, shut down British and French cables landing in the United States, and implement a press campaign against Britain and France.[6] As the United States, Britain, and France gradually worked down from this animosity toward a complicated settlement of the Atlantic cables, the agreement crashed apart when Japan refused to compromise over Yap Island and its cables, the other major controversy at the conference. When Wilson insisted that he had made an oral reservation at Versailles for Yap, the other powers turned to the files and insisted in return that the English-language notes contained no such reference (by quirk of accident, only Paul Mantoux, the French note taker, had been there on those days in 1919). The Japanese refused any reduction in their mandate. The United States and Japan would settle the Yap question separately, under the auspices of the Washington conference on arms limitation the next year.[7]

The preliminary conference soon broke up without formally concluding, and the general conference never convened. It was a great disappointment for U.S. officials, who had hoped to use the momentum of the war to remake the infrastructure of the world. But if the international approach would not work, the United States would still act in ways at home to protect and expand its cable and radio connections to the world.

In addition to the new cable industry and proposed Pacific cable, greater cable contact with Latin America remained a key concern for U.S. officials, but here British opposition remained steadfast. With the war over, the simmering conflict between U.S. and British cable companies at last boiled over. Western Telegraph, facing a threat in South America and an eventual U.S.-Brazilian cable, chose now to tie up its opponents in compromises. At the beginning of January, Sir John Denison Pender offered a deal first to Newcomb Carlton. The British cable director proposed a joint operation between North America and Brazil. For its part, Western Telegraph would lay a cable from northern Brazil to Barbados. The U.S. companies could then run cables to Barbados to create fast connections to Brazil. In exchange, they would abandon their own concessions from Brazil to Argentina. To make this fair, Western Telegraph would then sell off its own cable network on the West

Coast. This would split the continent between Britain in the east and the United States in the west. It was far from a capitulation, however, for Western Telegraph would gain access to the United States and Canada through Western Union's network. As he later explained to F. J. Brown of the British General Post Office, "We are convinced that a direct submarine cable connection will be made between North and South America in the near future . . . The advantages of working with the Western Union Company, with their vast network of Landlines in the United States, are considered of great importance and a *direct* connection to New York is essential. Communication via . . . [Western's original plan] . . . would not . . . meet these requirements."[8] In attempting to split the two U.S. firms, Pender had chosen his target carefully.

Of the two companies, Western Union was a lesser threat and a company more vulnerable to temptation. Unlike Central, Western Union lacked cable connections of its own to the southern continent. To purchase and lay the projected cable from Miami to Rio de Janeiro and then to Buenos Aires, Western Union would have to invest nearly $15 million and several years' patience to acquire the nearly seventy-five hundred nautical miles of cable needed. While Central worked only in the Americas, Western Union had ambitious plans to lay new cables to Asia and Europe. Such a lengthy and expensive South American cable represented a considerable investment in only one direction. Pender's proposal, meanwhile, promised the direct access to South America that Carlton sought, for only one-fifth the price. On February 26, 1919, Carlton and Pender signed the draft proposal.[9]

Carlton attempted to convince Merrill that the deal was the only optimal solution, but the head of Central rejected the compromise outright. "We feel we should be false to interests [of the] American Government and American commercial interests," he informed Carlton, "particularly because [a] foreign link in [an] American line [would be] recognized as [a] national blunder."[10] Merrill then warned the State Department of the offer and forwarded copies of all correspondence with Carlton about the matter through the rest of the year. State Department officials became as concerned as Merrill. Latin American Division head Herbert Stabler believed it was necessary for the United States to go as far as diplomatically possible to protect Central.[11]

Merrill made his refusal final on May 2, despite Carlton's persistent entreaties.[12] Central had already ordered twenty-five hundred nautical miles of submarine cable for the Buenos Aires to Rio de Janeiro and

Santos concessions that his company had fought so hard to win. This was an expensive undertaking: at well over $6.25 million, the price was double the prewar rate for cable. Another cable, destined to lie between Buenos Aires and Montevideo, would be ready in July. With victory in sight and the cables on order, Merrill was not about to capitulate. Informing Pender of Merrill's refusal, Carlton confessed that it was not clear to him what Merrill would do instead. Western Union was ready to expedite its plans to lay a cable to Barbados, and Central's participation was not essential. Perhaps to increase the pressure on Central, Western Union had also initiated plans to win a concession for a Panama-to-Peru cable. This would challenge Central in its own territory. Carlton's feeling was that Central would soon see the error of its decision: "[They] will want to join us when they realize our plans are definite and under way."[13]

On July 15, 1919, representatives of Western Union and Western Telegraph signed the agreement to connect Brazil and the United States by cable. Under the terms of the plan, Western Telegraph would start in Brazil, and Western Union would start in Miami, Florida. They would meet at a jointly maintained cable station on Barbados to exchange traffic and split the revenue. Although the two companies would refrain from making further deals with third parties, they left room for Central to join into the partnership later. If there were no agreement within a year, however, Western Union was free to challenge Central. Carlton could even ask Pender to extend his west coast cable network northward to Panama, where Western Union might land its own U.S.-Panama cable against Central's interests. However it was to be done, together the two companies would encircle South America and drive out Central.[14]

To complete the deal, Western Telegraph then bought out the Brazilian concession from Western Union, which then began to spend more than $2.7 million on the new cable venture. Carlton also pressed ahead with plans to extend Western Union's cables to the Pacific coast of South America. By November, company agents had acquired concessions in Peru to land cables from Panama and Chile. Central's own agents promptly challenged this attack in the Peruvian courts, while Merrill maintained his refusal to join with Pender and Carlton.[15]

The Brazil cable deal finalized, the South American cable issue took on greater importance at the State Department. It was not clear to what degree the Western Union–Western Telegraph collaboration would keep the South American cables under British influence. The question now arose, was the cable industry sufficiently different from other commercial enterprises that the U.S. government should insist on a policy of having cable connections to key locations solely in U.S. hands? Carlton assured nervous State Department officials that the contract protected the security of messages. U.S. Navy officers, disappointed that the cable deal did little to integrate the Caribbean more fully, suggested that the landing license in Miami be held up until Western Union agreed to run cables to the Virgin Islands, Puerto Rico, and the island of Hispaniola. But much remained unclear. Until the two companies moved forward with their plans and filed for cable-landing licenses, Carlton and Pender held the initiative.[16]

Western Telegraph's offensive against Central and South American Telegraph in South America continued unabated. Minor Brazilian officials began sniping at both the new Brazil-Cuba concession and Frank Carney's existing ones. Merrill and others believed that Western Telegraph had bribed these officials, because they were not questioning any of Western Telegraph's new cable contracts. At the beginning of July, with his patience and resources almost exhausted, Ambassador Morgan advised Frank Polk that the ambassador he could do no more against Western Telegraph in Brazil.[17]

At the same time, the British firm suffered a serious setback in Argentina. Merrill's representatives had cleverly exploited the wording of Western Telegraph's earlier cable concession between Uruguay and Argentina to win the right to lay a cable under the River Plate and to gain a fait accompli. The original concession for Western Telegraph granted it sole rights to Argentina's oceanic cables. Great Britain officially maintained that the Plate was open ocean. Both Argentina and Uruguay, meanwhile, maintained that it was a river. Central's agents argued that the U.S. cable between Montevideo and Buenos Aires was thus a river cable, not an oceanic one. Western Telegraph was thus in a bind. By objecting to the U.S. cable as an oceanic one, they would anger the Uruguayan and Argentine governments over the definition of the Plate. By conceding the U.S. cable, they would lose the chance to challenge any future concessions to Central. Repeated British protestations over this dilemma apparently only angered the Argentine foreign minister. Central's efforts had succeeded by appealing to the desire of Argentina to free itself from the British monopoly over its cable communications. On July 22, Central won its concession. Still, the vehemence with which the British company had fought Central impressed Stimson. Echoing Morgan in Brazil, Stimson recommended that the department lodge a protest with the British government about what he saw as extraordinary lengths taken to stop a U.S. company. In Washington, Frank Polk agreed.[18]

Polk attempted to rein in Western Telegraph from a different direction. On July 18, he instructed Ambassador John W. Davis in London to raise the matter with the Foreign Office. Western Telegraph had, "it appears, far exceeded proper methods of commercial rivalry." Davis was to secure relief "if possible . . . from opposition exceeding the bounds of friendly" business competition. The Foreign Office was not impressed. As one clerk concluded, "This seems rather vague—I don't know what the Americans want *us* [*sic*] to do, unless it is to ask the English Company to make friends with the Americans—!" Coming at a time when allegations swirled about British wartime cable espionage and when Anglo-American commercial rivalry was rising, however, no one could simply blink the matter away.[19]

At the suggestion of the U.S. Embassy, the Foreign Office invited Sir John Denison Pender on August 13 to refute the allegations. He defended Western Telegraph's actions without hesitation. His company, he argued, was only using the very same sorts of techniques that the Americans had used to secure their original concessions in South America, at British expense. The joint cable with Western Union was a perfectly rational business move to counter Central's efforts to divert traffic away from Western Telegraph. Pender again offered Central the chance to join the pool but pointed out that if the company refused, he "would continue to employ every means within his power to prevent the laying of competing cables." As for the allegations that Western Telegraph was behaving in an unfriendly manner, Pender simply noted that Central had to make use of one of his cable ships to lay their cables. The implication was clear: if he truly wished to stop Central, it would be very simple for him to do so. In reporting back to Polk, Ambassador Davis confidentially recommended that should these problems continue, it might be advisable for the State Department to refuse cable-landing permission at Miami.[20]

Pender's efforts to stop Central in Brazil, Argentina, and Uruguay proved inadequate. Between August and December, the last of Western

Telegraph's resistance collapsed. Central's new Argentina-Uruguay cable was in place by August 2. Although the cable was operational within two hours, administrative hurdles delayed the opening until December 18.[21] In Brazil, Central finally secured the necessary signatures and approvals to land cables from Uruguay and to lay new cables from Brazil to Cuba.[22] By the middle of 1920 the cables from Argentina to Uruguay and Brazil were open to the public. Full-paid traffic from New York could reach Montevideo in a half hour. It was now possible to send diplomatic, commercial, or personal messages rapidly all the way to Brazil without passing them through British control. After a six-year effort, the State Department and Central had worked together to drive back Western Telegraph's hold on the Atlantic coast of South America. It remained to be seen who would deliver on the other objective: a direct line between Brazil and the United States.[23]

The year 1919 saw direct intervention into the radio industry by the U.S. Navy, in a bid to protect and expand the nation's strategic communications. The result, the Radio Corporation of America (RCA), was intended to be the solution to a number of growing problems that converged in the months after the armistice. Most immediately, the navy faced the inevitable return of the commercial stations to their prewar owners as soon as Congress declared the war to be over. American Marconi stood to regain its international stations, but the navy's lingering distrust of the company had not abated. The war had shown the importance of having additional commercial capacity to augment naval radio in times of crisis. American Marconi's stations had not been up to this task, and they had no other real competitors. At the same time, General Electric was negotiating a contract to sell a large number of Alexanderson alternators, the most advanced transmitters at the moment, to British Marconi. Ambitious plans were afoot for British Marconi to revive its prewar radio network it had planned with the Americas and the rest of the world, for which the United States stations would be useful and the alternator vital. Countries from China to Argentina to Poland now clamored for high-power stations that would link them wirelessly to the rest of the world. The growing demand, however, very likely would exceed the available supply of suitable long-distance wavelengths. From the point of view of naval radio officers like

Stanford Hooper this situation foreshadowed significant problems for the United States. All of this international demand for wireless communications coincided with Hooper's ongoing interest in creating a single company to operate commercial international radio. A desire to protect wartime gains in the field of radio, reinforced by a perception of a closing window of opportunity, led to a new company intended to oversee the nation's international commercial radio ties and prevent a foreign power from controlling the nation's strategic links abroad.[24]

With peace, the U.S. Navy would lose its commercial high-power stations. Congress had not seen fit to validate Josephus Daniels's dream of having the government control radio operations in the country. But enterprising naval officers had extended some control when they could. Under pressure, American Marconi had sold the U.S. Navy its coastal stations. Federal Telegraph had yielded its stations and its influence as well. Hooper and his colleagues arranged for the alien property custodian, the federal government's trustee of seized enemy assets, to transfer to the navy the patents and stations of the Atlantic Communications Company, which included the station at Sayville. But the prize station at New Brunswick, with its Alexanderson alternator, would return to American Marconi. If the navy did nothing, American Marconi would resume its place as the leading radio company in the country. Its strong financial and technical position made it the company most capable of negotiating the complicated forest of patents that had grown up over the past few years. Through its interest in Pan-American Wireless Telegraph, American Marconi would also influence the development of U.S.–Latin American radio. All of this gave the company a considerable advantage against any potential competitor, to the navy's dismay.[25]

Another problem was the future of the Alexanderson alternator. The Marconi companies and General Electric had been discussing a deal since 1914. An initial agreement led to the 50 kw test device and the later 200 kw piece, which in 1917 had impressed naval radio officers at New Brunswick.[26] Both General Electric and the Marconi companies stood to gain much from a successful contract. So far General Electric had not received any payment for either alternator at New Brunswick. The tremendous research and manufacturing costs made a steady, long-term contract appealing. Though the U.S. Navy appreciated the technology, the only real offer from the government was like the one offered to Federal Telegraph: regular purchases of alternators from General Electric in exchange for the right to vet the company's sales of alternators to others.[27] This General Electric rejected. The Marconi companies, meanwhile, needed the alternator to revive transoceanic radio operations. The spark was outdated, and the Fuller improvements to the arc were unavailable. American Marconi was in an especially desperate situation now that international radio was going to be its only real source of income.[28] To deny the transmitter to potential rivals, the Marconi companies wanted an exclusive contract. Uncertain about the real value of the device, General Electric was hesitant to commit to a single client.[29] The deal on the table was for twenty-four 200-kw alternators, ten for British Marconi and fourteen for American Marconi. General Electric would ship two a month after the first year, effectively blocking competitors from acquiring any alternators until 1921. Unable to agree on a proper royalty, both sides continued negotiations in April 1919, in the absence of any better offer.[30]

The Marconi interest in the Alexanderson alternator was indicative of the growing worldwide demand for high-power stations. Britain revived prewar plans to connect the empire by a long-distance radio chain. France envisioned its own colonial radio network reaching all the way to southeast Asia. Italy, France, and other European powers saw these stations as a way to bypass British cable control and link directly with the United States and other countries. Belgian and Polish officials opened negotiations with the U.S. Navy to purchase high-power arc stations.[31] Both Sweden and Norway intended to establish contact with the United States by radio as soon as possible.[32] There was even discussion of building a special 1,000 kw arc station for the exclusive use of the new League of Nations.[33]

Linking with Latin America held great interest as well. British Marconi officials still envisioned creating a chain of stations from Britain to South America. In January the company received permission to build a station in England for work with Argentina, where a station was under construction.[34] In March British Marconi agents signed a contract with the Colombian government to build a station at Bogotá, which would serve as another link in the chain.[35] The plan called for a relay station on imperial territory at Barbados, Jamaica, or the British West Indies, to work with the Marconi station at Glace Bay, Nova Scotia, and through this station with Great Britain.[36] French and German companies also leapt forward to stake out their places in the radio game. The French General Wireless Radio Company chased concessions in Argentina and Venezuela.[37] Telefunken's agents were hard at work too, reviving concessions for stations at Cartagena and Buenos Aires.[38] The development of radio throughout Europe met with general U.S. approval. More stations meant more independent lines of communication beyond British cables. That development in Latin America, however, was not welcome at all.[39]

The United States had by 1919 the most expansive radio network of any power. It spanned the globe from Vladivostok to Constantinople. With the arrival of U.S., British, and Japanese forces in Siberia in late 1918, the demand for adequate cable contact with the rest of the world quickly outstripped the existing facilities.[40] The U.S. Navy had rapidly transplanted a 60 kw arc station from Hawaii at the end of September, and by October the following year those posted to what one observer called "a place the Lord certainly did forget" had added Vladivostok to the navy's radio network.[41] A set from the USS *Wilmington* enabled the U.S. Consulate General at Shanghai to extend the network down into China and connected it with that in the Philippines.[42] Working with these outposts in Asia and the Pacific Islands were Navy stations at Saint Paul in the Pribilof Islands, along the Alaskan coast, and stations from Seattle to San Diego.[43] The navy's high-power stations along the Atlantic coast now worked regularly with London, Lyon, and Rome, and handled commercial traffic with stations in Belgium, Germany, and Norway.[44] U.S. Navy patrols in the Adriatic stayed in constant contact through naval radio stations in France and Italy. Farther east, the USS *Sacramento* served as the radio relay ship for Admiral Mark L. Bristol's force at Constantinople. When the *Sacramento* left at the end of 1919, Frank Polk urged its swift replacement and the stationing of an additional ship still farther east at Batum on the Turko-Armenian border. Though not as robust as the cables, the navy's radio network enabled the United States to monitor diplomatic and military developments with a breadth and celerity never before imaginable.[45]

The growing chaos of worldwide radio compelled the imposition of order. The existing theoretical understanding of transmitting at the time was that radio was like a foghorn: for the signal to go far, it needed to be low and loud. That is, it needed to be of a long wavelength and from a high-power transmitter. By 1919 the available spectrum seemed to range from approximately one hundred meters to twenty thousand. Radio experts believed that stations working distances greater than two thousand miles—such as across an ocean—would likely use wavelengths between eight thousand and twenty thousand meters. Within these parameters, the Interallied Radio Commission (IARC) crafted in the spring of 1919 a rough plan of what the worldwide radio spectrum ought to look like, as a guide to further deliberations by member countries. The commission divided the spectrum into four main categories: commercial mobile, commercial fixed, military, and special (which included radio beacons and meteorological stations). The first of these categories, commercial mobile, included anything in use on ships or aircraft and ranged in sections from two hundred meters all the way up to five thousand meters for very large ships. As for the commercial fixed category, any wavelength that remained aside from military ones could be used by any country for domestic commercial work, provided it did not interfere with a neighboring country. Stations specifically handling international traffic, however, would be assigned an exclusive wavelength based on the distance covered and set aside for this purpose from the very long waves. At first glance it appeared that there would be plenty of wavelengths available in the eight-thousand- to the twenty-thousand-meter range to accommodate the growing number of stations.[46]

Determining how many stations could fit into this portion of the spectrum was difficult. The state of operation at the time and the very fact that adding a signal changes the wavelength meant that each wavelength in use required a band of additional wavelengths (the spacing waves) around it, to act as an interference barrier. To understand this concept, we can think of an audience in a concert hall or movie theater. Cruel managers might squash everyone closely together on long benches in order to sell the most number of tickets. Most people find this way of viewing the stage unpleasant and constricting. So in a gesture to propriety, everyone gets an individual seat, and the placement of the armrests between seats creates at least a little bit of room for everyone to make their inevitable movements. The question for theater owners has been how narrow the seats and armrests can be before everyone starts complaining. The same issue of spacing puzzled those fretting over radio.

By 1919 radio engineers believed that only a finite number of wavelengths were available in the range most useful for long-distance transmission. In time, steady technical improvements would allow progressively tighter bands, yielding more and more space. Until then, however, U.S. officials at the IARC suggested making the bands as tight as 0.5 percent on each side of a particular wavelength.[47] To push countries to make use of the most modern equipment and refined signals, the IARC also suggested that countries receive blocks of adjacent wavelengths.[48] How many long-distance wavelengths would each country get? General Gustave Ferrié, the French radio expert, suggested dividing wavelengths up according to the populations of the leading countries. Large nations with more than 30 million people might get two blocks, while smaller countries would get one. His list of countries tallied up to thirty-five blocks, with the remaining blocks available to be distributed on a first-come, first-served basis. How many blocks would there be? The spacing wave was key: the tighter the spacing wave, the more blocks available to the world. Working with either a 2.5 percent or 3 percent variance from eight thousand meters up, Ferrié calculated there would only be forty-three to fifty-four blocks in total.[49] This revealed real problems. There were already nine stations in operation between twelve thousand and twenty thousand meters on both sides of the North Atlantic. The U.S. Navy had more in the Pacific, and European powers had already announced plans to construct more high-power stations.[50] E. W. F. Alexanderson, whose alternator was the source of much interest, concluded that of these stations in use now, five were what he considered "first rate." By his calculation, there could be at most twelve such first-rate stations in the world. Until the transmitter and receiving technology could advance further, that left room at the time being for just seven more.[51]

Though the experts disagreed on an exact number, it was clear that there would be a limited number of long-distance stations. A problem on the minds of naval radio experts, not explicitly stated but implicitly understood, was that there was a closing window of opportunity to acquire the wavelengths most useful for direct radio contact with the United States and to assign them to those stations the navy could consider the best guardian of U.S. interests. If a foreign firm opened a station in the United States and occupied the best wavelengths, it would be next to impossible under present conditions for a U.S. company to challenge that firm through sheer commercial acumen with the few remaining wavelengths. Inactivity was not an option.

In the eyes of Secretary Daniels and selected senior officers, government control over all radio operations would be the magic pill to solve these various postwar radio problems. With such authority, the U.S. Navy would simply keep all commercial high-power stations, not need to worry about foreign influence over international radio, and be confident that commercial competition elsewhere would squander scarce wavelengths on redundant international circuits. Daniels's postwar attempt to win permanent radio control from Congress was as unsuccessful as before, but the experience was more searing. This time Republicans in the House, emboldened by electoral victory and popular discontent, dealt Daniels a severe blow. During the hearings, two congressmen pointedly criticized his wartime use of navy funds to purchase radio company assets without explicit authorization from Congress. Further discrediting the secretary was testimony from amateur groups and commercial firms, including E. J. Nally's angry retelling of the travails of Pan-American Wireless. The committee tabled the bill a month later.[52] The ire against Daniels spread to the rest of the House. House Minority Leader James R. Mann publicly called for Daniels's impeachment over the purchase of radio company assets.[53] The high-power station at Monroe, North Carolina, fell victim to this anger, its $3 million price tag and intended use for postwar commercial work its biggest liabilities.[54] Nor was that enough. Daniels's opponents attached an amendment to the Naval Appropriations Bill that rejected the requested $4.3 million to purchase more radio company assets and specifically banned Daniels from using any naval funds to buy these things.[55] Surprised by his singed fingers, Daniels became very cautious about touching the hot issue of national radio control again.[56]

The collapse of Daniels's latest attempt gave Hooper a chance to make his own move. Hooper had long believed that the United States was better served by having private companies handle international radio work and that the solution to the financial and technical problems was in the creation of a single powerful company possessing the necessary patents, wavelengths, and clout to compete with foreign radio companies. Neither American Marconi nor Pan-American Wireless would be this company. Hooper believed a new one, which would utilize the alternator, was necessary. First he gathered reinforcements. Captain D. W. Todd, who supported government ownership, was leaving for sea command in Europe. The slot of director of naval communications would now be vacant. Hooper prevailed upon Daniels to offer it to

Admiral W. H. G. Bullard, who was at sea in the Adriatic but who could be spared. Bullard would lend not only his rank to Hooper's cause in negotiations with private firms but also his experience: he had been Todd's predecessor. He also shared Hooper's views on long-distance radio. Bullard would return in early April to Washington via Paris, where Todd would brief him on the state of affairs.

The plan began to unfold in early April 1919. Writing to Franklin Roosevelt about the alternator at New Brunswick, General Electric vice president Owen D. Young added a careful, discreet warning that the negotiations with the Marconi companies would soon conclude. Hooper had been informed of this earlier by a source at General Electric and was developing a "big proposition" concerning the company and the alternators. Above all, it was essential that the Marconi companies not get access to the transmitter.[57] Having them control the alternator would, in Hooper's view, prevent the rise of any realistic competition and "be a grave menace to the safety of the United States." The British control of international cables only compounded the severity of the situation: "Should these negotiations [conclude] to the satisfaction of the British Marconi Company, the communications of the world would be controlled completely by this foreign country, with all the dangers which would be sure to ensue from such a condition." Hooper's office counseled Roosevelt to invite General Electric officials to a conference in Washington, but the scheduled meeting was aside when Admiral Bullard returned from Paris.[58] Hooper and Sweet briefed the admiral on the negotiations. What Bullard learned resonated with something that had happened in Paris. Bullard had met with Dr. Cary Grayson, Wilson's personal physician, and possibly Wilson himself, and received from them the vague exhortation to look into the radio situation and to safeguard the nation's interests. Confused at the time, Bullard now understood this situation to mean the negotiations between General Electric and the Marconi companies. To stop them, Hooper and Bullard took the train to New York to make the appeal to General Electric in person.[59]

Hooper and Bullard arrived at General Electric's office in New York on April 8. Meeting with senior officials, including Owen Young, Bullard presented the gist of the navy's concerns about the alternator contract and the possibility that through it the Marconi companies could come to exercise great control over international radio for the foreseeable future. During the break for lunch, Bullard took Young aside and told him what Young later described as a "state secret" and what helped to convince General Electric to abandon the contract.

Bullard explained to Young that in Paris Wilson had come to realize that three things determined international predominance: transportation, communications, and petroleum. Britain's lead in shipping was very strong, and the United States could not challenge it. The United States was sufficiently independent in petroleum. That left communications. British control over the submarine cables was now very great. The field of radio remained open. In order to remain independent in communications, the United States would have to have control over radio. If British Marconi were able to acquire the alternator, build its stations, and take up many of the limited wavelengths, no U.S. company could challenge Marconi. Britain would hold both cables and radio. It was Hooper who then outlined the navy's specific plan. General Electric or some other company would form an operating company to purchase the alternators and compete effectively with the Marconi interests. For its part, the U.S. Navy was prepared to transfer valuable patents from Federal Telegraph and others acquired during the war.[60] Though a new and ambitious proposal, it followed clearly and directly from the navy's earlier experiments with Federal Telegraph and Pan-American Wireless.

Hooper's proposal was attractive, and Bullard's words gave it the presidential imprimatur. General Electric would have a market for its alternators, a way out of the Marconi negotiations, and preservation of its sizable investments in Alexanderson's work. Sufficiently wooed, Young and the senior General Electric officials approved of the offer. The next day Hooper received a phone call in Washington: General Electric's deal with Marconi was off. A draft agreement for a federally chartered radio company gradually took shape over the next several weeks, at the hands of patent experts from the navy and General Electric. The company would create a subsidiary with 80 percent of its stock in American hands, staff the company with American citizens, and equip it with a brace of high-power stations for international work. To protect U.S. technology, the navy would have the right to veto the sales of radio equipment to foreign countries. A nonvoting representative of the government—a naval officer—would sit on the company's board to present the government's views. Most important, the draft charter would allow an exchange of radio-related patents between the navy and General Electric. This was crucial. No single company controlled all of the patents needed to build and operate a first-rate transmitting and receiving station. The U.S. Navy would give General Electric all of the patents the navy had acquired, which would allow the new company to build a complete station. Armed with the patents and shielded by the federal charter, this new company would be in a very strong position.[61]

The entire project nearly collapsed when Daniels caught word of it. Hooper and his associates had so far been acting with the tacit approval of Bullard and Roosevelt, the acting secretary while Daniels was in Paris. At no point, however, had Hooper or anyone else bothered to clear this monumental deal with Admiral Griffin, head of the Bureau of Steam Engineering and Hooper's superior; Admiral Benson, the chief of naval operations; or Secretary Daniels himself. All three were in Paris. It appears that the original plan was for Bullard and a General Electric official to take the draft contract to Paris for approval by Wilson and Daniels. When the secretary sent word that Daniels would be leaving Paris earlier than expected, it upset the plan and left the conspirators two paths. One was to wait until Daniels arrived in Washington, despite the danger that he would probably reject the contract. The other was to have Roosevelt approve it anyway and create a fait accompli to corner Daniels. But an accident of loyalty stayed Roosevelt's hand. Hooper, believing he should at least let Admiral Griffin know, cabled him in Paris to request authorization. Unconscious of the subterfuge, Griffin shared the message with Daniels. The secretary immediately cabled back that all policy questions were on hold until his return in mid-May.[62]

Arriving in Washington, Daniels refused to sign off on the plan after hearing Bullard's briefing. He would not do anything more until he had met with the cabinet and with congressional leaders to get their support in advance. Daniels remained unalterably opposed to anything but the idea of government control and told Young and other General Electric officials as much several days later. Hooper tried to enlist Griffin's help, but Daniels would not be swayed.[63]

General Electric needed Daniels's support only if the company were to win a federal charter. Nothing stopped Young and other company officials from going it alone without official sanction. There was also nothing stopping them from forming a joint company with American Marconi, which had the experience in operating commercial radio that General Electric certainly did not. Hooper did his best to nurture this deal, with threats and encouragement. E. J. Nally was told that the navy would scrap the New Brunswick station rather than see American Marconi get the alternator. Young learned that the navy would put the alternator in storage at the Brooklyn Navy Yard, freeze shipment of the second one from Schenectady, and view other General Electric contracts critically. Even though this would hurt General Electric and halt international commercial operations, Hooper made it clear that he was prepared to go this far.[64] Nally and Young did not call Hooper's bluff but instead began serious negotiations to form a joint company. American Marconi would provide the experience of its personnel. General Electric would provide the capital and equipment. In June company attorneys drew up the terms of a merger. General Electric would create a new company to buy out American Marconi completely at a fair price and General Electric would sell to this new company the alternators. Asked to review the proposal, Daniels agreed to release the alternator at New Brunswick from naval incarceration and even granted permission for General Electric to sell transmitters to British Marconi now that the U.S. stations would be under total American control. But there would be no federal charter or private monopoly. All that remained was to secure British Marconi's agreement.[65]

In August discussions in London between General Electric and Marconi company officials cleared the way for the ultimate demise of American Marconi and the formation of the Radio Corporation of America. Denied any share in the new company, Godfrey Isaacs agreed to give up to General Electric the shares in American Marconi. In exchange, General Electric and British Marconi would share the right to use each other's latest patents but not compete in each other's home territory (including the British Empire). In South America, they would form a new joint company under American control. In China the new U.S. company would not have competition from Marconi for U.S.-bound traffic. In all other parts of the world, the companies would cross-license their patents but be free to compete. This arrangement had the effect of putting British Marconi at the very edge of technology in return for granting the United States a place in international radio communications. For this, General Electric paid $3 million.[66]

RCA took shape in the final months of 1919. General Electric became the principal stockholder. In October, American Marconi officials took the necessary steps to subsume their operations under RCA's new banner. E. J. Nally would be head of operations as president of the company. To assuage fears that RCA was simply American Marconi in a new guise, Owen Young left his position with General Electric to become the new chairman of the board of RCA and to signal General Electric's strong commitment to the venture. Comforted by the existence of an American-controlled radio company, Admiral Griffin and Secretary Daniels authorized the release of the alternator at New Brunswick and the eventual return of the station to private hands. By November 20, the merger was complete. When President Wilson decreed the end of naval control over all radio operations the following March, it was now RCA that took over operations in Massachusetts, New York, California, and Hawaii. Whether or not RCA would meet navy's expectations, naval officers had no doubt that a financially sound company of reliable loyalty had emerged.[67]

From 1919 to 1920, RCA expanded operations quickly. The company opened regular commercial service with Britain, Norway, Germany, France, and Japan. Owen Young announced the purchase of six thousand acres on Long Island for a massive new radio station to be equipped with multiple alternators. Keeping a watchful eye on the company's affairs was Admiral Bullard, appointed by President Wilson as the federal representative to the board.[68] Hooper believed that the second-most important concern after RCA's creation was the preservation of wartime production of vacuum tubes, which were being used in receivers and would eventually replace the alternator. In early 1920 he guided General Electric and AT&T toward a patent exchange that would make available the most-advanced vacuum tubes to both the navy and RCA. The resulting agreement ensured both General Electric and AT&T could manufacture the most-advanced radio equipment, while AT&T would not face competition in the field of wireless telephony. AT&T then made a substantial investment in RCA. Following up on this, Owen Young negotiated similar deals with United Fruit and Westinghouse to obtain their patents in exchange for sizable investments. At the same time, Young used RCA's strong position to bind through negotiations British, French, and German radio companies in Latin America into a consortium controlled by RCA, even before regular commercial work had begun. As the Wilson administration left office, RCA had gained de facto control over much of the nation's research, manufacturing, and operations in radio and had secured the international connections that the navy wanted to be in U.S. hands. Though few asked it at the time, the only question that remained was how long the interests of the navy and RCA would remain in synch.

While RCA grew stronger in the spring of 1920, Western Union and Western Telegraph began the construction of their direct cable between the United States and Brazil. As this proceeded, officials in the State Department became concerned that when the two companies completed their work, they might be able to drive John Merrill's Central and South American Telegraph Company, now known as All America Cables, out of business in South America. Anxiety intensified when word arrived that Western Union was also planning a cable line down the Pacific coast from the Canal Zone to Peru, to meet a British cable at Callao and encircle South America. If this Western Union–Western Telegraph consortium succeeded, so the analysis went, it would overwhelm Merrill's All America company. If that happened, communications between the United States and Latin America would come under British control once again. So long as the British companies held exclusionary concessions in the region, U.S. companies would accept co-option or give up. Consequently, State Department officials concluded that they would have to oppose Western Union's attempts to land the new Brazil cable in the United States by whatever means necessary. Only with such leverage, they believed, could they force the British company to drop its exclusionary concessions in the region. The motivation was less the need to protect Merrill's All America Cables or hurt Western Union than the desire to prevent British companies from hindering the growth of U.S. international communications. The resulting clash would be a remarkable standoff with long-lasting effects.[69]

State Department officials moved carefully against Western Union through the spring and early summer of 1920. Frank Polk dispatched William Nye, the State Department's chief special agent, to Miami to report on the telegraph company's movements. The department solicitor warned the company that the president had to grant the customary (but not legally required) permit to land a cable.[70] With the help of the State Department, All America's counsel, Elihu Root Jr., drafted for Senator Frank Kellogg legislation to give the executive branch the formal authority to grant and enforce restrictions on cable-landing permits. With such a tool, the State Department could trade access to the United States for elimination of exclusive rights elsewhere, such as those the British companies enjoyed in South America.[71] When Newcomb Carlton asked the department in April about the state of the landing license application, he was informed that the British company's exclusionary concessions in Latin America prevented the approval. The next day Kellogg introduced the landing license bill in the Senate. But it was not clear that withholding the license would be enough. Root worried that Carlton might repeat what the French had done in 1897: seek permission after landing the cable and activating it. Consequently, the new secretary of state, Bainbridge Colby, decided to force the issue.[72]

At Colby's recommendation, President Wilson in mid July instructed the State, Justice, Navy, and War departments to cooperate in blocking Western Union from landing the cable at Miami.[73] Secretary of War Newton Baker placed soldiers in the army's Southeastern Department on alert to be ready to respond if necessary. Four U.S. Navy destroyers and a submarine chaser shadowed the cable ship *Colonia* as she sailed down the Florida coast toward Miami with the oceanic cable on board. Admiral Benton Decker, commandant of the Seventh Naval District, was to use "such force as may be necessary" to prevent Western Union from laying any cable within a three-mile limit of the coast. When Decker tried to negotiate with Western Union, Daniels abruptly replaced him with another admiral, Edwin Anderson.[74] The crew of the *Colonia*, prohibited from laying cable in U.S. waters, dropped the end of the cable outside the three-mile limit, along with a bright orange buoy, on August 11. Over the next ten days the crew laid the rest of the cable to Barbados. The *Cole*, a destroyer, shadowed her the entire way. Federal officials then turned their attention to the shore end, the three-mile long cable segment that would connect the deep-water end to a cable hut in Miami Beach. That piece lay in the hold of the cable tug *Robert C. Clowry*, which was in the area and also under naval observation.[75]

Newcomb Carlton became understandably frustrated. The entire cable was complete except for the last three miles. Western Union had invested millions in the operation so far and had given up its own concessions in Brazil in return. Moreover, Carlton was only doing what the Wilson administration itself had been asking of American companies since 1916. Indeed, William G. McAdoo, former treasury secretary and Wilson's son-in-law, now represented Western Union and reminded the administration of its earlier encouragement for what Western Union was doing. By the fall, Newcomb Carlton became desperate. It would be only a few hours' work to bring the shore end to the cable hut at Miami Beach and connect Miami to Brazil. The longer the delay, the greater the costs.

Company officials then investigated alternatives. They had a 1916 permit to lay a cable from Miami to Key West and then to Havana. By November, they were making preparations to run this cable out from Miami and then, instead of heading to Key West, connecting it with the Barbados cable out at sea. Rather than do this surreptitiously, however, Carlton intended to play to the press and motion picture cameras to show publicly the damages done to his company when the navy had stopped the laying of the cable. Learning of this in a cabinet meeting on November 23, Wilson ordered that all work be halted and the matter pushed into the courts. The necessary permits were revoked, the necessary workers halted. On November 24, *Subchaser-154* intercepted a Western Union barge along the causeway from Miami to Miami Beach. Landing two sailors armed with rifles, Lieutenant W. C. Murray stopped the company crew from running telegraph wire to the hut at Miami Beach. After a few tense hours, the supervisor informed Murray, "Well, I guess you are the master of the situation, with those men and guns." That afternoon Western Union attorneys marched into the Washington, D.C., federal courthouse to file lawsuits.[76]

The diplomatic and legal wrangling between the Wilson administration and Western Union intensified over the next four months. Western Union attorneys asked the court to block the government from stopping work on the cable, to let the company land the cable. Meanwhile, the *Robert C. Clowry*, Western Union's cable tug, moved cables near Havana, possibly in preparation to move the Barbados cable down to Cuba instead. At Colby's informal request, the Cuban government made it clear that Western Union could not reroute the lines to Havana and sent soldiers to guard the cable-landing locations. Wilson rejected offers from Carlton to work out a compromise. Instead, naval warships continued to patrol Miami Harbor and shadow the *Clowry* around Florida and Cuba. Carlton wanted the cable landed before Congress passed Kellogg's cable-landing act, which would give the Wilson administration the power to stop the cable completely. After Carlton testified to the Senate that he would flout presidential authority to get his cable landed, the Wilson administration filed a countersuit to stop Western Union from interfering with the executive's "duty to protect the national territory."[77]

As the court cases came before the Supreme Court, the clash peaked. On March 5, 1921, the *Clowry* eluded her guards and made it to sea near the buoyed Barbados cable. As the *Clowry* began to raise the cable, *Subchaser-154* caught up to the tug, and Ensign William Klapproth yelled at the captain to stop his work. When Captain H. M. Smith refused, Klapproth threatened force. Smith's answer was a curt "Go ahead." Klapproth ordered shots fired across the *Clowry*'s bow. Smith immediately halted. Arrested by the navy, Smith ventured that he would go right back out the next day. The next day another subchaser arrived at Miami to reinforce the guard, and Smith conceded the obvious. Why had this happened? March 5 was inauguration weekend, and Western Union appears to have tried to take advantage of the change in administration. The navy at Miami, however, had no change in orders.

As astonishing as the incident in Miami was, it did not derail either congressional passage of the cable-landing law in May or a settlement of the issue among the major companies in the months that followed. It did lead, significantly, to Western Union's withdrawal from the secret agreement to share cable traffic with Yardley's intelligence operation in New York, a move that may have permanently crippled the clandestine program. Still, forced by the new law to accede to State Department desires, Western Telegraph negotiated an abdication of exclusive rights in Latin America in exchange for All America waiving any similar rights in Chile and Peru. In return, on May 1, 1922, President Warren G. Harding granted Western Union permission to land its cable. By August the cable opened for business to Brazil, and the last subchaser departed. But for all the tensions of the recent years, the situation passed into lasting calm. In the subsequent years, there would be little new cable work by the major companies in Latin America, despite the grandiose plans advanced by Carlton and Merrill during the war. Nonetheless, the public and private efforts during and after the war to enhance cable connections between Latin America and the United States had partially succeeded and laid down precedents that would, through the Cable Landing License Act, remain in place to the present.[78]

In the years after the armistice, public and private attention in the United States to the state of worldwide communications lingered but dissipated gradually as the urgency of the war faded and the anticipated changes did not materialize. Personnel changes and policy confusion, compounded by Wilson's political and physical collapse, weakened the momentum that Breckinridge Long, Stanford Hooper, and others had generated. The preliminary conference on international communications, which was to have settled the agenda for the subsequent worldwide cable and radio congress, failed to resolve the fate of Germany's cables or Yap Island. The general conference never met. The experience further soured U.S. relations with Great Britain, Japan, and France.

Where the multilateral approach did not succeed, the private efforts of U.S. companies were marginally better. Though there were no improvements to Pacific communications, U.S. cable companies continued their push into Latin America. Central, changing its name to All America Cables, secured its long-sought concessions to Brazil but faced a new challenge from a collaboration between Western Union and Western Telegraph that would save the American firm funds badly needed for cable projects elsewhere. The Wilson administration, seeing in this collaboration the danger of greater British control over cable communications amid allegations that the wartime interceptions had not ceased and U.S. diplomatic traffic remained vulnerable, blocked Western Union from landing the cable at Miami. This strike at Western Telegraph by proxy created the unusual situation of the U.S. government using warships against its own citizens. The matter would be resolved by 1922, but the lingering antagonism between the United States and Great Britain would complicate subsequent clashes at the Azores over cable-landing rights and access by other U.S. cable companies to Europe.

Mindful of the cable situation and perceiving a closing window of opportunity, Stanford Hooper had seized the opportunity to block General Electric's negotiations to sell the Alexanderson alternator and to form with RCA the long-desired all-American international radio company. Yet by the end of 1921, Hooper and other naval radio officers had become very concerned about the extent to which RCA's interests were in line with those of the navy. RCA had transformed beyond Hooper's intentions into a powerful industrial conglomerate easily capable of co-opting its rivals. This development was at odds with the U.S. Navy's desire for a single international operator amid a multiplicity of research and manufacturing firms. Hooper even attempted to create a competitor by merging Westinghouse with the rump manufacturing arm of Federal Telegraph, with a view to having another company to manufacture equipment and operate international radio circuits. When Westinghouse joined the RCA cross-licensing deal instead, Hooper felt that Owen Young had betrayed him.[79] But with the growing use of the vacuum tube and the migration of radio into the shortwave part of the spectrum in the mid-1920s, the wartime concerns about finite numbers of long-distance stations evaporated. While RCA continued to play a predominant role in global wireless communications over the next several decades, handling up to 50 percent of all traffic on some routes, its relations with the U.S. Navy remained unsettled amid concern over its consolidated power.[80]

If anything, the breadth of these undertakings—carried out in the United States and abroad, in the fields of both radio and submarine cables, by officials in several different departments, and with multiple private companies—indicated how seriously those in the Wilson administration took the situation and how earnestly they believed their actions to be necessary. The United States would come away from the First World War having learned of the significance of cable and radio connections to world power. The interwar years would see substantial technological changes that would alter but not eliminate the problems that these officials had perceived. Only after another world war and an emerging geopolitical rivalry would there be the kind of sustained attention to these problems that officials during the Wilson administration had sought.

Conclusion

LIKE THE GLARE of sunlight in a darkened room, the experiences of World War I awakened U.S. officials to the broader requirements of being a world power. Among these were a large naval force, a strong military, a sturdy domestic base of industry and finance, and a corresponding system of transportation and communications to project this political, military, and economic influence across the seas. During this time, a select few public officials and private individuals came to appreciate the strategic importance of an international radio and submarine telegraph cable network serving the nation and to realize the network's inadequacies. They took it upon themselves to protect and expand these links to Europe, Latin America, and Asia. They believed that doing this and building up the domestic resources to support the network would lend significant advantages to a nation now taking its place among the great powers. However, things did not work out as supporters of the network had planned. For all the urgency of the war years and the activity during the armistice, federal efforts to meet the need for cable and radio links lost momentum in the final months of the Wilson administration. It would further weaken throughout the interwar years. Only with the onset of a second worldwide conflict twenty years later, a dramatic shift in the concepts and requirements of national security, and significant technological changes in the very nature of electrical communications would there come lasting, coordinated attention to the nation's international cable and radio ties.

Britain and Germany had both given considerable attention to the strategic importance of cables and radio before 1914. These nations, along with France, Holland, Spain, Italy, and Japan, had with varying success centrally directed the laying of cables and the construction of radio stations to meet strategic needs. Alert to the military and economic importance of these communications links, planners in both Britain and Germany strove to craft redundant routes to ensure a continuity of contact in the midst of conflict. In Britain's case, widely dispersed naval strength and an abundance of overseas territory made substantial reliance upon cables the best option. A plethora of cable supplies and repair ships ensured that wartime disruptions remained only temporary nuisances. Germany, which was likely to concede naval superiority across the globe and was short on colonies, chose to invest in a risky network of long-distance radio stations. Those in Africa and Asia proved vulnerable to destruction at the onset of war. The proliferation of German stations in the Americas became a cause for concern in the United States.

Moreover, both Britain and Germany took steps to destroy their opponent's communications links as a part of their war-fighting strategy. This electronic information warfare, on a scope and scale never before seen, directly affected the United States from the first hours of the war. Having forced the Central powers to use wireless or Allies' cables to reach beyond Europe, Britain used interception and cable censorship as part of an informational blockade, compounding the effects of the maritime blockade. Germany's bold but unsuccessful steps to attack cables on the high seas reflected a sophisticated understanding of their importance to effective coalition warfare. Together, these events forced upon the United States the realization that regardless of its moral or financial stake in any future war, the structure of the global cable and radio network and the nation's dependence upon lines of communication controlled by other powers placed the United States at a distinct and unpleasant disadvantage.

This imbalance became much more overt once the United States joined the war in April 1917. The initial assumption of military officers was that they could depend on the transatlantic cable network to provide continual contact with the expeditionary force in France. Given the weak state of transoceanic radio technology at the time, this was a realistic assumption. It soon became apparent to government officials, however, that these lines of communication were insecure. By the end of 1917, only half of the cables were still in operation. The implicit threat of submarines had deterred repair ships from doing routine cable maintenance or emergency repair work. There was a very real threat of submarine attacks on the cables themselves. Cable communications were easily vulnerable to further disruptions. The steadily increasing volume of war-related traffic, the limited number of alternate routes, and the money, resources, and time required to laying new transatlantic cables led the Navy to use the commercial high-power radio stations it had appropriated and to construct new stations for ensuring continual contact with Europe. In the end, the cable and radio system held, but had the war intensified or the German attacks succeeded, the situation would have been far more dire.

Beyond the question of how to stay in touch with forces in Europe, the war experience revealed for the United States several other significant aspects of the strategic importance of global communications. The imposition of censorship over the cables touching U.S. territory, the coordination of this with other forms of Allied censorship, and the creation of a wartime traffic monitoring group gave U.S. officials a taste of the great power to be gained from control of the cables. The Zimmermann telegram, regular interference with commercial and press communications, and allegations of British indiscretions with U.S. traffic were significant too. It became clear to many that should the United States wish to have secret, rapid contact with other countries in the future, it was essential to have direct cable contact, free of foreign influence whenever possible. In this light, diplomatic support for John Merrill's Central and South American Telegraph Company in its fight against Western Telegraph took on new importance. Just as important in this regard was the rapidly growing field of long-distance radio, a subject that had concerned the U.S. Navy since the turn of the century but that became more pressing after 1914. Fearful of foreign interference with both the developing domestic radio industry and stations around the Caribbean basin and across Latin America, the navy became closely involved in the evolution of this technology at home and abroad.

With these events in mind, U.S. officials took several important steps to correct the perceived imbalance in control of communications. Throughout the war, the United States maintained a diplomatic effort to keep European radio stations out of the Western Hemisphere. Internal disagreements within the navy over national radio policy, however, prevented the formation of a successful U.S.-controlled company capable of meeting the growing demand for long-distance radio service with North America. The State Department maintained its diplomatic support for the Central company in its fight to secure cable concessions in Brazil, Uruguay, and Argentina and to minimize British influence over U.S. cable connections there. At the same time, Breckinridge Long had initiated the first interdepartmental review of overall cable policy, out of frustration with the poor state of transpacific communications and with a view to implementing technical improvements and crafting a domestic cable industry from scratch.

These initiatives continued on into the armistice period. Guided by Long and Walter Rogers of the Committee on Public Information, President Wilson and Secretary Lansing halted the apportioning of German cables among the victors at Versailles and pushed for a postwar communication conference with which to undo the imbalances across the worldwide cable network. With the inevitable end of censorship, State Department and army officials created a peacetime cryptologic group and drafted secret agreements with cable companies to keep the flow of cable traffic coming into the United States. Long launched several efforts to develop a cable industry capable of meeting the growing need for submarine telegraph cable equipment and supplies, and pushed the Commerce Department to find solutions to the shortages of gutta-percha insulation. When Daniels's last efforts to win control over radio for the U.S. Navy failed, Commander Stanford Hooper was able to broker the creation of the Radio Corporation of America and invest it with sufficient assets to keep the United States at the forefront of radio communications.

Despite the momentum generated by the urgency of the World War I, these various efforts to craft a sustained program for bringing the United States into the center of global communications were unsuccessful. It took more than a year to organize a preliminary conference to discuss President Wilson's proposed international electrical communications conference. During these initial meetings, Britain, France, Japan, Italy, and the United States could not reach any agreement on distributing the German cables in such a way that would not leave the United States worse off than it had been before the war. The initial recommendations of the participants were ignored. The larger conference never convened. Meaningful negotiations over the imbalances in the worldwide cable and radio networks would not occur for another decade. Despite Breckinridge Long's hopes, the federal government never cornered the market on gutta-percha, discovered a pliable substitute, or jump-started a domestic cable industry. Although negotiations began in the first months of 1919 with interested parties in Europe, Commercial Cable and Western Union did not lay any new cables across the Atlantic until the mid-1920s, after further diplomatic and commercial fights with the British at the Azores.[1] Where the demand for service was greater, on the Pacific route, there would be no new submarine cable between the United States and Asia until 1964. Neither Commercial Pacific, the United States Senate, the Council on Foreign Relations, nor interested Japanese businesses could muster the energy or finances to put such a plan into motion. President Warren G. Harding dismissed the idea of any government support altogether in the years that followed. While RCA would draw a growing percentage of international traffic away from the cables, that market would become insignificant for the industrial giant compared with the growing domestic radio entertainment field. The cooperation between the cable companies and the joint intelligence operation of the State and War departments, meanwhile, lasted for about two years before Western Union withdrew from the agreement because of the fight to land a cable at Miami. Access to Japanese diplomatic traffic carried by the Mackay companies enabled the United States delegates to gain the advantage in negotiations during the Washington Arms Limitation Conference in late 1921 and early 1922, but this source too dried up as the 1920s went on and the urgency of the war years faded.[2] At the same time, U.S. cable company executives confirmed allegations that Britain continued to monitor international cable traffic in peacetime, prompting an admission from the British government that it regularly read diplomatic traffic but a vehement denial that it profited from access to commercial traffic.[3] Except for gains in communications in Latin America, the United States entered the 1920s worse off for cable communications than before the war, with an administration that paid only lip service to the need to improve the situation.[4]

Indeed, perhaps the sole success for the United States was the creation of permanent executive authority over cable landings on U.S. territory. The Cable Landing License Act of May 1921 was a tool for protecting U.S. strategic interests (by determining who could communicate with the United States) and for opening the international cable network up to competition (by threatening to withhold access to the remunerative U.S. market). The act's passage helped to compel Western Union to settle the Miami dispute and Western Telegraph to concede to a bargain to eliminate restrictive concessions in Latin America. But this development was relatively minor at the time; inapplicable to existing cables, the act brought only limited leverage to the few new cables laid through the rest of the interwar years.

Why, then, with its tremendous industrial power, financial resources, and involvement in world affairs, did the United States not sustain the wartime momentum and take a predominant position in global communications commensurate with its newfound role? What accounts for the difference between the United States on the one hand and Britain, Germany, and France on the other in incorporating strategic communications into foreign relations and military planning? The answer to this lies not in the interwar fate of individual projects or debates about corporate influences on foreign policymaking, but in both the deeper conditions that prevailed during the war and the nature of the United States at the time. Three interrelated answers present themselves: the inability to adapt individual enthusiasm into institutional attention, the misalignment of the nation's strategic and commercial interests, and exogenous factors particular to the United States, factors that together formed an insurmountable barrier to rapid success.

The first of these reasons was an organizational failure to transform the temporary interest and drive of individuals like Boaz Long, Stanford Hooper, Breckinridge Long, Walter Rogers, and John Merrill into a policy more permanent and adaptable to U.S. needs. In both Britain and Germany, high officials had already been coordinating diplomatic, military, and commercial requirements with the growing cable and radio networks since the late nineteenth century. Within the United States, this approach might have included the vesting of an existing official, department, interdepartmental committee, or new administrative body with permanent responsibility for or authority over communications. These had been Progressive solutions to other problems at the federal level, the Joint Army-Navy Board and the Interstate Commerce Commission being two such examples. However, no individual or group took up the mission of strategic communications. While Commander Hooper had made within the navy sweeping organizational changes regarding radio, national radio policy remained disorganized. The Commerce Department held licensing authority but was unable to evaluate the diplomatic or military implications of foreign-owned stations. The State Department, which could have evaluated these implications, deferred to the Navy Department. Yet divergent ideas within the navy about the best way to organize hemispheric radio led to the paradoxical and self-defeating dual endorsement of government control and U.S. commercial expansion across the hemisphere. This division within the navy paralyzed those private companies willing to take on the challenge. When Breckinridge Long began to coordinate cable policy, he found willing support from Walter Rogers, George Squier, and others alert to the broad significance of cable communications. But Long's interest came from a concern over larger diplomatic problems in the Pacific, not from any specific enthusiasm for submarine cables. After Long's departure in 1920 to Missouri for an unsuccessful Senate bid, cable affairs devolved to regional department heads. There was little coordination inside the State Department or with other departments, even though most agreed that the private companies could not—ought not to—be expected to coordinate policy themselves.

Further complicating this situation was the unresolved debate about national control over domestic communications, an ongoing issue that had pitted the U.S. Post Office against the commercial telegraph and telephone companies for more than a generation. The United States was exceptional in that it was the only country in the world at the time to permit domestic electrical communications to be in private hands. Albert Burleson's failed drive to consolidate the nation's electrical communications permanently under federal authority complicated the larger discussions about cable and radio policy. The postmaster general had become massively unpopular for his wartime censorship of the mails and the disastrous handling of the nationalized telephone and telegraph networks. But because he had taken the lead on domestic communications issues, it was natural and easy to presume that he should also head international communications issues, just as his counterparts in Britain, France, and elsewhere did. And Wilson accordingly did choose Burleson to head the interdepartmental effort in 1920 to organize the international communications conference. But the international cable and radio situation had become a matter of diplomatic, military, and commercial importance, ones which the U.S. Post Office, for all of its interest in domestic communications policy, was ill equipped to handle. Burleson's efforts needlessly squandered Wilson's weakened influence at a critical time. Burleson created suspicion and hesitation among the communications companies that were expected to cooperate and demonstrated the clear need for central direction from either the president or a designated representative. There would be no lasting central authority capable of considering the nation's diplomatic, military, and commercial interests into a strategic cable and radio policy until 1934, when the former assistant naval secretary—President Franklin D. Roosevelt—who had been favorable to Hooper's wild ideas, established the Federal Communications Commission.

The failure to designate any such central authority for coordinating cable and radio development with the nation's national security needs stemmed in part from the differing frames of reference the military, the State Department, and the cable and radio companies used when thinking about communications with the rest of the world and problem of integrating those worldviews. Such a disconnect was not unique to the question of strategic communications, however, and was symptomatic of a larger problem of coordinating policy and strategy among the army, navy, State Department, Congress, and others concerned with national security, a problem that would become particularly acute in the 1930s.[5]

Military planners cast defense of the country in terms of protecting the continent, its adjacent oceans, and the Panama Canal against any threats; forestalling further European intervention in the Western Hemisphere; protecting the Pacific territories; and preserving the territorial integrity of China. Doing so effectively required, among other things, the maintenance of continually reliable lines of communications. To meet the crushing demand for such communications in wartime, the armed services expected to augment their operations with the existing commercial systems. With some exceptions, the armed services encouraged the steady proliferation of U.S.-controlled cable connections to places of military significance. The greatest emphasis was on the Caribbean, particularly the islands and the Canal Zone, and across the Pacific to the Philippines. These were the places the army and the navy had to think most about defending. While the navy maintained its own strategic radio network to ensure continual contact with the fleet guarding the coasts, the success of RCA ensured that an additional commercial capacity existed to bolster that network in the event of another war.[6]

State Department officials developed a much broader perception of the need for cables and radios. Before 1914 diplomatic support for U.S. communications companies appears to have been no different than that given to firms selling machinery, cotton, or, perhaps, beeswax candles. The war made clear that control over cables and radio stations granted control over diplomatic, commercial, and press traffic, with potentially strategic consequences and that the network serving the United States was imbalanced. From the perspective of the State Department, having more cables or radio links to Asia, Latin America, and Europe was important in the abstract, regardless of the individual commercial necessity or military utility of a particular route. Ideally, diluting the power of the few countries controlling the global networks would make it easier for the citizens of the world to understand one another and to realize President Wilson's dreams of transforming international relations and spreading democracy. More pragmatically, the steady extension of cables and radios operated by U.S. firms would help to keep United States diplomatic and commercial information secure from foreign influence while making that of other countries available to the United States through the Cipher Bureau in New York. To this end, the view of those like Breckinridge Long and Walter Rogers was that the United States should see greater cable contact with all parts of the world, not just those areas central to national defense.

Commercial profitability, not utility for diplomacy or national defense, always guided the thinking of cable and radio company executives as they planned the extension of their lines abroad. Because of the great costs involved in laying new cables or constructing high-power radio stations, it made the most sense to follow the existing patterns of trade, where traffic returns would be greatest. Thus the greatest number of cables linked the United States with Europe, while only one went to the Philippines. John Merrill's Central and South American Telegraph Company ran lines across South America, with the intention of eventually reaching Brazil, the most lucrative market, not just Chile or Colombia. Federal Telegraph, Pan-American Wireless, and eventually RCA went primarily after direct long-distance connections to Brazil and Argentina, rather than building a network of smaller stations across Latin America or resting content with the sale of operating equipment to governments across the region. If necessary, compromise with foreign companies was perfectly acceptable even if it went against the interests of the U.S. government. Thus Mackay's Postal Telegraph and Commercial Cable companies joined with British and Danish companies to lay the transpacific cable. Thus Newcomb Carlton was willing to deal with Western Telegraph to reduce the costs of reaching Brazil. Thus British Marconi could seriously entertain the idea of acquiring Federal Telegraph. The greatest frustration came when the profit motive clashed with particular ideas held by federal officials of what the national interest was. This was the case with Western Union at Miami and with Federal Telegraph in 1918–1919. This kind of clash led to the passage of a law giving the executive branch some measure of influence over unequal cable concessions elsewhere in the world, but this law came at the expense of its target, Western Union, which withdrew from the signals intelligence operation in New York. On the issue of federal control over radio operations in the United States, Josephus Daniels vexed those U.S. companies pursuing regular connections to the Philippines, Panama, Latin America, and Asia. As Federal Telegraph and Pan-America Wireless found out, the persistent threat from the navy to expropriate the essential station in the United States immeasurably complicated efforts to construct expensive high-power stations both at home and abroad. With sufficient federal subsidies for cable or radio construction unlikely, at the end of the day cable and radio companies were not interested in expanding to places of diplomatic or military significance abroad unless the markets were commercially important and the lines suitably profitable.

Even if there had been a way to bring together the disparate interests of the military, the diplomats, and the businessmen, there were several additional factors that collectively formed high barriers to the rapid proliferation of cables and radio stations. One of the most unavoidable factors was the very real barrier of the major oceans surrounding North America. The great distances that at once provided "free security" against foreign invasion also became tremendous hurdles necessitating radio transmitters of significant power or cables of great length.[7] In the case of radio, Commander Hooper and naval radio officers managed to turn this liability into an asset. Eschewing the strategic vulnerabilities of a long chain of lower-power stations in indefensible Pacific territories, Hooper pushed radio equipment designers to come up with technology capable of leaping the thousands of miles between the United States and the Philippines with ease. As a result, he helped to drive the United States to the very fore of radio communications, a process not repeated in the more-conservative submarine telegraph industry. In the case of the cables, the effective operation of the cables required them to be as short as possible to minimize signal disruption. Thus U.S. cable companies could not reach Europe by cable without stopping along the way to renew the signal at intermediate points, the most accessible of which were British imperial territory. Across the Pacific, the limited number of suitable islands and the vast distances between them made the situation even worse. Under such circumstances, even the otherwise irrelevant island of Yap took on significant diplomatic importance. Despite the best wishes of federal officials, geographic realities frequently constrained strategic desires.[8]

These geographical barriers simply raised the basic costs of doing business. Even if federal officials could be certain that operations were in U.S. hands, passed through reliable neutral countries, or made use of the most-advanced equipment, the great distances involved always levied a significant toll. Thousands of miles of submarine telegraph cables and long-distance high-power radio stations were expensive, necessary investments before any operations could begin. The Western Union cable between Miami and Barbados ultimately cost the company around $3 million, considerably cheaper than the $15 million projected cost for a cable all the way to Brazil.[9] Estimates for the proposed five-thousand-mile transpacific cable ran to approximately $30 million. The high demand, limited supply, and absence of suitable substitutes for the essential gutta-percha insulation led to a doubling of the price during the war years and contributed to the reluctance of the U.S. cable companies to invest in their own cable research and manufacturing capacity. The massive Poulsen arc or Alexanderson alternator transmitters capable of reaching across the great oceans cost tens of thousands of dollars and were useless without the accompanying antenna array and operating equipment, which would push the cost into the hundreds of thousands of dollars. Beyond this, cable and radio companies in the United States faced additional costs in gathering and distributing traffic, services normally handled in other countries by a state telegraph authority. These investment costs, coupled with the technical expertise necessary for effective operation, represented significant barriers to a market not immediately remunerative to those brave enough to enter it.[10]

Finally, those U.S. cable or radio companies capable of hurdling these geographical and financial obstacles would still crash into other barriers erected in important locations overseas. Between exclusionary or monopoly concessions and discriminatory rate practices, British, French, and Japanese competitors could and did keep U.S. firms from encroaching on territory already staked out in Latin America, China, and essential cable-landing islands like the Azores and Yap. Security fears about the implications of allowing in foreign cable or radio stations, identical to those fears developing in the United States at this time, led Japan and Brazil to levy great restrictions on the ownership and operation of communications facilities. Altogether, these encumbrances made it much more difficult for the commercial companies that would operate the international cable and radio connections for the United States to realize dreams of wiring the world, dreams held by farsighted U.S. officials.

For historians who study the foreign relations of the United States in the early twentieth century, these efforts made by U.S. officials to protect and expand the nation's international communications infrastructure in support of changing diplomatic, military, and commercial ambitions is an important if overlooked story. It illustrates the extent to which the United States was not prepared for the world role President Wilson dreamt for it, at levels deeper than simply diplomatic participation in the League of Nations or the maintenance of a navy second to none. The national will, as reflected in administrative disunity, congressional apathy, and commercial hesitancy, was not sufficient to sustain the political momentum, financial support, and strategic clarity essential for transforming the nation's cable and radio network from a regional to a global one, as Great Britain and Germany had done nearly two decades earlier. Individual enthusiasm from national figures for the power of technology and its ability to draw the world closer together led to few concrete achievements in the 1920s of the sort that did justice to the original dreams. Only with the tremendous responsibilities generated by World War II and the cold war that followed would federal officials and commercial firms finally confront these issues in a lasting manner.[11]

What makes this story different from other accounts of the evolution of U.S. foreign affairs or the transformation of U.S. economic influence abroad is the strategic importance of communications to world power. Whether the president actually made the observation Admiral Bullard attributed to him, Wilson's insight was apt: control of communications, transportation, and energy were, in the modern era, necessary prerequisites for global predominance. Understanding the rise of the United States in the twentieth century requires tracing how this nation passed from the periphery to the center of world communications and transportation networks and how it gathered tremendous, if not preponderant, influence over energy and financial markets. We might term these four factors strategic goods, distinct from and far more important because of their diplomatic and military utility than the agricultural, industrial, or consumer goods more commonly associated with the expansion of U.S. trade in the late nineteenth and early twentieth centuries.

Analysis of these factors, especially communications, indicates that a corporatist approach to the study of international relations in the 1920s may not be entirely helpful, because it overemphasizes cooperation and engagement, when often co-option or disengagement occurred instead. When U.S. officials perceived the strategic importance of international communications during and after the World War I, they specifically opposed stability, harmony, and collaboration between U.S. and foreign cable or radio companies, as Western Union and American Marconi could easily attest. In doing so, federal officials backed companies that could co-opt or drive away their foreign competitors and bring the United States into the center of international communications networks. After 1921, however, the Republican administrations' approach to cable and radio matters largely lacked this wartime concern for the diplomatic and military importance of communications. Significantly, the Republican administrations also gave surprisingly minimal attention to the commercial importance of international communications, given the well-recognized utility of expanded cable and radio links to international commerce and the long-standing pressure from merchants on both coasts for improvements to those links. This suggests not a pursuit of stability, harmony, and international collaboration, or a devolution to private actors in pursuit of clear objectives, but instead a curious disengagement from a complex subject. If the business of America was business, why was more not done to make that business easier to conduct abroad? In addition, it would be a mistake to assume that U.S. communications firms were all acting on the same side toward a collaborative goal: as Western Union and RCA would demonstrate, firms could come to be starkly at odds with the desires of government officials and their chosen actors. Moreover, historians should be very careful to discern the internal bureaucratic struggles that hindered implementation of coherent policies, particularly in times of rapid shifts in technology that solved military problems. Thus, the strategic rather than economic implications of changes in communications technology injected a different set of variables that could seem irrational to more pragmatic or economically minded observers yet were nonetheless significant to decision makers at the time.[12]

The experiences of World War One, from the submarine cable attacks to the high-power radio chain and the fight to win cable access in Latin America, all offered several lasting questions that have resonated to this day. Who has control over the nation's important communications links? Is the United States at the center or the periphery of global communications? Are the networks that serve the country aligned with its larger commercial and strategic needs? Is there an excess of international commercial capacity, to be available in an emergency? Is the system redundant and robust enough to survive attacks? Where is it vulnerable? Is the research, development, and manufacturing capability in place to sustain these networks and keep the United States at the forefront? Are those who do this work U.S. citizens or are they friendly to U.S. interests? In some form or another, the answers to these questions shaped the successive construction of global communications networks that were centered in the United States but that linked the entire world through the twentieth century. Indeed, what is the Internet but the latest iteration of a series of attempts to organize the world's communications networks in ways that will be redundant and survivable and that will link places of strategic and commercial importance? As this country sheds the last of its cold war–era outlooks and adjusts to meet new strategic realities in an age of global insurgency and stateless enemies, these questions are just as important today as they were a century ago.

Abbreviations

Primary Sources

Notes

Acknowledgments

Index

Abbreviations

BFDC Bureau of Foreign and Domestic Commerce
CNO Chief of Naval Operations
CW Cable and Wireless Archives
DNC Director of Naval Communications
FRUS Foreign Relations of the United States
GB Records of the General Board
HOYC Herbert O. Yardley Collection
LOC Library of Congress
NARA National Archives and Record Administration
NMAH National Museum of American History
OCSO Office of Chief Signal Officer
OFSN Office Files of the Secretary of the Navy
ONI Office of Naval Intelligence
PRO Public Record Office
RG Record Group
SecNav Secretary of the Navy
SecState Secretary of State
SDDF State Department Decimal Files, 1910–1929
WUC Western Union Collection

Primary Sources

Archive and Manuscript Collections

United States

National Archives and Record Administration,
College Park, Maryland, and Washington, D.C.
- Record Group [hereafter, RG] 38, Records of the Chief of Naval Operations
  - Director of Naval Communications
    - Office Files of Captain David W. Todd, 1916–1919
    - Office Files of Rear Admiral W. H. G. Bullard, 1919–1921
    - Division of Naval Communications, Classified Correspondence, 1917–1926
  - Office of Naval Intelligence
    - Naval Attaché Registers, 1886–1939
    - Formerly Confidential Correspondence, 1913–1924
- RG 40 General Records of the Department of Commerce
  - Office of the Secretary, General Correspondence, 1903–1950
- RG 43 Records of International Conference, Commissions, and Expositions
  - Records of the Preliminary International Conference on Electrical Communications
- RG 80, Records of the Office of the Secretary of the Navy
  - Office Files of the Secretary of the Navy
    - General Correspondence, 1896–1915, 1916–1926
    - Formerly Classified Correspondence, 1917–1919
  - Records of the General Board, Subject Files, 1900–1947
  - Index and Register to Formerly Classified Correspondence of the Chief of Naval Operations and the Secretary of the Navy, 1919–1927 (Microfilm Publication M 1141)
  - Formerly Classified Correspondence of the Chief of Naval Operations and the Secretary of the Navy, 1919–1927 (Microfilm Publication M 1140)

RG 59, Records of the Department of State
   Central Decimal Files, 1910–1929
   Records of the Office of Counselor and the Chief Special Agent, 1915–1928
      Classified Records of the Office of the Counselor, 1916–1927
      Classified Case Files, 1916–1926
RG 111 Records of the Office of the Chief Signal Officer
   General Correspondence, 1889–1917
   General Correspondence, 1917–1940
RG 151 Records of the Bureau of Domestic and Foreign Commerce
   General Records, 1914–1958
RG 165 Records of the War Department General and Specific Staffs
   War College Division: General Correspondence, 1903–1919
RG 242 National Archives Collection of Foreign Records Seized, 1675–1983
   Records of the German Navy, 1850–1945 (Microfilm Publication T 1022)
RG 407 Records of the Adjutant General's Office, 1917–
   War Department Annual Reports
RG 457 Papers of the National Security Agency
   Records of the Predecessors of the National Security Agency
   Historical Cryptographic Collection
   Herbert O. Yardley Collection

Manuscripts Division, Library of Congress, Washington D.C.

   Rear Admiral Stanford C. Hooper Papers
   Leland Harrison Papers
   Breckinridge Long Papers
   Norman H. Davis Papers

Archives Center, National Museum of American History, Smithsonian Institution

   George H. Clark Radio Collection
   Western Union Collection

Manuscripts and Archives, Sterling Memorial Library, Yale University

   Frank L. Polk Papers

Department of Rare Books and Special Collections, Princeton University Library

   Council on Foreign Relations Archives

Bentley Historical Library, University of Michigan

   George O. Squier Papers

United Kingdom

National Archives of the UK

Public Record Office, Kew

ADM 1
ADM 116
ADM 137
ADM 223
CAB 2
CAB 4
CAB 5
CAB 16
CAB 17
CAB 21
CAB 27
CAB 35
CAB 37
CAB 42
DEFE 1
FO 368
FO 371

Post Office [Consignia] Archives, Freeling House, Mount Pleasant Complex, London

Cable and Wireless Archives, Porthcurno Telegraph Museum, Porthcurno, Cornwall

Published Government Documents

Bourne, Kenneth, and D. Cameron Watt. *British Documents on Foreign Affairs: Reports and Papers from the Foreign Office Confidential Print.* Part 2: *From the First to the Second World War.* Series C: North America, 1919–1939. Frederick, Md.: University Publications of America, 1981.

United States. Army Security Agency. *Historical Background of the Signal Security Agency.* 3 vols. Washington, D.C.: Army Security Agency, 1946.

United States. Committee on Public Information. *Complete Report of the Chairman of the Committee on Public Information.* Washington, D.C.: Government Printing Office, 1920.

United States. Congress. House. Committee on Interstate and Foreign Commerce. *Cable Landing Licenses: Hearings on S. 535.* 67th Congress., 1st sess., May 10–13, 1921.

United States. Congress. Senate. Committee on Interstate Commerce. *Cable Landing Licenses: Hearings on S.4301.* 66th Congress., 3rd Sess., December 15, 16, 1920, January 10, 11, 1921.

United States. Congress. Senate. *Hearings Before a Subcommittee of the Committee on Naval Affairs.* U.S. Senate, Washington, D.C. 66th Congress, August 1919.

United States. Department of the Navy. Bureau of Engineering. *History of the Bureau of Engineering, Navy Department, During the World War.* Washington, D.C.: Government Printing Office, 1922.

United States. Department of the Navy. Office of Naval Records and Library. Historical Section. *German Submarine Activities on the Atlantic Coast of the United States and Canada.* Washington, D.C.: Government Printing Office, 1920.

United States. Department of the Post Office. *Government Control and Operations of Telegraph, Telephone, and Marine Cable Systems, August 1, 1918 to July 31, 1918.* Washington, D.C.: Government Printing Office, 1921.

United States. Department of State. *Foreign Relations of the United States.* Washington, D.C.: Government Printing Office, 1914–1922.

Woodward, E. L. and Rohan Butler, eds. *Documents on British Foreign Policy, 1919–1939.* First series. London: HMSO, 1966.

Notes

Introduction

1. Rudyard Kipling, "The Deep-Sea Cables," *Verses, 1889–1896*, www.gutenberg.org (accessed 25 October 2007).

1. The Information Network and the Outbreak of War

1. Many writers, citing Barbara Tuchman's *The Zimmermann Telegram* (New York, 1958), have suggested that the cable ship *Telconia* cut these cables. It did not. The *Alert* did. See J. Bordeaux, Submarine Superintendent, Dover, to Secretary, GPO, August 7, 1914, POST 56/55, Post Office (Consignia) Archives, London.
2. Bordeaux to Secretary, GPO, August 7, 1914.
3. On the early history and working of submarine telegraphy, the most recent thorough treatment is Ken Beauchamp, *History of Telegraphy* (London, 2001). There had been earlier transatlantic attempts in 1857 and 1858. On the transatlantic cable, the standard account is Bern Dibner, *The Atlantic Cable* (Norwalk, Conn., 1959). See John Griesemen, *Signal and Noise* (New York, 2003) for a literary treatment.
4. Verne published the work in 1873, the year after Eastern Telegraph linked Australia to Britain by cable. For Fix's use of the cable, see Jules Verne, *Around the World in Eighty Days* (New York, 1988), 18–27.
5. During the relief of the diplomatic compound, the Royal Navy arranged for new cables to be laid to the port of Tientsin. Foreign cable firms used the crisis to secure new, lengthy concessions to solidify control over China's external communications and freeze out potential competitors. See Daniel Headrick, *The Invisible Weapon: Telecommunications and International Politics, 1851–1945* (New York, 1991), 60, 98.
6. On the effects of the introduction of telegraphy, particularly cables, to diplomacy in the nineteenth century, see David P. Nickles, *Under the Wire: How Telegraphy Changed Diplomacy* (Cambridge, Mass., 2003).

7. On the globalization phenomenon of the late nineteenth century, of which the cables were an important part, see Kevin H. O'Rourke and Jeffrey G. Williamson, *Globalization and History* (Cambridge, Mass., 1999).
8. On the absolute necessity of synchronized time for measuring the world and the role of cables in this, see Peter Galison, *Einstein's Clocks, Poincaré's Maps: Empires of Time* (New York, 2003).
9. On the importance of the cables to the Krakatoa story, see Simon Winchester, *Krakatoa: The Day the World Exploded: August 27, 1883* (New York, 2003).
10. This led to a plot to seize Neckar Island, in the Hawaiian Islands, for the British. See W. D. Alexander, "The Story of the Transpacific Cable," *Annual Report of the Hawaii Historical Society*, 1910, 50–81.
11. On British cable strategy, see Paul M. Kennedy, "Imperial Cable Communications and Strategy, 1870–1914," in Paul M. Kennedy, ed., *War Plans of the Great Powers, 1880–1914* (London, 1979), 75–98.
12. Censorship has largely come to mean the prior control of information disseminated to a mass audience. In practice, especially in this period, it was the examination and manipulation of information in all forms, principally telegrams and letters but also the press. For this work, censorship will refer by and large to the examination and manipulation of information passing by cable or radio in a telegram.
13. No one has covered this subject in its entirety. The best survey has been Headrick, *Invisible Weapon*. An American economic perspective is Michael Hogan, *Informal Entente: The Private Structure of Cooperation in Anglo-American Economic Diplomacy, 1918–1928* (Columbia, Mo., 1977). For the postwar perspective in Latin America, see Joseph Tulchin, *The Aftermath of War: World War I and U.S. Policy Toward Latin America* (New York, 1971). The history of technology perspective on radio is covered by Hugh G. J. Aitken, *The Continuous Wave: Technology and American Radio, 1900–1932* (Princeton, N.J., 1985), and Susan J. Douglas, *Inventing American Broadcasting, 1899–1922* (Baltimore, 1987). These works are, as a whole, reasonably correct in their narrative but their conclusions are collectively inadequate. None, although Headrick and Aitken have come closest, effectively explained the military and security perspective that framed the problems associated with international communications. The anxieties that policy makers had over cables and radios stemmed from a variety of concerns, at once as much economic as diplomatic, technological, or military. The proper understanding of this story, therefore, requires its analysis from a multiplicity of perspectives and the inclusion of new evidence.
14. The president of Western Union estimated that 95 percent of the operators on its transatlantic cables were British. Statement of Newcomb Carlton before Subcommittee of Interstate Commerce Committee, December 15, 1920, Senate Committee on Interstate Commerce, *Cable Landing Licenses: Hearings on S. 4301*, 66th Congress, 3rd sess., 1920–1921, 108.
15. The standard cable landing license granted by the British government contained a clause permitting a government designee to take over the cables or to inspect the messages, transiting them in times of emergency. This applied equally to all cables, regardless of ownership.
16. An Italian, Gugliemo Marconi had pioneered and marketed the first practicable radio equipment in 1898, and he formed a company that bore his

name in Britain. Here I will refer to the company by its shortened name, and unless otherwise indicated, this will refer to the company, not the man himself.
17. G. S. Graham, "Imperial Cable Communications," in E. A. Benians, et al., eds., *Cambridge History of the British Empire*, vol. 3: *The Empire Commonwealth, 1870–1919* (Cambridge, Mass., 1959), 473–475.
18. These transmitters were sets using 14 kw of power and having a range of around eight hundred miles. The Admiralty had these medium-range transmitters and receivers installed on all battleships and first-rate cruisers before installing short-range sets for ship-to-ship work.
19. "Wireless Telegraphy: Note on the Strategic Aspect of Wireless Telegraphy," Secretary of the Committee of Imperial Defense, September 14, 1906, National Archives of the UK: Public Record Office [hereafter, PRO]/CAB 17/92, Kew. The Russo-Japanese War and the voyage of Admiral Rozhdestvenski's fleet in 1905 confirmed the utter necessity of such a communications network for long-distance force projection. British control of the cables compelled the admiral to send messages by French cable, which complicated his ability to stay in contact with his superiors. See Constantine Pleshakov, *The Tsar's Last Armada: The Epic Voyage to the Battle of Tsushima* (New York, 2003).
20. As one official wrote, "No other Department of State is competent to form a judgment of the national requirements, or to determine to what extent the aims of other Powers may conflict with those requirements. The aspects of the question which naturally present themselves to the Post Office are of subordinate importance, and are not worth consideration as compared with the national security." See "Wireless Telegraphy," PRO/CAB 17/92.
21. This Admiralty emphasis on ship-shore radio, the focus on medium-distance communications (under one thousand miles), and the Admiralty's antagonistic relationship with the Marconi company prevented Britain from becoming the leader in the field of long-distance radio communications.
22. Nicholas Lambert, "Strategic Command and Control for Maneuver Warfare: Creation of the Royal Navy's 'War Room' System, 1905–1915," *Journal of Military History* 69 (April 2005): 361–410; "Wireless Telegraphy: Note on the Strategic Aspect of Wireless Telegraphy," Secretary of the CID, September 14, 1906, PRO/CAB 17/92.
23. Memorandum by Hankey, July 15, 1914, W.T. 8, and memorandum by Admiralty War Staff, July 14, 1914, W.T. 7, Subcommittee on Empire's Wireless Telegraph Communications, 1914, PRO/CAB 16/32. Some of these stations would be built during the war but only after Germany's surface raiders, the original threat, had been destroyed.
24. Kenneth R. Haigh, *Cableships and Submarine Cables* (London, 1978), 321; Jorma Ahvenainen, *The History of the Caribbean Telegraphs before the First World War* (Helsinki: 1996), 94–109.
25. On the Dutch and Japanese cables in the Pacific, see Jorma Ahvenainen, *The Far Eastern Telegraphs* (Helsinki, 1991), and Daqing Yang, *Technology of Empire: Telecommunications and Japanese Imperialism, 1930–1945* (Cambridge, Mass., 2003).
26. The German cable-manufacturing industry and operating companies all came into being within this next decade. From the efforts of the wire rope and cable company Felten und Guilleaume Carlswerk A.G., the German

Imperial Post Office, and a leading Cologne bank came the cable-making firm Norddeutsche Seekabelwerke and five associated companies, which operated German overseas cables.

27. Headrick, *Invisible Weapon*, 87–89.
28. Headrick, *Invisible Weapon*, 105–111; Haigh, *Cableships*, 328–336. Interestingly, Franco-German distrust of the British cable system allowed these two countries to cooperate in laying cables abroad. Once Germany had finished the cable to Liberia, the French then laid their own cables from there to connect the French West African colonies for a fraction of the cost. The two governments also agreed on a cable from Emden to Brest, to add to the transatlantic network.
29. Slaby-Arco-AEG and Braun-Siemens-Halske were the two leading German companies in radio research and manufacturing. The long name for Telefunken was the Gesellschaft für drahtlose Telegraphie.
30. Headrick, *Invisible Weapon*, 120. Marconi could not counter the argument that such a practice was necessary to ensure safety at sea. The role of wireless in the *Titanic* disaster in 1912 evaporated any further opposition.
31. Nicholas Hiley, "Strategic Origins of Room 40," *Intelligence and National Security* 2, no. 2 (April 1987): 254.
32. A. E. Seelig to Dr. L. W. Austin, July 26, 1915, with map, enclosed in Griffin to Bullard, July 30, 1915, 12479–568:169, General Correspondence, 1916–1926, Office Files of the Secretary of the Navy, Record Group [hereafter, RG] 80, National Archives and Records Administration [hereafter, NARA], Washington, D.C.
33. Raw decryptions of transmissions from Nauen to Sayville, January to March 1917, "1917 Intercepts, Chilean and German," PRO/ADM 223/781.
34. "Report of the Standing Sub-Committee of the Committee of Imperial Defense: Submarine Cable-Communications in Time of War," December 1911, PRO/CAB 38/19/56; Kennedy, "Imperial Cable Communications." The suggestion of Admiralty preparations comes from Hiley, "Strategic Origins of Room 40."
35. The companies under Western Union influence included the Anglo-American Company, the Direct United States Cable Company, and the American Telegraph and Cable Company. On how Western Union came to acquire such control, see Headrick, *Invisible Weapon*, 101–102.
36. Cables went out from landings at Saint John's, Hearts Content, or Bay Roberts in Newfoundland or at Harbor Grace, Canso, or Halifax in Nova Scotia. Landlines or short cables connected these places with the United States.
37. On the Collins Overland Line, see for example, Charles Vevier, "The Collins Overland Line and American Continentalism," *Pacific Historic Review* 28, no. 3 (August 1959): 237–253.
38. Mackay also controlled the Postal Telegraph Company, the only domestic rival to Western Union. His submarine cables were an extension of that rivalry.
39. On the Pacific cable, see Ahvenainan, *Far Eastern Telegraphs*, 168–172; on the Caribbean basin cables before 1914, see Ahvenainan, *History of Caribbean Telegraphs*. See also Ahvenainan, *The European Cable Companies in South America before the First World War* (Helsinki, 2004).
40. Squier commanded the U.S. Army cable ship *Burnside* during its 1900–1902 Philippines operations.

41. Squier also delivered a paper before the American Institute of Electrical Engineers on December 27, 1899, regarding the Pacific cable as a government operation. Captain George O. Squier, "The Influence of Submarine Cables upon Military and Naval Supremacy" (lecture delivered in 1900 to the Naval War College); subsequently published in *National Geographic,* Naval War College Archives, RG 8, XCOC, Box 81, 1900–1910. I am indebted to Professor John B. Hattendorf for his assistance here.
42. See Hooper to Commander in Chief, Atlantic Fleet, May 21, 1913, and General Board to Secretary of the Navy, March 14, 1914, in "Secrecy of Radio Communications," File 419, Subject Files, 1900–1947, Records of the General Board, RG 80, NARA.
43. Proceedings of the joint naval and military committee, 6 October 1914, PRO/CAB 5/5/3/113C. There was also some concern about the use on German commercial ships of wireless sets that might be used to coordinate cruiser attacks from neutral harbors, because on the evening of August 4 German commercial ships had been instructed by wireless to seek the closest neutral harbor. The German cable ship *Stephan* fled for Vigo, and the *Frankenwald* went to Bilbao. Their radio sets helped to convey messages to the German embassy in Madrid. Sir Julian S. Corbett, *History of the Great War: Naval Operations,* vol. 1 (London, 1920), 42.
44. "Report on the Opening of the War," November 1, 1914, PRO/CAB 17/102B; Corbett, *History,* 128.
45. Corbett, *History,* 130–132; Hiley, "Strategic Origins," 259–260. The Liberian government ordered the German stations closed. See David Nickles, "The Struggle over Liberia's Telecommunications during the First World War" (paper presented at Society of Historians of American Foreign Relations annual conference, June 2001).
46. Note on Pacific Islands, August 17, 1914, Proceedings of the joint naval and military committee, PRO/CAB 5/3/11C; Corbett, *History,* 143; Hiley, "Strategic Origins," 259–260. On the importance of Yap for coordinating the movements of Spee's cruisers, see Peter Overlack, "The Force of Circumstance: Graf Spee's Options for the East Asian Cruiser Squadron in 1914," *Journal of Military History* 60 (October 1996): 657–682.
47. These included the Admiralty station at Stockton as well as various General Post Office and Marconi stations along the coast. Patrick Beesly, *Room 40: British Naval Intelligence, 1914–1918* (San Diego, 1982), 9.
48. On the origins of British code breaking and signals intelligence relative to the outbreak of war, see Hiley, "Strategic Origins," 248–255; Beesly, *Room 40,* 129–133.
49. "Colombian Neutrality: Control of Wireless Telegraphy," memorandum, March 10, 1915, PRO/FO 881/10541; Nickles, "Struggle over Liberia's Telecommunications."
50. Corbett, *History,* 331.
51. "Cable History of World War I Written in 1919," POST 56/55, Post Office (Consignia) Archives, London.
52. Admiralty Memorandum on the Importance of the Establishment of British Owned High Power Wireless Stations in South America, May 17, 1916, PRO/CAB 42/14/2; Corbett, *History,* 404–405.
53. Memorandum by Edwin S. Montagu, January 14, 1916, PRO/CAB 37/140/

32; Artur Kunert, *Geschichte der deutschen Fernmeldekabel,* vol 2: *Telegraphen-Seekabel* (Cologne-Mülheim, 1962), 353; Lansing and Woolsey to Secretary of State, December 8, 1920, 811.73/588, State Department Decimal Files, 1910–1929 [hereafter, SDDF], RG 59, NARA.

54. "Cables between Portugal and Brazil," minute, September 20, 1917, PRO/FO 395/159/182805; Erye Crowe to Pierre Cambon, August 22, 1914, PRO/ADM 116/1371; Nickles, "Struggle over Liberia's Telecommunications." There were concerns as well that the Brazilians might retaliate by canceling the landing rights of British cables in its territory.

55. Letters of August 1914, Valentia Cable Station letterbook, Western Union Collection [hereafter, WUC], National Museum of American History [hereafter, NMAH], Washington, D.C.

56. Bulgaria connected by landline to the Eastern Telegraph Company cables landing in Greece and Turkey.

57. Between 1911 and 1913, Britain had made secret arrangements with France and Russia to establish radio contact between their countries as backup in case the cables failed. These were to be secondary, not primary, interallied strategic communications routes. See "Action Taken by the Post Office as Regards Establishing Wireless Telegraph Communications with France," PRO/CAB 4/4/33/141-B, and papers relating to "Telegraph with Russia," March 7, 1913, PRO/CAB 4/5/173-B. Additionally, the French established two radio links with Russia, from Bobrurysk to Paris and from Bobrurysk to Sevastopol to Bizerta to Paris. It is likely that for information-security purposes they would have relied on the cables. On the French-Russian radio link, see Robert A. Doughty, "French Strategy in 1914: Joffre's Own," *Journal of Military History* 67 (April 2003): 435.

58. The cable ran from Peterhead in the United Kingdom to the Russian port of Alexandrovsk and utilized cables that were originally earmarked for a U.S. company and that were part of the German cables in the English Channel. When the cable ship returned to Britain, it was down to five tons of condemned fresh water and its coal had frozen solid. See "Cable History of World War I."

59. "Russian Cables" file, PRO/ADM 116/1569, and minutes of the War Committee, October 26, 1916, PRO/CAB 42/22/8. The extension went from Alexandrovsk to the Gulf of Archangel.

60. Cables connected at Cocos Island from Mauritius, Batavia, and Perth.

61. Corbett, *History,* 290, 380. The station superintendent managed to get a message out before capture that the *Emden* was there, which allowed Allied pursuers to catch her. See Dan van der Vat, *Gentlemen of War: The Amazing Story of Captain Karl von Müller and the SMS Emden* (New York, 1984).

62. It appears that Germany preserved the transatlantic cables in order use them to communicate with agents and diplomats in the Americas, despite the risk that the British would intercept and decrypt the German traffic.

63. Colonel Heftye, Director General Norwegian Telegraphs, to Commander Kettlewell, Royal Navy, August 18, 1915, POST 56/114, BT Archives, London. This cable ran between Newbiggen, United Kingdom, and Arendal, Norway.

64. F. J. Brown to Foreign Office, August 9, 1915, and related correspondence, PRO/FO 368/1372/J541/109909.

65. Ships from the first Sondergruppe der Nordesee-Vorpostenflottillee carried out this work. Kunert, *Geschichte,* 711.
66. One of these was the *U-47,* which began cable war training in Emden but later moved to Pola, Austria. Ironically, it later accidentally severed Austrian cables that entered the harbor there, while practicing with new equipment.
67. The U-boat may have been ten to twenty feet above the cable at this point. The higher the ship rose, the greater weight of cable it pulled, and the more work the vessel performed. In fact, given the relative weight of the cable and boat, it may not have been possible for a U-boat to surface while grappling a deep-sea cable.
68. The Lucas cutting and holding grapple was one such piece of equipment that could do this work, although it was not designed for use on a submarine. See Eastern Associated Telegraph Companies, *Telegraph Cable Engineering,* vol. 2 (London, 1927), 59–60. I am indebted to Barney Finn for his help here.
69. Kunert, *Geschichte,* 709–713; War Diary of Third U-Flotilla, 1.10.1916 to 15.10.1918, Roll 89, T1022, Records of the German Navy, 1850–1945, Collection of Foreign Records Seized, 1941–, RG 242, NARA. I am grateful to Daniel Headrick and Lorenz Lüthi here.
70. Insurance premiums for cable ships reflect this estimated danger. When Western Union chartered a British cable ship in 1916, they had to pay more than $9,000 in premiums for a $643,200 policy on the ship; similar work in 1917, after the United States had joined the war, required a premium of over $30,000, for a $1.2 million policy. The company also had to carry separate insurance on the cable in the hold. Series 2, Executive Committee Minutes, October 26, 1916, and July 24, 1917, WUC, NMAH.
71. "Cable History of World War I"; Secretary of the Navy [hereafter, SecNav] to Secretary of State [hereafter, SecState], September 17, 1917, 5806–145, General Correspondence, 1916–1926, RG 80, NARA.

2. Neutrality and Vulnerability

1. The outdated French cables also had censorship, aligned with Britain's.
2. Keith Clark, *International Communications* (New York, 1931), 163–164; Hugh Barty-King, *Girdle Round the World* (London, 1979), 163–164; James Schwoch, *The American Radio Industry and Its Latin American Activities, 1900–1939* (Urbana, 1990), 36.
3. Memorandum of conversation among Dover, Ward, and Goldhammer, August 7, 1914; see, for example, Dover to Sir John Denison-Pender, August 6, 1914, "First World War Censorship," folder Section 6: North America, Eastern and Associated Records, Cable and Wireless Archives [hereafter, CW]; memorandum by Edwin Montague, January 14, 1916, PRO/CAB 37/140/32; Artur Kunert, *Geschichte der deutschen Fernmeldekabel,* 2: *Telegraphen-Seekabel* (Cologne-Mülheim, 1962), 353.
4. George P. Oslin, *The Story of Telecommunications* (Macon, Ga., 1992), 277–278; H. T. Taft to SecState, August 11, 1914, *Foreign Relations of the United States* [hereafter, FRUS] 1914, Supplement, 504–505.
5. WANGSPIER (the war is evidently about to commence), CABESTROS (the cable between——and——has been cut), BICHOSO (New York), BETT-

LEREI (Berlin), WANGGUNST (expect the war to continue for some time). Formulated from ABC Code, 5th ed. (1901), International Cable Register, 1917, WUC, NMAH.
6. With additional blank code words, the ABC Code was versatile. The owner of the copy in the National Museum of American History used his blank code words to refer to transporting hippopotami.
7. Such practices continue today, as seen with special phone numbers or Internet domain names. The letterheads of prominent companies in the 1910s often carried their cable addresses.
8. "British Announcement to the International Telegraph Bureau, 3rd August, 1914," quoted in War Trade Intelligence Department, "Report on Cable Censorship during the Great War, 1914–1918," PRO/DEFE 1/402.
9. Memorandum from Sir Edward Grey to Walter Hines Page restating notice given from outbreak of war, February 2, 1915, enclosed in Page to Bryan, February 3, 1915, FRUS 1915, Supplement, 707.
10. Taft to SecState Bryan, August 11, 1914, FRUS 1914, Supplement, 505.
11. British Consul, Pernambuco to Admiralty, December 23, 1916, PRO/ADM 223/779.
12. See copies of traffic from "Chilean Diplomatic," PRO/ADM 223/786, and "1917 Intercepts, Chilean and German," PRO/ADM 223/781. Such arrangements were in place before the war. Nick Lambert has uncovered that Admiral Sir John Fisher had an agreement with the Eastern Telegraph Company when he was in command of the British fleet based at Malta.
13. Not all copies of traffic came from direct control of the cables. In Mexico City, the British chargé d'affaires gained access to cables through a contact at a central telegraph office. Patrick Beesly, *Room 40: British Naval Intelligence* (San Diego, 1982), 211.
14. Kirby Lumber Company to SecState, August 5, SecState to Kirby Lumber Company, August 7, and Lansing to Kirby Lumber Company, September 1, 1914, FRUS 1914, Supplement, 503–505.
15. Taft to SecState, August 11, 1914, FRUS 1914, Supplement, 504–505.
16. Lansing to Page, August 28, 1915, ibid., 722–723.
17. Taft to SecState, August 11, 1914, ibid., 505.
18. "Secrecy of Radio Communication," File 419, Subject Files, 1900–1947, Records of the General Board, RG 80, NARA.
19. Colville Barclay to SecState, August 4, and Page to SecState, August 5, 1914, FRUS 1914, Supplement, 667–668.
20. Executive Order No. 2011, August 5, and Bryan to Page, August 7, 1914, FRUS 1914, Supplement, 668–669.
21. Bryan to Page, August 11, 1914, and German Chargé d'Affaires, Haniel, to SecState, August 11, 1914, FRUS 1914, Supplement, 669–670.
22. Memorandum by the Counselor for the Department of State on the Use by Belligerents of Wireless Stations and Submarine Telegraph Cables on Neutral Territory, August 12, 1914, FRUS, The Lansing Papers, 1914–1920, vol. 1, 152–156. The guiding document was the Hague Convention of 1907. The conflicting guidelines were Article 3, which prohibited belligerents from building military stations in neutral territory, and Article 8, which did not require neutrals to prohibit their use. See also Lansing to Bryan, September 2, 1914, 811.741/41, SDDF, RG 59, NARA.

23. Ambassador James Gerard to SecState, August 30, 1914, FRUS 1914, Supplement, 677; Arthur S. Link, *Wilson,* vol. 3: *The Struggle for Neutrality, 1914–1915* (Princeton, N.J., 1960), 58–60.
24. Executive Order No. 2042, September 5, 1914, FRUS 1914, Supplement, 678.
25. Linwood S. Howeth, *History of Communications-Electronics in the United States Navy* (Washington, D.C., 1963), 225.
26. Franklin Roosevelt to SecState, September 8, 1914, 811.741/43, SDDF, RG 59, NARA.
27. Susan J. Douglas, *Inventing American Broadcasting, 1899–1922* (Baltimore, 1987), 270.
28. Crammond Kennedy to SecState, February 22, 1915, 811.74/84, and W. G. Sharp to SecState, February 22, 1915, 811.74/87, SDDF, RG 59, NARA.
29. E. F. Sweet, Acting Secretary of Commerce, to SecState, September 28, 1914, 81.74/76, SDDF, RG 59, NARA.
30. Memorandum by Robert Lansing with memorandum from Captain Gaunt, British Embassy, August 28, 1914, with copies of transmissions from Sayville to German cruisers off the U.S. coast, 811.741/41.5, SDDF, RG 59, NARA.
31. Memorandum from British Embassy, September 18, 1914, 811.741/52, SDDF, RG 59, NARA.
32. Along the Atlantic coast alone there were stations at Boston, Siasconset, and South Wellfleet in Massachusetts; New York; Atlantic City; Cape May; Philadelphia; Baltimore; Cape Hatteras and Seagate, North Carolina; Savannah; and Jacksonville and Miami, Florida, from 1913 onwards. Similar stations existed along the Gulf and Pacific coasts.
33. Howeth, *History of Communications-Electronics,* 227.
34. The American Marconi station (known as South Wellfleet) on Cape Cod had to take over from Siasconsett the radio traffic for ships on approach to New York.
35. Daniels to SecState, October 19, 1914, 811.741/75, SDDF, RG 59, NARA.
36. War Trade Intelligence Department, "Report on Cable Censorship during the Great War, 1914–1918," 117.
37. Taft to SecState, August 11, 1914, and Bryan to Page, August 23, 1914, 504–506; Edward Grey to Page, August 23, enclosed in Page to Bryan, August 24, 1914, 508; Bryan to Page, September 5, 1914, and Lansing to Page, September 26, 508–509; Page to Bryan, (n.d. but probably October 13, 1914), 511; Lansing to Page, October 14, 1914, 512; Page to Lansing, October 30, 1914, 513, FRUS 1914, Supplement.
38. War Trade Intelligence Department, "Report on Cable Censorship during the Great War, 1914–1918," 117–118.
39. Bryan to Nelson Page, November 10, 1914, 514; Stovall, Minister to Switzerland, to SecState, November 5, 1914, and November 11, 1914, and President of Swiss Confederation to Swiss Minister, November 12, 1914, copy passed to SecState, November 18, 1914, 513–514 and 515, and Nelson Page to Bryan, December 2, 1914, 519, FRUS 1914, Supplement.
40. Bryan to W. H. Page, November 12, 515; Nelson Page to Bryan, November 27, 519; Bryan to W. H. Page, December 2, with cable from Madrid Embassy, November 27, 1914, 519, FRUS 1914, Supplement.
41. Herrick to Bryan, November 22, Page to Bryan, November 25, and Bryan to Page, December 3, 1914, 518 and 520, FRUS 1914, Supplement.

42. See the correspondence among Bryan, Page, and Gerard between December 3 and 18, 1914, as well as Elliot H. Goodwin, Secretary, Chamber of Commerce of the United States of America, to SecState, December 11, 1914, FRUS 1914, Supplement, 521–528.
43. Page to Bryan, December 17, 21, and 23, 1914, FRUS 1914, Supplement, 527, 529, and 530.
44. Page to Bryan, January 7, and Bryan to Page, January 9, 1915, FRUS 1915, Supplement, 698–699.
45. Page to Bryan, January 20, and Bryan to Page, January 21, 1915, FRUS 1915, Supplement, 701.
46. Correspondence between Bryan and Page, January 25 to February 3, 703–705; Page to Lansing, August 24, 1915, 708–709; and memorandum from Spring-Rice to Bryan, February 19, 1915, 723, FRUS 1915, Supplement.
47. Emil Sauer, Consul at Göteborg, to SecState, January 21, 1915, FRUS 1915, Supplement, 706–707.
48. Bryan's approval was conditional, provided that the messages did not relate to contraband or financial transactions with belligerents.
49. U.S. Navy radio commercial traffic records for this period reveal that the practice proliferated by radio. Swedish diplomats made great use of this in radio messages to Washington, as did Danish, Norwegian, Austrian, and German diplomats. See naval radio blanks collected in 811.741/–, SDDF, RG 59, NARA.
50. Bryan to Sauer, Consul in Göteborg, February 26; Morris, Minister in Sweden, to Bryan, March 4; Page to Bryan, March 9; and Bryan to Page, March 16, 1915, FRUS 1915, Supplement, 710–712.
51. Page to SecState, April 14; Lansing to Page, May 5; SecState to Page, May 13; Van Dyke to SecState, June 8; Lansing to Page, June 15; Page to SecState, June 17; and Page to SecState, June 28, 1915, FRUS 1915, Supplement, 714–715 and 718–720.
52. See Thomas A. Bailey, "The United States and the Blacklist during the Great War," *Journal of Modern History* 6 (March 1934): 14–35, and Ethel C. Phillips, "American Participation in Belligerent Commercial Controls 1914–1917," *American Journal of International Law* 27 (October 1933): 675–696, esp. 683–684.
53. War Trade Intelligence Department, "Report on Cable Censorship during the Great War, 1914–1918," 25. The report states, "The whole business entailed an enormous amount of labour and correspondence; but it was intended, and proved to be, an object lesson of the power of the cable censorship." The French subsequently applied the same technique to a Swiss bank, with similar results.
54. This represented a major upgrade in power and range of transmission. George H. Clark, *Radio in Peace and War,* 250, Box 289, George H. Clark Collection, NMAH.
55. George H. Clark, *Radio in Peace and War,* 251–252; Apgar's materials are in 12479–568, General Correspondence, 1916–1926, Office Files of the Secretary of the Navy [hereafter, OFSN], RG 80, NARA.
56. Entry for June 28, 1915, in Josephus Daniels, *The Cabinet Diaries of Josephus Daniels, 1913–1921,* ed. E. David Cronon (Lincoln, Neb., 1963), 100; William C. Redfield, Secretary of Commerce, to Secretary Lansing, June 28,

1915, 811.741/226, SDDF, RG 59; Lansing to Wilson, June 28, 1915, 811.741/269b, and Wilson to Lansing, July 2, 1915, 811.741/503, SDDF, RG 59; George H. Clark, *Radio in War and Peace*, 251; Bullard to Officer-in-Charge, Sayville Radio Station, October 25, 1915, 12479–568:169, General Correspondence, 1916–1926, OFSN, RG 80, NARA.
57. Link, *Wilson: Struggle for Neutrality, 1914–1915*, 105.
58. On Brazil in particular, see Emily Rosenberg, "Anglo-American Economic Rivalry in Brazil during World War I," *Diplomatic History* 2 (Spring 1978): 131–152. See also David M. Kennedy, *Over Here: The First World War and American Society* (New York, 1980), 299–308.
59. On the Wilson administration and shipping, see Jeffrey J. Safford, *Wilsonian Maritime Democracy, 1913–1921* (New Brunswick, 1978). See also Mark T. Gilderhus, *Pan American Visions: Woodrow Wilson in the Western Hemisphere, 1913–1921* (Tucson, 1986), 72–73, for the push to improve U.S. shipping in 1916 as part of the preparedness movement.
60. The inadequate French Caribbean cable connected Haiti to the northern coast of South America down to Brazil. It failed completely in 1917; see James A. Scrymser, *Personal Reminiscences in Times of Peace and War* (privately printed, 1915), 67–106.
61. Annual Report for Western Union, 1920, 17–19. These concerns remained throughout the neutrality period. Delegates from many America countries to the International High Commission in Buenos Aires in April 1916 identified improved cable connections and cheaper rates as one of their key goals. On wartime hemispheric economic relations, see Gilderhus, *Pan American Visions*, 70–74, and David Healy, *Drive to Hegemony: The United States in the Caribbean, 1898–1917* (Madison, Wis., 1988), 166–170.
62. Dispatch of Consul General, Rio de Janeiro, October 23, 1917, in "Brazilian Cables," Register No. 9494, File B-10-g, Naval Attaché Reports, Office of Naval Intelligence [hereafter, ONI], RG 38, NARA.
63. Bryan to American Legation, Buenos Aires, August 20, and Bryan to American Legation, Buenos Aires, September 4, 1914, 835.73/19 and 835.73/20, SDDF, RG 59, NARA.
64. Morgan to George Lorillard, August 11, 1914, 835.73/28, SDDF, RG 59, NARA.
65. Lorillard to SecState, October 13 and December 23, 1914, 835.73/32 and 835.73/33; Wright to Long, October 18, 1915, 835.73/39, SDDF, RG 59, NARA.
66. F. J. Stimson to SecState, November 17, 1915, 835.73/42, SDDF, RG 59, NARA.
67. Fred Ward to W. Dover, November 12, 1915, and message for Colonel G. Wright, enclosing cable from Buenos Aires Superintendent, January 30, 1917, in "First World War Censorship" folder, Section 6: North America, Eastern and Associated Records, CW.
68. Alexander Benson, Chargé, to SecState, January 29, 1917, 832.73/97, and memorandum from Scrymser to Lansing, September 23, 1916, 835.73/66, SDDF, RG 59; Dispatch of Consul General, Rio de Janeiro, October 23, 1917, in "Brazilian Cables," Register No. 9494, File B-10-g, Naval Attaché Reports, ONI, RG 38, NARA.
69. Merrill to SecState, March 11, SecState to Merrill, April 7, 833.73/9, and Merrill to SecState, April 19, 1916, 833.73/10, SDDF, RG 59, NARA.

70. Merrill to SecState, June 9, 1916, 833.73/13, Scrymser to Lansing, September 22, 1916, 835.73/64, and Merrill to SecState, March 9, 1917, 835.73/46, SDDF, RG 59, NARA.
71. The British government used these two lengths to create the Britain-Russia cable in January 1915 and an Montevideo–Falklands Islands cable in August 1915. See Submarine Cables Manufactured and Laid, Telegraph Construction and Maintenance record book, book 3, vol. 2, 1912–1920, microfilm copy, NMAH, and "Cable History of the War," 1919, POST 56/55, Post Office (Consignia) Archives, London.

3. Security and Radios

1. Hooper had support for his ideas from Badger and his chief of staff, Commander Charles F. Hughes.
2. Hooper to Badger, May 21, 1913, "Secrecy of Radio Communication" [hereafter, "Secrecy"], File 419, Subject Files, 1900–1947, Records of the General Board [hereafter, GB], RG 80, NARA.
3. Griffin to Superintendent, Naval Radio Service (hereafter, NRS), June 2, and Report of Naval Attaché Symington, September 12, 1913, "Secrecy."
4. S. W. Bryant to Operations, October 23, 1913, and Franklin Roosevelt to Bryant, October 28, 1913, "Secrecy."
5. General Board Report to Secretary Daniels, March 14, 1914, and Griffin to Superintendent, NRS, October 13, 1913, "Secrecy."
6. Hooper notebook, Box 40, Hooper Papers, Library of Congress (hereafter, LOC), Washington, D.C.; Bullard to SecNav, March 28, 1914, Griffin to Operations, May 19, and Hooper memorandum, June 12, 1914, Serial No. 276, Subject File 419, GB, RG 80, NARA.
7. General Board recommendation, November 17, 1914, Serial No. 276, Subject File 419, GB, RG 80, NARA.
8. Hooper, transcript of memoirs, Box 37, 493, Box 38, 601, and Hooper notebook, Hooper Papers, LOC; United States, Department of the Navy, Bureau of Engineering, *History of the Bureau of Engineering, Navy Department, During the World War* (Washington, D.C., 1922), 11–13; Paul Wilson Clark, "Major General George Owen Squier: Military Scientist," (PhD diss., Case Western University, 1974), 220–223, 244; George H. Clark, *Radio in Peace and War,* Box 289, p. 154, George H. Clark Collection, NHAH; and draft of Hooper biography, 5, Folder 21, Box 14, George H. Clark Radioana Collection, NMAH.
9. Memorandum from Lieutenant S. C. Hooper, USN, to Colonel Squier, Military Attaché in London, November 26, 1914, enclosed in dispatch by Squier of December 8, 1914, No. 8759–18, War College Division. General Correspondence, 1903–1919, Records of the War Department, General and Special Staffs, RG 165, NARA.
10. Memorandum from Hooper to Squier, November 26, 1914, in dispatch by Squier.
11. Hooper, transcript of memoirs, Box 38, 590, Hooper Papers, LOC; SecNav to Captain Bullard, December 5, 1914, and General Board to Senior Member, Board on Organization, December 23, 1914, Serial No. 276, Subject File 419, GB, RG 80, NARA.

12. Confidential Report of the Board on Organization, U.S. Naval Radio Service, February 20, 1915, Subject File 419, Serial No. 276, GB, RG 80, NARA; Hooper notes, Box 40, Hooper Papers, LOC.
13. The Board on Organization revised its conclusions in early 1916. The superintendent became a director. The title of the office changed from "Radio Service" to "Naval Communications" to reflect that messages might not always go by radio. The message, not the medium, became paramount. See Revised Board on Reorganization Report, July 14, 1916, Subject File 419, Serial No. 276, GB, RG 80, NARA; Linwood C. Howeth, *A History of Communications-Electronics in the United States Navy* (Washington, D.C., 1963), 233.
14. Some of these stations already existed, and Hooper's plan called for boosting their power to cover a greater area. The stations were Puget Sound, Washington; Cordova, Alaska; Saint Paul, Pribilof Islands, Alaska; Mare Island, California; Guam; and Apia, American Samoa.
15. Confidential Report of the Board on Organization, U.S. Naval Radio Service, February 20, 1915, Subject File 419, Serial No. 276, GB, RG 80, NARA; Hooper notes, Box 40, Hooper Papers, LOC.
16. Susan J. Douglas, *Inventing American Broadcasting, 1899–1922* (Baltimore, 1987), 132–134, 259; Hugh Aitken, *The Continuous Wave: Technology and American Radio, 1900–1932* (Princeton, N.J., 1985), 149, 157.
17. Captain Bullard to Admiral Dewey, January 4, 1915, and General Board (Dewey) to Captain Bullard, January 8, 1915, Serial No. 276, Subject File 419, GB, RG 80, NARA.
18. George H. Clark, *History*, 217–220.
19. Ibid., 221–222.
20. Clark, *History*, 226; Aitken, *Continuous Wave*, 157; Howeth, *History*, 223, citing Clark; Unsigned memorandum on the background of the Southern Federal Telegraph Company, May 11, 1916, 832.74/22, RG 59, NARA; Hooper notes, Folder February–December 1917, Box 1, Hooper Papers, LOC.
21. On the story of the search for the continuous wave, see Aitken, *Continuous Wave*. On the adoption of radio technology by the United States Navy before World War I, see Douglas, *Inventing*, and Howeth, *History*.
22. The use of a radio on board the *Republic* allowed the rescue of over twelve hundred passengers after it collided with the *Florida* in January 1909; this led to the Wireless Ship Act of June 24, 1910, which required ships carrying more than fifty passengers going farther than two hundred miles over open ocean to have a radio on board. The *Titanic* disaster of April 14, 1912, might have been less horrific had several ships closer to her than the *Carpathia* had their radios on or operators monitoring for distress signals. This led to revision of the Wireless Ship Act and a new law, the Radio Act of August 13, 1912, which made a sweeping set of organizational changes to radio in the United States. It established the right of the government to regulate radio operators and regulate the spectrum in accordance with the larger needs of the nation. On the *Titanic* disaster and the radio regulations of 1910–1912, see Douglas, *Inventing*, chap. 7.
23. Of the 479 radios installed on American-flagged ships in 1913, 217 were Marconis. Clark notes, Box 101 and Box 112, Folder 2, Clark Radioana Collection, NMAH. On the consolidation of American Marconi's position, see

Elizabeth M. Kruse, "Property from the Sky: The Creation of Property Rights in the Radio Spectrum in the United States," (PhD diss., University of Massachusetts, Amherst, 2002), 143–145.

24. By 1912 regulations in place meant that civilians could use two sections of the available spectrum. This was from six hundred meters and below, or sixteen hundred meters and above. Six hundred to sixteen hundred meters was the purview of governments around the world. Ship-shore radio work occurred at three hundred and six hundred meters, while international or long-distance radio work went on above sixteen hundred. Amateurs could work only below two hundred meters.

25. An Australian engineer, C. F. Elwell, acquired the rights to use the arc in the United States and its territories in 1909. His company, the Federal Telegraph Company of Palo Alto, California, formed in 1911 to exploit the U.S. patent for this device. On the arc, see Aitken, *Continuous Wave*, 122–151. Griffin to Operations, May 19, 1914, Serial No. 276, Subject File 419, GB, RG 80, NARA.

26. Aitken, *Continuous Wave*, 318–319; Steadman, Van Praugh, and Gaylor to Foreign Office, July 14, 1919, PRO/FO 368/2176/f103384; Clark Notes, Folder 2, Box 112, Clark Radioana Collection, NMAH. On lock-in, see M. Mitchel Waldrop, *Complexity* (New York, 1992), 35–41.

27. Hooper memorandum, June 12, 1914, Serial No. 276, Subject File 419, GB, RG 80, NARA.

28. Hooper memorandum, June 12, 1914, General Board to Board on Organization, December 23, 1914, and Report of Board on Organization, February 20, 1915, in Subject File 419, GB, RG 80, NARA; *Annual Report of the Secretary of the Navy, 1914* (Washington, D.C., 1914), 19.

29. A. B. Cole to Captain Bullard, January 20, 1916, and Navy Solicitor Graham Egerton to Bullard, February 7, 1916, 12479–841, General Correspondence, 1916–1926, OFSN, RG 80, NARA.

30. President of General Board (Dewey) to SecNav, June 5, 1915, and subsequent file, Serial No. 276, Subject File 419, GB, RG 80, NARA; Bullard to Chief of Naval Operations [hereafter, CNO], May 17, 1916, enclosing Adjutant General W. M. Wright to H. P. Veeder, May 12, 1916, 12479–715:12, General Correspondence, 1916–1926, OFSN, RG 80, NARA; entry for June 29, 1915, The *Cabinet Diaries of Josephus Daniels, 1913–1921,* ed. E. David Cronon (Lincoln, Neb., 1963), 101.

31. Bullard to Daniels, March 9, 1916, 26509–139:4, General Correspondence, 1916–1926, OFSN, RG 80, NARA.

32. Approved Report on Organization, U.S. Navy Radio, July 14, 1916, in File 419, GB, RG 80, NARA.

33. George T. Davis, *Navy Second to None: The Development of Modern American Naval Policy* (Westport, Conn., 1971), 213–232; Todd to Bullard, August 29, November 22, and December 1, 1916, Todd Files, Director of Naval Communications [hereafter, DNC], RG 38, NARA; Howeth, *History,* 314.

34. Captain D. W. Todd to Captain S. S. Robinson, March 3, 1917, Box 3, Todd Files, DNC, RG 38; memorandum from Todd to CNO, December 15, 1916, 26256–324:3, General Correspondence, 1916–1926, RG 80, NARA.

35. Memorandum from Todd to CNO, December 15, 1916, 26256–324:3, Gen-

eral Correspondence, 1916–1926, OFSN, RG 80; Todd to Bullard, December 19, 1916, Todd Files, DNC, RG 38, NARA.
36. Daniels to Representative J. W. Alexander, December 29, 1916, 26256–324:2, General Correspondence, 1916–1926, OFSN, RG 80, NARA.
37. Memorandum by Leland Harrison for Lester H. Woolsey, January 27, 1917, 811.741/457, SDDF, RG 59, NARA.
38. Lansing to Representative Alexander, February 8, 1917, Box 3, Todd Files, DNC, RG 38, NARA.
39. Howeth, *History,* 316; "Radio Communication," hearings before the House Committee on Merchant Marine and Fisheries, January 11–13, 15–19, 23–26, 1917; Hooper, transcript of memoirs, Box 37, 117, Hooper Papers, LOC; Captain Todd to Captain S. S. Robinson, March 3, 1917, Box 3, Todd Files, DNC, RG 38. See also Daniels–Charles D. Wolcott correspondence, 26256–324, General Correspondence, 1916–1926, OFSN, RG 80 for an instance of Daniels's going after a high-profile critic of the plan. Daniels to Senator B. R. Tillman, January 23, 1917, and Daniels to Tillman, February 19, 1917, 26256–324, General Correspondence, 1916–1926, OFSN, RG 80, NARA. Douglas, *Inventing,* 274.
40. On the early corporate use of radio in Latin America, see James Schwoch, *The American Radio Industry and Its Latin American Activities, 1900–1939* (Urbana, Ill., 1990), 15–21.
41. A. E. Seelig to Dr. L. W. Austin, July 26, 1915, with map, enclosed in Griffin to Bullard, July 30, 1915, 12479–568:169, General Correspondence, 1916–1926, RG 80, NARA.
42. Morgan to SecState, December 8, 1915, 810.74/26, SDDF, RG 59, NARA.
43. Oscar Milmore to SecState, October 25, 1915, 810.74/7, Perry Beldon to SecState, November 6, 1915, 810.74/8, McGoodwin to SecState, December 15, 1915, 810.74/11, Minister at Colombia to SecState, December 17, 1915, 810.74/35, all SDDF, RG 59, NARA; Schwoch, *American Radio Industry,* 20.
44. "Colombian Neutrality: Control of Wireless Telegraphy," Foreign Office memorandum, March 10, 1915, PRO/FO 881/10541; Manning, Consul at Barranquilla, to SecState, October 3, 1914, FRUS 1914, Supplement, 681; memorandum by Boaz Long, April 20, 1918, 810.74/108, SDDF, RG 59 NARA.
45. Von Heinz Bonatz, *Die Deutsche Marine-Funkaufklärun, 1914–1945* (Darmstadt, 1970), 62. See also Geoffrey Bennett, *Coronel and the Falklands* (Edinburgh, 2000), appendix 2, 170–171. On Cradock, see Julian Corbett, *History of the Great War: Naval Operations,* vol. 1 (New York, 1920), 314; Patrick Beesly, *Room 40: British Naval Intelligence, 1914–1918* (San Diego, 1982), 73–74.
46. For example, in Argentina the British minister wanted German engineers removed from the government stations, while in Paraguay Britain pushed to have the German engineers actually expelled from the country. Stimson to SecState, November 24, 1915, 810.74/15, Milmore to SecState, October 25, 1915, 810.74/7, SDDF, RG 59, NARA.
47. On the importance of the Panama Canal and the defense of the Caribbean in U.S. strategic thinking before World War I, see Richard D. Challener, *Admirals, Generals, and American Foreign Policy* (Princeton, N.J. 1973), 35–36. For a different view, see Nancy Mitchell, *The Danger of Dreams: German and American Imperialism in Latin America* (Chapel Hill, N.C., 1999).

48. SecNav to SecState, November 22, 1913, 819.74/35, SDDF, RG 59, NARA.
49. On the granting of authority, see Price to SecState, August 14, 1914, 819.74/56, and Price to SecState, August 29, 1914, 819.74/59, SDDF, RG 59, NARA. For additional information on the negotiations between the Panamanian government and the United States government, see FRUS 1914, 1036–1052, and 1915, 1155–1161. On the naval radio stations in Panama, see General Estimate of the Radio Station, Canal Zone, and Republic of Panama, October 16, 1916, 12479A-407:56, General Correspondence, 1916–1926, OFSN, RG 80, NARA.
50. On telegraphy's effects on diplomacy, see David Nickles, *Under the Wire: How the Telegraph Changed Diplomacy* (Cambridge, Mass., 2003).
51. Memorandum by Boaz Long, February 2, 1918, PD 177, M1140, RG 80, memorandum by Long, April 20, 1918, 810.74/108, and memorandum by Long to Nelson Johnson, April 3, 1919, 810.74/97, SDDF, RG 59, NARA.
52. Daniels to McAdoo, December 3, 1915, 12479–833, General Correspondence, 1897–1915, OFSN, RG 80, NARA.
53. SecNav to SecState, June 16, 1915, 810.74, SDDF, RG 59, NARA.
54. This conference met between December 27, 1915, and January 8, 1916. On the importance of the Pan-American Scientific Conference in the context of Wilson's Pan-American program, see Mark Gilderhus, *Pan American Visions: Woodrow Wilson in the Western Hemisphere, 1913–1921* (Tucson, 1986), 68–71.
55. Memorandum from solicitor to Boaz Long, August 9, 1915, 810.74, memorandum from Wright to Long, October 13, 1915, 811.74/58, SDDF, RG 59, NARA; circular letter to all U.S. diplomatic officers in Latin America from SecState, October 13, 1915, FRUS 1915, 24.
56. This was to form the first body of information on radio in the hemisphere that any department had yet gathered.
57. Minutes of an informal conference on radio communication in the Western Hemisphere, January 7, 1916, FRUS 1916, 976–979.
58. Mexico, because it suffered from domestic political instability, and Panama, because the United States controlled its radio, were not informed of this proposal. Acting SecState to Ambassador Stimson, et al., with memorandum of the navy, enclosed, March 15, 1916, FRUS 1916, 5–10.
59. Roosevelt to Lansing, June 12, 1916, 12479A-267, General Correspondence, 1916–1926, OFSN, RG 80, NARA.
60. Franklin Roosevelt to SecState, September 24, 1915, 12479A-249:1, General Correspondence, 1897–1915, OFSN, RG 80, NARA.
61. Bullard to Daniels, June 9, 1916, 12479A-267, General Correspondence, 1916–1926, OFSN, RG 80, NARA.
62. Bullard to Daniels, June 9, 1916, 12479A-267, SecNav to SecState, November 23, 1915, transmitting report, 12479A-250:2, Roosevelt to Lansing, June 12, 1916, 12479A-267, Daniels to Lansing, April 9, 1917, 12479A-275:2, and Operations to Flag, Santo Domingo, May 12, 1917, 12479A-275:3, all in General Correspondence, 1916–1926, OFSN, RG 80, NARA.
63. Bullard to CNO, November 3, 1915, and accompanying documents, November–December 1915, Serial 437, File 419, GB, RG 80, NARA.
64. Merrill to Secretary of War Newton Baker, March 8, 1917, and SecNav to Secretary of Commerce, March 21, 1917, 12479–928, Carlton to SecNav,

May 25, 1917, and Daniels to Carlton, June 7, 1914, 12479-970, General Correspondence, 1916–1926, OFSN, RG 80; McAdoo to Lansing, September 11, 1916, 810.74/79, SDDF, RG 59, NARA.
65. Revised Board on Reorganization Report, July 14, 1916, Subject File 419, Serial No. 276, GB, RG 80, NARA; Howeth, *History*, 233.
66. Chauncy Eldridge to SecState, November 5, 1915, enclosed in 12479-249:2-3, General Correspondence, 1916–1926, OFSN, RG 80, NARA.
67. Morgan to SecState, August 24, 1915, 832.74/6, McGoodwin to Lansing, June 15, 1916, and William Philips to Federal Holdings, July 21, 1916, 831.74/9, Schoenfeld to SecState, January 22, 1916, 833.74/15, memorandum by Wright, October 29, 1915, 831.74/4, Preston McGoodwin to SecState, December 17, 1915, 831.74/7, all in SDDF, RG 59, NARA.
68. Schoenfeld to SecState, December 11, 1915, 833.74/13, and January 22, 1916, 833.74/15, SDDF, RG 59, NARA.
69. Eldridge to Lansing, December 11, 1915, 832.74/18, SDDF, RG 59, NARA.
70. Daniels to Lansing, November 7, 1916, 12479A-249:44, General Correspondence, 1916–1926, OFSN, RG 80, NARA.
71. Alvey Adee to SecNav, July 5, 1916, and Daniels to SecState, July 12, 1916, 12479A-249:33, General Correspondence, 1916–1926, OFSN, RG 80; and McGoodwin to SecState, July 28, 1917, 831.74/19, SDDF, RG 59, NARA.
72. Morgan to SecState, August 24, 1915, 832.74/6, E. J. Nally to SecState, September 16, 1915, 832.74/8, Polk to Morgan, September 23, 1915, 832.74/6, and Lansing to Nally, October 9, 1915, 832.74/8, all in SDDF, RG 59, NARA.
73. E. J. Nally to Lansing, November 4, 1915, 832.74/9, and memorandum by J. Butler Wright, October 26, 1915, 832.74/10, SDDF, RG 59, NARA.
74. SecNav to SecState, November 18, 1915, 12479-249:2-3, General Correspondence, 1916–1926, RG 80, NARA.
75. Wright to Adee, November 23, 1915, Adee to Wright, November 29, 1915, 832.74/13a, and Memorandum by J. Butler Wright, December 2, 1915, 832.74/15, SDDF, RG 59; SecState to SecNav, January 14, 1916, 12479-249:2, General Correspondence, 1916–1926, OFSN, RG 80, NARA.
76. Sweden turned to Telefunken after rejecting Marconi's demand for a fifty-year operating license; Sweden repeatedly requested assistance from the United States in testing the station after it was built, but U.S. Navy officials were reluctant to open yet another radio connection during the war. Aitken, *Continuous Wave*, 335; "German Activity in Wireless," memorandum by Isaacs, December 11, 1915, in Montagu memorandum, PRO/CAB 37/140/32; memorandum from Todd to Bullard, March 6, 1919, Bullard Files, DNC, RG 38, NARA.
77. "German Activity in Wireless."
78. Isaacs to Algernon Law, January 3, 1916, PRO/FO 368/1664/*f*1843/2433; Spring-Rice to Foreign Office [hereafter, FO], January 15, 1916, *f*1843/8974; and Isaacs to FO, February 14, 1916, with accompanying minutes, *f*1843/29420. Isaacs tried again in 1916 but failed. See Admiralty memorandum on the Importance of the Establishment of British Owned High Power Wireless Stations in South America, May 17, 1916, and Minutes of War Committee, May 18, 1916, PRO/CAB 42/14/2; FO to Peel, August 22, and Peel to FO, August 23, 1916, PRO/FO 368/1494/*f*10728/161793 and PRO/FO 368/1494/*f*10728/166999; minutes on letter of September 6,

1916, PRO/FO 368/1494/*f*10788/176941; O'Driscoll to Isaacs, October 24, 1916, PRO/FO 368/1494/*f*10728/237169.
79. The Board on Organization had encouraged an agreement with the United Fruit Company on this matter and noted such an agreement between Tropical Radio and the superintendent of the Naval Radio Service by early 1916. See Approved Report, July 14, 1916, Folder 1914–1915, File 419, GB, RG 80, NARA.
80. Memorandum by Boaz Long, February 2, 1918, PD 177, RG 80; memorandum by Boaz Long, April 20, 1918, 810.74/108, SDDF, RG 59, NARA.

4. At War in Europe

1. The story of the Zimmermann telegram has been well covered. See Christopher Andrew, *For the President's Eyes Only: Secret Intelligence and the American Presidency from Washington to Bush* (New York, 1996), 40–46; Patrick Beesly, *Room 40: British Naval Intelligence, 1914–1918* (San Diego, 1982), 204–224; David Kahn, *Codebreakers* (New York, 1996), 284–297. See also Barbara Tuchman, *The Zimmermann Telegram* (New York, 1958), and Friedrich Katz, *The Secret War in Mexico: Europe, the United States, and the Mexican Revolution*, with portions translated by Loren Goldner (Chicago, 1981), 350–366.
2. Memorandum on the message of Zimmermann to the German Minister to Mexico, March 4, 1917, in Arthur S. Link, ed., *The Papers of Woodrow Wilson*, vol. 41: *January 24–April 6, 1917* (Princeton, N.J., 1983), 321–327. See especially David Nickles, *Under the Wire: How the Telegraph Changed Diplomacy* (Cambridge, Mass., 2003), 142–150, esp. notes 25–33.
3. "Transatlantic Electrical Communications," Report of the Chief Signal Officer, *Annual Report of the War Department* (Washington, D.C., 1919), vol. 1, 1013.
4. Joseph Tulchin, *Aftermath of War: World War I and U.S. Policy Toward Latin America* (New York, 1971), 16.
5. Original History Sheets, U Type Submarines *U-106* to *U-164*, entry for *U-155*, and Report of Interrogation of Seaman Huck Charles (Submarine Stoker), *U-155*, in French, attached, Naval Intelligence Division, PRO/ADM 137/3915.
6. See Spring-Rice to Foreign Office, October 12, 1916, PRO/FO 372/910/*f*122691/204141.
7. *Annual Report of the War Department*, 1013; memorandum from Philip Patchin, Division of Foreign Intelligence, for Frank Polk, July 19, 1917, 811.74/133, SDDF, RG 59, NARA.
8. Naval Attaché, Paris, to DNC, August 17, 1917, in Todd Files, DNC, RG 38, NARA.
9. Sharp, Ambassador in Paris, to SecState, April 28, 1917, with enclosed Protocols of April 13 and 19, 1917, 811.74/124, SDDF, RG 59, NARA.
10. The Pisa station also went by the name Coltano. The Rome station used a 350 kw arc transmitter, with improvements by the former Federal Telegraph engineer C. F. Elwell. It could transmit to Massawa and New York. See B. Micchiardi, G. Pession, and G. Ballauri, "The Rome Radio Telegraphic Station," abstract, *Science Abstracts* (1920): 358, and C. F. Elwell, "Poulsen Arc Installations," abstract, *Science Abstracts* (1920): 278. See also "Develop-

ments of Poulsen Wireless System Shown," *Electrical Review,* September 6, 1919, 397.
11. "Navy Radio," Senate Document 248, Statement to Accompany S. 4038, March 8, 1920, 66th Congress, 2nd sess., copy found in file 26256–324, General Correspondence, 1916–1926, OFSN, RG 80, NARA.
12. On January 20, 1918, exclusive service began between Tuckerton and Rome.
13. Sharp to SecState, April 28, 1917, with enclosed Protocols of April 13 and 19, 1917, 811.74/124, and Sharp to SecState, May 2, 1917, with Protocol of April 27, 1917, 811.74/125, SDDF, RG 59, NARA.
14. Sharp to SecState, May 29, 1917, 832.74/27, Jusserand to Lansing, June 19, 1917, 811.74/130, Daniels to Lansing, June 6, 1917, 832.74/28, SDDF, RG 59, NARA.
15. Polk to Jusserand, July 19, 1917, in FRUS 1918, Supplement 2, 837–838.
16. SecNav to SecState, June 4, 1917, 12479A-301, General Correspondence, 1916–1926, OFSN, RG 80, NARA.
17. Carlton to Daniels, June 9, 1917, and Daniels to Carlton, June 15, 1917, 6694–309, General Correspondence, 1916–1926, OFSN, RG 80, NARA.
18. Russel in *Annual Report of the War Department,* 1013.
19. Russel to Pershing, August 23, 1917, in *Annual Report of the War Department,* 1013–1014.
20. Martin Gilbert, *The First World War: A Complete History* (New York, 1994), 339; Paul G. Halpern, *A Naval History of World War I* (Annapolis, Md., 1994), 358.
21. See memorandum for Commander Sayles from Colonel Russell, August 15, 1917, Todd Files, DNC, RG 38, NARA.
22. General Pershing to Adjutant General of the Army, August 29, cited in *Annual Report of the War Department,* 1014. Pershing made virtually no reference to these matters in his memoirs. See John J. Pershing, *My Experiences in the World War,* vol. 1 (New York, 1931), 324. An examination of several other standard accounts of Pershing, his role in the war, and the AEF failed to turn up any references to these events.
23. G. M. Yorke to Squier, September 24, 1917, File 676.4, General Correspondence, 1917–1940, Office of the Chief Signal Officer, RG 111, NARA.
24. Carlton's confidant was Lord Northcliffe, head of the British Mission to the United States in 1917. Lord Northcliffe to C. J. Phillips, October 13, 1917, et al., in "Capacity of Atlantic Cables," PRO/FO 368/1845/f198724.
25. Data from memorandum of March 22, 1918, in Register 9494C, File B-10-g, Naval Attaché Registers, ONI, RG 38, NARA.
26. *Annual Report of the War Department,* 1014; the Signal Corps originally envisioned its own seven-station network. See Hooper, transcript of memoirs, Box 38, 834, Hooper Papers, LOC.
27. Frank Polk to Clarence Mackay, October 4, 1917, and draft cable to Embassy, London, October 4, 1917, Folder 339, Box 10, Series 1 (Correspondence), Polk Papers, Archives and Manuscripts Collection, Sterling Memorial Library, Yale University [hereafter, Polk Papers]; Page to SecState, October 24, 1917, 811.73/56, SDDF, RG 59, NARA.
28. Dispatch of R. H. Jackson, May 21, 1918, in Force Commander, France, to DNC, June 1, 1918, Box 5, Confidential Correspondence, 1917–1926, Divi-

sion of Naval Communications; Todd to Sims, July 10, 1918, Todd Files, DNC, RG 38, NARA.

29. The navy had fifty-five ship-shore and radio compass stations at the outbreak of the war along the Atlantic, Gulf, Pacific, and Alaskan coasts. During the war, it built sixty-nine more stations, of which fifteen were radio compass stations. All told, the U.S. Navy operated seventy-eight radio stations, of which fifty were along the lower contiguous coastline or the Great Lakes. The ship-shore network included seven stations in Alaska, eight scattered in the Pacific, and seven in the Caribbean. It was the most sophisticated regional network anywhere in the world at the time. See list of commercial radio stations taken over under executive order of April 6, 1917, 12479–568:119, General Correspondence, 1916–1926, OFSN, RG 80, NARA.

30. Linwood S. Howeth, *A History of Communications-Electronics in the United States Navy* (Washington, D.C., 1963), 237. The navy also gained control over the Federal Telegraph stations and indirect control over the Caribbean network of Tropical Radio.

31. Report of the Board on Organization, July 14, 1916, File 419, GB, RG 80, NARA; Howeth, *History*, 237, 290; Hugh G. J. Aitken, *The Continuous Wave: Technology and American Radio, 1900–1932* (Princeton, N.J., 1985), 159.

32. The meeting occurred aboard the USS *Chicago* in New London, Connecticut. Colonel John J. Carty to Chief Signal Officer (CSO), July 7, 1918, in Register No. 18439, File B-10-g, Naval Attaché Registers, ONI, RG 38; memorandum on October 8, 1917, meeting, Item 49, Box 3, Confidential Correspondence, 1917–1926, Division of Naval Communications, RG 38, NARA; Hooper, transcript of memoirs, Box 38, 834, Hooper Papers; *Annual Report of the War Department*, 1015.

33. There was an American Marconi station at Marion/Chatham, Massachusetts, but it was incomplete at the war's outbreak. The navy instructed American Marconi to continue building and testing the station, but signal interference at the site caused too many problems for the station ever to work effectively.

34. Aitken, *Continuous Wave*, 311; Vice Admiral Sir Arthur Richard Hezlet, *The Electron and Sea Power* (New York, 1975), 156.

35. Howeth, *History*, 238–239; "Navy Radio."

36. Howeth, *History*, 248, 290.

37. Daniels to SecState, August 9, 1917, 811.74/136, SDDF, RG 59, NARA; Howeth, *History*, 238–239.

38. Dispatch of R. H. Jackson, May 21, 1918, in Force Commander, France, to DNC, June 1, 1918, Box 5, Confidential Correspondence, 1917–1926, Division of Naval Communications, RG 38, NARA.

39. Pannill to Hooper, April 16, 1918, Box 2, Hooper Papers, LOC.

40. U.S. Navy, Office of Naval Records and Library, *German Submarine Activities on the Atlantic Coast of the United States and Canada* (Washington, D.C., 1920), 121–122.

41. Secretary of War to SecNav, December 14, 1917, 28754–29:17, Formerly Confidential Correspondence, 1917–1919, and SecNav to Chief of the Bureau of Steam Engineering, June 28, 1918, 12479–1056, General Correspondence, 1916–1926, OFSN, RG 80, NARA.

42. Report of August 3, 1917, "U.K.-Verband, Kabelschneide- und Minenan-

gelegenheiten, Juli 1917–August 1918," 2, Bundesarchiv-Militärarchive, Freiburg, Germany (BAMA) RM 5/6439.

43. Report of Korvettekapitän E. Winkler (n.d. but late summer 1917), 6–16, "U.K.-Verband, Kabelschneide- und Minenangelegenheiten, Juli 1917–August 1918." E. Winkler no relation to the author of this work.
44. On March 7–8, 1918, the *U-155* hit cables off of the Spanish coast again, while off the west coast of Africa the *U-153* and *U-154* joined forces to attack British cables in April. Allied forces, alerted by urgent warnings from Liberia, caught up with the *U-154* after it raided Monrovia. See *U-155* history sheet, and Huck interrogation, PRO/ADM 137/3915; *U-153* logbook, entries for April, 1918, Roll 64, Microfilm Publication T-1022, Records of the German Navy, 1850–1945, RG 242, NARA; Chargé Bundy, Monrovia, to SecState, April 10, 1918, and subsequent documents, FRUS 1918, Supplement 1, 740–750.
45. CNO to Commandant, Marine Corps, June 21, 1918, 28754–29:38, Formerly Confidential Correspondence, 1917–1919, OFSN, RG 80, NARA.
46. U.S. Navy, *German Submarine Activities*, 119–120. See also Michael L. Hadley and Roger Sarty, *Tin Pots and Pirate Ships: Canadian Naval Forces and German Sea Raiders, 1880–1918* (Montreal, 1991), 243, 286–287; Henry J. James, *German Subs in Yankee Waters, First World War* (New York, 1940), 32–34.
47. Report of June 27, 1918, 95, "U.K.-Verband, Kabelschneide- und Minenangelegenheiten, Juli 1917–August 1918."
48. Chief of Admiral Staff to Nauen, January 11, 1918, and Chief of Admiral Staff to Marine Attaché, Hague, Christiana, Stockholm, Copenhagen, 59–60, "U.K.-Verband, Kabelschneide- und Minenangelegenheiten, Juli 1917–August 1918."
49. Report on March 29, 1918, cable cutting, 75, "U.K.-Verband, Kabelschneide- und Minenangelegenheiten, Juli 1917–August 1918."
50. The campaign against Allied communications is almost entirely unmentioned in standard accounts of World War I naval history by English-language authors.
51. Memorandum on the subject of interference in transatlantic radio messages, April 17, 1918, in Item 49, Box 3, Confidential Correspondence, 1917–1926, Division of Naval Communications, RG 38, NARA. The jamming occurred on March 30, 1918.
52. Colonel F. R. Curtis to Colonel J. J. Carty, May 22, 1918, and Carty to Curtis, July 7, 1918, in Register No. 18439, File B-10-g, Naval Attaché Registers, ONI, RG 38, NARA.
53. Minute by T. A. M. Craven on NID to DNC, June 18, 1918, Confidential Communications, 1917–1926, Division of Naval Communications, RG 38, NARA. Properly, the station was to be at Monroe, North Carolina.
54. Federal Telegraph had meanwhile constructed the arcs for the station. They sat—weighing eighty tons each—unused for many years in the company warehouse. The powerful magnets at the core of the arc transmitters later became part of Dr. E. O. Lawrence's cyclotron at Stanford University in the 1930s and contributed to the birth of the atomic era.
55. Howeth, *History*, 238–239; "Organization of the U.S. High Power Radio Detachment, Lafayette Radio Station, Croix d'Hins," (n.d. but in file for January 6, 1919), 12479–1072, General Correspondence, 1916–1926, OFSN, RG

80, NARA. On its postwar fate, see Daniels to Lansing, November 24, 1919, with enclosures, FRUS 1918, Supplement 2, 840–842. Negotiations continued on into the 1920s: see also FRUS 1921, vol. 1, 957–962.

56. Clarence Mackay to Frank Polk, March 23, 1917, with enclosures, Folder 339, Box 10, Series 1, Polk Papers.
57. Robert Lansing, *War Memoirs of Robert Lansing* (Indianapolis, 1935), 86 and 318. With no operatives under its direct control, the State Department borrowed agents from other departments to carry out missions. J. M. Nye of the Treasury Department's Secret Service was in charge. Some time around the point when Polk's position of counselor became that of undersecretary, the Bureau of Secret Intelligence became U-1.
58. Andrews, *For the President's Eyes Only*, 37.
59. Beesly, *Room 40*, 236–237.
60. Josephus Daniels, *The Cabinet Diaries of Josephus Daniels, 1913–1921*, ed. E. David Cronon (Lincoln, Ill., 1963), 141.
61. There was substantial censorship over the international mails as well, but for the purposes of this study censorship refers only to the monitoring of the cables and radio systems because these were the faster and more important routes over which to send intelligence.
62. Howeth, *History*, 296.
63. Intercept of German diplomatic traffic, Santiago, Chile, to Lima, Peru, July 6, 1917, "1917 Intercepts, Chilean and German," PRO/ADM 223/781.
64. Report of Captain J. H. Trye, British Cable Censor Liaison Officer, April 4, 1919, appendix 3, Report on Cable Censorship During the Great War, 1914–1918, PRO/DEFE 1/402.
65. SecNav to SecState, October 31, 1917, 28639–118: 60, General Correspondence 1916–1926, OFSN, RG 80, NARA.
66. SecNav to J. C. Willever, July 28, 1917, 28639–118, General Correspondence 1916–1926, OFSN, RG 80, NARA. In total, at the height of the war the censors screened some twenty-five thousand messages a day across the U.S. end of the cable network.
67. Report of Captain J. H. Trye.
68. Standard recent accounts of the early history of U.S. signals intelligence include David Alvarez, *Secret Messages: Codebreaking and American Diplomacy, 1930–1945* (Lawrence, Kans., 2000), and Stephen Budiansky, *Battle of Wits: The Complete Story of Codebreaking in World War II* (New York, 2000); see also David Kahn's *Codebreakers* (New York: Scribner, 1996), and his recent biography of Herbert Yardley, *The Reader of Gentlemen's Mail: Herbert O. Yardley and the Birth of American Codebreaking* (New Haven: Yale, 2004).
69. The navy briefly had its own code-breaking section, but after little success the navy passed this work to MI-8. Beesly, *Room 40*, 247.
70. The State Department supplied several of its code clerks to the U.S. Army, which had entered the war with no official code -making or -breaking section. See Kahn, *Codebreakers*, 326.
71. Because MI-8 drew upon other sources, such as postal mail and messages smuggled in person by spies, we should not consider it to be connected solely with cable censorship. More interesting, and less well known by intelligence historians, is who in the State or War departments made use of what MI-8 uncovered.

72. Report of Captain J. H. Trye; Beesly, *Room 40*, 248. At its peak, MI-8 had 151 staff members, including 24 civilian cryptanalysts. See Kahn, *Codebreakers*.
73. This support is not surprising. James Scrymser, the founder and president of the company, had been a Union officer in the Civil War and often expressed his desire to assist the government before World War I.
74. Commander A. B. Hoff, Chief Cable Censor, to Commander Todd, August 13, 1917, in Todd Files, DNC, RG 38, NARA.
75. Woolsey to Merrill, October 29, 1917, and Merrill to Harrison, December 12, 1917, "Censorship," Box 7, Classified Case Files, 1916–1926, Entry 349, Office of the Counselor/Undersecretary of State and Chief Special Agent, RG 59, NARA.
76. Copy of Count Luxburg cable, July 20, 1917, War Report of War Trade Intelligence Department, appendix 1, 121, PRO/DEFE 1/402; Beesly, *Room 40*, 239–240.
77. Brazil and the United States had initially discussed Brazil's entry into the war on the side of the Allies in the weeks that followed the U.S. declaration of war. Brazil broke relations with Germany and eventually removed its neutrality to allow the United States access to Brazil's ports. See Mark T. Gilderhus, *Pan American Visions: Woodrow Wilson in the Western Hemisphere, 1913–1921* (Tucson, 1986), 97–98, 106.
78. The United States also dispatched censors for joint operations with the Allies at Shanghai, Nagasaki, Paris, and Lisbon. See Report of Captain J. H. Trye; SecNav to SecState, October 6, 1917, and May 7, 1918, 28639-118:44, 28639-118:128, General Correspondence 1916–1926, OFSN, RG 80, NARA; Colonel A. Churchill to Sir Adam Block, September 12, 1917, PRO/FO 395/159/181960.
79. Claims of interference to cable messages are filed generally in 811.731, SDDF, but the complaints largely concerned interference, not allegations of information being passed to competitors. See, as examples, Francis, Petrograd, to SecState, June 28, 1917, 811.731/163, on U.S. Steel's complaints, and American Consul, Athens, to SecState, September 21, 1917, 811.731/255, on Colt, SDDF, RG 59, NARA.
80. Robertson to SecState, December 20, 1917, 835.738/1, SDDF, RG 59, NARA.
81. Assistant Director of Naval Intelligence to Leland Harrison, June 21, 1918, 811.73/85, SDDF, RG 59, NARA. The assistant naval attaché may have been Captain F. K. Hill, USN Retired, who served May 1917 to July 1920 and testified to the Senate Interstate Commerce Committee on the matter on December 16, 1920; see Senate Committee on Interstate Commerce, *Cable Landing Licenses: Hearings on S. 4301*, 66th Congress, 3rd sess., 1920–1921, 182 [hereafter, Senate Hearings].
82. William Phillips to Edwin V. Morgan, July 12, 1918, 811.73/85, SDDF, RG 59, NARA.
83. Morgan to SecState, August 26, 1918, 811.73/92, and March 22, 1918, 832.731/10, SDDF, RG 59, NARA.
84. Testimony of Carlton before Senate, December 15, 1920, Senate Hearings, 130.
85. Robertson to SecState, October 22, 1918, 835.738/2, SDDF, RG 59, NARA.
86. Captain D. W. Todd to Captain William Strother Smith, September 7, 1917, Box 3, Todd Files, DNC, RG 38, NARA.

87. This principle of induction continues to be the basis for more-sophisticated methods of tapping today. Van Eyck phreaking is one method of doing this involving computer monitors. See, for example, Neal Stephenson, *Cryptonomicon*, (New York: Eos, 1999).
88. Report of Colonel John J. Carty to Chief Signal Officer, July 9, 1918, Confidential Report on A Method of Tapping Submarine Cables, April 30, 1918, and statement of Carty for the Interallied Radio Commission, from Naval Attaché's Report No. 18439, File B-10-g, Attaché Reports, 1886–1939, ONI, RG 38, NARA.
89. Report of the Chief Signal Offficer, Annual Report of the War Department (Washington, D.C., 1919), vol. 1, 1019; Colonel Carty, July 9, 1918.
90. U.S. Naval Force Commander in France to DNC, June 1, 1918, covering letter from R. H. Jackson, Staff Representative, May 21, 1918, Box 5, Confidential Correspondence, 1917–1926, Division of Naval Communications, RG 38, NARA.
91. On cold war operations, see Sherry Sontag and Christopher Drew, with Annette Lawrence Drew, *Blind Man's Bluff: The Untold Story of American Submarine Espionage* (New York, 1998), esp. 158–163 and 214–220.
92. Tulchin, *Aftermath of War*, 59.

5. In Pursuit of Cables to Asia and the Americas

1. Alexander Benson to SecState, March 20, 1917, Lansing to Benson, March 22, 1917, and Benson to Lansing, April 10, 1917, FRUS 1918, 45–47.
2. This was the Compañía Telegráfico-Telephónica de la Plata, a subsidiary of the Deutsche Sud Amerikanische Telegraphen Gesellschaft, which operated the German cable from Liberia to Brazil.
3. Merrill to Lansing, April 30, 1917, 835.73/49, May 3 and July 20, 1917, 835.73/51, SDDF, RG 59, NARA.
4. On Admiral Caperton's mission, see David Healy, "Admiral William B. Caperton and United States Naval Diplomacy in South America, 1917–1919," *Journal of Latin American Studies* 8 (November 1976): 297–323.
5. Stimson to SecState, August 1, 1917, 835.73/54, SDDF, RG 59, NARA.
6. Merrill to Breckinridge Long, November 23, 1917, 835.73/58, SDDF, RG 59, NARA.
7. See data provided in "Cable Communications, Uruguay," Register No. 9836, File B-10-g, Naval Attaché Reports, ONI, RG 38; Confidential Consular Report, Montevideo, May 18, 1918, 833.73/31, SDDF, RG 59, NARA.
8. Merrill to SecState, June 9, 1916, 833.73/13, SDDF, RG 59, NARA.
9. Morgan to SecState, August 16, 1917, FRUS 1918, 49; Carlton to Polk, August 28, and Polk to Auchincloss, August 31, 1917, Folder 96, Box 3, Series I, Polk Papers, Archives and Manuscripts Collection, Sterling Memorial Library, Yale University [hereafter, Polk Papers]; Long diary, March 22, 1917, Long Papers, LOC [hereafter, Long Papers]; see also Robert Quirk, *An Affair of Honor: Woodrow Wilson and the Occupation of Vera Cruz* (New York, 1962), 34–45.
10. He signed the decree on October 24. Stimson to SecState, February 24, 835.73/60, Merrill to SecState, March 27, 835.73/63, Adee to Merrill, November 5, 835.73/83, Wadsworth, Chargé in Montevideo, to SecState,

March 8, 1918, 833.73/29, SDDF, RG 59, NARA; Merrill to SecState, March 23, and Stimson to Lansing, April 2, 9, and 10, 1918, FRUS 1918, 39, 41–43.
11. Lansing to Jeffery, Minister in Montevideo, February 7, 1917, 833.73/14, Jeffery to SecState, April 19, and Lansing to Jeffery, October 25, 1917, 833.73/21, Merrill to SecState, October 16, 1917, 833.73/22, all in SDDF, RG 59, NARA. On Scrymser's fear of Britain blocking German traffic after the war, see memorandum from Scrymser to Merrill, January 15, 833.73/17, and Merrill to Phillips, January 20, 1917, 833.73/16, SDDF, RG 59, NARA.
12. Lansing to Stimson, December 28, 1917, 835.73/59, SDDF, RG 59, NARA.
13. Merrill to SecState, July 18, 1918, 811.73/80, SDDF, RG 59, NARA.
14. Morgan to SecState, July 13 and October 31, 1917, 832.73/110 and 832.73/119, SDDF, RG 59, NARA.
15. W. S. Robertson, General Superintendent, South America, to E. Steer Hodson, January 29, 1917, "Revision of Brazilian Concession" folder, Western Telegraph Company records, CW.
16. Morgan to SecState, October 25, 1917, FRUS 1918, 50.
17. Jorma Ahvenainen, *The History of the Caribbean Telegraphs before the First World War* (Helsinki, 1996), 146–157.
18. Morgan to SecState, November 26 and December 12, 1917, FRUS 1918, 57–58 and 62–63.
19. Merrill to Lansing, February 12, 1918, 811.74/146, SDDF, RG 59, NARA.
20. Ibid; Morgan to SecState, December 12, 1917.
21. Merrill to SecState, April 16, 1918, and June 4, 1918, 832.73/144 and /150, SDDF, RG 59, NARA; Lansing to Morgan, April 19, 1918, and Vice Consul in Charge at Rio de Janeiro, Momsen, to Lansing, November 30, 1918, FRUS 1918, 65 and 74.
22. Morgan to SecState, March 14, 1918, 832.73/139, SDDF, RG 59, NARA; Morgan to Lansing, May 17, Carlton to Lansing, May 31, and Polk to Morgan, June 5, 1918, FRUS 1918, 66, 70–71.
23. The regular rate was thirty-four cents per word; it became fifty-eight cents per word. Merrill to Lansing, November 7, 1917, Lansing to Stimson, March 29, 1918, Morgan to Lansing, August 13, 1918, and Lansing to Morgan, September 27, 1918, FRUS 1918, 51, 41, 72–74; Merrill to SecState, March 27, 1918, 835.73/63, SDDF, RG 59, NARA.
24. Note of October 11, 1917, in "First World War Censorship" folder, Section 6: North America, Eastern and Associated Records, CW.
25. Report of the Special Committee, August 1, 1918, in Merrill to Gordon Auchincloss, September 27, 1918, 811.731/711, SDDF, RG 59, NARA.
26. Radio Scrapbook 2, Box 295, Clark Radioana Collection, NMAH.
27. Memorandum by F. R. Eldridge, Chief, Far Eastern Division, Bureau of Foreign and Domestic Commerce, September 6, 1919, 811.73/144, SDDF, RG 59, NARA.
28. Office of Naval Intelligence Report, February 13, 1919, Box 10, Confidential Correspondence, 1917–1926, Division of Naval Communications, RG 38, NARA.
29. For complaints on the U.S. end, see, for example, "Complaints of Delay Made by Silk Trade," *New York Times*, July 22 and August 5, 1917, and "Delays Bother U.S. Importers of Far East Goods," *New York Times*, September 9, 1917.

30. Memorandum by Long, "Japanese Series No. 2," July 17, 1917, Box 183, Long Papers.
31. SecNav to SecState, July 27, 1917, 28639–118:3, General Correspondence, 1916–1926, OFSN, RG 80, NARA; memorandum by Long, "Japanese Series No. 6," August 3, 1917, and "Japanese Series No. 11," November 13, 1917, Box 183, and Diary Entries for August 23, September 13, October 18 and November 13, 1917, Box 1, Long Papers.
32. On the Committee on Public Information, see James R. Mock and Cedric Larson, *Words That Won the War: The Story of the Committee on Public Information, 1917–1919* (Princeton, N.J., 1939). On the Foreign Section, see pp. 73, 239–251. See also *Complete Report of the Chairman of the Committee on Public Information* (Washington, D.C., 1920), 108–127. The various press agencies usually had agreements with the cable companies to send a minimum daily or weekly amount of press traffic, for which they received a reduced rate but also preferential treatment against other wire services. In this environment U.S. news agencies Associated Press and United Press had a difficult time securing more than a fraction of the share that Reuters, Havas, or Wolff had of the international news wire market.
33. Roy Watson Curry records that Rogers initially brought this to the attention of Colonel House, who directed him to the State Department (and thus Long). See Roy Watson Curry, *Woodrow Wilson and Far Eastern Policy, 1913–1921* (New York, 1968), 209, citing letter from Rogers to George Creel in the Wilson papers.
34. The general manager of United Press, W. W. Hawkins, later explained that the United Press had a similar problem getting news into South America via the British cables. The number of words is mentioned in Minutes of the Second Meeting of the Interdepartmental Committee on Communications across the Pacific, August 27, 1918, "Pacific Communications" folder, File 676.4, "Pacific and Alaska Miscellaneous Materials," General Correspondence, 1917–1940, Office of Chief Signal Officer [hereafter, OCSO], RG 111, NARA.
35. Memorandum by Walter S. Rogers to Frank L. Polk, June 19, 1917, 811.73/43, and Rogers to Auchincloss, October 6, 1917, 811.73/64, SDDF, RG 59, NARA. If we think of news as a perishable commodity like fruit or meat, then international news sent by news agencies must have been one of the few parts of international trade not covered by the tariff systems constructed by nation-states. Instead, news—through the rates cable companies and governments charged for sending messages in the press category—fell under the purview of the International Telegraph Union, whose interest was interoperability (internationally recognized rates) but not equality (elimination of preferential rates).
36. Colonel House had informed President Wilson of Rogers's initial findings in May. See House to Wilson, May 11, 1917, Wilson Papers, vol. 2, 118, cited in Curry, *Woodrow Wilson*, 175.
37. As early as March 28, 1917, Polk and Breckinridge Long had discussed using this Peking station and the navy's Pacific radio chain in place of the cables if they were cut by the Germans. See entry of March 28, 1917, Long diary, Box 1, Long Papers.
38. Rogers to Polk, June 19, 1917, 811.74/131, and Rogers to President Wilson, June 21, 1917, 811.74/131, SDDF, RG 59, NARA.

39. SecNav to SecState, August 21, 1917, 28639-103, General Correspondence, 1916-1926, OFSN, RG 80, NARA.
40. SecNav to SecState, July 16, 1917, 28639-103, General Correspondence, 1916-1926, OFSN, RG 80, NARA.
41. SecNav to SecState, July 16, 1917.
42. These were the British Eastern Extension, part of Pender's British cable conglomerate, and the Danish Great Northern Telegraph Company.
43. Memorandum from Edward T. Williams, State Department China expert, to Lansing, September 11, 1917, 811.73/43, SDDF, RG 59, NARA.
44. Memorandum on interallied radio conference, June 22, 1917, 28754-29:5, Formerly Confidential Correspondence, 1917-1919, OFSN, RG 80, NARA.
45. Notes by Clark from Federal Telegraph Company records, Folder 3, Box 101, Clark Radioana Collection, NMAH; SecNav to Secretary of Commerce, June 22, 1916, 12479-874, General Correspondence, 1916-1926, OFSN, RG 80, NARA.
46. Samuel Flagg Bemis, "The Yap Island Controversy," *Pacific Review* 2 (September 1921): 314-315.
47. Daniels to SecState, May 15 and May 28, 1918, 811.74/149a, SDDF, RG 59, NARA; *Annual Report of the Secretary of the Navy, 1918* (Washington, D.C., 1919); memorandum of conversation with Japanese Chargé d'Affaires, March 9, 1918, Folder 393, Box 28, Polk Papers; memorandum by Long, May 29, memorandum of conversation with Mr. Tanaka, May 7, memorandum of conversation with Japanese Chargé d'Affaires, January 26, and supplemental memorandum, March 9, 1918, Box 183, Long Papers.
48. Polk to George Ward, April 18, 1918, and Ward to Polk, May 3, 1918, 894.733/1, SDDF, RG 59, NARA.
49. Entry of June 27, 1918, Long diary, Box 1, Long Papers; Mackay to Polk, June 19, and Long to Ward, June 26, 1918, 894.733/2 and 894.7331, SDDF, RG 59; Copies of dispatches, July 1918, File 676.4, "Pacific Cables, 1917-1924" folder, General Correspondence, 1917-1940, OCSO, RG 111, NARA. On the Pacific Cable situation, see Jorma Ahvenainen, *The Far Eastern Telegraphs* (Helsinki, 1991).
50. SecNav to SecState, July 31, 1918, 12479A-333, General Correspondence, 1916-1926, OFSN, RG 80, NARA; Office of Naval Intelligence to Operations, June 18, 1918, Confidential Correspondence, 1917-1926, Division of Naval Communications, RG 38, NARA; Minutes of First Meeting of Interdepartmental Committee, August 10, 1918, Folder 240, Box 25, Series 3, Polk Papers.
51. Long and Rogers found support for this program from the nascent Council on Foreign Relations, a committee that resolved that "it should be the policy of the United States Government . . . to establish additional cable communications" with those countries of international and commercial importance, even if the commercial demand for such service is not yet enough to compel private interests to lay such a cable. They circulated their resolution to several senior officials, including President Wilson. See Douglas Dunbar, Secretary, Council on Foreign Relations, to Frank N. Doubleday, July 25, 1918, "Communications Committee, 1918-1919," Box 412, Council on Foreign Relations Collection, Department of Rare Books and Special Collections, Princeton University Library.

52. Rogers, Todd, Squier, and Patchin all provided reports. Patchin's report is missing from the files and his role in State Department intelligence remains unclear.
53. Report on the Study of Present Routes of Communication between the United States, China, Japan, and other Asiatic Countries, August 9, 1918, "Pacific Communications" folder, and Report of Walter S. Rogers, August 24, 1918, "Pacific Cables, 1917–1924" folder, File 676.4, Pacific and Alaska Miscellaneous Material, General Correspondence, 1917–1940, OCSO, RG 111; memorandum for Long from Captain Todd, "Interest of Navy Department in Cable Communications," enclosed in memorandum regarding transpacific communications, August 29, 1918, Box 17, Confidential Correspondence, 1917–1926, Division of Naval Communications, RG 38; memorandum on the Cable Situation in the Pacific Area and the Military Necessity for Improved Communications across the Pacific Between America and the Continent of Asia, General George O. Squier (n.d. but before August 27, 1918), 811.73/382, SDDF, RG 59, NARA.
54. See memorandum by Long in Patchin to Todd, August 30, 1918, Todd Files, 1916–1919, DNC, RG 38, NARA. Notes of a meeting on Interdepartmental Committee for Communications across the Pacific, August 10, 1918, Folder 240, Box 25, Series 3, Polk Papers.
55. Memorandum of a meeting of the Interdepartmental Committee on Pacific Communications, October 9, 1918, 574.D1/188, SDDF, RG 59, NARA.
56. These were Lieutenant P. E. D. Nagle, the navy's supervisor of cable communications at New York, and Captain A. A. Clokey, the Signal Corps' chief of the cable engineering section. Gano Dunn to Breckinridge Long, August 29, 1918, "Pacific Communications" folder, File 676.4, Pacific and Alaska Miscellaneous Material, and Gano Dunn to Colonel E. Russel, March 30, 1921, File 676.4, "Pacific Cables, 1917–1924," folder, General Correspondence, 1917–1940, OCSO, RG 111, NARA.
57. F. B. Jewett to Squier, August 10, 1918, File 676.4, General Correspondence, 1917–1940, OCSO, RG 111, NARA; Squier to Kennelly, January 21, and Kennelly to Squier, January 27, 1919, Squier Papers, Bentley Historical Library, University of Michigan.
58. Dunn to Squier, February 15, 1919, "Cable Problems—Pacific Cables," File 676.6, General Correspondence, RG 111, NARA.
59. Dunn to Long, November 8, 1918, Box 33, Long Papers; Gano Dunn to Squier, October 30, 1918, File 676.4, "Pacific Cables, 1917–1924," folder, General Correspondence, 1917–1940, OCSO, RG 111, NARA.
60. Bernard Finn, "Submarine Telegraphy: A Study in Technical Stagnation" (paper presented before Communications under the Sea Conference, Dibner Institute for History of Science and Technology, Massachusetts Institute of Technology, April 19, 2002).
61. These included the Safety Insulated Wire Company of New York City, Kerite Insulated Wire and Cable Company, the Okonite Company, the Standard Underground Cable Company, and the Western Electric Company.
62. W. W. Hawkins, General Manager of the United Press Association, to Phillip W. Patchen, Chief of Bureau of Intelligence, State Department, August 28, 1918, "Pacific Communications" folder, File 676.4, General Correspondence, 1917–1940, OCSO, RG 111, NARA.

63. Report of the Special Committee, August 1, 1918, enclosed in Merrill to Gordon Auchincloss, September 27, 1918, 811.731/711, SDDF, RG 59, NARA.
64. Britain had six plants; France had one, Italy two, Norway one, and Germany two.
65. Report of the Special Committee, August 1, 1918.
66. Ibid.
67. Ibid.
68. Notes of a meeting on the Interdepartmental Committee for Communications across the Pacific, August 10, 1918, Folder 240, Box 25, Series 3, Polk Papers; Minutes of the Second Meeting of the [Committee], August 27, 1918, "Pacific Communications" folder, File 676.4, "Pacific and Alaska Miscellaneous Materials," General Correspondence, 1917–1940, OCSO, RG 111; Breckinridge Long to S. W. Stratton, Director, Bureau of Standards, August 29, 1918, 811.73/94b, SDDF, RG 59, NARA.
69. Report of the Special Committee, August 1, 1918, in Merrill to Gordon Auchincloss, September 27, 1918, 811.731/711, SDDF, RG 59, NARA.
70. Ninety-one percent comes from data on existing capacity in October 1917 (2.4 million maximum weekly load or 342,900 average maximum daily load) and daily minimums of the final six months of the war (never less than 23,300 words per day of government traffic or 287,000 words per day of commercial) and with never fewer than seven cables operational. Part of the delays could also be traced to the influenza outbreak. See memorandum of March 22, 1918, in Register 9494C, File B-10-g, Naval Attaché Registers, Office of Naval Intelligence, RG 38, NARA, and Lieutenant P. E. D. Nagle to Gano Dunn, December 6, 1918, Long Papers.
71. Carlton to Lansing, July 2, 1918, 811.73/79, SDDF, RG 59, NARA.

6. Radio, the Navy, and Latin America

1. Arthur C. Clarke, *Profiles of the Future* (New York, 1962), chap. 2.
2. Lansing to Daniels, March 31, 1917, 12479–942, and memorandum by Leland Harrison, April 16, 1917, 12479A-286:2, General Correspondence, 1916–1926, OFSN, RG 80, NARA.
3. Germany also pursued a chain of stations in China at this time, but historians have not yet explored this story. Foreign Office memorandum quoted in Friedrich Katz, *Secret War in Mexico: Europe, the United States, and the Mexican Revolution*, with portions translated by Loren Goldner (Chicago, 1981), 417.
4. The committee continued, "The preparation of machines, equipment and antennae must immediately be set in motion, for the three major stations to be established in Mexico, in China, and in South America, either in Brazil or Uruguay, regardless of whether they will be in operation during the war." Conclusions of an interdepartmental committee, February 14, 1917, quoted in Katz, *Secret War,* 420.
5. As the Mexico City station could not transmit back to Nauen, apparently the German agents sent their most urgent messages by cable from the United States to Spain. From there the messages would go by radio to Nauen. Eventually U.S. censors discovered the ruse and stopped it. Katz, *Secret War,* 422.

6. Memorandum for Boaz Long from Todd, April 12, 1918, 810.74/104, SDDF, RG 59, NARA; Translated decryptions of wireless messages from Nauen to Sayville, January 7, February 1, and March 4, 1917, PRO/ADM 223/781; Leland Harrison to Lieutenant Colonel Ralph Van Deman, October 10, 1917, Field 041—State Department, General Correspondence, 1917–1940, OCSO, RG 111, NARA; Katz, *Secret War*, 418–421.
7. Memoranda in File 20950-847, Box 6, Confidential "Suspect" and General Correspondence Files, 1913–1926, Entry 78A, ONI, RG 38; McGoodwin to SecState, January 31, 1916, 831.74/8, and November 23, 1917, 831.74/25, SDDF, RG 59, NARA.
8. Memorandum for Boaz Long from Todd, April 12, 1918, 810.74/104; memorandum on wireless concessions granted in Latin America, July 3, 1919, 810.74/98, SDDF, RG 59, NARA.
9. On German wartime propaganda in Mexico and Latin America, see Katz, *Secret War*, 441–445. Part of the concern was that such stations might help German U-boats operating from secret Central American bases. See Charles H. Harris and Louis R. Sadler, *The Archaeologist Was a Spy: Sylvanus G. Morley and the Office of Naval Intelligence* (Albuquerque, 2003).
10. Many of the local Mexican stations apparently had a German engineer in charge. American Ambassador, Mexico, to SecState, March 13, 1917, and Harrison memorandum, April 16, 1917, "Wickersham-Wireless" folder, Box 15, and Letter to Randolph Robertson, "Robertson, Randolph, Reports from Mexico" folder, Box 13, Classified Case Files, 1916–1926, Entry 349, Office of the Counselor, RG 59; ONI to DNC, February 2, 1918, PD 177, M1140, RG 80, NARA.
11. Memorandum for Lansing from Boaz Long, April 20, 1918, and dispatch of March 28, 1918, from Curtis in Lansing to Wilson, April 25, 1918, 810.74/108, SDDF, RG 59, NARA.
12. William Broch to Pan-American Wireless T&T Co., July 29, 1918, in Box 2, Hooper Papers, LOC [hereafter, Hooper Papers]; Long memorandum, April 20, 1918. See also Katz, *Secret War*, 422.
13. Harrison Memorandum, April 16, 1917, "Wickersham-Wireless" folder, Box 15, Entry 349, Counselor Files, RG 59; Stimson to SecState, April 27 and May 11, and Lansing to American Embassy, Mexico and Panama, May 15, 1917, 835.74/10 and 833.74/12, SDDF, RG 59, NARA. See also Katz, *Secret War*, 421–422, although he reports having found little documentary evidence in the German records on this project.
14. Copy of Count Luxburg cable, July 20, 1917, appendix 1, 121, War Report of War Trade Intelligence Department, PRO/DEFE 1/402; Stimson to Lansing, May 16, 1917, 835.74/14, SDDF, RG 59; memoranda in file 20950-876, Box 6, Confidential "Suspect" and General Correspondence Files, 1913–1926, Entry 78A, ONI, RG 38; Merrill to Todd, June 28 and July 25, 1917, Todd Files, DNC, RG 38; Stimson to Lansing, September 19, 1917, 835.74/20, SDDF, RG 59, NARA.
15. Memorandum for Boaz Long from Todd, April 12, 1918, 810.74/104, data from memorandum from Todd, April 12, 1918, cited in Long memorandum, n.d. but April 1918, 810.74/108, Robbins to Lansing, July 24, 1918, 835.74/24, SDDF, RG 59, NARA; E. J. Nally of American Marconi and Pan-

American Telegraph was reporting the same thing. See Nally to Todd, September 17, 1918, Todd Files, DNC, RG 38, NARA.
16. Memoranda in file 20950–876, Box 6, Confidential "Suspect" and General Correspondence Files, 1913–1926, Entry 78A, ONI, RG 38, NARA. On the German countermeasures, see Katz, *Secret War,* 430. Roger Lancelyn Green, *A. E. W. Mason* (London: Max Parrish, 1952), 154. On the monitoring of German radio traffic, as well as copies of traffic, see Mexican intercepts received from State Department, 1918–1919, Document 39, Box 38, Herbert O. Yardley Collection [hereafter, HOYC], and Box 793, Historical Cryptographical Collection, RG 457, NARA.
17. Green, *A. E. W. Mason,* 149–154. Katz, *Secret War,* 439. Katz (or his translator) mistakes the use of "audion bulbs" for lamps and illumination rather than as electrical signal amplification.
18. Green, *A. E. W. Mason,* 149–154.
19. Memorandum for Lansing from Boaz Long, April 20, 1918, 810.74/108, SDDF, RG 59, NARA.
20. Price to SecState, December 16, 1916, 810.74/88, SDDF, RG 59, NARA. Almonte telegram forwarded under diplomatic cover, May 22, 1917, PRO/FO 368/1873/ƒ102655. Almonte worked hard; U.S. diplomats reported his presence in Brazil, Uruguay, Argentina, Panama, Ecuador, Venezuela, Costa Rica, and Honduras between 1915 and 1917.
21. Daniels to SecState, March 14, Polk to Daniels, April 11, and Daniels to SecState, April 20, 1917, 12479A-285, General Correspondence, 1916–1926, OFSN; SecNav to SecState, May 21, 1917, PD 177, M1140, RG 80, NARA.
22. Memorandum for Boaz Long from Todd, April 12, 1918, 810.74/104, memorandum for Lansing from Boaz Long, April 20, 1918, 810.74/108, SDDF, RG 59, NARA; Young to Foreign Office, June 12, 1917, PRO/FO 368/1873/ƒ133367.
23. Memorandum from Isaacs, February 12, 1917, PRO/FO 368/1873/ƒ34796.
24. Victor Wellesley to Admiralty and Treasury, March 8, 1917, PRO/FO 368/1873/ƒ34796; Isaacs to Maurice de Bunsen, June 27, 1917, PRO/FO 368/1873/ƒ129212; Marconi to Foreign Office, March 31, 1917, and accompanying minutes, PRO/FO 368/1873/ƒ68645, Treasury to Foreign Office, March 20, 1917, PRO/FO 368/1873/ƒ59706, and "Wireless Scheme in Brazil," minute sheet, June 27, 1917, PRO/FO 368/1873/ƒ129212; Treasury to Foreign Office, July 25, 1917, PRO/FO 368/1873/ƒ147472.
25. Isaacs to Undersecretary of State, Foreign Office, August 13, 1917, PRO/FO 368/1873/ƒ159762.
26. Isaacs to Undersecretary of State, Foreign Office, August 13, and Foreign Office to Spring Rice, August 21, 1917, PRO/FO 368/1873/ƒ159762, Isaacs to Foreign Office, August 23, 1917, PRO/FO 368/1873/ƒ165557, Admiralty to the Foreign Office, August 29, 1917, PRO/FO 368/1873/ƒ169702, and Minutes of a meeting of September 3, 1917, PRO/FO 368/1873/ƒ172529.
27. Isaacs to de Bunsen, September 17, and circular letter to British diplomats in Latin America, November 12, 1917, PRO/FO 368/1873/ƒ181522.
28. Daniels to Lansing, April 12, 1917, 12479A-292, and SecNav to SecState, September 4, 1917, 4881–90, General Correspondence, 1916–1926, OFSN, RG 80; memorandum for Boaz Long from Todd, April 12, 1918, 810.74/

104, and McGoodwin to SecState, November 23, 1917, 831.74/25, SDDF, RG 59; memoranda in File 20950–847, Box 6, Confidential "Suspect" and General Correspondence Files, 1913–1926, Entry 78A, ONI, RG 38; memorandum for Boaz Long from Todd, April 12, 1918, 810.74/104, and Memorandum on Wireless Concessions Granted in Latin America, July 3, 1919, 810.74/98, SDDF, RG 59, NARA.

29. President Alfonso Cabrera had requested *this* radio station. He had come to believe his enemies would have the submarine telegraph cable cut once he broke relations with Germany. The station was built in April 1917. SecNav to SecState, September 14, 1916, 12479A-270, General Correspondence, 1916–1926, OFSN, RG 80; Leavell to SecState, April 1, 1917, 811.74/115, and Daniels to SecState, April 25, 1917, 811.74/120, SDDF, RG 59, NARA.

30. Operational by the summer of 1918, the Port-au-Prince station remained a part of the navy's network until 1923. See SecNav to SecState, December 6, 1917, 1479–1052, General Correspondence, 1916–1926, OFSN, RG 80, NARA.

31. It appears that this was very closely held information. One officer wrote, "The foregoing is confidential . . . Please destroy this letter or put it where no one will see it but yourself, on account of the information about State Department dope." Lieutenant Commander Reed M. Fawell to Lieutenant E. H. Loftin, April 21, 1917, Todd Files, DNC, RG 38, NARA.

32. There were stations at Swan Island, Truxillo [*sic*], and Tela, Honduras; Bluefields, Nicaragua; Bocas del Toro, Panama; Port Limon, Costa Rica; and Santa Marta, Colombia. The powerful stations were at New Orleans, Swan Island, and Santa Marta, rated at 50 kw with a range of nine hundred miles. George S. Davis, Tropical Radio Company, to Fawell, March 6, 1918, PD 117–34, M1140, RG 80, NARA.

33. Memorandum for SecNav from Benson, March 12, 1918, PD 177–6, M1140, RG 80, and memorandum for Lansing from Boaz Long, April 20, 1918, 810.74/108, SDDF, RG 59, NARA.

34. SecNav to SecState, May 21, 1917, PD 177, M1140, RG 80; memorandum for Boaz Long from Todd, April 12, 1918, 810.74/104, and memorandum for Lansing from Boaz Long, April 20, 1918, 810.74/108, SDDF, RG 59, NARA; Young to Foreign Office, June 12, 1917, PRO/FO 368/1873/*f*133367; memorandum by Boaz Long, Division of Latin American Affairs, February 2, 1918, and ONI to DNC, February 2, 1918, PD 177, M1140, RG 80, NARA (emphasis in original).

35. Based along the coast and not the political centers of the countries in which they had been located, the Tropical Radio stations served U.S. but not Central American political interests. memorandum for Lansing from Long, April 20, 1918, 810.74/108, SDDF, RG 59; Daniels to SecState, June 15, 1917, 12479A-286, General Correspondence, 1916–1926, OFSN, RG 80; memorandum by Boaz Long, February 2, and Stabler to Lansing, February 11, 1918, PD 177, M1140, RG 80, NARA.

36. Unsigned memorandum for the CNO, March 2, 1918, PD 177, M1140, RG 80, NARA.

37. SecNav to SecState, March 11, 1918, and memorandum for SecNav from Benson, March 12, 1918, PD 177–6, M1140, RG 80, NARA.

38. Entry for March 12, 1918, Josephus Daniels, *The Cabinet Diaries of Josephus Daniels, 1913–1921*, ed. E. David Cronon (Lincoln, Neb., 1936), 290.

39. Memorandum for Boaz Long from Todd, April 12, 1918, 810.74/104, and memorandum from Long to Stewart Johnson, April 3, 1919, 810.74/97, SDDF, RG 59, NARA.
40. Memorandum from Boaz Long to Lansing, April 20, with summary dated April 22, 1918, 810.74/108, SDDF, RG 59, NARA.
41. Lansing to Wilson, April 25, 1918, 810.74/108, SDDF, RG 59, NARA.
42. Boaz Long to Skinner, July 27, 1920, 810.74/108, SDDF, RG 59, NARA. I am indebted to Long: "[This memo] should be preserved and entered into the files because the papers attached to it . . . might serve as a valuable aid to anyone desirous to study the question of wireless control. It might be important as well as interesting for any such student to know of the following difference of opinion." Indeed.
43. Hooper, transcript of memoirs, Box 37, 117, Hooper Papers; Nally to Isaacs, July 27, in Isaacs to Under Secretary of State, Foreign Office, August 13, 1917, PRO/FO 368/1873/fl59762.
44. Memorandum on Basis of Radio Organization, enclosed in Hooper to Todd, July 30, 1917, Box 2, Todd Files, DNC, RG 38, NARA.
45. Linwood S. Howeth, *A History of Communications-Electronics in the United States Navy* (Washington, D.C., 1963), 253–259; Hooper to Sweet, January 24, 1919, Box 2, Hooper Papers; Hugh Aitken, *The Continuous Wave: Technology and American Radio, 1900–1932* (Princeton, N.J., 1985), 286–287. The negotiations began in October and culminated in November after the armistice.
46. Susan J. Douglas, *Inventing American Broadcasting, 1899–1922* (Baltimore, 1987), 276; on the close coordination of the Bureau of Steam Engineering with equipment beyond just that for radio, see United States, Department of the Navy, Bureau of Engineering, *History of the Bureau of Engineering, Navy Department, During the World War* (Washington, D.C., 1922), and Howeth, *History,* chaps. 21–24.
47. Hooper, transcript of memoirs, Box 37, 423 and 428, and "Biographical Material" folder, Box 44, Hooper Papers. United States, *History of the Bureau of Engineering,* 17; abstracts of Hooper to Nally, February 22, and Nally to Hooper, March 1, 1917, in personal letters of E. J. Nally, Box 16, Series 4, and Annual Report of American Marconi, Box 104, Series 5, Clark Radioana Collection NMAH. On the markup permitted American Marconi, see Howeth, *History,* chap. 24.
48. Hooper to Sweet, May 21, 1917, Box 1, Hooper Papers; Nally to Isaacs, July 27, 1917, enclosed in Isaacs to Foreign Office, August 13, 1917, PRO/FO 368/1873/fl59762; RCA brochure, "New Era of Communications," November 12, 1932, Box 110, Clark Radioana Collection.
49. In response to two patent suits challenging the patent suspension, the navy Department in April 1918 issued a circular letter to all manufacturers, indemnifying them from any damages for patent infringement for the duration of the war. This was later known as the "Farragut Letter"—damn the patents, full manufacturing ahead. See Roosevelt to Sheffield and Betts, for example, April 3, 1918, Box 295, Clark Radioana Collection; see also Howeth, *History,* chap. 21.
50. Hooper to Bastedo, November 3, 1917, Box 1, Hooper Papers. Nally also suggested to the U.S. House Merchant Marine and Fisheries Committee in December 1918 that "an official of the Navy Department suggested the ad-

visability of the organization of an entirely separate company to exploit long-distance wireless communication with South America." See Annual Report of the Marconi Company of America, 1918, Box 105, Clark Radioana Collection. Compare Aitken, *Continuous Wave,* 290–292, on the Federal-Marconi combination here.

51. Nally to Isaacs, July 27, 1917, enclosed in Isaacs to Foreign Office, August 13, 1917, PRO/FO 368/1873/f159762, and Nally to Isaacs, August 10, 1917, enclosed in Isaacs to Foreign Office, August 27, 1917, PRO/FO 368/1873/f167787.
52. Memorandum by Griggs for Nally, July 24, 1917, enclosed in Isaacs to Foreign Office, August 13, 1917, PRO/FO 368/1873/f159762; and Steadman to Isaacs, September 22, 1917, PRO/FO 368/1873/f213398.
53. Some at Federal Holdings believed that the innovations of Fred A. Kolster, a radio engineer, had made the use of the Fleming valve for signal reception unnecessary. Some in the Bureau of Standards radio laboratories apparently backed this view. Steadman to Isaacs, September 22, 1917, intercepted copy in hands of the Foreign Office, PRO/FO 368/1873/f213398.
54. Steadman to Isaacs, November 17, 1917, intercepted copy, PRO/FO 368/1873/f213398.
55. O'Driscoll to Isaacs, September 23, 1917, intercepted copy, PRO/FO 368/1873/f235842.
56. Steadman to Isaacs, September 22, 1917, intercepted copy, PRO/FO 368/1873/f213398.
57. Memorandum of conversation, October 7, 1917, "Pan American" folder, Box 17, Confidential Correspondence, 1917–1926, Division of Naval Communications, RG 38; Todd to Bullard, October 11, 1917, Todd Files, DNC, RG 38, NARA.
58. Each Marconi company received 18,750 shares, and Federal received 12,500 of the total 50,000.
59. The legal particulars are in 810.74/74, SDDF, RG 59, NARA.
60. Undated memorandum by State Department Solicitor (likely September–November 1917), 811.74/74, SDDF, RG 59, NARA.
61. Hooper to Bastedo, November 3, 1917, Box 1, Hooper Papers. See also Aitken, *Continuous Wave,* 290–292.
62. Steadman to Lansing, October 28, 1917, 811.74/141a, Lansing to Steadman, November 2, 1917, and memorandum by Herbert Stabler, October 25, 1917, 811.74/143, all in SDDF, RG 59, NARA.
63. SecNav to SecState, November 24, 1917, PD177–6, M1140, RG 80, NARA.
64. Morgan to SecState, July 26, 1918, 832.74/39, SDDF, RG 59, NARA.
65. Nally's testimony before the Merchant Marine and Fisheries Committee of the House of Representatives, December 1918, reprinted in the Marconi Wireless Telegraph Company of America Annual Report, 1918, Folder 1, Box 105, Clark Radioana Collection.
66. Hooper, transcript of memoirs, Box 37, 430 and 109, Hooper Papers; Aitken, *Continuous Wave,* 292–295. See also memorandum of conversation, October 7, 1917, "Pan American" folder, Box 17, Confidential Correspondence, 1917–1926, Division of Naval Communications, RG 38, NARA.

67. Aitken, *Continuous Wave*, 292, suggests that this was American Marconi's second attempt to get at the arc patents and equipment under Federal Telegraph's control. The archival records clarify that both efforts were part of the same divestiture of commercial radio operations.
68. This letter was dated April 12. Waller to Chief of Bureau of Steam Engineering, April 18, 1918, 8247-383, General Correspondence, 1916-1926, OFSN, RG 80, NARA.
69. Pannill to Hooper, April 16, 1918, Box 2, Hooper Papers. The price of $1.64 million was incredibly low for the ten stations. The two Marconi high-power stations in Hawaii and San Francisco alone had a book value of nearly $2.27 million. See Bureau of Steam Engineering to DNC, "Estimated Cost of Purchasing High-Power Trans-Oceanic and Coastal Stations not owned by the Government," August 28, 1919, reprinted in *United States Senate, Hearings Before a Subcommittee of the Committee on Naval Affairs, United States Senate, 66th Congress, August 1919* (Washington, D.C., 1919), 79; Waller to Chief of Bureau of Steam Engineering, April 18, 1918, 8247-383, General Correspondence, 1916-1926, OFSN, RG 80, NARA. Compare Aitken, *Continuous Wave*, 293-294.
70. Roosevelt to Waller, April 19, 1918, 8247-383, General Correspondence, 1916-1926, OFSN, RG 80, NARA; copy of Federal Telegraph-U.S. Navy contract, May 15, 1918, in Box 2, Hooper Papers.
71. See Aitken, *Continuous Wave*, 295-296. On the damage to American Marconi, compare Aitken, 301: "To think of the navy's actions in acquiring the Federal patents as denying to the Marconi organization access to continuous wave technology is a considerable overstatement." Aitken did not discover or account for the equally important interest of senior naval officials in gaining government control of radio by eliminating the commercial operators, a reverse application of the Radio Act of 1912.
72. See Aitken, *Continuous Wave*, 296-297.
73. Memorandum of October 28, 1918, covering memorandum by Waller of the Federal Company, October 25, 1918, Folder 421, and memorandum from Stabler to Polk, December 2, 1918, Folder 422, Box 28, Series 3, Polk Papers; Nally's testimony, reprinted in Annual Report of Pan-American Wireless, 1918.
74. Isaacs to Sweet, August 1, 1918, 10191-125, General Correspondence, 1916-1926, OFSN, RG 80, NARA.
75. Hooper to Sweet, November 9, 1918, and Hooper to Sweet, November 27, 1918, Box 2, Hooper Papers; Colville Barclay to William Phillips, November 5, 1918, and Phillips to Barclay, December 16, 1918, 811.74/163, SDDF, RG 59, NARA.
76. Aitken, *Continuous Wave*, 157 and 312; Howeth, *History*, 238-239. The New Brunswick station carried the most traffic with Europe through March 1920.

7. The Quest for Independence

1. Martin Gilbert, *The First World War: A Complete History* (New York, 1994), 495.
2. Extract of Report of Lieutenant Brown, June 1919, no. 67; complaints from British manufacturers on telegraphic delays, July 1919, and A. Calthorpe to

Secretary of State for Foreign Affairs, July 24, 1919, No. 100, PRO/CAB 35/2; F. J. Brown to Foreign Office, September 2, 1919, No. 110, War Office to Secretary, ICC, November 4, 1919, No. 163, PRO/CAB 35/3; §24: Censorship during the Armistice, 69, "Report on Cable Censorship during the War, 1914–1918," PRO/DEFE 1/402.

3. See §24: Censorship during the Armistice, p. 69; Josephus Daniels, *The Cabinet Diaries of Josephus Daniels, 1913–1921*, ed. E. David Cronon (Lincoln, Neb., 1963), 348 and 354; Polk to Colonel House, December 7, 1918, 811.731/778a, and Daniels to SecState, November 11, 1918, 811.731/515, SDDF, RG 59, NARA.

4. Memorandum by Long, November 25, 1918, Box 183, Long Papers, LOC [hereafter, Long Papers]; SecNav to SecState, December 18, 1918, 28639–316, General Correspondence, 1916–1926, OFSN, RG 80, NARA; "Protest against Cable Censorship," *New York Times*, December 18, 1918, 17; "Censoring of Cables to Far East to End," *New York Times*, December 20, 1918, 22; "Says Britain Clings to Cable Censor," *New York Times*, December 28, 1918, 18.

5. "Say Censors Hurt Trade," *New York Times*, January 25, 1919, 13; "Say Cable Delays Hamper Business," *New York Times*, March 3, 1919, 22; "Double Censorship of Cables to Cease," *New York Times*, March 5, 1919, 9; "Protest to Lansing on Cable Holdup," *New York Times*, April 12, 1919, 22.

6. See Wilson to McCormick, with enclosure, March 28, and McCormick to Wilson, April 1, 1919, in Arthur S. Link, ed., *The Papers of Woodrow Wilson*, vol. 56 (Princeton, N.J., 1987), 372–374 and 514–515; Wilson to McCormick, with enclosure, April 16, and McCormick to Wilson, with enclosure, April 17, 1919, in Link, *Papers of Woodrow Wilson*, vol. 57, 423 and 448–449. Report of Captain J. H. Trye, RN, Liaison Officer, April 4, 1919, in "Report on Cable Censorship during the War, 1914–1918," PRO/DEFE 1/402.

7. Press Release, Office of Chief Cable Censor, April 18, 1919, 811.731/726, SDDF, RG 59; SecNav to SecState, July 22, 1919, 28639–394, and Roosevelt to Senator McCormick, August 6, 1919, 28639–407, General Correspondence, 1916–1926, OFSN, RG 80, NARA; §24: Censorship during the Armistice, 69–71.

8. Mackay to Polk, January 16, 1919, Folder 342, Box 10, Series I, Polk Papers, Archives and Manuscript Collection, Sterling Memorial Library, Yale University [hereafter, Polk Papers].

9. Yardley to F. W. Allen, December 25, 1918, quoted in Wayne G. Barker, *The History of Codes and Ciphers in the United States During the Period Between the World Wars*, part 1: *1919–1929*, (Laguna Hills, Calif., 1979), 44–47.

10. A. B. Coxe to Assistant Chief of Staff for Northeastern Department, April 22, 1920, "History of Certain Radio Tractor Units" folder, and documents in "Correspondence re: Permanent Organization For Cipher Work," Box 777, Historic Cryptographical Collection, RG 457, NARA.

11. Yardley to Colonel A. G. Campbell and Yardley to H. F. Taff, Commercial Superintendent, Western Union, November 11, 1919, Yardley to Brigadier General M. Churchill, November 21, 1919, and Yardley to Campbell, April 15, 1920, "Yardley NY Correspondence" folder, Box 99, HOYC, RG 457, NARA.

12. Harrison's successors included William Lee Hurley and Arthur Bliss Lane. This description comes from a memorandum by Lane to Alexander Kirk,

(n.d. but after May 1924), Folder 205, Box 10, Entry 344, Classified Records of the Office of the Counselor, 1916–1927, RG 59, NARA.

13. Submarine Cables Manufactured and Laid, Telegraph Construction and Maintenance record book, book 3, vol. 2, 1912–1920, microfilm copy, NMAH; George Ward to Lansing August 9, 1917, 811.73/51, Ward to Lansing, November 3, 1917, 811.73/60, and memorandum by Woolsey, November 6, 1917, 811.73/66, SDDF, RG 59, NARA.

14. Rogers to Wilson, January 30, 1919, and Wilson to Rogers, January 31, 1919, in Link, *Papers of Woodrow Wilson,* vol. 54, 381–382 and 400; Long to Rogers, February 4, 1919, Box 59, Long Papers.

15. Breckinridge Long to Lansing, November 25, 1918, and Colonel House to Long, December 15, 1918, FRUS Paris Peace Conference [hereafter, PPC], 1919, vol. 1, 535–538; memorandum on Wire and Radio Communications, Walter S. Rogers, February 12, 1919, in Ray Stannard Baker, ed., *Woodrow Wilson and World Settlement,* vol. 3, (Garden City, N.J., 1923), 425–426. Radio was to be discussed at an international conference postponed since 1917. See also Outlines of Communications Program, Walter S. Rogers, in Winslow to Long, September 19, 1918, 574.D1/188, SDDF, RG 59; memorandum for CNO Benson from DNC Todd, November 6, 1918, PD-177, Classified Correspondence of the CNO, Secretary of the Navy, 1919–1927, M1140, RG 80, NARA; and Hooper to Captain Todd, November 8, 1918, Book 3, Box 296, Clark Radioana Collection, NMAH.

16. Memorandum by Breckinridge Long, December 14, 1918, FRUS PPC, vol. 2, 512–515. See also Werner Levi, "American Attitudes toward Pacific Islands, 1914–1919," *Pacific Historical Review* 17 (1948): 55–64; Timothy P. Maga, "Prelude to War? The United States, Japan, and the Yap Crisis, 1918–1922," *Diplomatic History* 9 (Summer 1985): 215–231.

17. On the Liberia incident, see Richard C. Bundy to SecState, November 18, 1918, and subsequent diplomatic exchanges, FRUS 1919, vol. 2, 504–512.

18. The French company would have redirected the German cable either to Dakar or Conakry. Since it was not long enough, they would have had to splice in extra sections, and these would have come from the Conakry–Monrovia cable, thereby cutting the sole remaining cable connection that Liberia had. Polk to Robert Woods Bliss, Chargé in France, January 11, 1919, Bliss to Polk, January 14 and January 15, 1919, and Polk to Sharp, February 24, 1919, FRUS 1919, vol. 2, 513–517 and 525–526.

19. Appendix D of Minutes of the Second Meeting of the Thirteenth Session of the Supreme War Council, February 8, 1919, FRUS PPC, 1919, vol. 3, 941–942. Includes a list of all German cables captured, severed, or diverted; Naval Clauses for Peace With Germany, appendix to Minutes of the Seventeenth Session of the Supreme War Council, March 6, 1919, PPC, vol. 4, 250.

20. Minutes of the Seventeenth Session of the Supreme War Council, March 6, and Minutes of the Second Meeting of the Seventeenth Session of the Supreme War Council, March 7, 1919, PPC, vol. 4, 226–228 and 254–255.

21. Summary of First and Second Meetings of International Committee Considering International Law and Cables, March 11 and 16, 1919, Box 29, Norman H. Davis Papers, LOC [hereafter, Davis Papers]. The idea of protecting submarine telegraph cables had first been established by international convention in 1884. The issue of submarine telegraph cables in

wartime had then become a matter for international legal attention after the Spanish-American War.

22. Minutes of the Meeting of the Council of Ten, March 24, 1919, FRUS PPC, vol. 4, 460–470. U.S. companies Western Union and Commercial Cable did operate the majority of transatlantic cables between the Western Hemisphere and Great Britain. The concern of U.S. officials was that the British Empire controlled the content through censorship because the cables terminated in British imperial territory.

23. Minutes of the Meeting of the Council of Ten, March 24, 1919.

24. Notes of a Conversation between President Wilson and MM Clemenceau, Balfour, and Orlando, April 15, 1919, and Notes of a Conversation between President Wilson and MM Clemenceau, Lloyd George, and Orlando, April 18, 1919, in *The Deliberations of the Council of Four (March 24–June 28, 1919): Notes of the Official Interpreter, Paul Mantoux*, vol. 1, translated and edited by Arthur S. Link (Princeton, N.J., 1992), 250–251 and 274; notes of a meeting at President Wilson's house, April 21, and notes of a meeting at President Wilson's house, April 25, 1919, FRUS PPC, vol. 5, 109 and 241.

25. Secretary's notes of a conversation of the foreign ministers, April 30, 1919, FRUS PPC, vol. 4, 641–654.

26. Secretary's notes of a conversation held in M. Pichon's room, May 1, 1919, FRUS PPC, vol. 4, 483–492.

27. Timothy Maga, "Prelude to War?" 222, has confused Lansing's appearance before this body with his testimony before the Senate Foreign Relations Committee. Lansing was in Paris, not in Washington; based upon this discrepancy, Maga's larger arguments about Henry Cabot Lodge, Wilson, and Yap Island are in doubt.

28. Secretary's notes of a conversation held in M. Pichon's room, May 2, 1919, FRUS PPC, vol. 4, 493–500.

29. Secretary's notes of a conversation held in M. Pichon's room, May 2, 1919, FRUS PPC, vol. 4, 493–500; Notes of a meeting at President Wilson's residence, May 3, 1919, FRUS PPC, vol. 5, 437–438.

30. Rogers to Wilson, May 27, 1919, Box 8, Confidential Correspondence, 1917–1926, Division of Naval Communications, RG 38, NARA.

31. See David Hochfelder, "Constructing an Industrial Divide: Western Union, AT&T, and the Federal Government, 1876–1971," *Business History Review* 76 (Winter 2002): 705–732.

32. Post Office Department, *Government Control and Operation of Telegraph, Telephone, and Marine Cable Systems, August 1, 1918, to July 31, 1919* (Washington, D.C., 1921), 72–75.

33. Report of Captain J. H. Trye, RN, the British Cable Censor Liaison Officer, April 4, 1919, Appendix 3, Report on Cable Censorship during the Great War, 1914–1918, PRO/DEFE 1/402; Daniels to Wilson, November 19, 1918, 12479–1189, General Correspondence, 1916–1926, OFSN, RG 80, NARA. Vail loved the idea of government control. See "Would Put Wires Under One Head; Cables Likewise," *New York Times*, December 9, 1918, 1. See also "Wire System: Discussion of Electrical Intelligence," letter of Theodore N. Vail, in response to request of Hon. John A. Moon, Chairman, Committee on Post Office and Post Roads, House of Representatives, December 30,

1918, photocopy in author's possession. I am grateful to Richard John of the University of Illinois, Chicago.
34. Post Office Department, *Government Control and Operation,* 72–75; see also *New York Times* coverage of the matter from November 17, 1918, to early February, 1919.
35. Memorandum for Admiral Bullard of a meeting with Postmaster Burleson by Captain Todd, March 15, 1919, Box 4, Todd Files, DNC, RG 38, NARA; Tumulty to Wilson, enclosing message from Burleson, March 14, 1919, in Baker, *Woodrow Wilson and World Settlement,* vol. 3, 425–426. Hugh Aitken's suggestion that this document and Rogers's of February 12 shaped Wilson's thinking is incorrect; the lines had been draw well before Burleson's attempt to trace them again. See Hugh Aitken, *The Continuous Wave: Technology and American Radio, 1900–1932* (Princeton, N.J., 1985), 262–263.
36. Long to Dunn, December 11, 1918, Box 33, and entry for December 11, 1918, Long diary, Box 1, Long Papers.
37. See copies of telegrams in Gano Dunn Correspondence File, Box 33, and Long diary, Box 1, Long Papers; Preliminary Report of the Interdepartmental Committee on Communications, February 1, 1919, Box 30, Davis Papers.
38. Burleson to SecState, February 21, 1919, 811.73/116, SDDF, RG 59, NARA; Long to Newcomb Carlton, for example, July 19, 1919, Box 44, Long Papers; memorandum for MacElwee, August 18, 1919, File 78332, General Correspondence, 1903–1950, Office of the Secretary, Department of Commerce, RG 40, NARA.
39. SecState to Secretary of Commerce, January 15, 1919, File 78332, General Correspondence, 1903–1950, Office of the Secretary, Department of Commerce, RG 40, NARA.
40. Long to Julius Lay, February 26, 1919, 811.73/151, SDDF, RG 59, NARA.
41. John Cutter, Acting Chief of the Industrial Cooperation Service, to Secretary of Commerce, January 31, 1919, File 78332, General Correspondence, Department of Commerce, RG 40; Leroy Clark to Cutter, February 3, 1919, "Rubber-Gutta Percha Cables," File 254.0, General Records, 1914–1958, Bureau of Foreign and Domestic Commerce [hereafter, BFDC], Department of Commerce RG 151; Redfield to Polk, February 5, 1919, 811.73/146, SDDF, RG 59, NARA.
42. See memoranda of February 7 and 14, 1919, by Acting Trade Advisor Julius G. Lay, and minutes of April 9, 1919, meeting, Folder 798, Box 35, Series 3, Polk Papers; memorandum for Dr. MacElwee from Frank R. Rutter, May 15, 1919, File 78332, General Correspondence, 1903–1950, Office of the Secretary, Department of Commerce, RG 40, NARA; entry for February 17, Long diary, Box 2, Long Papers; Long to Julius Lay, February 26, 1919, 811.73/151, SDDF, RG 59, NARA. See also Burton I. Kaufman, *Efficiency and Expansion: Foreign Trade Organization in the Wilson Administration, 1913–1921* (Westport, Conn., 1974).
43. Long to Redfield, March 7, 1919, 811.73/111c, SecState to Secretary of Commerce, March 7, 1919, and Secretary of Commerce to SecState, March 8, 1919, 811.73/119, SDDF, RG 59; memorandum for R. L. Stancill by John Cutter, April 22, 1919, and R. S. MacElwee to Secretary of Commerce, June 25, 1919, File 78332, General Correspondence, RG 40, NARA.

44. R. S. MacElwee to Secretary Redfield, May 16, 1919, File 78332, General Correspondence, RG 40, NARA; memorandum by John Cutter, June 24, 1919, cited in Clarence Mackay to Senator Frank Kellogg, June 7, 1921, "Deegan" folder, Box 4, Harrison Papers, LOC; Secretary Redfield to Mark O. Prentiss, May 19, 1919, File 7833, General Correspondence, RG 40, NARA.
45. B. S. Cutler to Redfield, May 24, 1919, File 78332, General Correspondence, RG 40, NARA.
46. Emphasis in original. Cutler to Casey, June 2, 1919, "Rubber-Gutta Percha Cables."
47. Cutler to Carr, July 31, 1919, File 254.0, General Records, BFDC, RG 151, NARA.
48. R. S. MacElwee to J. S. Fowler, October 22, 1919, File 543, General Records, BFDC, RG 151, NARA.
49. Ibid.
50. Eldridge to Fowler, December 2, 1919, File 254.0, General Records, BFDC, RG 151, NARA.
51. R. S. MacElwee to J. S. Fowler, October 22, 1919.
52. John Cutter to F. R. Eldridge, May 26, and Cutler to Redfield, June 4, 1919, File 254.0, General Records, BFDC, RG 151; memorandum of S. W. Stratton to Secretary of Commerce, July 1, 1919, File 78332, RG 40, NARA.
53. A. L. Salt, Western Electric, to Eldridge, November 25 and December 6, 1919, File 254.0, General Records, RG 151, NARA; testimony of P. E. D. Nagle, "Pacific Cable Construction," in *Hearings before the Subcommittee of the Committee on Commerce*, Congress, 1st sess., on S. 1651, 1919–1920, 84 and 119.
54. Mark O. Prentiss, Council on Foreign Relations, to Secretary Redfield, May 7, 1919, File 78332, General Correspondence, 1903–1950, RG 40; see also correspondence in "Rubber-Gutta Percha Cables,"
55. See "Brief Summary of the Findings of the Communications Committee of the Council on Foreign Relations . . ." September 23, 1919, Correspondence File, 1919, Communications Committee, Box 412, Council on Foreign Relations Papers, Seeley G. Mudd Manuscript Library, Princeton University, Princeton, New Jersey.
56. Breckinridge Long to Julius Lay, February 26, 1919, 811.73/151, SDDF, RG 59, NARA.
57. Newcomb Carlton to Hon. H. W. Lamar, Post Office Department, April 14, 1919, 811.73/127, and Secretary of Commerce to SecState, July 18, 1919, 894.73/7, SDDF, RG 59; Chief Cable Censor, San Francisco, to Navy Department, April 11, 1919, 28639–373, General Correspondence, 1916–1926, OFSN, RG 80.
58. On the need for redundancy, see Confidential Report on Pacific Cable Situation, August 15, 1919, enclosed in F. R. Eldridge to J. V. A. MacMurray, September 6, 1919, 811.73/144, SDDF, RG 59, NARA.
59. Entry for May 5, 1919, Long diary, Box 2, and memorandum by Long of conversation with Japanese Chargé Debuchi, July 1, 1919, Box 183, Long Papers.
60. See testimony on "Control of Navy Radio Stations for Commercial Purposes," before the Committee on Naval Affairs, U.S. Senate, Thursday, September 4, 1919, Box 294, Series 100, Clark Radioana Collection, NMAH.

61. Daniels to SecState, July 21, 1919, 894.73/8, and Baker to SecState, July 23, 1919, 894.73/9, SDDF, RG 59, NARA.
62. A. P. Winston to Breckinridge Long, September 25, 1919, 811.73/149; see also Ray Atherton, Minister at Tokyo, to SecState, September 18, 1919, 894.73/12, SDDF, RG 59, NARA.
63. Memorandum of conversation by Long, September 23, 1919, 811.73/149, SDDF, RG 59, NARA.
64. Copies of the hearings on the cable bill, held September 22 and 26 and November 14, 1919, are in "Pacific Communications" folder, File 676.4, Cable Problems–Pacific Cables, General Correspondence, 1917–1940, OCSO, RG 111, NARA.
65. SecState to President Wilson, July 24, 1919, 811.73/326a, SDDF, RG 59, NARA. Commerce Department officials had to correct Jones's estimates. The cable would more likely cost $30 million for five thousand miles of cable. Redfield to Jones, July 9, 1919, File 78332, General Correspondence, 1903–1950, Office of the Secretary, Department of Commerce, RG 40, NARA.
66. Acting Chief Signal Officer to Senator Jones, November 25, and Lieutenant Colonel B. O. Lenoir to General Squier, October 7, 1919, File 676.4, Cable Problems–Pacific Cables, General Correspondence, 1917–1940, OCSO, RG 111, NARA; "Pacific Cable Construction," 119.
67. Memorandum on Senate Bill 1651 and Matter Pertaining to the Construction, Maintenance, and Operation of a Pacific Cable, June 30, 1919, File 78332, General Correspondence, 1903–1950, Office of the Secretary, Department of Commerce, RG 40; Secretary of Commerce to SecState, July 18, 1919, 894.73/7, SDDF, RG 59, NARA.
68. Memorandum of conversation by Long, September 23, 1919, 811.73/149, SDDF, RG 59, NARA.
69. George Ward, Vice President, Commercial Pacific Cable Company, to Senator Jones, enclosed in Jones to Acting Chief Signal Officers, November 21, 1919, File 676.4 Cable Problems–Pacific Cables, General Correspondence, 1917–1940, OCSO, RG 111, NARA.
70. See Thomas J. Knock, *To End All Wars: Woodrow Wilson and the Quest for a New World Order* (Princeton, N.J., 1995).

8. The Illusion of Success

1. Report of "Washington Congress" Subcommittee of the Imperial Communications Committee, June 30, 1920, No. 288, PRO/CAB 35/4.
2. James Schwoch, *The American Radio Industry and Its Latin American Activity, 1900–1939* (Urbana, Ill., 1990), 61–64.
3. Lansing to Wilson, December 23, 1919, 574.D1/13, and Edith Bolling Wilson to Lansing, December 24, 1919, 574.D1/150, memorandum by Merle-Smith of conversation with Postmaster General Burleson, September 20, 1920, 574.D1/153, SDDF, RG 59, NARA.
4. Nagle to Harrison, September 19, 1922, "CO" folder, Box 3, Harrison Papers, LOC.
5. Statement of Norman Davis before the Preliminary Conference on Communications, October 8, 1920, Box 9, Davis Papers, LOC.

6. Colby to Wright, November 4 and 5, 1920, FRUS 1920, vol. 1, 137; Wilson to Seymour, November 11, 1920, PRO/FO 371/4574/A7942/661/45; Admiralty to FO, November 16, 1920, and unsigned minute, PRO/FO 371/4575/A8057/661/45; Geddes to Curzon, November 3, 1920, A7732/661/45, and Geddes to Curzon, November 5, 1920 PRO/FO 414/246/A7773/661/45; Geddes to Curzon, November 29, 1920, PRO/FO 414/246/A8365/661/45.
7. Colby to Davis, November 9, and Davis to Colby, November 17, and Bell to Colby, November 19, 1920, FRUS 1921, vol. 2, 263–264.
8. Denison Pender to F. J. Brown, General Post Office, May 23, 1919, "Western Telegraph–Western Union" folder, Miscellaneous Reports and Accounts Box, Western Telegraph Company records, CW (emphasis in original).
9. Western Union Annual Report, 1920, WUC, NMAH; draft memorandum of February 26, 1919, Miami Cable File, "Western Telegraph–Western Union" folder, Miscellaneous Reports and Accounts Box, Western Telegraph Company Records, CW.
10. Merrill to Carlton, February 11, 1919, in Senate Committee on Interstate Commerce, *Cable Landing Licenses: Hearings on S. 4301*, 66th Congress, 3rd sess., 1920–1921, 63 [hereafter, Senate Hearings].
11. Merrill to SecState, April 9, 1919, 811.73/134, SDDF, RG 59, NARA; collected complete correspondence relating to this is reprinted in Senate Hearings, 61–67; memorandum from Stabler to Lay, February 15, 1919, with notes, 811.731/767, SDDF, RG 59, NARA.
12. Merrill to Carlton, May 2, 1919, in memorandum from Chief Special Agent Nye to Woolsey, February 28, 1920, 811.73/195, SDDF, RG 59, NARA.
13. Merrill to SecState, February 11 and February 24, 1919, 835.73/89 and 835.73/91, SDDF, RG 59, NARA; Carlton to S. J. Goddard, European Representative of Western Union, for Pender, May 8, 1919, "Western Telegraph–Western Union" folder, Miscellaneous Reports and Accounts Box, Western Telegraph Company Records, CW.
14. Copy of Agreement between Western Telegraph Co. and the Western Union Telegraph Company, July 15, 1919, WUC, NMAH.
15. The cable cost about $2.6 million for 1,679 nautical miles, while the land and equipment in Barbados as well as the services of the cable engineers Clark, Forde, and Taylor was around $125,000. There were other miscellaneous expenses as well. Directors and Stockholders Minutes, Box 184, entries for June 10, October 14, November 11, 1919, and January 13, 1920, WUC, NMAH; Attaché Report of April 20, 1921, File B-10-g, Naval Attaché Registers, ONI, RG 38, NARA.
16. Memorandum from Winston to Lay, July 11, 1919, 811.73/134, and Assistant Secretary Franklin Roosevelt to SecState, September 2, 1919, 811.73/141, SDDF, RG 59, NARA.
17. Merrill to SecState, June 14, 1919, 811.73, SDDF, RG 59, NARA; Polk to Morgan, June 21, Morgan to Gama, with enclosed memorandum, June 24, and Morgan to Acting SecState, July 1, 1919, FRUS 1919, vol. 1, 193–200.
18. Remarks of Ambassador Stimson to SecState Lansing, January 19, 1920, and dispatches of Stimson on April 16 and of Chargé Wells on July 22, 1919, FRUS 1919, vol. 1, 174 and 181; the unsuccessful efforts of the British minister, Sir Reginald Tower, can be followed in PRO/FO 368/2049/ƒ3384, ƒ29605, ƒ40987, and ƒ46580; memorandum from Breckinridge Long to

Frank Polk, December 28, 1918, covering Stimson to SecState, December 10, 1918, 835.73/85, SDDF, RG 59, NARA.

19. [Italics in original] Polk to Davis, London, July 18, 1919, FRUS 1919, vol. 1, 200–201; Aide-Mémoire of J. Butler Wright, July 23, 1919, and covering Minute Sheet, July 26, PRO/FO 371/4334/f108305.

20. Minute Sheet, July 26, 1919, PRO/FO 371/4334/f108305; Davis to Polk, August 13, 1919, FRUS 1919, vol. 1, 202–203.

21. Stimson to SecState, January 19, 1920, FRUS 1919, vol. 1, 181–182.

22. Chargé Wadsworth to SecState, December 2 and December 16, 1919, in FRUS 1919, vol. 1, 204.

23. On diplomatic efforts to secure cable concessions, see FRUS 1919, vol. 1, 172–183.

24. The standard account of the formation of RCA is Hugh G. J. Aitken's masterful *The Continuous Wave: Technology and American Radio, 1900–1932* (Princeton, N.J., 1985). If there is a fault to his work, it is that he did not examine U.S. Navy records.

25. Hooper for Admiral Griffin, Chief of Bureau of Steam Engineering, May 22, 1919, Box 2, Hooper Papers, LOC [hereafter, Hooper Papers]; Lieutenant Commander E. H. Loftin, quoted in Gleason L. Archer, *History of Radio to 1926* (New York, 1938), 162; "New Era of Communications," RCA Brochure, November 12, 1932, Box 110, Clark Radioana Collection, NMAH.

26. Hooper notes to George H. Clark, *Radio in Peace and War*, Clark Radioana Collection 8; Aitken, *Continuous Wave*, 302–310.

27. Aitken, *Continuous Wave*, 313–314.

28. E. J. Nally to A. G. Davis, April 1, 1924, quoting Nally's diary for 1919, Box 290; RCA In-House account of the History of Marconi and the Creation of RCA, prepared for W. A. Weagant, October 1932, Box 101, Clark Radioana Collection, NMAH.

29. The navy blocked any sales to Italy, France, and Sweden. See Aitken, *Continuous Wave*, 320 and 335.

30. Anson W. Burchard to E. W. Rice Jr. et al., March 26, 1919, Box 50, Clark Radioana Collection.

31. Memorandum from A. P. Winston for Lay, September 9, 1919, 811.74/174, SDDF, RG 59; Daniels to Eugene Stalinger, Polish Ministry of Post and Telegraphs, September 22, 1919, 12479A-372, and Daniels to SecState, October 27, 1919, 12479A-372:3, General Correspondence, 1916–1926, OFSN, RG 80, NARA; Schwoch, *American Radio Industry*, 58–60.

32. SecNav to SecState, July 8, 1918, 12479A-326, SecState to SecNav, March 12, 1919, 12479A-349, SecNav to T. Engset, Secretary General, Telegraph Administration, Norwegian Government, September 12, 1919, 12479A-349:3, General Correspondence, 1916–1926, OFSN, RG 80; Daniels to SecState, April 19, 1917, 811.74/117, W. A. F. Ekengren to SecState, May 2, 1917, 811.74/121, Daniels to SecState 811.74/122, SDDF, RG 59; memorandum for Bullard from Todd, March 6, 1919, Bullard Files, DNC, RG 38, NARA; Aitken, *Continuous Wave*, 334–336.

33. Schwerin to SecState, April 9, 1919, 811.74/171, SDDF, RG 59, NARA; Beal to Federal Telegraph Company, October 17, 1919, Box 118, Clark Radioana Collection. With Beal's encouragement, Federal Telegraph officials were going to use the arc transmitter built for the navy's North Carolina station.

34. General Post Office to Marconi Company, January 15, 1919, PRO/CAB 21/210; C. Mallet to Curzon, November 16, 1922, PRO/FO 371/7177/A7471/7471/2.
35. "Confidential Memorandum Concerning Cable and Radio Telegraphic Communications with Mexico, Central and South America, and the West Indies," prepared for the second Pan American Financial Conference, January 19–24, 1920, Box 1, Confidential Correspondence, 1917–1926, Division of Naval Communications, RG 38, NARA; H. M. Minister to Bogotá to the Foreign Office, July 15, 1919, No. 106, PRO/CAB 35/3; Johnson, Caracas, to SecState, May 11, 1919, Folder 424, Box 28, Series 3, Polk Papers, Archives and Manuscript Collection, Sterling Memorial Library, Yale University [hereafter, Polk Papers].
36. Marconi Company to Secretary, Imperial Communications Committee, September 10, 1919, PRO/CAB 21/210. On Lord Milner's lament that there was no firm imperial radio policy, see Conclusions of the Eighth Meeting of the ICC, October 2, 1919, and Extracts from the Finance Committee of the Cabinet Minutes, November 6, 1919, PRO/CAB 21/210.
37. "Radio Situation in South America," Register No. 13014, File B-7-e, Naval Attaché Registers, ONI, RG 38, NARA; Johnson, Caracas, to SecState, May 11, 1919; "Confidential Memorandum Concerning Cable and Radio Telegraphic Communications," 41.
38. SecNav to SecState, December 13, 1919, 12479A-378, General Correspondence, 1916–1926, OFSN, RG 80, NARA; Tower to Foreign Office, March 17, 1919, PRO/FO 371/3505/f11334/63271.
39. See, for example, Radio Stations: Argentina, Register No. 2213-A, File B-7-e, Naval Attaché Registers, ONI, RG 38; Daniels to Lansing, November 12, 1919, 12479A-362:1, and Daniels to Lansing, December 13, 1919, 12479A-377, General Correspondence, 1916–1926, OFSN, RG 80; Roosevelt to SecState, April 1, 1919, 835.74/32, and Lansing to Secretary of Commerce, November 22, 1919, 831.74/36, SDDF, RG 59, NARA; Johnson, Caracas, to SecState, May 11, 1919; memorandum for Polk, May 14, 1919, Folder 424, Box 28, Series 3, Polk Papers.
40. George F. Kennan, *Soviet-American Relations*, vol. 2: *Decision to Intervene* (Princeton, N.J., 1989), 414–415, and Betty M. Unterberger, *America's Siberian Expedition, 1918–1920* (Durham, N.C., 1956).
41. The necessary equipment for the 300 kw station was in Petrograd. SecNav to Bureau of Steam Engineering, September 26, 1918, 12479–1160, General Correspondence, 1916–1926, OFSN, RG 80; Short History of Vladivostok Naval Radio Station to Accompany Intelligence Report of Commander-in-Chief, U.S. Asiatic Fleet, November 4, 1918, ONI Register No. 12896, ONI, RG 38, NARA; Quote from Rodman to Lieutenant A. Y. Tuel, March 3, 1919, Box 2, Hooper Papers.
42. Walter S. Rogers to Todd, August 11, and Todd to Rogers, August 12, 1918, Todd Files, DNC, RG 38; Daniels to Bureau of Steam Engineering, October 21, 1918, and Theodore Roosevelt, Acting SecNav, to SecState, March 25, 1921, 12479–1171, General Correspondence, 1916–1926, OFSN, RG 80, NARA.
43. Franklin Roosevelt to Representative Julius Kahn, June 24, 1919, 12479–1304, General Correspondence, 1916–1926, OFSN, RG 80, NARA.

44. Activity Report to DNC, January 1920, prepared by Lieutenant Commander Loftin, 12479-1518, General Correspondence, 1916–1926, OFSN, RG 80, NARA.
45. Daniels to SecState, December 18, 1919, PD 177-4, M1140, and Polk to SecNav, December 26, 1919, 12479A-379, General Correspondence, 1916–1926, OFSN, RG 80, NARA.
46. Notes of the Meeting of the IARC on April 7, 1919, PRO/CAB 35/2; Reports of the Meeting of the IARC on August 27, 1919, No. 104, and Report of the Meeting of the IARC on September 5, 1919, No. 136, PRO/CAB 35/3.
47. For example, the wavelength of 11,000 meters would have a band from 10,945 to 11,055 meters.
48. U.S. presentation of September 8, 1919, No. 159, PRO/CAB 35/3.
49. Appendix 17, Minutes of the IARC, August 25, 1919, No. 159, PRO/CAB 35/3.
50. Data from IARC Protocol of August 25, 1919, No. 159, PRO/CAB 35/3.
51. E. W. F. Alexanderson, "Transatlantic Radio Communication," *Proceedings of the American Institute of Electrical Engineers* 38 (October 1919): 1077–1093.
52. Archer, *History of Radio,* 157–159; Aitken, *Continuous Wave,* 281–282; Susan J. Douglas, *Inventing American Broadcasting, 1899–1922* (Baltimore, 1987), 282–285.
53. "Wants Daniels Ousted," *New York Times,* January 30, 1919, 3.
54. Daniels to Representative Swager Shirly, Chairman, House Appropriations Committee, January 11, 1919, 12479-1188:4, General Correspondence, 1916–1926, OFSN, RG 80, NARA.
55. Douglas, *Inventing,* 283–284; diary entry for January 29, 1919, Josephus Daniels, *The Cabinet Diaries of Josephus Daniels, 1913–1921,* ed. E. David Cronon (Lincoln, 1963), 372 [hereafter, Daniels diary]; Hooper to Sweet: "The radio bill, as usual, came to naught." Hooper to Sweet, January 24, 1919, Box 2, Hooper Papers.
56. Aitken, *Continuous Wave,* 366. There was one more attempt later that summer. See, for example, memorandum of conversation by Long with Commander Woodworth, June 3, 1919, Box 183, memorandum from Rogers to Long, July 26, 1919, Box 59, Long Papers, LOC; Samuel Bryant to Todd, October 16, 1919, Todd Files, DNC, RG 38, NARA.
57. E. P. Edwards to Hooper, November 20, 1920, Box 3, Hooper Papers; Aitken, *Continuous Wave,* 330; Hooper's access to this information through Edwards was so valuable and privileged that Nally was absolutely convinced the only way the navy could have learned of the deal was by reading his every cable to Isaacs in London. E. J. Nally to A. G. Davis, April 1, 1924, Box 290, Clark Radioana Collection.
58. Memorandum from Bureau of Steam Engineering to SecNav, April 4, 1919, Box 8, Confidential Correspondence, 1917–1926, DNC, RG 38, NARA.
59. E. J. Nally to Davis, April 1, 1924, Box 290, Clark Radioana Collection; Aitken, *Continuous Wave,* 331–334. Aitken has done a remarkable job of clarifying the role of President Wilson and the formation of RCA as best as can be done. Aitken notes that Arthur Link, at his request, could not find anything in Grayson's diary or the Wilson papers. Grayson testified to his role in 1928. See Archer, *History of Radio,* 155.
60. Aitken, *Continuous Wave,* 340–341; Archer, *History of Radio,* 164; Josephine

Young Case and Everett Needham Case, *Owen D. Young and American Enterprise: A Biography* (Boston, 1982), 178–180.
61. Aitken, *Continuous Wave*, 344–350.
62. Knapp to Opnav, with enclosed cable from Daniels, May 3, 1919, 12479-1287, General Correspondence, 1916–1926, OFSN, RG 80, NARA; Aitken, *Continuous Wave*, 352–353.
63. Daniels may have urged Young to sound out Henry Cabot Lodge on the matter. See Archer, *History of Radio*, 170; Entry of May 23, 1919, Daniels diary, 416; memorandum for the Chief, Bureau of Steam Engineering, May 22, 1919, Box 2, Hooper Papers.
64. Nally to A. G. Davis, April 1, 1924, quoting Nally's diary entries for 1919, Box 290, Clark Radioana Collection, NMAH; Aitken, *Continuous Wave*, 367–369.
65. Case and Case, *Owen D. Young*, 183–185; Aitken, *Continuous Wave*, 380–386, esp. 374–375.
66. Aitken, *Continuous Wave*, 394; Case and Case, *Owen D. Young*, 181; see also memorandum for Captain D. W. Todd from E. B. Woodward, February 18, 1919, 12479-568:203, General Correspondence, 1916–1926, OFSN, RG 80, NARA.
67. Aitken, *Continuous Wave*, 414–415; Admiral Griffin to SecNav, November 17, 1919, 12479-258:169, General Correspondence, 1916–1926, OFSN, RG 80, NARA.
68. Daniels to Secretary of State, June 2, 1920, 12479-1481, General Correspondence, 1916–1926, OFSN, RG 80, NARA; Nally to Wilson, January 3, 1920, quoted in Archer, *History of Radio*, 183–184; *New York Times*, May 16, 1920.
69. Polk to Baker, February 25, 1920, 811.73/184, SDDF, RG 59, NARA.
70. Memorandum from Office of Chief Special Agent William Nye to Woolsey, February 28, 1920, 811.73/195, SDDF, RG 59, NARA; Frank Polk to Western Union, 25 March, 1920, Exhibit D, D.C. Court Case file, U.S. vs. W.U.Tel.Co. case, Box B-69A, Law Department Files, [hereafter, Court Case], WUC.
71. Elihu Root Jr. to Frank Polk, April 7, 1920, Folder 422, Box 12, Series 1, Polk Papers.
72. Memorandum by Vallance, April 28, 1920, 811.73/193, Merrill to Colby, September 28, 1920, 811.73/261, minutes of a conference, May 21, 1920, 811.73/378, Root to Vallance, May 29, 1920, 811.73/200, Nielsen to Colby, July 17, 1920, 811.73/258, all in SDDF, RG 59; memorandum concerning cable situation in South America, May 27, 1920, Division of Naval Communications, Classified Correspondence, 1917–1926, Box 9, RG 38, NARA.
73. Colby to Wilson, July 17, and Wilson to Colby, July 20, 1920, FRUS 1920, vol. 2, 686–687.
74. Memorandum by Vallance, July 31, 1920, FRUS 920, vol. 2, 687–689; Miami–Barbados Paying Out Log, CS *Colonia* records, WUC; CNO to Commandant, August 2, 1920, PD 177-5, M1140, RG 80; Colby to Western Union, August 3, 1920, 811.73/229a, SDDF, RG 59; entry of August 4, 1920, Daniels diary, 542–543; Daniels to Anderson, to Decker, August 4, 1920, PD177-5, M1140, RG 80, NARA. Anderson had been commander of the cable-cutting operations in Cuba during the War of 1898.
75. Miami–Barbados Paying Out Log; logbooks of *Subchaser 154*, USS *Satterlee* and *Cole*, RG 45, NARA.

76. Minutes of Executive Committee, November 1 and 9, 1920, Stockholders Minutes, and Colby to Carlton, November 24, 1920, Court Case; Colby to Baker, November 19, 1920, 81.73/355, SDDF, RG 59; entry for late November 1920, Daniels diary, 566–567; SecNav to Commandant, November 22, Commandant to OPNAV, and Latimer to OPNAV, November 24, 1920, 27014–20:68–72, OFSN, RG 80; logbook of *Subchaser 154*, RG 45; Murray to Commandant, November 25, 811.73/448, and Vallance memorandum, November 25, 811.73/594, RG 59, NARA. Apparently McAdoo's personal appeal offended Wilson.
77. Long to Colby, November 29, and Colby to Long, December 2, 1920, FRUS 1920, vol. 2, 68–69; entry of December 7, 1920, Daniels diary, 572; Transcript of Record for Supreme Court, Court Case.
78. Murray report, in Latimer to CNO, March 7, 27014–20:128, and Harrison to SecNav, May 11 and August 22, 1922, 27014–20:168, OFSN, RG 80, and Commandant to OPNAV, copy to State Department, March 7, 1921, 811.73/592, SDDF, RG 59, NARA.
79. Hooper to Young, December 2 and December 11, 1920, and September 20, 1921, Box 3, Hooper Papers; Case and Case, *Owen D. Young*, 219–221, 224.
80. Robert Sobel, *ITT: The Management of Opportunity* (New York, 1982), 62; Leslie B. Tribolet, *The International Aspects of Electrical Communications in the Pacific Area* (Baltimore, 1929), 196–197.

Conclusion

1. Commercial Cable laid its new cable in 1923. Western Union's cables followed in 1924, 1926, and 1928. These were the last telegraph cables across the North Atlantic. On the Azores fight, see Michael Hogan, *Informal Entente: The Private Structure of Cooperation in Anglo-American Economic Diplomacy, 1918–1928* (Colombia, Mo., 1977), 119–125. The full story of submarine cable development in the interwar period, like its predecessor during the war years, is not well understood. Hogan's account is valuable but now inadequate.
2. The role of signals intelligence allowing the U.S. to know the Japanese positions on naval arms limitation is well covered. See, for example, David Kahn, *Codebreakers* (New York, 1996), esp. 358–359.
3. We know very little about this monitoring of U.S. traffic, but it was extensive. See, for example, Admiral Bristol to SecState, December 15, 1920, No. 5034, Intercepted Diplomatic Traffic, November 22 to December 31, 1920, PRO/HW 12/17. Files on the formation of the Government Code and Cipher School(GC&CS) can be found in PRO/ADM 1/8637/55; John Ferris, "Whitehall's Black Chamber: British Cryptology and the Government Code and Cypher School, 1919–1929," *Intelligence and National Security* 2, no. 1 (January 1987), 54–91; Christopher Andrew, *Her Majesty's Secret Service: The Making of the British Intelligence Community* (New York, 1986), 259–261; Keith Jeffrey and Alan Sharp, "Lord Curzon and Secret Intelligence," in Christopher Andrew and Jeremy Noakes, eds., *Intelligence and International Relations, 1900–1945* (Exeter, 1987), 108.
4. Hoover to Senator Wesley Jones, April 27, Harding to Hughes, July 12, and

Hughes to Harding, July 19, 1921, 811.7394C73/3 and 811.7394C73/6, SDDF, RG59, NARA.
5. The Joint Army-Navy Board was a prime example of this problem, and the Joint Chiefs of Staff, the Department of Defense, and the National Security Council were examples of how these disconnects were supposed to be dealt with. On the lack of effective tools for coordinating strategy and policy in the prewar and interwar period, see Richard Challener, *Admirals, Generals and American Foreign Policy* (Princeton, N.J., 1973); George Baer, *One Hundred Years of Sea Power: The U.S. Navy, 1890–1990* (Stanford, Calif., 1994), esp. chaps. 6 and 7; and Brian McAllister Linn, *Guardians of Empire: The U.S. Army and the Pacific, 1902–1940* (Chapel Hill, N.C., 1997), esp. chap. 7.
6. On the strategic outlook of the United States during the interwar period, see Allan R. Millett and Peter Maslowski, *For the Common Defense: A Military History of the United States of America*, rev. ed. (New York, 1994), 380–412; on these changing notions of the security of the United States, see Frank Ninkovitch, *Modernity and Power: A History of the Domino Theory in the Twentieth Century* (Chicago, 1994), 1–68.
7. On the idea of "free security," see C. Vann Woodward, "The Age of Reinterpretation," *American Historical Review* 66 (October 1960): 2–8.
8. The advent of signal repeaters in the 1950s would obviate the need to lay cables across the shortest possible distance.
9. In current dollars, roughly $34.5 million and $173 million. These costs are comparable to submarine fiber optic cable projects today.
10. This situation abroad was ironically at odds with the situation at home, where the geographic enormity and the permissive regulatory environment of the United States made possible the creation of the powerful private domestic communications telephone and telegraph network. On this, see the important work by Paul Starr, *The Creation of the Media: Political Origins of Modern Communications* (New York, 2004), esp. 227–230.
11. See the case study of Elihu Root Sr. in Walter LaFeber, "Technology and U.S. Foreign Relations," *Diplomatic History* 24 (Winter 2000), 1–19. LaFeber focuses on technology as an abstract analytical category of U.S. foreign relations, like that of race or ideology, rather than distinguishing between technological change that had economic or social implications (electric lighting or canned goods) and technology that helped to solve existing military or strategic problems (communications technology, metallurgy, explosives chemistry, or naval architecture) and thus had more immediate diplomatic implications. Continuity of interest among high officials does not mean continuity of engagement, despite what LaFeber implies.
12. Michael J. Hogan, "Corporatism," in Michael J. Hogan and Thomas G. Paterson, eds., *Explaining the History of American Foreign Relations*, 2nd ed. (New York, 2004), 137–148; Hogan, *Informal Entente;* John Lewis Gaddis, "The Corporatist Synthesis: A Skeptical View," *Diplomatic History* 10 (Fall 1986): 357–362; Thomas J. McCormick, "Drift or Mastery? A Corporatist Synthesis for American Diplomatic History," *Reviews in American History* 10 (December 1982): 318–330.

Acknowledgments

RESEARCHING AND WRITING A BOOK are monumental activities for any author. Each activity incurs successive debts of gratitude that are difficult to repay. It is no different for me. Through the seven years that this project has occupied my life, a great many individuals have lent their time and effort to see that I reached the end of the project. Though I cannot mention everyone, I ought to identify those whose assistance has been especially important.

Foremost is John Lewis Gaddis. His throwing a sophomore into a graduate-level colloquium on U.S. foreign relations meant my removal from the normal course of undergraduate life. John's approach to history—characterized by thoroughness, an open mind, and respect for the larger picture—has shaped my own approach to life. The students from that class have gone on to become professors themselves; their willingness to tolerate an upstart in their midst has meant more to me than they will ever know. Through it all Lorenz Lüthi has been an invaluable friend. At Yale, Paul Kennedy, Donald Kagan, Jon Butler, and Theodore Bromund each lent their particular encouragement to the project. Jon Sumida, Bernard Finn, Nicholas Lambert, David Nickles, Daniel Headrick, Jim Schwoch, and Richard John all shared their own work and taught me the larger significance of what I was piecing together. Faculty at the United States Naval Academy, the University of Maryland, College Park, and Wright State University have all been especially supportive. Zach Kincade created excellent maps. There are others, family and friends, to whom I owe innumerable personal debts, far more than I can express here—you know who you are.

I also gratefully acknowledge the financial and archival support that made this work possible. This support includes Yale's International Security Studies; the Smith Richardson Foundation; a Smithsonian Fellowship; a Yale Center for International and Area Studies Henry Hart Rice Research Fellowship; and the Yale Graduate School of Arts and Sciences John F. Enders Grant. Archivists at the following places gave of their time to help me: the Archive Center of the National Museum of American History; the Porthcurno Telegraph Museum in Porthcurno, Cornwall; the National Archives in Washington, D.C., and at College Park, Maryland; the Library of Congress; the Public Record Office, Kew Gardens, London; Sterling Memorial Library, Yale University; Bentley Historical Library, University of Michigan; Seeley G. Mudd Manuscript Library, Princeton University; and the Bundesarchiv-Militärarchiv, Freiburg. Their documents are noted in the footnotes. Much of the secondary literature has been removed from the bibliography, but I am happy to provide this to any interested reader.

Most importantly, I must thank my wife, Heather. Her faith and devotion sustained me through this entire project. Was it worth it? Elliot and Spencer think so.

Index

Admiralty, 5, 41, 112, 117–119, 122, 124; and command and control, 13–14, 66, 83, 103; and German communications, 22–25, 49, 27–28, 170, 267; and interest in British Marconi, 94, 174–175. *See also* Royal Navy

Adriatic Sea, 31, 251, 255

Alaska, 19, 21, 68, 152–155, 160, 202, 235, 251

Alert, 5–6, 11, 17, 22, 289n1

Alexanderson, E. W. F., 114–115, 248–250, 253, 256, 264, 276

All America Cables, 212, 260–261, 263. *See also* Central and South American Telegraph Company; John Merrill

Almonte, J. J., 173

Alternator transmitter, 120, 248–250, 253–259, 264; and Telefunken, 51; as improvement in radio, 114–116, 202, 240

American Expeditionary Force (AEF), 3, 105–107, 110–111, 115–116, 131, 307n22

American Marconi. *See* Marconi Wireless Telegraph Company of America

American Samoa, 68, 153, 202

Anderson, Edwin, 261

Annapolis, 115–116, 120, 200, 202

Apgar, Charles, 51–52

Arc transmitters, 68–76, 93, 186, 188–189, 195–204; as improvement in radio, 16, 68–76, 97, 114–115, 120; and transatlantic communications, 42, 114–115; and European interest in, 74, 108, 120, 189, 200–201, 250; and Royal Navy, 83, 201. *See also* C. F. Elwell; Federal Telegraph; Fuller improvements

Argentina, 18, 53–59, 90, 275; and American radio firms, 93, 99, 188, 190, 194–195, 198, 248; and British Marconi, 250; and communications intelligence, 39, 126, 128; and German radios, 82, 167, 169–170; and submarine telegraph cables, 36, 137, 140–145, 243, 246–247, 269

Arlington, 68–69, 115

Ascension Island, 10, 39, 83, 139, 142–143

Asquith, Herbert, 25

Astraea, 23

AT&T, 112, 159, 165, 185, 226, 229, 234, 259; and tapping submarine telegraph cables, 131–132

Atlantic Communications Company, 21, 51–52, 61–62, 96; and Latin America, 16, 43, 167–168

Australia, 6–9, 13, 24, 29, 147, 186, 289n4

339

Austria-Hungary, 27, 53
Azores, 26–28, 35, 54, 127, 277; and cable cutting by German warships, 106, 117–119; and German cables, 5, 15, 17, 36, 214–215; and Anglo-American relations, 222, 264, 270

Badger, Charles J., 61
Baker, Newton, 208, 261
Balfour, Arthur, 104, 174, 219–224
Baltic Sea, 28, 30, 117
Barbados, 142, 243, 245, 250, 261–263, 276
Barclay, Colville, 41
Beijing. *See* Peking
Belgium, 5, 65, 136, 250–251
Bell, Edward, 104, 122, 125
Belmar, 94
Benson, William S., 87, 112, 138, 180, 193, 219, 225, 257
Berlin, 15–16, 37, 41, 46, 52, 70, 104, 167
Bermuda, 10, 39, 142
Birmingham, 63
"Black Chamber." *See* MI-8
Black Sea, 29, 251
de Bon, Ferdinand, 220, 224
Bonin Islands, 20
Boston, 8, 43, 77
Boxer Rebellion, 7
Brazil, 53, 54–59, 90, 112, 203, 274–277; and British Marconi, 174–175; and communications intelligence, 39, 127; and German communications, 16–18, 28, 36, 167; government control of communications in, 81–82, 93–94; and interest in radio communications, 81–82, 94–95, 109–110, 178; object of cable attention, 137–145, 161, 164, 217–218, 224, 243–248, 260–265, 269; and U.S. radio firms, 81, 181, 195
British Marconi. *See* Marconi Wireless Telegraph Company, Ltd.
Brown, F. J., 244
Bryan, William Jennings, 39–41, 45–49, 56, 62, 82
Bryant, Samuel W., 62
Bullard, W. H. G., 76–77, 79–80, 87, 89–92, 95, 99, 180, 191, 278; and the formation of RCA, 255–259

Bundy, Richard C., 218
Bureau of Foreign and Domestic Commerce, 231–234
Bureau of Standards, 231, 234
Burlson, Albert, 208–209, 226–229, 242, 272–273

Cameroon, 16, 23–24
Canada, 9, 18, 35, 143, 214, 244; and radio, 13, 95, 190; and censorship, 125. *See also* Newfoundland
Canary Islands, 15, 26–27
Caperton, William B., 139, 312n4
Carlton, Newcomb, 92; and communications intelligence, 125, 130; and government control of cables, 227–229; and wartime deterioration of cables, 110–111; and joint cable to Brazil, 243–246, 261–263, 275. *See also* Western Union
Carney, Frank, 57–59, 140–144, 256
Carr, Wilbur, 231–232
Cartagena, 43, 54, 78, 81–82, 168–169, 251
Cartier, François, 108–109
Carty, J. J., 112, 114, 119, 131–133
Cavite, 68, 70–71, 148, 153–154
Central and South American Telegraph Company, 92, 238; and cable industry problems, 160–164, 229, 233; and cables to South America, 54–59, 137–146, 244–248, 264, 268; and communications intelligence, 104, 125, 130. *See also* All America Cables; John Merrill; James Scrymser
Chamber of Commerce, 46
Chile, 39, 53, 90, 93, 195, 275; and cable connections, 55, 161, 245, 263; and German radios, 27, 82–83, 167, 169
China, 40, 96, 112, 273, 277; and cable connections, 7–8, 15, 20, 147–148, 151–158, 216, 235; and radio connections, 16, 147–148, 151–158, 202–203, 248, 251, 258
Churchill, Marlborough, 211
Cipher Bureau. *See* MI-8
Robert C. Clowry, 133, 261–263
Cocos Island, 29
Colby, Bainbridge, 261–262

Cole, 261
Collins Overland Line, 19
Colombia, 85, 92, 144, 178, 250, 275; and German radios, 16, 27, 43, 78, 81–83, 167–168; and Tropical Radio, 97, 181
Colonia, 261
Colt Firearms Company, 128
Commerce Department, 42, 51, 94, 230–234
Commercial Cable Company, 18, 20, 156, 241, 270, 275; and effects of war on operations, 36, 37, 112, 214; and communications intelligence, 211–212, 270. *See also* Commercial Pacific Cable Company; Clarence Mackay; Postal-Telegraph
Commercial Pacific Cable Company, 20, 76, 112, 147–149, 234, 270; and reluctance to improve, 155–158, 229, 235–236. *See also* Commercial Cable Company; Clarence Mackay; Postal-Telegraph
Committee on Public Information (CPI), 115–116, 150, 156, 269
Compagnie Universelle de Télégraphie et Téléphonie (CUTT), 42
Conger, Edwin, 7
Constantinople, 102, 203, 251
Copenhagen, 46
Coronel, Battle of, 25, 83
Costa Rica, 81, 97, 166, 169, 177, 181
Council of Foreign Ministers, 222
Council of Four, 221
Council of Ten. *See* Supreme War Council
Council on Foreign Relations, 208, 234, 270
Cradock, Christopher, 83
Crane, Charles R., 151
Creel, George, 123, 150–151
Cutler, B. S., 232
Cutter, John, 230–233

Dacia, 32
Dakar, 28, 118, 325n18
Daniels, Josephus, 66, 69, 86–95, 110, 153, 173, 227, 275; and concern over German radio stations, 42, 52, 62–63; and government control of radio, 71, 75–80, 98–99, 120, 177, 203–204, 249–254, 269; and opposition to commercial radio firms, 180, 182, 186, 193–199; and Battle of Miami, 261; and Pan-American, 193–199, 203–204; and neutrality, 42, 44, 52; and censorship, 122, 150, 208–209; and the creation of RCA, 257–259
Davis, John W., 247
Decker, Benton, 261
Denison Pender, John, 12, 20, 145, 243–247
Denmark, 28, 30, 47, 49, 73, 163, 190
Dodge, Washington, 191, 195–197
Dominican Republic, 23, 91–92, 97, 123, 180, 202
Dresden, 41
Dunn, Gano, 159–160, 229, 231
Dyke, Henry van, 49

Eastern Extension Telegraph Company, 20, 156
Eastern Telegraph Company, 6, 9, 12, 17, 20, 36, 206; and communications intelligence, 39, 145, 296n12. *See also* John Denison-Pender; Eastern Extension Telegraph Company; Western Telegraph Company
Eckhardt, Heinrich von, 103–104
Economic Liaison Committee, 231
Eilvese, 42
Eldridge, Chauncy, 93, 99
El Salvador, 86–87, 94, 97–98, 166; and German radio interests, 168–169, 179; and Marconi companies, 173–174; and Tropical Radio, 179–182. *See also* Boaz Long
Elwell, C. F., 108, 302n25, 306n10. *See also* Federal Telegraph Company; Fuller improvements
Emden (German cruiser), 29
Emden (city), 10, 18, 106, 292n28, 295n66
English Channel, 5–6, 17, 23, 26, 31, 117
Egypt, 7, 13, 206
Ewing, Sir Alfred, 25

Fairfax, 189
Falklands Islands, 30, 83
Fanning Island, 29
Federal Telegraph Company, 42, 73, 76–77, 108, 120, 174, 238; reorganization, 185, 188–199; in South America, 93–97, 99, 168, 170, 176–177, 275; and U.S. Navy, 69–71, 113–114, 148, 154, 203, 249–250, 256, 265; and combination with American Marconi, 185–192, 201. *See also* C. F. Elwell; Fuller improvements; Pan-American
Ferrié, Gustave, 108, 110, 253
Foreign Office, Great Britain, 17, 23, 41, 45, 83, 96, 112, 167, 175–176, 247
French Telegraph Cable Company, 56, 143
Fuller improvements (to arc), 73, 174, 189–190, 195–201, 250

Galveston, 46, 123, 145
Gaunt, Captain Guy, 43, 82
General Board, 62, 64, 91, 180
General Electric, 4, 70, 81, 114, 131, 159, 185, 231; and postwar negotiations with Marconi companies, 248–250, 264; and formation of RCA, 255–259. *See also* Owen D. Young
General Post Office, 5, 13–14, 22, 32, 112, 175, 244
German East Africa, 16, 23
German South West Africa, 23–24
Germany: information warfare, 12, 28–32, 117–121, 125–128, 133, 267; and destruction of its communications network, 3, 5–6, 16–17, 22–24, 26–28, 37, 40–43, 103–105, 123, 136–137, 170–172, 208; development of strategic communications network, 2, 14–17, 40–44, 50–52, 166–172, 266–267, 271, 277
Gherardi, Bancroft, 159
Gibraltar, 10, 13, 69, 106, 118
Goeben, 29
Göteborg, 48
Great Britain: information warfare, 5–7, 12, 16–17, 82–83, 103, 121, 126, 170–172, 242, 267; and communications intelligence, 25–26, 39–40, 44–50, 103–104, 121, 124–127; and damage to its communications network, 28–32, 106–107, 112, 117–119; and development of strategic communications network, 8–14, 174–176, 266–268
Great Northern Telegraph Company, 14, 20, 28, 153, 156, 275
Grey, Sir Edward, 44–49
Griffin, Robert S., 62–63, 66, 183, 195, 257, 259
Griggs, John W., 188
Guatemala, 86, 89, 90, 97, 122, 173–174, 178, 181
Gutta-percha, 6, 12, 13, 15, 146–147, 164; and effect of supply on South American cables, 59–60, 160–162; and effect of supply on U.S. policy, 230–234, 269–270, 276

Haiti, 39, 122–123, 178, 180, 202
Hall, Reginald "Blinker," 25, 103–104, 125–126
Harrison, Leland, 78, 122, 125, 211–212
Havas, 8, 151, 215
Herrick, Myron T., 46
Hochfrequenz-Machinen Aktiengesellschaft für Drahtlose Telegraphie (HOMAG), 42
Honduras, 97, 181
Hooper, Stanford C., 194, 196, 264–265; and collaboration with radio companies, 75, 97, 99, 175; and concern about German radios in Western Hemisphere, 61–64; creation of RCA, 249, 254–259, 269; and improvement of naval radio, 21–22, 63–80, 114, 153, 276; and shaping of radio policy, 67–71, 75–80, 182–190, 199–201, 204, 271–273; wartime observation of European radio by, 64–67
Hurley, Edward, 208

Iceland, 30
Indian Ocean, 6, 9, 29, 30
Industrial Cooperation Service, 230–231, 233
Interallied Radio Commission, 108–109, 241, 252–253

International Telegraph Union, 58, 241
International Telegraph Bureau, 38
Internet, 4
Ireland, 28, 36, 136
Irigoyen, Hipólito, 141
Irving National Bank, 50
Isaacs, Godfrey, 95–96, 174–176, 187, 189, 190, 200–202, 258
Ishii Kikujiro, 155
Italy, 45, 47–49, 108–109, 163, 219, 221, 225, 240, 250, 267, 269

Jackson, Henry B., 23
Japan, 13–15, 108, 112, 239–241, 251, 259; censorship, 124, 208–209; and interest in German Pacific cables, 158, 214, 216, 243, 269, 277; and interest in improved contact with the United States, 20, 149–155, 235–236, 270; and influence on U.S. cable connections, 213–217, 221–222, 235, 277; and Paris Peace Conference, 219, 221–225; and postwar communications conference, 264; as target of U.S. communications intelligence, 212; and Zimmermann telegram, 103, 105; cable and radio network of, 14, 163, 147–149, 267
Jeffery, Robert E., 141
Jerram, Martyn, 24
Jewett, F. B., 159
Jones, Wesley L., 235–236

Kamina, 10, 16, 18, 23–24, 70
Karlsruhe, 41
Kellogg, Frank, 261, 263
Kennelly, Arthur, 159
Kipling, Rudyard, 1
Krakatoa, 8

Lansing, Robert, 3, 41–42, 45, 52, 58, 125, 155; and Paris Peace Conference, 213–214, 219–225, 237, 269; and cables to South America, 130, 137–138, 141, 143, 145; radio connections with South America, 87, 90, 93–95, 169, 179, 181–182; radio policy, 78; and censorship, 45, 49, 227; communications intelligence, 104,
122, 126, 170; and communications conference, 240–242
Lay, Julius, 231
League of Nations, 215, 217, 237, 243, 250, 277
LeClair, H. P., 194–195
Libau, 29
Liberia, 15, 16, 23–24, 26–28, 203, 217–218, 224
Long, Boaz, 86, 88, 94, 97, 169, 173, 177–178, 194, 271
Long, Breckinridge, 241, 264, 269–272, 274; and concern over transpacific communications, 149–150, 155–162; and Paris Peace Conference, 214–217, 224–231; and government intervention in cables, 137, 164, 209, 226, 228–231, 235–238
Loucks, William D., 188–189, 197
Lusitania, 52

Mackay, Clarence (son), 156, 211, 214, 227–229, 236, 241, 270, 275; and cooperation in communications intelligence, 122, 125. *See also* Commercial Cable Company; Commercial Pacific Cable Company; Postal-Telegraph
Mackay, John (father), 20
Madrid, 46
Manila, 20, 146, 152, 216, 232, 234
Marconi Wireless Telegraph Company, Ltd., 13, 15–16, 74, 180, 240, 248, 250; access to new technology, 199–202, 255–256, 258; and South America, 94–95, 172–177, 203, 259; and attempts to purchase U.S. companies, 174–177, 275; Pan-American Wireless, 187–190, 192; and RCA, 258–259. *See also* Godfrey Isaacs, Marconi Wireless Telegraph Company of America
Marconi Wireless Telegraph Company of America, 51, 65, 74, 113–114, 147–148, 150; opposition from the U.S. Navy, 43–44, 60, 77, 254; as important manufacturer, 184–185; and expansion across the Americas, 94–95, 172–176, 204; Pan-American Wireless, 176, 185–197; postwar uncertainty, 248, 278; negotiations with

Marconi Wireless *(continued)*
  General Electric, 249–250, 258–259.
  See also Marconi Wireless Telegraph
  Company, Ltd.; Edward J. Nally
Mason, A. E. W., 171–172
McAdoo, William G., 55, 87, 262
McCormick, Vance, 208–209
McKenna, Reginald, 25
Mediterranean, 6, 9, 14, 66, 106, 118, 136, 206.
Memphis, 46
Merrill, John, 260, 263, 268, 271, 274; assistance to State Department, 125–126; and South America, 58–59, 130, 140–146, 244–246; cable supply problems, 59, 153, 158, 161–162. *See also* All America Cables; Central and South American Telegraph Company
Mexico, 18, 63, 101, 103–104, 123, 126; U.S. radio interests in, 91–92, 180–181; German radio interests in, 16, 81, 167–173; as object of intelligence operations, 171–172, 211–212
Mexico City, 103–104, 167–173, 212
MI-8, 124–125, 211–213, 237, 263, 270, 274–275
Miami, 47, 244–247, 260–264, 270–271, 275–276
Monarch, 32
Monroe Doctrine, 175, 184, 187, 237
Monrovia, 16, 18, 27–28, 218. *See also* Liberia
Morgan, Edwin, 94, 129–130, 140–145, 246–247
Morris, Ira Nelson, 49
Morse, Samuel F. B., 6

Nally, Edward J., 94–96, 175, 185–189; and Pan-America, 192, 194–198, 254; and RCA, 258–259
Nauen, 16, 23–27, 109, 121; and the United States, 43, 51, 104, 108, 116, 119; and Mexico, 167–172
Netherlands, 14–15, 17, 24, 30, 48–49, 65, 128, 163
Netherlands Antilles, 144
Netherlands East Indies, 15, 24, 128, 231–232
Netherlands Overseas Trust, 49

New Brunswick, 108, 114–116, 202, 204, 249, 255, 258
Newfoundland, 35, 48, 65, 143, 292n36
New Orleans, 46, 123
New Zealand, 9, 24, 29
News Industry, 7–8, 59, 151, 215. *See also* Havas; Reuters; Wolff
North Sea, 13, 22, 28, 30, 117
Norway, 28–30, 49, 60, 96, 250–251, 259
Nova Scotia, 133, 142, 250
Nürnberg, 29
Nye, William, 260

Oliver, Henry, 25
O'Shaughnessy, Nelson, 144

Pacific Cable Board, 9
Page, Walter Hines, 44–47, 104, 112
Pan American Financial Conference (1915), 55
Pan American Scientific Conference (1916), 88
Pan-American Wireless Telegraph and Telephone Company, 181, 191–199, 203–204, 249, 254, 256, 275
Panama Canal, 109, 113, 123, 178, 260; importance to U.S. security, 67–68, 84, 97–98, 273; and U.S. naval radio, 51, 67–69, 84–87, 90, 202; and rumors of German activity, 166, 170
Paraguay, 58, 82, 169, 181
Paris Peace Conference, 207, 213–225
Patchin, Philip, 157, 316n52
Peking, 7, 152, 154, 202, 314n37. *See also* China
Pernambuco, 10, 18, 39, 54, 127, 130
Pershing, John J., 107, 110, 112, 136, 146, 307n22
Peru: cable connections to, 39, 245, 260, 263; radio connections to, 16, 82–83, 93, 167, 169, 195
Philips, William, 129
Pichon, Stephen, 218
Polk, Frank, 104, 151, 155–156, 218, 241, 251, 260; and monitoring of cable traffic, 122, 208, 211–213; and radio policy, 180, 193, 198; and South American cables, 246–247
Portugal, 26–27, 36–37, 106, 118, 127

Post Office, United States, 76, 213, 226–228, 272–273
Postal-Telegraph, 122, 160, 212, 275. *See also* Commercial Cable Company; Commercial Pacific Cable Company; Clarence Mackay
Poulsen, Valdemar, 73, 174, 189–190
Prentiss, Mark, 209, 232
Puerto Rico, 21, 39–40, 71, 97, 114, 123, 202, 246

Qingdao. *See* Tsingtao

Radio Act of 1912, 21, 62–63, 73
Radio Corporation of America, 4, 163, 248, 258, 269. *See also* Owen D. Young
Redfield, William C., 52, 55, 232
Reinsch, Paul, 154, 157–158
Republic, 72
Reuters, 8, 151, 215
Robertson, W. Henry, 128, 130–131
Robertson, W. S., 142–143
Rogers, Walter S., 151–152, 237–238, 241, 269, 271–272, 274; and the interdepartmental communications committee, 156–157, 214–217; and Paris Peace Conference, 214–217, 224–225
Rome, 46, 108, 251
Room 40, 25–26, 103–104, 122, 125–126, 171. *See also* Reginald Hall; MI-8
Roosevelt, Franklin D., 44, 52, 62, 87, 90–91, 99, 273; and Pan-American Wireless, 193, 196–197; and the Radio Corporation of America, 255, 257
Root, Elihu, Jr., 261
Royal Navy, 17, 27–30, 112, 170, 201; and use of radio, 13, 23, 66, 108. *See also* Admiralty
Russel, Edgar, 105, 107–108, 110
Russia, 19, 95, 128, 151–153, 203, 212, 236; and cable connections: 28–30, 37, 118, 164

St. Petersburg, 29
Sacramento, 251
Salem, 69
San Diego, 68, 70–71, 148, 154, 251

San Francisco, 20, 76, 123, 146, 148–149, 155, 229, 234–235
Satellites, 2, 4
Sauer, Emil, 48
Sayles, W. L., 110
Sayville, 26, 43, 51–52, 60–63, 91; under Navy control, 104, 109, 113–116, 202, 204, 249; as perceived German outpost, 16, 21, 41–42, 67, 79
Scott, James Brown, 219
Scrymser, James, 18–19, 54–58, 92. *See also* Central and South American Telegraph Company; James Merrill
Sevastopol, 29, 294n57
Shanghai, 20, 146–147, 152, 154, 203, 235, 251; and German cable, 24, 158, 216
Sharp, William G., 48
Shirley, James J., 140–141
Shortwave, 4
Siasconsett, 44
Siberia, 15, 19, 29, 152–154, 157, 202, 251
Signal Corps, United States Army, 20, 105, 111, 113, 160, 212, 235; and tapping submarine telegraph cables, 131, 133. *See also* Edgar Russel; George O. Squier
Singapore, 9, 11, 12, 231–233
South Africa, 9, 24, 39
Spain, 25, 27, 47, 125, 170–171, 267; and cable connections, 5, 15, 119, 127, 163, 212; and war with the United States, 19–20, 123
Spanish-American War, 3, 19–20, 123, 158, 326
Spark transmitter, 51, 69, 71, 75, 77, 85, 200–201, 250; and Marconi companies, 16, 72, 74, 94–95, 148, 173
Spee, Maximilian von, 24–25, 27, 30, 83
Spring-Rice, Cecil, 96
Squier, George O., 20–22, 111–112, 131, 185, 229, 272; posting to London, 65; as chief signal officer, 105; and interdepartmental communications committee, 156–159
Stabler, Herbert, 179, 192–193, 198, 244
Steadman, Sydney, 176, 189–190, 193, 200

Stimson, Frederic J., 56–58, 139, 141, 170, 247
Suffolk, 44
Suppression, 17, 35, 38–40, 44–47, 50, 207, 209
Supreme War Council (Council of Ten), 219–221
Sweden, 26, 28, 30, 48–49, 96, 104, 126, 250
Sweet, George C., 120, 194, 200–202, 255
Switzerland, 38, 45–47, 49, 58

Telefunken: 15–16, 21, 96–97, 99; and Argentina, 170, 251; and Latin America, 27, 78, 81–83, 88, 93, 99, 179–182, 187; and Mexico, 81, 167–171; and rumor of Federal Telegraph purchase, 96; and El Salvador, 86, 94, 166, 168–169, 181; and the United States, 16, 51, 61–62
Telegraph Construction and Maintenance Company, 146, 160, 230
Telephony, 4, 184, 226–227, 272, 336n10
Tenerife, 26–27
Third International Radio Telegraphic Conference, 72, 85
Titanic, 21, 72
Todd, D. W., 182–184, 254–255; and Federal Telegraph, 190–191, 195; and government control of radio, 77–78, 80, 98, 183, 198–199; and interdepartmental communications committee, 156–157; and wartime censorship, 123–124, 227
Togoland, 16, 23, 70
Tower, Reginald, 128
Triumph, 24
Tropical Radio Company, 81, 86, 88, 241; and collaboration with the U.S. government, 91–92, 97, 173, 178–182. *See also* United Fruit Company
Trye, J. H., 124, 227
Tsingtao, 16, 19, 24
Tuckerton, 41–43, 60, 109, 113–116, 119, 202, 204

U-directorate, 212–213. *See also* MI-8
United Fruit Company, 80–81, 92, 178, 180, 241, 259. *See also* Tropical Radio Company
United Kingdom. *See* Great Britain
United Press Association, 151–152, 161
Uruguay, 18, 82, 93, 144, 177, 195, 269; and Anglo-American cable rivalry, 53–59, 137–141, 246–248; and German radio, 167, 169
U.S. Steel, 128

Vacuum tubes, 132, 171–172, 184, 188–189, 259, 265
Varna, 29
Veeder, Howard P., 186, 190–191
Venezuela, 16, 81, 93–94, 144, 166–169, 177, 181, 251
Veracruz, 63–64, 66, 68, 74–75, 171
Verne, Jules, 7, 289n4
Versailles. *See* Paris Peace Conference
Vladivostok, 11, 102, 202, 251

Waller, Charles W., 190–192, 195–198
War Trade Board, 209
Ward, George, 155, 236
Western Electric, 133, 159, 185, 234; and tapping submarine telegraph cables, 133
Western Telegraph Company, 55, 129, 164, 260, 268, 271, 275; and censorship, 58, 123, 145; and communications intelligence, 39; and rivalry with Central company, 56–59, 137–145, 263–264; and Western Union deal, 243–248, 260. *See also* John Denison-Pender; Eastern Telegraph Company; Eastern Extension Telegraph Company
Western Union, 18, 92, 104, 115, 163–164, 278–279; and the Battle of Miami, 260–264; and cables to South America, 137–138, 140, 142–144, 243–247, 260–264; and communications intelligence, 122, 125, 130, 133, 212, 270, 275; and deterioration of North Atlantic cables, 110–112; and development of the cable industry, 160, 231; and government control

of communications, 228–229; and problems in 1914; 37, 39–40, 46; and Wilson administration encouragement, 55, 262

Westinghouse, 81, 259, 265

Wilmington, 251

Wilson, Woodrow, 3, 63, 151–152, 180, 259, 272; and American entry in 1917, 100–105, 135; and beginning of war in 1914, 41–43, 52; and government control of communications, 113, 122–123, 158, 226–227, 259; and greater U.S. role in the world, 147, 150, 207, 236–237, 240–243, 277; and the Miami incident, 261–263; and Paris Peace Conference, 207, 213–215, 217, 220–225, 240–243, 256, 269; and support for improved communications abroad, 3, 55, 60, 88, 140

Wolff press agency, 8, 151, 215

Yap island, 15–16, 19, 24, 158; as diplomatic problem, 214, 216, 243, 264, 276–277; and Paris Peace Conference, 221–225

Yardley, Herbert, 124–125, 211–213, 263

Young, Owen, 255–259, 265

Zimmermann telegram, 101, 104–105, 122, 126, 268